EXPLORING MICROSOFT® WORD 97

EXPLORING MICROSOFT® WORD 97

Robert T. Grauer / Maryann Barber

University of Miami

Prentice Hall, Upper Saddle River, New Jersey 07458

Acquisitions Editor: Carolyn Henderson
Assistant Editor: Audrey Regan
Editorial Assistant: Lori Cardillo
Executive Marketing Manager: Nancy Evans
Editorial/Production Supervisor: Greg Hubit
Project Manager: Lynne Breitfeller
Senior Manufacturing Supervisor: Paul Smolenski
Manufacturing Coordinator: Lisa DiMaulo
Manufacturing Manager: Vincent Scelta
Senior Designer/Interior and Cover Design: Suzanne Behnke
Composition: GTS Graphics

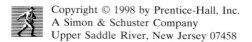

Copyright © 1998 by Prentice-Hall, Inc.
A Simon & Schuster Company
Upper Saddle River, New Jersey 07458

ISBN 0-13-754201-1

Prentice-Hall International (UK) Limited, London
Prentice-Hall of Australia Pty. Limited, Sydney
Prentice-Hall Canada Inc., Toronto
Prentice-Hall Hispanoamericana, S.A., Mexico
Prentice-Hall of India Private Limited, New Delhi
Prentice-Hall of Japan, Inc., Tokyo
Simon & Schuster Asia Pte. Ltd., Singapore
Editora Prentice-Hall do Brasil, Ltda., Rio de Janeiro

Printed in the United States of America

10 9 8 7 6 5 4 3 2 1

CONTENTS

2

Gaining Proficiency: Editing and Formatting 51

3

Enhancing a Document: The Web and Other Resources 105

4

Advanced Features: Outlines, Tables, Styles, and Sections   151

5

Desktop Publishing: Creating a Newsletter   205

6

Creating a Home Page: Introduction to HTML   241

To Marion, Benjy, Jessica, and Ellie

—Robert Grauer

To Frank, Jessica, and My Parents

—Maryann Barber

PREFACE

We are proud to announce the third edition of the *Exploring Windows* series in conjunction with the release of Microsoft Office 97. There is a separate book for each major application—*Word 97, Excel 97, Access 97,* and *PowerPoint 97*—as well as a book on Windows 95, and, eventually, Windows 97. There are also two combined texts, *Exploring Microsoft Office 97 Professional, Volumes I* and *II. Volume I* contains the introductory chapters from each application, supplementary modules on Internet Explorer and Windows 95, and a PC Buying Guide. It is designed for the instructor who seeks to cover the basics of all Office applications in a single course, but who does not need the extensive coverage that is provided in the individual books. *Volume II* consists of the advanced chapters from each application and was developed for the rapidly emerging second course in PC applications. The complete set of titles appears on the back cover.

Exploring Microsoft Word 97 is a revision of our existing book on *Microsoft Word for Windows 95.* It reflects the new features in Word 97 such as the automatic grammar check, Office Art, and support of the Web. It also contains an entirely new chapter on creating a home page using commands that are built into Word 97. In addition, we have revised the end-of-chapter material to include a greater number of practice exercises and case studies.

Our most significant change, however, is the incorporation of the Internet and World Wide Web throughout the text. Students learn Office applications as before, and in addition are sent to the Web as appropriate for supplementary exercises. Students can download the practice files (or "data disk") from the *Exploring Windows* home page (***www.prenhall.com/grauer***). This site also contains additional practice exercises and case studies, which can be downloaded to supplement the text. The icon at the left of this paragraph appears throughout the text whenever there is a Web reference.

Each book in the *Exploring Windows* series is accompanied by an Instructor's Resource Manual with solutions to all exercises, PowerPoint lectures, and the printed version of our test bank. (The Instructor's Resource Manual is available on a CD-ROM, which contains a Windows-based testing program.) Instructors can also use the Prentice Hall Computerized Online Testing System to prepare customized tests for their courses and may obtain Interactive Multimedia courseware as a further supplement.

The *Exploring Windows* series is part of the Prentice Hall custom binding program, enabling you to create your own text by selecting any module(s) in *Office Volume I* to suit the needs of a specific course. You could, for example, create a custom text consisting of the introductory (essential) chapters in Word, Excel, and Internet Explorer. You get exactly the material you need, and students realize a cost saving. You can also take advantage of our ValuePack program to shrink-wrap multiple books together. If, for example, you are teaching a course that covers Excel and Access, and you want substantial coverage of both applications, a ValuePack results in significant savings for the student.

We look forward to continuing to provide quality textbooks for all of your Microsoft Office requirements.

FEATURES AND BENEFITS

Exploring Microsoft Word 97 is written for the computer novice and assumes no previous knowledge about Windows 95. A detailed supplement introduces the reader to the operating system and emphasizes the file operations he or she will need.

An introductory section on Microsoft Office 97 emphasizes the benefits of the common user interface. Although the text assumes no previous knowledge, some users may already be acquainted with another Office application, in which case they can take advantage of what they already know.

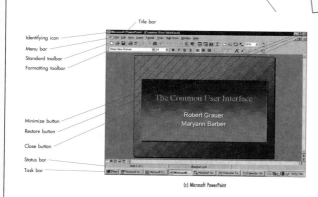

(c) Microsoft PowerPoint

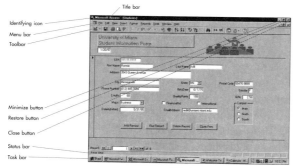

FIGURE 1   The Common User Interface (continued)

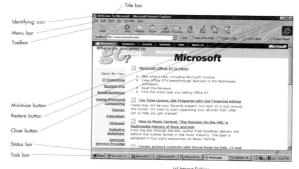

(e) Internet Explorer

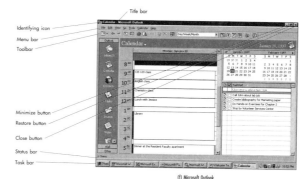

(f) Microsoft Outlook

FIGURE 1   The Common User Interface (continued)

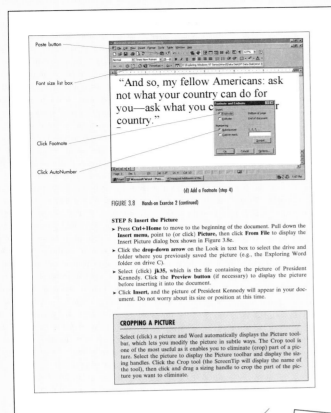

Paste button

Font size list box

Click Footnote

Click AutoNumber

"And so, my fellow Americans: ask not what your country can do for you—ask what you c... r country."

(d) Add a Footnote (step 4)

FIGURE 3.8   Hands-on Exercise 2 (continued)

STEP 5: Insert the Picture

➤ Press **Ctrl+Home** to move to the beginning of the document. Pull down the **Insert menu**, point to (or click) **Picture**, then click **From File** to display the Insert Picture dialog box shown in Figure 3.8e.

➤ Click the **drop-down arrow** on the Look in text box to select the drive and folder where you previously saved the picture (e.g., the Exploring Word folder on drive C).

➤ Select (click) **jk35**, which is the file containing the picture of President Kennedy. Click the **Preview button** (if necessary) to display the picture before inserting it into the document.

➤ Click **Insert**, and the picture of President Kennedy will appear in your document. Do not worry about its size or position at this time.

CROPPING A PICTURE

Select (click) a picture and Word automatically displays the Picture toolbar, which lets you modify the picture in subtle ways. The Crop tool is one of the most useful as it enables you to eliminate (crop) part of a picture. Select the picture to display the Picture toolbar and display the sizing handles. Click the Crop tool (the ScreenTip will display the name of the tool), then click and drag a sizing handle to crop the part of the picture you want to eliminate.

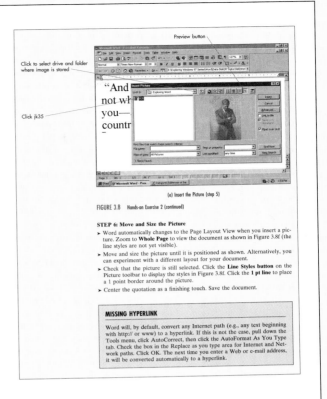

Preview button

Click to select drive and folder where image is stored

Click jk35

"And not wh you— countr

(e) Insert the Picture (step 5)

FIGURE 3.8   Hands-on Exercise 2 (continued)

STEP 6: Move and Size the Picture

➤ Word automatically changes to the Page Layout View when you insert a picture. Zoom to **Whole Page** to view the document as shown in Figure 3.8f (the line styles are not yet visible).

➤ Move and size the picture until it is positioned as shown. Alternatively, you can experiment with a different layout for your document.

➤ Check that the picture is still selected. Click the **Line Styles button** on the Picture toolbar to display the styles in Figure 3.8f. Click the **1 pt line** to place a 1 point border around the picture.

➤ Center the quotation as a finishing touch. Save the document.

MISSING HYPERLINK

Word will, by default, convert any Internet path (e.g., any text beginning with http:// or www) to a hyperlink. If this is not the case, pull down the Tools menu, click AutoCorrect, then click the AutoFormat As You Type tab. Check the box in the Replace as you type area for Internet and Network paths. Click OK. The next time you enter a Web or e-mail address, it will be converted automatically to a hyperlink.

A total of 18 in-depth tutorials (hands-on exercises) guide the reader at the computer. Each tutorial is illustrated with large, full-color screen captures that are clear and easy to read. This example is taken from Chapter 3, which describes how to download resources from the Web for inclusion in a Word document.

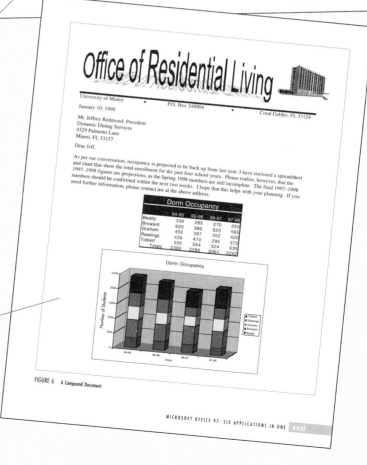

FIGURE 6   A Compound Document

Object Linking and Embedding is stressed throughout the series, beginning in the introductory section on Microsoft Office, where the reader is shown the power of this all-important technology. Appendix A, on pages 283–300, provides additional information.

5. Form design: The tables feature is ideal to create forms as shown by the document in Figure 4.17, which displays an employment application. Reproduce the document shown in the figure or design your own application. Submit the completed document to your instructor.

Computer Consultants, Inc.
Employee Application Form

Last Name:	First Name:	Middle Name:

Address:

City:	State:	Zip Code:	Telephone:

Date of Birth:	Place of Birth:	Citizenship:

Highest Degree Attained: 　High School Diploma 　Bachelor's Degree 　Master's Degree 　Ph.D.	List Schools Attended (include years attended):

List Specific Computer Skills:

List Relevant Computer Experience:

References (list name, title, and current mailing address):

1.

2.

3.

FIGURE 4.17　Document for Practice Exercise 5

---

6. Graphics: A table may contain anything—text, graphics, or numbers as shown by the document in Figure 4.18, which displays a hypothetical computer advertisement. It's not complicated; in fact, it was really very easy; just follow the steps below:
   a. Create a 7 × 4 table.
   b. Merge all of the cells in row one and enter the heading. Merge all of the cells in row two and type the text describing the sale.
   c. Use the Clip Gallery to insert a picture into the table. (Various computer graphics are available in the Business and Technology categories.)
   d. Enter the sales data in rows three through seven of the table; all entries are centered within the respective cells.
   e. Change the font, colors, and formatting, then print the completed document. Use any format you think is appropriate.

Of course, it isn't quite as simple as it sounds, but we think you get the idea. Good luck and feel free to improve on our design. Color is a nice touch, but it is definitely not required. You might also make your table more realistic by going to the Web and searching for current prices and configurations. Go to the Exploring Windows home page (www.prenhall.com/grauer), click on Additional Resources, then click the link to PC Buying Guide as one source of information.

Computers To Go

Our tremendous sales volume enables us to offer the fastest, most powerful series of Pentium and Pentium Pro computers at prices almost too good to be true. Each microprocessor is offered in a variety of configurations so that you get exactly what you need. All configurations include a local bus video, a 17-inch monitor, a mouse, and Windows 95.

Capacity	Configuration 1 16 Mb RAM 1.6 Gb Hard Drive	Configuration 2 32 Mb RAM 2.5 Gb Hard Drive	Configuration 3 64 Mb RAM 4 Gb Hard Drive
Pentium w/MMX – 166 MHz	$1,599	$2,199	$3,099
Pentium w/MMX – 200 MHz	$1,799	$2,399	$3,299
Pentium Pro – 180 MHz	$1,999	$2,599	$3,499
Pentium Pro – 200 MHz	$2,199	$2,799	$3,699

FIGURE 4.18　Document for Practice Exercise 6

Every chapter contains a variety of assignments to avoid repetition from one semester to the next. The exercises vary in scope and difficulty and encourage students to create attractive documents. These examples are taken from Chapter 4, which describes the Tables feature.

Every chapter also contains a number of less-structured case studies to challenge the student. The Web icon appears throughout the text whenever the student is directed to the World Wide Web as a source of additional material.

CASE STUDIES

The Letterhead

A well-designed letterhead adds impact to your correspondence. Collect samples of professional stationery, then design your own letterhead, which includes your name, address, phone, and any other information you deem relevant. Include a fax number and/or e-mail address as appropriate. Using your imagination, design the letterhead for your planned career. Try different fonts and/or the Format Border command to add horizontal line(s) under the text. Consider a graphic logo, but keep it simple. You might also want to decrease the top margin so that the letterhead prints closer to the top of the page.

An Ad for Travel

The Clip Gallery includes the maps and flags of many foreign countries. It also has maps of all 50 states as well as pictures of many landmarks. Design a one-page flyer for a place you want to visit, either in the United States or abroad. Collect the assignments, then ask your instructor to hold a contest to decide the most appealing document. It's fun, it's easy, and it's educational. Bon voyage!

The Cover Page

Use WordArt and/or the Clip Gallery to create a truly original cover page that you can use with all of your assignments. The cover page should include the title of the assignment, your name, course information, and date. (Use the Insert Date and Time command to insert the date as a field so that it will be updated automatically every time you retrieve the document.) The formatting is up to you. Print the completed cover page and submit it to your instructor, then use the cover page for all future assignments.

The Résumé

Use your imagination to create a résumé for Benjamin Franklin or Leonardo da Vinci, two acknowledged geniuses. The résumé is limited to one page and will be judged for content (yes, you have to do a little research on the Web) as well as appearance. You can intersperse fact and fiction as appropriate; for example, you may want to leave space for a telephone and/or a fax number, but could indicate that these devices have not yet been invented. You can choose a format for the résumé using the Résumé Wizard, or better yet, design your own.

File Compression

Photographs add significantly to the appearance of a document, but they also add to its size. Accordingly, you might want to consider acquiring a file compression program to facilitate copying large documents to a floppy disk in order to transport your documents to and from school, home, or work. You can download an evaluation copy of the popular WinZip program at www.winzip.com. Investigate the subject of file compression, then submit a summary of your findings to your instructor.

Chapter 6 describes how to create a home page using tools that are built into Word 97. The student learns how to incorporate graphics and tables into a Web page, and how to insert hyperlinks to other pages on the Web or on a corporate Intranet.

Chapter 5 covers the basics of desktop publishing. Students not only learn the mechanics of Word, but are also taught the basics of graphic design. This unique combination of concepts and key strokes is one of the distinguishing features of our series.

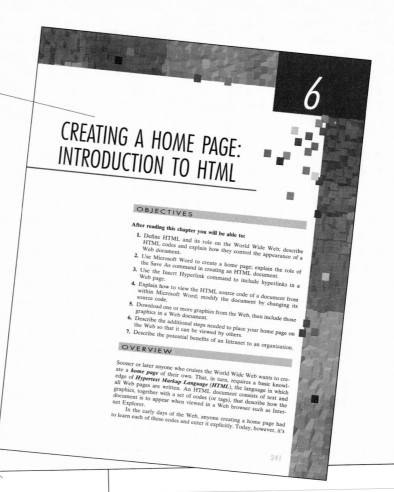

6

CREATING A HOME PAGE: INTRODUCTION TO HTML

OBJECTIVES

After reading this chapter you will be able to:

1. Define HTML and its role on the World Wide Web; describe HTML codes and explain how they control the appearance of a Web document.
2. Use Microsoft Word to create a home page; explain the role of the Save As command in creating an HTML document.
3. Use the Insert Hyperlink command to include hyperlinks in a Web page.
4. Explain how to view the HTML source code of a document from within Microsoft Word; modify the document by changing its source code.
5. Download one or more graphics from the Web, then include those graphics in a Web document.
6. Describe the additional steps needed to place your home page on the Web so that it can be viewed by others.
7. Describe the potential benefits of an Intranet to an organization.

OVERVIEW

Sooner or later anyone who cruises the World Wide Web wants to create a *home page* of their own. That, in turn, requires a basic knowledge of *Hypertext Markup Language (HTML)*, the language in which all Web pages are written. An HTML document consists of text and graphics, together with a set of codes (or tags), that describe how the document is to appear when viewed in a Web browser such as Internet Explorer.

In the early days of the Web, anyone creating a home page had to learn each of these codes and enter it explicitly. Today, however, it's

241

The essence of *desktop publishing* is the merger of text with graphics to produce a professional-looking document without reliance on external services. Desktop publishing will save you time and money because you are doing the work yourself rather than sending it out as you did in traditional publishing. That is the good news. The bad news is that desktop publishing is not as easy as it sounds, precisely because you are doing work that was done previously by skilled professionals. Nevertheless, with a little practice, and a basic knowledge of graphic design, which we include in this chapter, you will be able to create effective and attractive documents.

Our discussion focuses on desktop publishing as it is implemented in Microsoft Word. We show you how to design a multicolumn document, how to import clip art and other objects, and how to position those objects within a document. The chapter also reviews material from earlier chapters on bullets and lists, borders and shading, and section formatting, all of which will be used to create a newsletter.

THE NEWSLETTER

The chapter is built around the newsletter in Figure 5.1. The newsletter itself describes the basics of desktop publishing and provides an overview of the chapter. The material is presented conceptually, after which you implement the design in two hands-on exercises. We provide the text and you do the formatting. The first exercise creates a simple newsletter from copy that we provide. The second exercise uses more sophisticated formatting as described by the various techniques mentioned within the newsletter. Many of the terms are new, and we define them briefly in the next few paragraphs.

A *reverse* (light text on a dark background) is a favorite technique of desktop publishers to emphasize a specific element. It is used in the *masthead* (the identifying information) at the top of the newsletter and provides a distinctive look to the publication. The number of the newsletter and the date of publication also appear in the masthead in smaller letters.

A *pull quote* is a phrase or sentence taken from an article to emphasize a key point. It is typically set in larger type, often in a different typeface and/or italics, and may be offset with parallel lines at the top and bottom.

A *dropped-capital letter* is a large capital letter at the beginning of a paragraph. It, too, catches the reader's eye and calls attention to the associated text.

Clip art, used in moderation, will catch the reader's eye and enhance almost any newsletter. It is available from a variety of sources including the *Microsoft Clip Gallery*, which is included in Office 97. Clip art can also be downloaded from the Web, but be sure you are allowed to reprint the image. *Borders and shading* are effective individually, or in combination with one another, to emphasize important stories within the newsletter. Simple vertical and/or horizontal lines are also effective. The techniques are especially useful in the absence of clip art or other graphics and are a favorite of desktop publishers.

Lists, whether bulleted or numbered, help to organize information by emphasizing important topics. A *bulleted list* emphasizes (and separates) the items. A *numbered list* sequences (and prioritizes) the items and is automatically updated to accommodate additions or deletions.

All of these techniques can be implemented with commands you already know, as you will see in the hands-on exercise, which follows shortly.

Creating a Newsletter

Volume I, Number 1   Spring 1997

Desktop publishing is easy, but there are several points to remember. This chapter will take you through the steps in creating a newsletter. The first hands-on exercise creates a simple newsletter with a masthead and three-column design. The second exercise creates a more attractive document by exploring different ways to emphasize the text.

Clip Art and Other Objects

Clip art is available from a variety of sources. You can also use other types of objects such as maps, charts, or organization charts, which are created by other applications, then brought into a document through the Insert Object command. A single dominant graphic is usually more appealing than multiple smaller graphics.

Techniques to Consider

Our finished newsletter contains one or more examples of each of the following desktop publishing techniques. Can you find where each technique is used, and further, explain, how to implement that technique in Microsoft Word?

1. Pull Quotes
2. Reverse
3. Drop Caps
4. Tables
5. Styles
6. Bullets and Numbering
7. Borders and Shading

Newspaper-Style Columns

The essence of a newsletter is the implementation of columns in which text flows continuously from the bottom of one column to the top of the next. You specify the number of columns, and optionally, the space between columns. Microsoft Word does the rest. It will compute the width of each column based on the number of columns and the margins.

Beginners often specify margins that are too large and implement too much space between the columns. Another way to achieve a more sophisticated look is to avoid the standard two-column design. You can implement columns of varying width and/or insert vertical lines between the columns.

The number of columns will vary in different parts of a document. The masthead is typically a single column, but the body of the newsletter will have two or three. Remember, too, that columns are implemented at the section level and hence, section breaks are required throughout a document.

Typography

Typography is the process of selecting typefaces, type styles, and type sizes, and is a critical element in the success of any document. Type should reinforce the message and should be consistent with the information you want to convey. More is not better, especially in the case of too many typefaces and styles, which produce cluttered documents that impress no one. Try to limit yourself to a maximum of two typefaces per document, but choose multiple sizes and/or styles within those typefaces. Use boldface or italics for emphasis, but do so in moderation, because if you use too many different elements, the effect is lost.

A pull quote adds interest to a document while simultaneously emphasizing a key point. It is implemented by increasing the point size, changing to italics, centering the text, and displaying a top and bottom border on the paragraph.

Use Styles as Appropriate

Styles were covered in the previous chapter, but that does not mean you cannot use them in conjunction with a newsletter. A style stores character and/or paragraph formatting and can be applied to multiple occurrences of the same element within a document. Change the style and you automatically change all text defined by that style. You can also use styles from one edition of your newsletter to the next to ensure consistency.

Borders and Shading

Borders and shading are effective individually or in combination with one another. Use a thin rule (one point or less) and light shading (five or ten percent) for best results. The techniques are especially useful in the absence of clip art or other graphics and are a favorite of desktop publishers.

FIGURE 5.1   The Newsletter

Acknowledgments

We want to thank the many individuals who helped bring this project to fruition. We are especially grateful to our editor at Prentice Hall, Carolyn Henderson, without whom the series would not have been possible. Cecil Yarbrough and Susan Hoffman did an outstanding job in checking the manuscript and proofs for technical accuracy. Suzanne Behnke developed the innovative and attractive design. John DeLara and David Nusspickel were responsible for our Web site. Carlotta Eaton of Radford University and Karen Vignare of Alfred University wrote the Instructor Manuals, and Dave Moles produced the CD. Paul Smolenski was senior manufacturing supervisor. Lynne Breitfeller was project manager. Greg Hubit was in charge of production and kept the project on target from beginning to end. Nancy Evans, our marketing manager at Prentice Hall, developed the innovative campaigns that made the series a success. Lori Cardillo, editorial assistant at Prentice Hall, helped in ways too numerous to mention. We also want to acknowledge our reviewers who, through their comments and constructive criticism, greatly improved the *Exploring Windows* series.

Lynne Band, Middlesex Community College
Stuart P. Brian, Holy Family College
Carl M. Briggs, Indiana University School of Business
Kimberly Chambers, Scottsdale Community College
Alok Charturvedi, Purdue University
Jerry Chin, Southwest Missouri State University
Dean Combellick, Scottsdale Community College
Cody Copeland, Johnson County Community College
Larry S. Corman, Fort Lewis College
Janis Cox, Tri-County Technical College
Martin Crossland, Southwest Missouri State University
Paul E. Daurelle, Western Piedmont Community College
David Douglas, University of Arkansas
Carlotta Eaton, Radford University
Raymond Frost, Central Connecticut State University
James Gips, Boston College
Vernon Griffin, Austin Community College
Michael Hassett, Fort Hays State University
Wanda D. Heller, Seminole Community College
Bonnie Homan, San Francisco State University
Ernie Ivey, Polk Community College
Mike Kelly, Community College of Rhode Island
Jane King, Everett Community College

John Lesson, University of Central Florida
David B. Meinert, Southwest Missouri State University
Bill Morse, DeVry Institute of Technology
Alan Moltz, Naugatuck Valley Technical Community College
Kim Montney, Kellogg Community College
Kevin Pauli, University of Nebraska
Mary McKenry Percival, University of Miami
Delores Pusins, Hillsborough Community College
Gale E. Rand, College Misericordia
Judith Rice, Santa Fe Community College
David Rinehard, Lansing Community College
Marilyn Salas, Scottsdale Community College
John Shepherd, Duquesne University
Helen Stoloff, Hudson Valley Community College
Margaret Thomas, Ohio University
Mike Thomas, Indiana University School of Business
Suzanne Tomlinson, Iowa State University
Karen Tracey, Central Connecticut State University
Sally Visci, Lorain County Community College
David Weiner, University of San Francisco
Connie Wells, Georgia State University
Wallace John Whistance-Smith, Ryerson Polytechnic University
Jack Zeller, Kirkwood Community College

A final word of thanks to the unnamed students at the University of Miami, who make it all worthwhile. And most of all, thanks to you, our readers, for choosing this book. Please feel free to contact us with any comments and suggestions.

Robert T. Grauer
rgrauer@umiami.miami.edu
www.bus.miami.edu/~rgrauer
www.prenhall.com/grauer

Maryann Barber
mbarber@homer.bus.miami.edu
www.bus.miami.edu/~mbarber

MICROSOFT OFFICE 97: SIX APPLICATIONS IN ONE

OVERVIEW

Word processing, spreadsheets, and data management have always been significant microcomputer applications. The early days of the PC saw these applications emerge from different vendors with radically different user interfaces. WordPerfect, Lotus, and dBASE, for example, were dominant applications in their respective areas, and each was developed by a different company. The applications were totally dissimilar, and knowledge of one did not help in learning another.

The widespread acceptance of Windows 3.1 promoted the concept of a common user interface, which required all applications to follow a consistent set of conventions. This meant that all applications worked essentially the same way, and it provided a sense of familiarity when you learned a new application, since every application presented the same user interface. The development of a suite of applications from a single vendor extended this concept by imposing additional similarities on all applications within the suite.

This introduction will acquaint you with *Microsoft Office 97* and its four major applications—*Word, Excel, PowerPoint,* and *Access.* The single biggest difference between Office 97 and its predecessor, Office 95, is that the Internet has become an integral part of the Office suite. Thus, we also discuss *Internet Explorer,* the Web browser included in Office 97, and *Microsoft Outlook,* the e-mail and scheduling program that is built into Office 97. The icon at the left of this paragraph appears throughout the text to highlight references to the Internet and enhance your use of Microsoft Office. Our introduction also includes the Clip Gallery, WordArt, and Office Art, three tools built into Microsoft Office that help you to add interest to your documents. And finally, we discuss Object Linking and Embedding, which enables you to combine data from multiple applications into a single document.

Our primary purpose in this introduction is to emphasize the similarities between the applications in Office 97 and to help you transfer your knowledge from one application to the next. You will find the same commands in the same menus. You will also recognize familiar toolbars and will be able to take advantage of similar keyboard shortcuts. You will learn that help can be obtained in a variety of ways, and that it is consistent in every application. Our goal is to show you how much you already know and to get you up and running as quickly as possible.

TRY THE COLLEGE BOOKSTORE

Any machine you buy will come with Windows 95 (or Windows 97), but that is only the beginning since you must also obtain the application software you intend to run. Some hardware vendors will bundle (at no additional cost) Microsoft Office as an inducement to buy from them. If you have already purchased your system and you need software, the best place to buy Microsoft Office is the college bookstore, where it can be obtained at a substantial educational discount.

MICROSOFT OFFICE 97

All Office applications share the ***common Windows interface*** with which you may already be familiar. (If you are new to Windows 95, then read the appendix on the "Essentials of Windows.") Microsoft Office 97 runs equally well under Windows 95, Windows 97, or Windows NT.

Figure 1 displays a screen from each major application in Microsoft Office—Word, Excel, PowerPoint, and Access. Our figure also includes screens from Internet Explorer and Microsoft Outlook, both of which are part of Office 97. Look closely at Figure 1, and realize that each screen contains both an application window and a document window, and that each document window has been maximized within the application window. The title bars of the application and document windows have been merged into a single title bar that appears at the top of the application window. The title bar displays the application (e.g., Microsoft Word in Figure 1a) as well as the name of the document (Web Enabled in Figure 1a) on which you are working.

All six screens in Figure 1 are similar in appearance even though the applications accomplish very different tasks. Each application window has an identifying icon, a menu bar, a title bar, and a minimize, maximize or restore, and a close button. Each document window has its own identifying icon, and its own minimize, maximize or restore, and close button. The Windows taskbar appears at the bottom of each application window and shows the open applications. The status bar appears above the taskbar and displays information relevant to the window or selected object.

Each major application in Microsoft Office uses a consistent command structure in which the same basic menus are found in all applications. The File, Edit, View, Insert, Tools, Window, and Help menus are present in all six applications. The same commands are found in the same menus. The Save, Open, Print, and Exit commands, for example, are contained in the File menu. The Cut, Copy, Paste, and Undo commands are found in the Edit menu.

The means for accessing the pull-down menus are consistent from one application to the next. Click the menu name on the menu bar, or press the Alt key plus the underlined letter of the menu name; for example, press Alt+F to pull down the File menu. If you already know some keyboard shortcuts in one application, there is a good chance that the shortcuts will work in another application. Ctrl+Home and Ctrl+End, for example, move to the beginning and end of a document, respectively. Ctrl+B, Ctrl+I, and Ctrl+U boldface, italicize, and underline text. Ctrl+X (the "X" is supposed to remind you of a pair of scissors), Ctrl+C, and Ctrl+V will cut, copy, and paste, respectively.

Title bar

Identifying icon

Menu bar

Standard toolbar

Formatting toolbar

Minimize button

Restore button

Close button

Status bar

Task bar

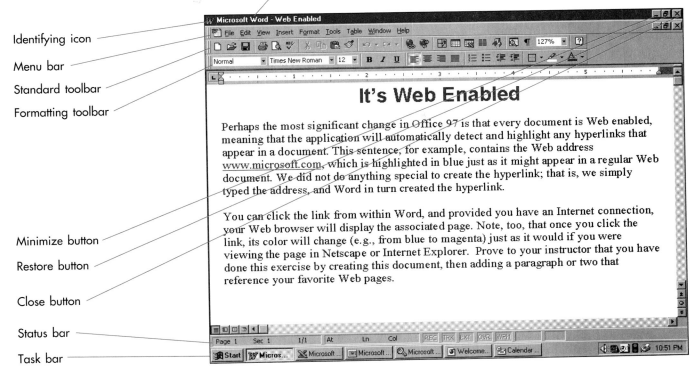

(a) Microsoft Word

Title bar

Identifying icon

Menu bar

Standard toolbar

Formatting toolbar

Minimize button

Restore button

Close button

Status bar

Task bar

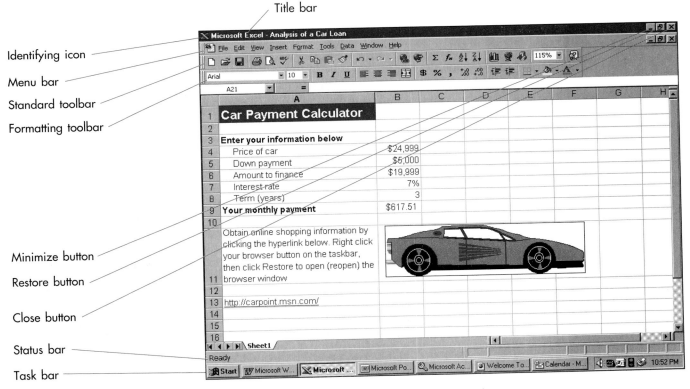

(b) Microsoft Excel

FIGURE 1   The Common User Interface

Title bar

Identifying icon

Menu bar

Standard toolbar

Formatting toolbar

Minimize button

Restore button

Close button

Status bar

Task bar

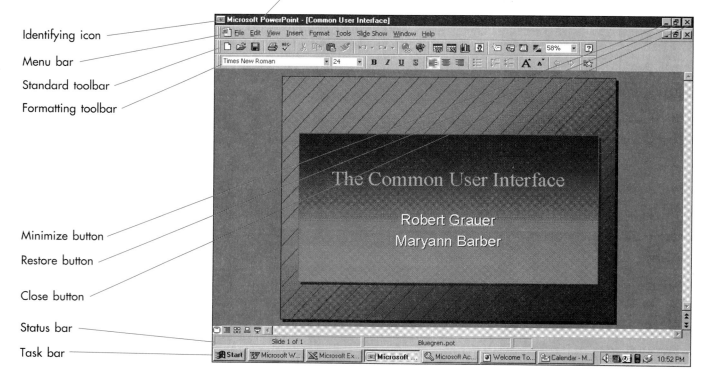

(c) Microsoft PowerPoint

Title bar

Identifying icon

Menu bar

Toolbar

Minimize button

Restore button

Close button

Status bar

Task bar

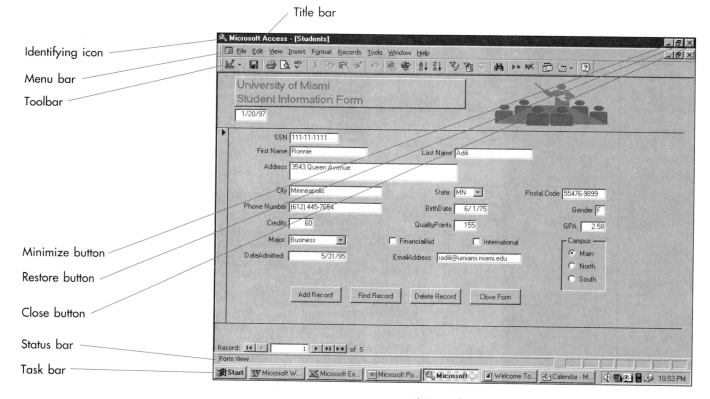

(d) Microsoft Access

FIGURE 1   The Common User Interface (continued)

Title bar

Identifying icon

Menu bar

Toolbar

Minimize button

Restore button

Close button

Status bar

Task bar

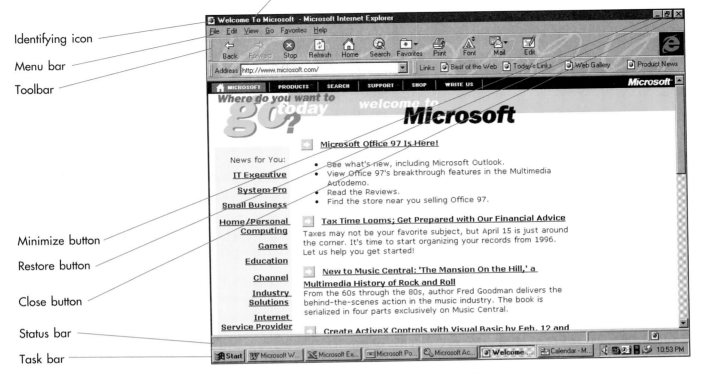

(e) Internet Explorer

Title bar

Identifying icon

Menu bar

Toolbar

Minimize button

Restore button

Close button

Status bar

Task bar

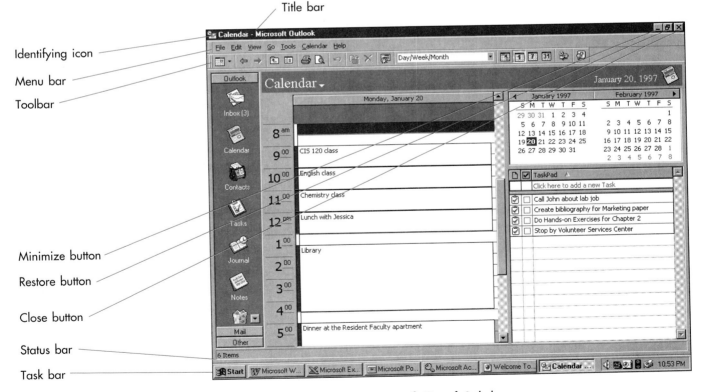

(f) Microsoft Outlook

FIGURE 1   The Common User Interface (continued)

The four major applications use consistent (and often identical) dialog boxes. The dialog boxes to open and close a file, for example, are identical in every application. All four applications also share a common dictionary. The AutoCorrect feature (to correct common spelling mistakes) works identically in all four applications. The help feature also functions identically.

There are, of course, differences between the applications. Each application has unique menus and toolbars. Nevertheless, the Standard and Formatting toolbars in the major applications contain many of the same tools (especially the first several tools on the left of each toolbar). The **Standard toolbar** contains buttons for basic commands such as Open, Save, or Print. It also contains buttons to cut, copy, and paste, and these buttons are identical in all four applications. The **Formatting toolbar** provides access to common operations such as boldface or italics, or changing the font or point size; again, these buttons are identical in all four applications. ScreenTips are present in all applications.

STANDARD OFFICE VERSUS OFFICE PROFESSIONAL

Microsoft distributes both a Standard and a Professional edition of Office 97. Both versions include Word, Excel, PowerPoint, Internet Explorer, and Outlook. Office Professional also has Microsoft Access. The difference is important when you are shopping and you are comparing prices from different sources. Be sure to purchase the version that is appropriate for your needs.

Help for Office 97

Several types of help are available in Office 97. The most basic is accessed by pulling down the Help menu and clicking the Contents and Index command to display the Help Contents window as shown in Figures 2a and 2b. (The Help screens are from Microsoft Word, but similar screens are available for each of the other applications.) The **Contents tab** in Figure 2a is analogous to the table of contents in an ordinary book. It displays the major topics in the application as a series of books that are open or closed. You can click any closed book to open it, which in turn displays additional books and/or help topics. Conversely, you can click any open book to close it and gain additional space on the screen.

The **Index tab** in Figure 2b is similar to the index of an ordinary book. Enter the first several letters of the topic to look up, such as "we" in Figure 2b. Help then returns all of the topics beginning with the letters you entered. Select the topic you want, then display the topic for immediate viewing, or print it for later reference. (The Find tab, not shown in Figure 2, contains a more extensive listing of entries than does the Index tab. It lets you enter a specific word, then it returns every topic that contains that word.)

The **Office Assistant** in Figure 2c is new to Office 97 and is activated by clicking the Office Assistant button on the Standard toolbar or by pressing the F1 function key. The Assistant enables you to ask a question in English, then it returns a series of topics that attempt to answer your question.

Additional help can be obtained from the Microsoft Web site as shown in Figure 2d, provided you have access to the Internet. The easiest way to access the site is to pull down the Help menu from any Office application, click Microsoft on the Web, then click Online Support. This, in turn, will start the Internet Explorer and take you to the appropriate page on the Web, where you will find the most current information available as well as the most detailed support. You can, for example, access the same knowledge base as that used by Microsoft support engineers when you call for technical assistance.

Topic may be viewed or printed by clicking appropriate command button

Double click closed book to open it and display additional help topics

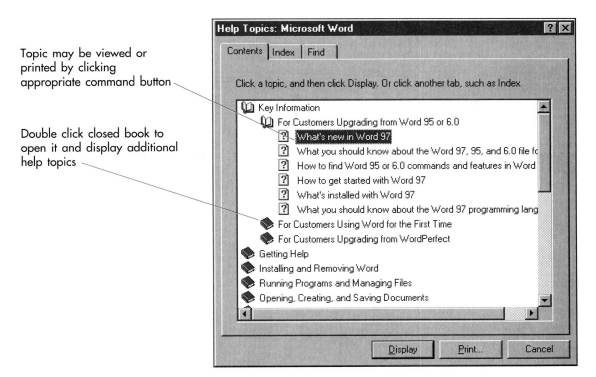

(a) Contents Tab

Type the first few letters in the topic to look up

Select the desired topic

Click Display button to view the information

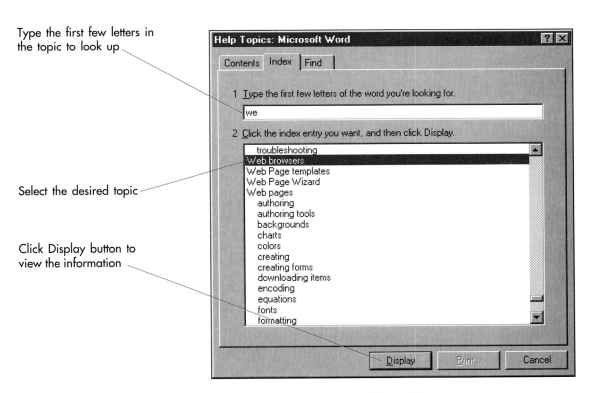

(b) Index Tab

FIGURE 2   Help with Microsoft Office

Help screen contains links to additional information

Click any topic to display the help screen

Enter your question, then click the Search button

Office Assistant (other images are available)

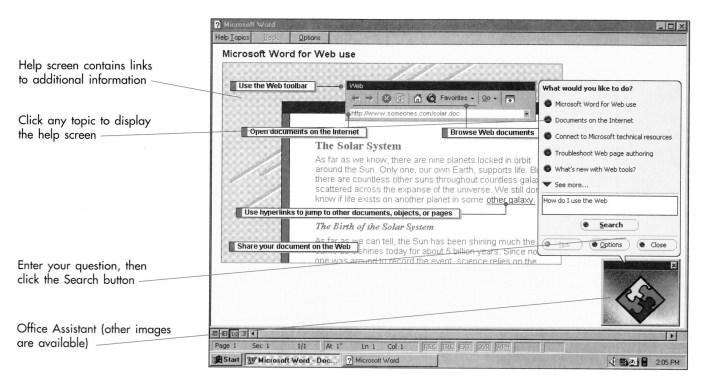

(c) The Office Assistant

Internet Explorer opens automatically

Web address

Link to Frequently Asked Questions

Click the link to desired information

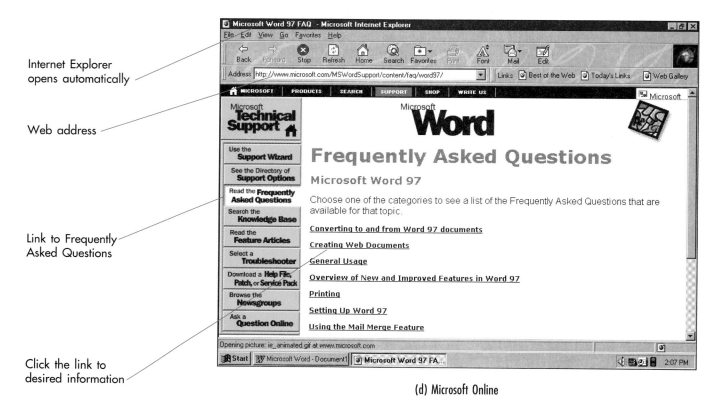

(d) Microsoft Online

FIGURE 2   Help with Microsoft Office (continued)

Office Shortcut Bar

The *Microsoft Office Shortcut Bar* provides immediate access to each application within Microsoft Office. It consists of a row of buttons and can be placed anywhere on the screen. The Shortcut Bar is anchored by default on the right side of the desktop, but you can position it along any edge, or have it "float" in the middle of the desktop. You can even hide it from view when it is not in use.

Figure 3a displays the Shortcut Bar as it appears on our desktop. The buttons that are displayed (and the order in which they appear) are established through the Customize dialog box in Figure 3b. Our Shortcut Bar contains a button for each Office application, a button for the Windows Explorer, and a button for Bookshelf Basics.

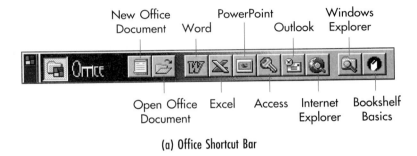

(a) Office Shortcut Bar

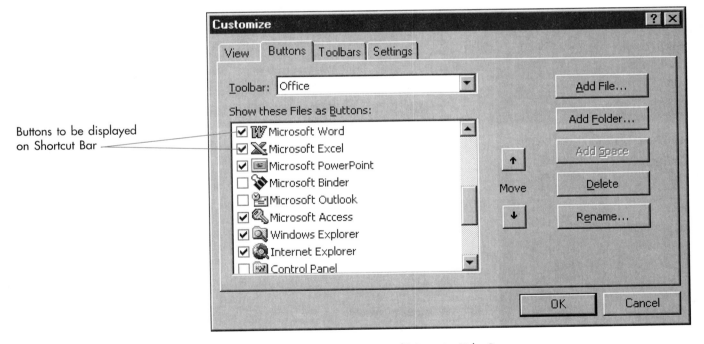

Buttons to be displayed on Shortcut Bar

(b) Customize Dialog Box

FIGURE 3   Microsoft Office Shortcut Bar

Docucentric Orientation

Our Shortcut Bar contains two additional buttons: to open an existing document and to start a new document. These buttons are very useful and take advantage of the "docucentric" orientation of Microsoft Office, which lets you think in terms

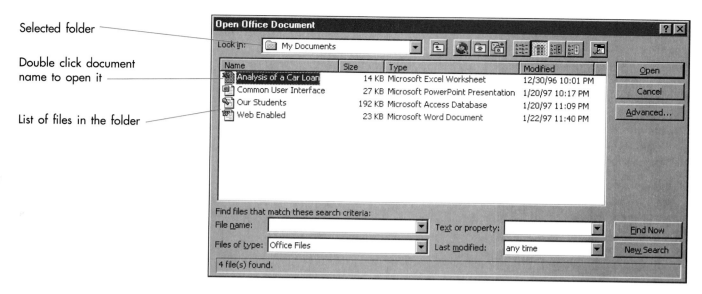

Selected folder

Double click document
name to open it

List of files in the folder

(a) Open an Existing Document

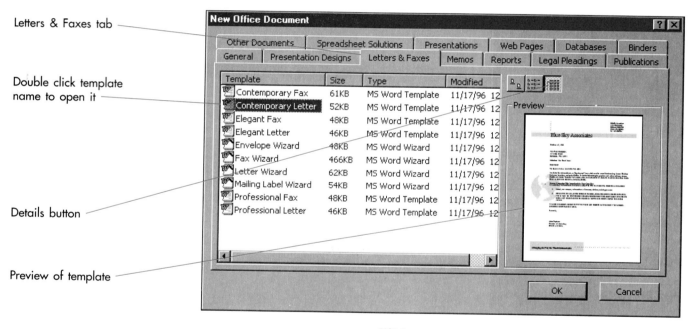

Letters & Faxes tab

Double click template
name to open it

Details button

Preview of template

(b) Start a New Document

FIGURE 4   Document Orientation

of a document rather than the associated application. You can still open a document in traditional fashion, by starting the application (e.g., clicking its button on the Shortcut Bar), then using the File Open command to open the document. It's easier, however, to locate the document, then double click its icon, which automatically loads the associated program.

Consider, for example, the Open dialog box in Figure 4a, which is displayed by clicking the Open a Document button on the Shortcut Bar. The Open dialog box is common to the major Office applications, and it works identically in each application. The My Documents folder is selected in Figure 4a, and it contains four documents of various file types. The documents are displayed in the Details view, which shows the document name, size, file type, and date and time the document was last modified. To open any document—for example, "Analysis of a Car Loan"—just double click its name or icon. The associated application (Microsoft Excel in this example) will be started automatically; and it, in turn, will open the selected workbook.

The "docucentric" orientation also applies to new documents. Click the Start a New Document button on the Office Shortcut Bar, and you display the New dialog box in Figure 4b. Click the tab corresponding to the type of document you want to create, such as Letters & Faxes in Figure 4b. Change to the Details view, then click (select) various templates so that you can choose the one most appropriate for your purpose. Double click the desired template to start the application, which opens the template and enables you to create the document.

CHANGE THE VIEW

The toolbar in the Open dialog box contains buttons to display the documents within the selected folder in one of several views. Click the Details button to switch to the Details view and see the date and time the file was last modified, as well as its size and type. Click the List button to display an icon representing the associated application, enabling you to see many more files than in the Details view. The Preview button lets you see a document before you open it. The Properties button displays information about the document, including the number of revisions.

SHARED APPLICATIONS AND UTILITIES

Microsoft Office includes additional applications and shared utilities, several of which are illustrated in Figure 5. The *Microsoft Clip Gallery* in Figure 5a has more than 3,000 clip art images and almost 150 photographs, each in a variety of categories. It also contains a lesser number of sound files and video clips. The Clip Gallery can be accessed from every Office application, most easily through the Insert Picture command, which displays the Clip Gallery dialog box.

The *Microsoft WordArt* utility adds decorative text to a document, and is accessed through the Insert Picture command from Word, Excel, or PowerPoint. WordArt is intuitive and easy to use. In essence, you choose a style for the text from among the selections in the dialog box of Figure 5b, then you enter the specific text in a second dialog box (which is not shown in Figure 5). It's fun, it's easy, and you can create some truly dynamite documents that will add interest to a document.

Office Art consists of a set of drawing tools that is found on the Drawing toolbar in Word, Excel, or PowerPoint. You don't have to be an artist—all it takes is a little imagination and an appreciation for what the individual tools can do. In Figure 5c, for example, we began with a single clip art image, copied it several times within the PowerPoint slide, then rotated and colored the students as shown. We also used the AutoShapes tool to add a callout for our student.

Microsoft Bookshelf Basics contains three of the nine books available in the complete version of Microsoft Bookshelf (which is an additional cost item). The *American Heritage Dictionary,* the *Original Roget's Thesaurus,* and the *Columbia Dictionary of Quotations* are provided at no charge. An excerpt from the *American Heritage Dictionary* is illustrated in Figure 5d. Enter the word you are looking for in the text box on the left, then read the definition on the right. You can click the sound icon and hear the pronunciation of the word.

Choose the type of object

Choose the category

Choose the image

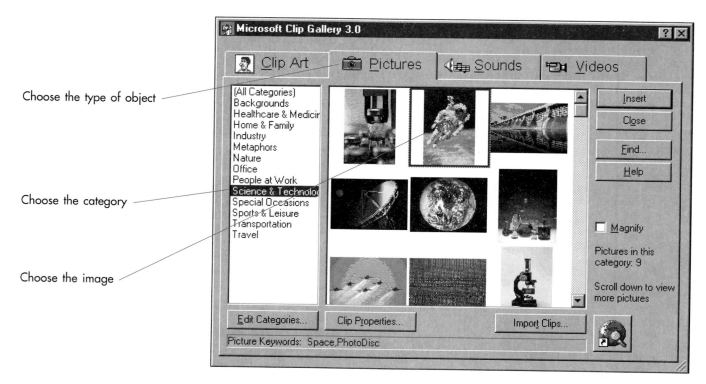

(a) Microsoft Clip Gallery

Select the style to display a
second dialog box in which
you enter your text

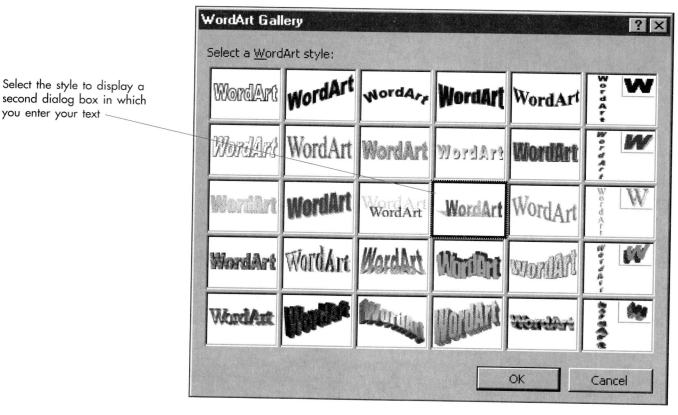

(b) WordArt

FIGURE 5   Shared Applications

Color objects in clip art

Create callout

Callout tool

Drawing toolbar

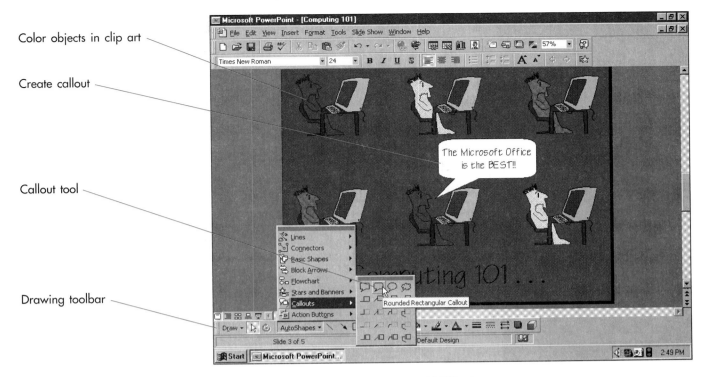

(c) Office Art

Enter word

Click to
hear pronunciation

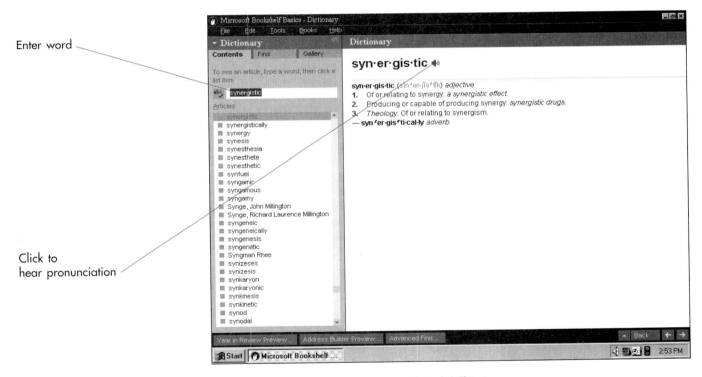

(d) Bookshelf Basics

FIGURE 5   Shared Applications (continued)

OBJECT LINKING AND EMBEDDING

The applications in Microsoft Office are thoroughly integrated with one another. They look alike and they work in consistent fashion. Equally important, they share information through a technology known as **_Object Linking and Embedding (OLE)_,** which enables you to create a **_compound document_** containing data (objects) from multiple applications.

The compound document in Figure 6 was created in Word, and it contains objects (a worksheet and a chart) that were created in Excel. The letterhead uses a logo that was taken from the Clip Gallery, while the name and address of the recipient were drawn from an Access database. The various objects were inserted into the compound document through linking or embedding, which are actually two very different techniques. Both operations, however, are much more sophisticated than simply pasting an object, because with either linking or embedding, you can edit the object by using the tools of the original application.

The difference between linking and embedding depends on whether the object is stored within the compound document (**_embedding_**) or in its own file (**_linking_**). An _embedded object_ is stored in the compound document, which in turn becomes the only user (client) of that object. A _linked object_ is stored in its own file, and the compound document is one of many potential clients of that object. The compound document does not contain the linked object per se, but only a representation of the object as well as a pointer (link) to the file containing the object. The advantage of linking is that the document is updated automatically if the object changes.

The choice between linking and embedding depends on how the object will be used. Linking is preferable if the object is likely to change and the compound document requires the latest version. Linking should also be used when the same object is placed in many documents so that any change to the object has to be made in only one place. Embedding should be used if you need to take the object with you (to a different computer) and/or if there is only a single destination document for the object.

Office of Residential Living

| University of Miami | • | P.O. Box 248904 | • | Coral Gables, FL 33124 |

January 10, 1998

Mr. Jeffrey Redmond, President
Dynamic Dining Services
4329 Palmetto Lane
Miami, FL 33157

Dear Jeff,

As per our conversation, occupancy is projected to be back up from last year. I have enclosed a spreadsheet and chart that show the total enrollment for the past four school years. Please realize, however, that the 1997–1998 figures are projections, as the Spring 1998 numbers are still incomplete. The final 1997–1998 numbers should be confirmed within the next two weeks. I hope that this helps with your planning. If you need further information, please contact me at the above address.

Dorm Occupancy

	94-95	95-96	96-97	97-98
Beatty	330	285	270	250
Broward	620	580	620	565
Graham	450	397	352	420
Rawlings	435	470	295	372
Tolbert	550	554	524	635
Totals	2385	2286	2061	2242

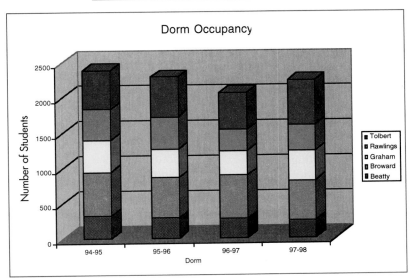

FIGURE 6   A Compound Document

The common user interface requires every Windows application to follow a consistent set of conventions and ensures that all applications work basically the same way. The development of a suite of applications from a single vendor extends this concept by imposing additional similarities on all applications within the suite.

Microsoft distributes both a Standard and a Professional edition of Office 97. Both versions include Word, Excel, PowerPoint, Internet Explorer, and Outlook. Office Professional also has Microsoft Access. The single biggest difference between Office 97 and its predecessor, Office 95, is that the Internet has become an integral part of the Office suite.

Help for all Office applications is available in a variety of formats. The Help Contents window provides access to a Contents and Index tab in which you look up specific topics. The Office Assistant enables you to ask a question in English. Still additional help is available from the Microsoft Web site, provided you have access to the Internet.

Microsoft Office includes several additional applications and shared utilities that can be used to add interest to a document. The Clip Gallery has more than 3,000 clip art images, 150 photographs, and a lesser number of sound files and video clips. WordArt enables you to create decorative text, while Office Art consists of a powerful set of drawing tools.

The Microsoft Office Shortcut Bar provides immediate access to each application in Microsoft Office. The Shortcut Bar is fully customizable with respect to the buttons it displays, its appearance, and its position on the desktop. The Open a Document and Start a New Document buttons enable you to think in terms of a document rather than the associated application.

Object Linking and Embedding (OLE) enables you to create a compound document containing data (objects) from multiple applications. Linking and embedding are different operations. The difference between the two depends on whether the object is stored within the compound document (embedding) or in its own file (linking).

KEY WORDS AND CONCEPTS

Common Windows
    interface
Compound document
Contents tab
Docucentric orientation
Embedding
Formatting toolbar
Index tab
Internet Explorer
Linking
Microsoft Access

Microsoft Bookshelf
    Basics
Microsoft Clip Gallery
Microsoft Excel
Microsoft Office
    Professional
Microsoft Office
    Shortcut Bar
Microsoft Outlook
Microsoft PowerPoint
Microsoft Standard
    Office

Microsoft Word
Microsoft WordArt
Object Linking and
    Embedding (OLE)
Office Art
Office Assistant
Online help
Shared applications
Standard toolbar

MICROSOFT® WORD 97: WHAT WILL WORD PROCESSING DO FOR ME?

After reading this chapter you will be able to:

1. Define word wrap; differentiate between a hard and a soft return.
2. Distinguish between the insert and overtype modes.
3. Describe the elements on the Microsoft Word screen.
4. Create, save, retrieve, edit, and print a simple document.
5. Check a document for spelling; describe the function of the custom dictionary.
6. Describe the AutoCorrect feature; explain how it can be used to create your own shorthand.
7. Use the thesaurus to look up synonyms and antonyms.
8. Explain the objectives and limitations of the grammar check; customize the grammar check for business or casual writing.
9. Differentiate between the Save and Save As commands; describe various backup options that can be selected.

OVERVIEW

Have you ever produced what you thought was the perfect term paper only to discover that you omitted a sentence or misspelled a word, or that the paper was three pages too short or one page too long? Wouldn't it be nice to make the necessary changes, and then be able to reprint the entire paper with the touch of a key? Welcome to the world of word processing, where you are no longer stuck with having to retype anything. Instead, you retrieve your work from disk, display it on the monitor and revise it as necessary, then print it at any time, in draft or final form.

This chapter provides a broad-based introduction to word processing in general and Microsoft Word in particular. We begin by presenting (or perhaps reviewing) the essential concepts of a word processor, then show you how these concepts are implemented in Word. We show you how to create a document, how to save it on disk, then retrieve the document you just created. We introduce you to the spell check and thesaurus, two essential tools in any word processor. We also present the grammar check as a convenient way of finding a variety of errors but remind you there is no substitute for carefully proofreading the final document.

THE BASICS OF WORD PROCESSING

All word processors adhere to certain basic concepts that must be understood if you are to use the programs effectively. The next several pages introduce ideas that are applicable to any word processor (and which you may already know). We follow the conceptual material with a hands-on exercise that enables you to apply what you have learned.

The Insertion Point

The *insertion point* is a flashing vertical line that marks the place where text will be entered. The insertion point is always at the beginning of a new document, but it can be moved anywhere within an existing document. If, for example, you wanted to add text to the end of a document, you would move the insertion point to the end of the document, then begin typing.

Word Wrap

A newcomer to word processing has one major transition to make from a typewriter, and it is an absolutely critical adjustment. Whereas a typist returns the carriage at the end of every line, just the opposite is true of a word processor. One types continually *without* pressing the enter key at the end of a line because the word processor automatically wraps text from one line to the next. This concept is known as *word wrap* and is illustrated in Figure 1.1.

The word *primitive* does not fit on the current line in Figure 1.1a, and is automatically shifted to the next line, *without* the user having to press the enter key. The user continues to enter the document, with additional words being wrapped to subsequent lines as necessary. The only time you use the enter key is at the end of a paragraph, or when you want the insertion point to move to the next line and the end of the current line doesn't reach the right margin.

Word wrap is closely associated with another concept, that of hard and soft returns. A *hard return* is created by the user when he or she presses the enter key at the end of a paragraph; a *soft return* is created by the word processor as it wraps text from one line to the next. The locations of the soft returns change automatically as a document is edited (e.g., as text is inserted or deleted, or as margins or fonts are changed). The locations of the hard returns can be changed only by the user, who must intentionally insert or delete each hard return.

There are two hard returns in Figure 1.1b, one at the end of each paragraph. There are also six soft returns in the first paragraph (one at the end of every line except the last) and three soft returns in the second paragraph. Now suppose the margins in the document are made smaller (that is, the line is made longer) as shown in Figure 1.1c. The number of soft returns drops to four and two (in the first and second paragraphs, respectively) as more text fits on a line and fewer lines are needed. The revised document still contains the two original hard returns, one at the end of each paragraph.

The original IBM PC was extremely pr

The original IBM PC was extremely primitive

primitive cannot fit on current line

primitive is automatically moved to the next line

(a) Entering the Document

The original IBM PC was extremely primitive (not to mention expensive) by current standards. The basic machine came equipped with only 16Kb RAM and was sold without a monitor or disk (a TV and tape cassette were suggested instead). The price of this powerhouse was $1565. ¶
You could, however, purchase an expanded business system with 256Kb RAM, two 160Kb floppy drives, monochrome monitor, and 80-cps printer for $4425. ¶

Hard returns are created by pressing the enter key at the end of a paragraph.

(b) Completed Document

The original IBM PC was extremely primitive (not to mention expensive) by current standards. The basic machine came equipped with only 16Kb RAM and was sold without a monitor or disk (a TV and tape cassette were suggested instead). The price of this powerhouse was $1565. ¶
You could, however, purchase an expanded business system with 256Kb RAM, two 160Kb floppy drives, monochrome monitor, and 80-cps printer for $4425. ¶

Revised document still contains two hard returns, one at the end of each paragraph.

(c) Completed Document

FIGURE 1.1   Word Wrap

Toggle Switches

Suppose you sat down at the keyboard and typed an entire sentence without pressing the Shift key; the sentence would be in all lowercase letters. Then you pressed the Caps Lock key and retyped the sentence, again without pressing the Shift key. This time the sentence would be in all uppercase letters. You could repeat the process as often as you like. Each time you pressed the Caps Lock key, the sentence would switch from lowercase to uppercase and vice versa.

The point of this exercise is to introduce the concept of a ***toggle switch,*** a device that causes the computer to alternate between two states. The Caps Lock key is an example of a toggle switch. Each time you press it, newly typed text will change from uppercase to lowercase and back again. We will see several other examples of toggle switches as we proceed in our discussion of word processing.

Insert versus Overtype

Microsoft Word is always in one of two modes, ***insert*** or **overtype.** (The insert mode is the default and the one you will be in most of the time.) Text that is entered into a document during the insert mode moves existing text to the right to accommodate the characters being added. Text entered from the overtype mode replaces (overtypes) existing text. Regardless of which mode you are in, text is always entered or replaced immediately to the right of the insertion point.

The insert mode is best when you enter text for the first time, but either mode can be used to make corrections. The insert mode is the better choice when the correction requires you to add new text; the overtype mode is easier when you are substituting one or more character(s) for another. The difference is illustrated in Figure 1.2.

Figure 1.2a displays the text as it was originally entered, with two misspellings. The letters *se* have been omitted from the word *insert,* and an *x* has been erroneously typed instead of an *r* in the word *overtype.* The insert mode is used in Figure 1.2b to add the missing letters, which in turn moves the rest of the line to the right. The overtype mode is used in Figure 1.2c to replace the *x* with an *r.*

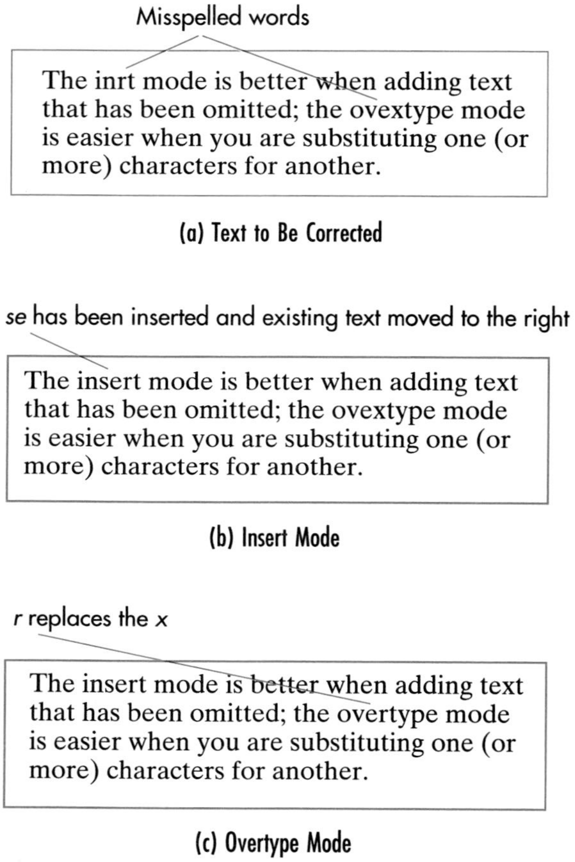

Misspelled words

The inrt mode is better when adding text that has been omitted; the ovextype mode is easier when you are substituting one (or more) characters for another.

(a) Text to Be Corrected

se has been inserted and existing text moved to the right

The insert mode is better when adding text that has been omitted; the ovextype mode is easier when you are substituting one (or more) characters for another.

(b) Insert Mode

r replaces the *x*

The insert mode is better when adding text that has been omitted; the overtype mode is easier when you are substituting one (or more) characters for another.

(c) Overtype Mode

FIGURE 1.2   Insert and Overtype Modes

Deleting Text

The backspace and Del keys delete one character immediately to the left or right of the insertion point, respectively. The choice between them depends on when you need to erase a character(s). The backspace key is easier if you want to delete a character immediately after typing it. The Del key is preferable during subsequent editing.

You can delete several characters at one time by selecting (dragging the mouse over) the characters to be deleted, then pressing the Del key. And finally, you can delete and replace text in one operation by selecting the text to be replaced and then typing the new text in its place.

LEARN TO TYPE

The ultimate limitation of any word processor is the speed at which you enter data; hence the ability to type quickly is invaluable. Learning how to type is easy, especially with the availability of computer-based typing programs. As little as a half hour a day for a couple of weeks will have you up to speed, and if you do any significant amount of writing at all, the investment will pay off many times.

INTRODUCTION TO MICROSOFT WORD

We used Microsoft Word to write this book, as can be inferred from the screen in Figure 1.3. Your screen will be different from ours in many ways. You will not have the same document nor is it likely that you will customize Word in exactly the same way. You should, however, be able to recognize the basic elements that are found in the Microsoft Word window that is open on the desktop.

There are actually two open windows in Figure 1.3—an application window for Microsoft Word and a document window for the specific document on which you are working. Each window has its own Minimize, Maximize (or Restore), and Close buttons. Both windows have been maximized, and thus the title bars have been merged into a single title bar that appears at the top of the application window and reflects the application (Microsoft Word) as well as the document name (Word Chapter 1). A menu bar appears immediately below the title bar. Vertical and horizontal scroll bars appear at the right and bottom of the document window. The Windows taskbar appears at the bottom of the screen and shows the open applications.

Microsoft Word is also part of the Microsoft Office suite of applications, and thus shares additional features with Excel, Access, and PowerPoint, that are also part of the Office suite. *Toolbars* provide immediate access to common commands and appear immediately below the menu bar. The toolbars can be displayed or hidden using the Toolbars command in the View menu.

The *Standard toolbar* contains buttons corresponding to the most basic commands in Word—for example, opening a file or printing a document. The icon on the button is intended to be indicative of its function (e.g., a printer to indicate the Print command). You can also point to the button to display a *ScreenTip* showing the name of the button. The *Formatting toolbar* appears under the Standard toolbar and provides access to common formatting operations such as boldface, italics, or underlining.

The toolbars may appear overwhelming at first, but there is absolutely no need to memorize what the individual buttons do. That will come with time. We

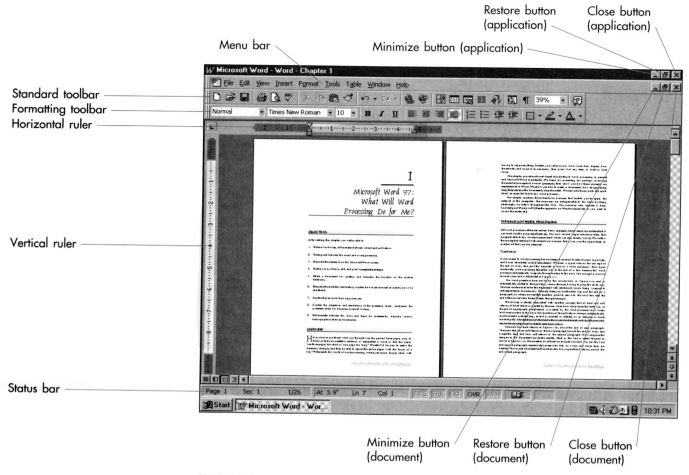

Restore button (application)

FIGURE 1.3   Microsoft Word

suggest, however, that you will have a better appreciation for the various buttons if you consider them in groups, according to their general function, as shown in Figure 1.4a.

The **horizontal ruler** is displayed underneath the toolbars and enables you to change margins, tabs, and/or indents for all or part of a document. A **vertical ruler** shows the vertical position of text on the page and can be used to change the top or bottom margins.

The **status bar** at the bottom of the document window displays the location of the insertion point (or information about the command being executed.) The status bar also shows the status (settings) of various indicators—for example, OVR to show that Word is in the overtype, as opposed to the insert, mode.

HELP FOR MICROSOFT WORD

Office 97 offers help from a variety of sources. You can pull down the Help menu as you can with any Windows application and/or you can click the Office Assistant button on the Standard toolbar. You can also go to the Microsoft Web site to obtain more recent, and often more detailed, information. You will find the answer to frequently asked questions, and you can access the same Knowledge Base used by Microsoft support engineers.

Starts a new document, opens an existing document, or saves the document in memory

Prints the document or previews the document prior to printing

Checks the spelling and grammar of the document

Cuts, copies, or pastes the selected text; copies the formatting of the selected text

Undoes or redoes a previously executed command

Inserts a hyperlink or toggles the display of the Web toolbar on and off

Draws a table, inserts a table, inserts an Excel worksheet, creates columns, or toggles the display of the Drawing toolbar on and off

Toggles the Document map feature on and off, toggles the nonprinting characters on and off, or changes the zoom percentage

Displays the Office Assistant. (The lightbulb indicates the Assistant has a suggestion)

(a) Standard Toolbar

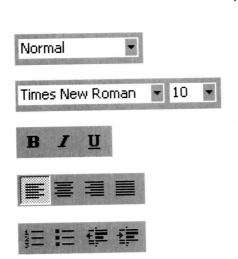

Applies a specific style to the selected text

Changes the typeface, or changes the type size

Toggles boldface, italics, and underline on and off

Aligns left, center, right, or full (justified)

Creates a numbered or bulleted list; decreases or increases the indent

Creates a border, applies highlighting to the selected text, or applies color to the selected text

(b) Formatting Toolbar

FIGURE 1.4   Toolbars

The *File menu* is a critically important menu in virtually every Windows application. It contains the Save and Open commands to save a document on disk, then subsequently retrieve (open) that document at a later time. The File menu also contains the Print command to print a document, the Close command to close the current document but continue working in the application, and the Exit command to quit the application altogether.

The *Save command* copies the document that is being edited (the document in memory) to disk. The Save As dialog box appears the first time that the document is saved so that you can specify the file name and other required information. All subsequent executions of the Save command save the document under the assigned name, replacing the previously saved version with the new version.

The Save As dialog box requires a file name (e.g., My First Document in Figure 1.5a), which can be up to 255 characters in length. The file name may contain spaces and commas. (Periods are permitted, but discouraged, since they are too easily confused with DOS extensions.)

The dialog box also requires the specification of the drive and folder in which the file is to be saved as well as the file type that determines which application the file is associated with. (Long-time DOS users will remember the three-character extension at the end of a file name—for example, DOC—to indicate the associated application. The extension may be hidden in Windows 95 according to options set through the View menu in My Computer or the Windows Explorer.

The *Open command* brings a copy of a previously saved document into memory enabling you to work with that document. The Open command displays the Open dialog box in which you specify the file to retrieve. You indicate the drive (and optionally the folder) that contains the file, as well as the type of file you want to retrieve. Word will then list all files of that type on the designated drive (and folder), enabling you to open the file you want.

The Save and Open commands work in conjunction with one another. The Save As dialog box in Figure 1.5a, for example, saves the file *My First Document* onto the disk in drive A. The Open dialog box in Figure 1.5b brings that file back into memory so that you can work with the file, after which you can save the revised file for use at a later time.

The toolbars in the Save As dialog and Open dialog boxes have several buttons in common that enable you to list the files in different ways. The Details view is selected in both dialog boxes and shows the file size as well as the date and time a file was last modified. The List button displays only the file names, and hence more files are visible at one time. The Preview button lets you see a document before you open it. The Properties button displays information about the document including the number of revisions.

SEARCH THE WEB

Microsoft Office 97 enables you to open and/or search for a Web document without having to exit from the application. Pull down the File menu and click the Open command to display the Open dialog box, from where you can click the Search the Web button. Your Web browser will open automatically and connect you to a search page in which you enter keywords, provided you have an Internet connection.

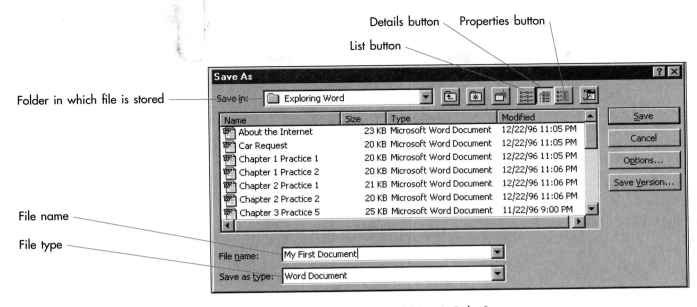

Details button   Properties button

List button

Folder in which file is stored ——— Save in:

File name

File type

(a) Save As Dialog Box

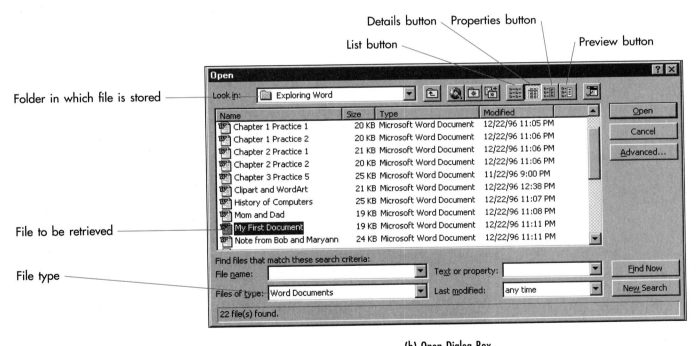

Details button   Properties button

List button   Preview button

Folder in which file is stored ———

File to be retrieved ———

File type ———

(b) Open Dialog Box

FIGURE 1.5   The Save and Open Commands

LEARNING BY DOING

Every chapter contains a series of hands-on exercises that enable you to apply what you learn at the computer. The exercises in this chapter are linked to one another in that you create a simple document in exercise one, then open and edit that document in exercise two. The ability to save and open a document is critical, and you do not want to spend an inordinate amount of time entering text unless you are confident in your ability to retrieve it later.

My First Document

Objective: To start Microsoft Word in order to create, save, and print a simple document. To execute commands via the toolbar or from pull-down menus. Use Figure 1.6 as a guide in doing the exercise.

STEP 1: Welcome to Windows

➤ Turn on the computer and all of its peripherals. The floppy drive should be empty prior to starting your machine. This ensures that the system starts from the hard disk, which contains the Windows files, as opposed to a floppy disk, which does not.

➤ Your system will take a minute or so to get started, after which you should see the Windows desktop in Figure 1.6a. Do not be concerned if the appearance of your desktop is different from ours.

➤ You may see additional objects on the desktop in Windows 95 and/or the active desktop content in Windows 97. It doesn't matter which operating system you are using because Office 97 runs equally well under both Windows 95 and Windows 97 (as well as Windows NT).

➤ You may see a Welcome to Windows 95/Windows 97 dialog box with command buttons to take a tour of the operating system. If so, click the appropriate button(s) or close the dialog box.

(a) The Windows Desktop (step 1)

FIGURE 1.6   Hands-on Exercise 1

STEP 2: Obtain the Practice Files

➤ We have created a series of practice files (commonly called a "data disk") for you to use throughout the text. Your instructor will make these files available to you in a variety of ways:

- You can download the files from our Web site if you have access to the Internet and World Wide Web (see boxed tip).
- The files may be on a network drive, in which case you can use the Windows Explorer to copy the files from the network to a floppy disk.
- There may be an actual "data disk" that you are to check out from the lab in order to use the Copy Disk command to duplicate the disk.

➤ Check with your instructor for additional information.

STEP 3: Start Microsoft Word

➤ Click the **Start button** to display the Start menu. Click (or point to) the **Programs menu,** then click **Microsoft Word** to start the program.

➤ Close the Office Assistant if it appears. (The Office Assistant is illustrated in step 6 of this exercise.)

➤ If necessary, click the **Maximize button** in the application window so that Word takes the entire desktop as shown in Figure 1.6b. Click the **Maximize button** in the document window (if necessary) so that the document window is as large as possible.

➤ Do not be concerned if your screen is different from ours as we include a troubleshooting section immediately following this exercise.

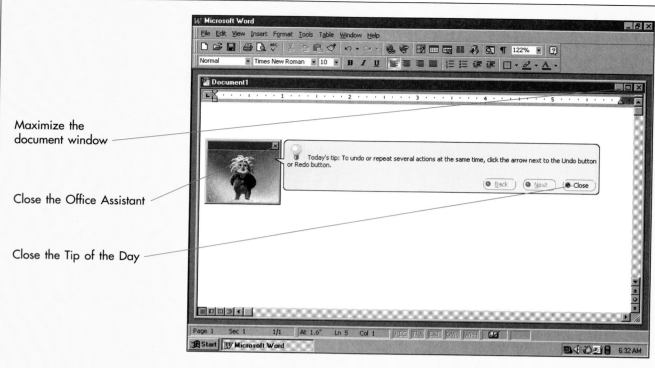

Maximize the document window

Close the Office Assistant

Close the Tip of the Day

Today's tip: To undo or repeat several actions at the same time, click the arrow next to the Undo button or Redo button.

(b) Start Word (step 3)

FIGURE 1.6   Hands-on Exercise 1 (continued)

CHOOSE YOUR OWN ASSISTANT

You can choose your own personal assistant from one of several available images. Click the Office Assistant button on the Standard toolbar to display the Assistant, click the Options button to display the Office Assistant dialog box, click the Gallery tab, then click the Next button repeatedly to cycle through the available images. Click OK to select the image and close the dialog box. (The Office 97 CD is required for certain characters.)

STEP 4: Create the Document

➤ Create the document in Figure 1.6c. Type just as you would on a typewriter with one exception; do *not* press the enter key at the end of a line because Word will automatically wrap text from one line to the next.

➤ Press the **enter key** at the end of the paragraph.

➤ You may see a red or green wavy line to indicate spelling or grammatical errors respectively. Both features are discussed later in the chapter.

➤ Point to the red wavy line (if any), click the **right mouse button** to display a list of suggested corrections, then click (select) the appropriate substitution.

➤ Ignore the green wavy line (if any).

Show/Hide ¶ button (displays/
hides nonprinting characters)

Press the enter key at the end
of the paragraph

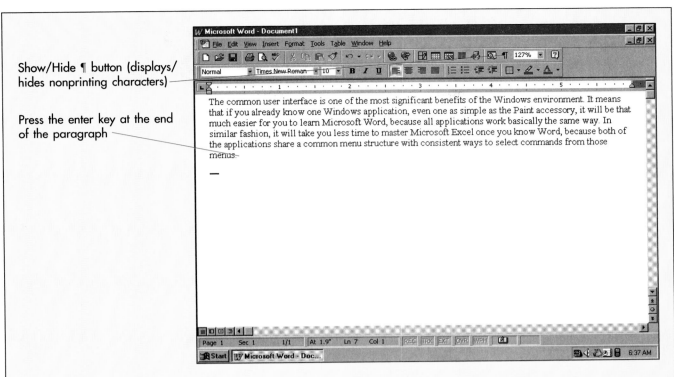

(c) Create the Document (step 4)

FIGURE 1.6   Hands-on Exercise 1 (continued)

WHAT HAPPENED TO THE INS KEY?

Every previous version of Word has used the Ins key to toggle between
the Insert and Overtype modes. Unfortunately this simple technique no
longer works in Word 97, as the key has been disabled. Instead, Microsoft
directs you to pull down the Tools menu, click the Options command,
select the Edit tab, then check (clear) the box for Overtype (Insert) mode.
Fortunately, we found our own toggle switch—double click the OVR indicator on the status bar to switch back and forth between the two modes.

STEP 5: Save the Document

➤ Pull down the **File menu** and click **Save** (or click the **Save button** on the Standard toolbar). You should see the Save As dialog box in Figure 1.6d. If necessary, click the **Details button** so that the display on your monitor more
closely matches our figure.

➤ To save the file:

• Click the **drop-down arrow** on the Save In list box.

• Click the appropriate drive, drive C or drive A, depending on whether or
not you installed the data disk on your hard drive.

• Double click the **Exploring Word folder,** to make it the active folder (the
folder in which you will save the document).

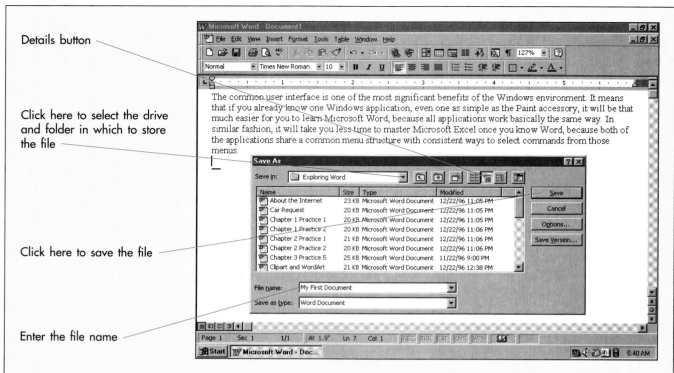

Details button

Click here to select the drive and folder in which to store the file

Click here to save the file

Enter the file name

(d) Save the Document (step 5)

FIGURE 1.6   Hands-on Exercise 1 (continued)

- Click and drag over the default entry in the File name text box. Type **My First Document** as the name of your document. (A DOC extension will be added automatically when the file is saved to indicate that this is a Word document.)
- Click **Save** or press the **enter key.** The title bar changes to reflect the document name.
- ➤ Add your name at the end of the document, then click the **Save button** on the Standard toolbar to save the document with the revision. This time the Save As dialog box does not appear, since Word already knows the name of the document.

CHANGE THE DEFAULT FOLDER

The default folder is the folder where Word opens (saves) documents unless it is otherwise instructed. To change the default folder, pull down the Tools menu, click Options, click the File Locations tab, click Documents, and click the Modify command button. Enter the name of the new folder (for example, C:\Exploring Word), click OK, then click the Close button. The next time you access the File menu, the default folder will reflect these changes.

STEP 6: The Office Assistant

➤ Click the **Office Assistant button** on the Standard toolbar to display the Office Assistant. (You may see a different character than the one we have selected.)

➤ Enter your question—for example, **How do I print a document?**—as shown in Figure 1.6e, then click the **Search button** to look for the answer.

➤ The size of the dialog box expands as the Assistant suggests several topics that may be appropriate to answer your question.

➤ Click the first topic, **Print a document,** which in turn displays a help screen with detailed information. Read the help screen, then close the Help window.

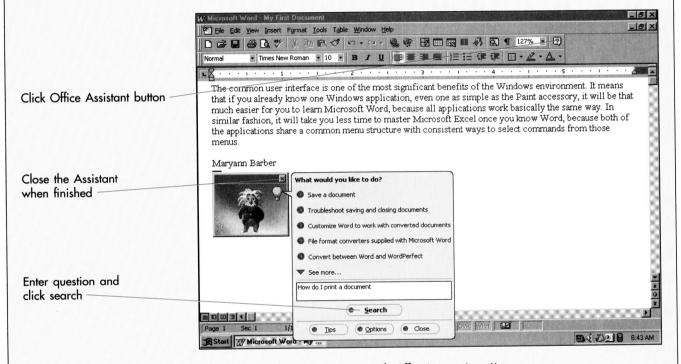

Click Office Assistant button

Close the Assistant when finished

Enter question and click search

(e) The Office Assistant (step 6)

FIGURE 1.6   Hands-on Exercise 1 (continued)

TIP OF THE DAY

You can set the Office Assistant to greet you with a "Tip of the Day" whenever you start Word. If the Office Assistant is not visible, click the Office Assistant button on the Standard toolbar to start the Assistant, then click the Options button to display the Office Assistant dialog box. Check the Show the Tip of the Day at the startup box, then click OK. The next time you start Word, you will be greeted by the Assistant, who will offer you a tip of the day.

STEP 7: Print the Document

➤ You can print the document in one of two ways:

- Pull down the **File menu.** Click **Print** to display the dialog box of Figure 1.6f. Click the **OK command button** to print the document.

- Click the **Print button** on the Standard toolbar to print the document immediately without displaying the Print dialog box.

Print button

Click here to print the file

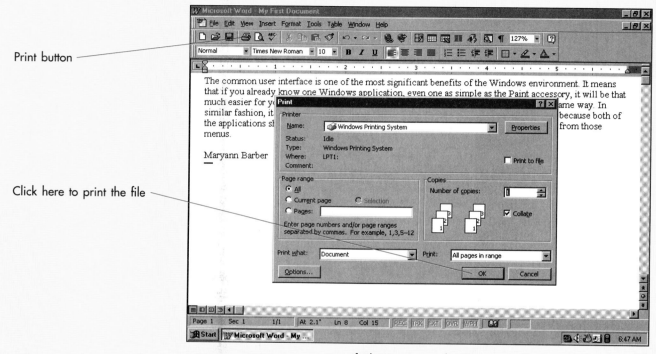

(f) The Print Command (step 7)

FIGURE 1.6   Hands-on Exercise 1 (continued)

ABOUT MICROSOFT WORD

Pull down the Help menu and click About Microsoft Word to display the specific release number and other licensing information, including the product serial number. This help screen also contains two very useful command buttons, System Information and Technical Support. The first button displays information about the hardware installed on your system, including the amount of memory and available space on the hard drive. The Technical Support button provides telephone numbers for technical assistance.

STEP 8: Close the Document

➤ Pull down the **File menu.** Click **Close** to close this document but remain in Word. (Click **Yes** if prompted to save the document.) The document disappears from the screen, but Word is still open.

➤ Pull down the **File menu** a second time. Click **Exit** to close Word if you do not want to continue with the next exercise at this time.

We trust that you completed the hands-on exercise without difficulty, and that you were able to create, save, and print the document in Figure 1.6. There is, however, one area of potential confusion in that Word offers different views of the same document, depending on the preferences of the individual user. It also gives you the option to display (hide) its various toolbars. Thus your screen will not match ours exactly, and, indeed, there is no requirement that it should. The *contents* of the document, however, should be identical to ours.

Figure 1.6 displayed the document in the *Normal view.* Figure 1.7 displays an entirely different view called the *Page Layout view.* Each view has its advantages. The Normal view is generally faster, but the Page Layout view more closely resembles the printed page as it displays top and bottom margins, headers and footers, graphic elements in their exact position, a vertical ruler, and other elements not seen in the Normal view. The Normal view is preferable only when entering text and editing. The Page Layout view is used to apply the finishing touches and check a document prior to printing. Note, too, that each view can be displayed at different magnifications.

Your screen may or may not match either figure, and you will undoubtedly develop preferences of your own. The following suggestions will help you match the screens of Figure 1.6:

- If the application window for Word does not take the entire screen, and/or the document does not take the entire window within Word, click the Maximize button in the application and/or the document window.

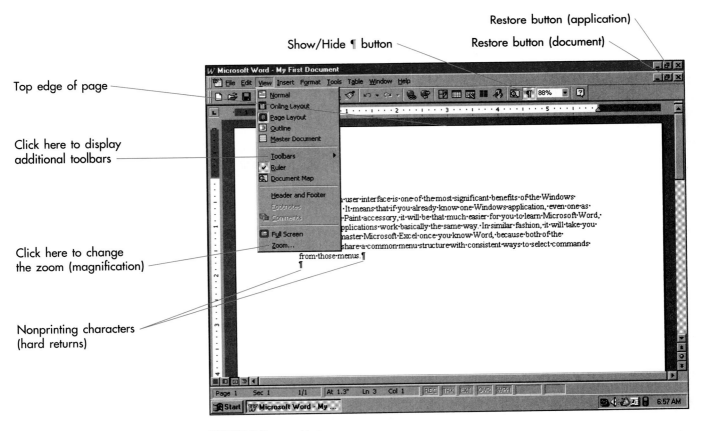

FIGURE 1.7   Troubleshooting

- If the text does not come up to the top of the screen—that is, you see the top edge of the page (as in Figure 1.7)—it means that you are in the Page Layout view instead of the Normal view. Pull down the View menu and click Normal to match the document in Figure 1.6c.

- If the text seems unusually large or small, it means that you or a previous user elected to zoom in or out to get a different perspective on the document. Pull down the View menu, click Zoom, then click Page Width so that the text takes the entire line.

- If you see the ¶ and other nonprinting symbols, it means that you or a previous user elected to display these characters. Click the Show/Hide ¶ button on the Standard toolbar to make the symbols disappear.

- If the Standard or Formatting toolbar is missing and/or a different toolbar is displayed, pull down the View menu, click Toolbars, then click the appropriate toolbars on or off. If the ruler is missing, pull down the View menu and click Ruler.

- The automatic spell check may (or may not) be implemented as indicated by the appearance (absence) of the open book icon on the status bar. If you do not see the icon, pull down the Tools menu, click Options, click the Spelling and Grammar tab, then check the box for Check Spelling as you type.

THE WRONG KEYBOARD

Microsoft Word facilitates conversion from WordPerfect by providing an alternative (software-controlled) keyboard that implements WordPerfect conventions. If you are sharing your machine with others, and if various keyboard shortcuts do not work as expected, it could be because someone else has implemented the WordPerfect keyboard. Pull down the Tools menu, click Options, then click the General tab in the dialog box. Clear the check box next to Navigation keys for WordPerfect users to return to the normal Word keyboard.

HANDS-ON EXERCISE 2

Modifying an Existing Document

Objective: To open an existing document, revise it, and save the revision. To demonstrate the Undo command and online help. Use Figure 1.8 as a guide in doing the exercise.

STEP 1: Open an Existing Document

➤ Click the **Start menu.** Click (or point to) the **Program menu,** then click **Microsoft Word** to start the program. Close the Office Assistant if it appears.

➤ Maximize the application window (if necessary). Maximize the document window as well.

➤ Pull down the **File menu** and click **Open** (or click the **Open button** on the Standard toolbar). You should see a dialog box similar to the one in Figure 1.8a. (The Exploring Word folder is not yet selected.)

➤ To open a file:
- Click the **Details button** to change to the Details view. Click and drag the vertical border between columns to increase (or decrease) the size of a column.
- Click the **drop-down arrow** on the Look In list box.
- Click the appropriate drive, drive C or drive A, depending on the location of your data.
- Double click the **Exploring Word folder** to make it the active folder (the folder in which you will save the document).
- Click the **down arrow** in the Name list box, then scroll until you can select **My First Document** from the first exercise. Click the **Open command button** to open the file.

➤ Your document should appear on the screen.

Details button

Click here to select the drive and folder in which the file is stored

Click and drag here to change column width

Click the file to be retrieved

Click here to open the file

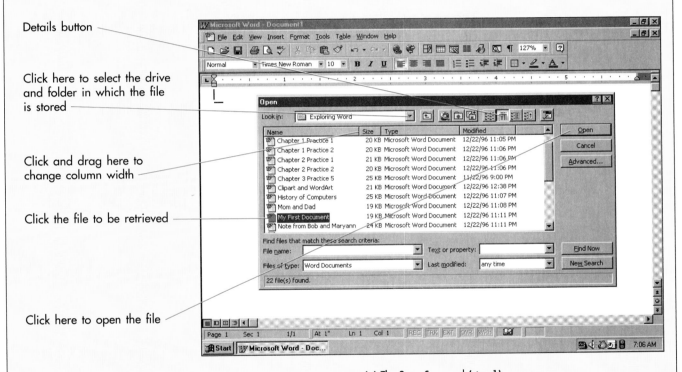

(a) The Open Command (step 1)

FIGURE 1.8   Hands-on Exercise 2

THE MOST RECENTLY OPENED FILE LIST

The easiest way to open a recently used document is to select the document directly from the File menu. Pull down the File menu, but instead of clicking the Open command, check to see if the document appears on the list of the most recently opened documents at the bottom of the menu. If so, you can click the document name rather than having to make the appropriate selections through the Open dialog box.

STEP 2: The View Menu (Troubleshooting)

➤ Modify the settings within Word so that the appearance of your document matches Figure 1.8b.

- To change to the Normal view, pull down the **View menu** and click **Normal** (or click the **Normal View** button at the bottom of the window).

- To change the amount of text that is visible on the screen, click the **drop-down arrow** on the Zoom Control box on the Standard toolbar and select **Page Width.**

- To display (hide) the ruler, pull down the **View menu** and toggle the **Ruler command** on or off. End with the ruler on.

➤ There may still be subtle differences between your screen and ours, depending on the resolution of your monitor. These variations, if any, need not concern you at all as long as you are able to complete the exercise.

Zoom box (click to change magnification)

Horizontal ruler

Page Layout button

Normal View button

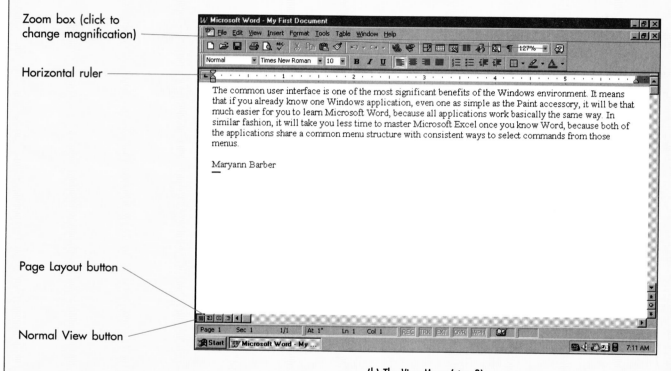

(b) The View Menu (step 2)

FIGURE 1.8   Hands-on Exercise 2 (continued)

DISPLAY (HIDE) TOOLBARS WITH THE RIGHT MOUSE BUTTON

Point to any visible toolbar, then click the right mouse button to display a shortcut menu listing the available toolbars. Click the individual toolbars on or off as appropriate. If no toolbars are visible, pull down the View menu, click Toolbars, then display or hide the desired toolbars.

STEP 3: Display the Hard Returns

➤ The **Show/Hide ¶** button on the Standard toolbar functions as a toggle switch to display (hide) the hard returns (and other nonprinting characters) in a document.

➤ Click the **Show/Hide ¶ button** to display the hard returns as in Figure 1.8c. Click the **Show/Hide ¶ button** a second time to hide the nonprinting characters. Display or hide the paragraph markers as you see fit.

Save button

Show/Hide button

ScreenTip (displayed when you point to a toolbar button)

Hard returns

Add a sentence

Modifications to the document

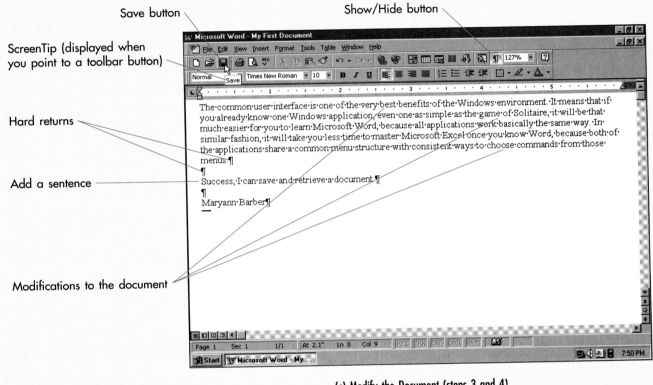

(c) Modify the Document (steps 3 and 4)

FIGURE 1.8   Hands-on Exercise 2 (continued)

SCREENTIPS

Point to any button on any toolbar and Word displays a ScreenTip containing the name of the button to indicate its function. If pointing to a button has no effect, pull down the View menu, click Toolbars, then click Customize to display the Customize dialog box. Click the Options tab, check the box to Show ScreenTips on Toolbars, then close the dialog box.

STEP 4: Modify the Document

➤ Press **Ctrl+End** to move to the end of the document. Press the **up arrow key** once or twice until the insertion point is on a blank line above your name. If necessary, press the **enter key** once (or twice) to add blank line(s).

➤ Add the sentence, **Success, I can save and retrieve a document!,** as shown in Figure 1.8c.

➤ Make the following additional modifications to practice editing:
- Change the phrase *most significant* to **very best.**
- Change *Paint accessory* to **game of Solitaire.**
- Change the word *select* to **choose.**

➤ Switch between the insert and overtype modes as necessary. Double click the **OVR indicator** on the status bar to toggle between the insert and overtype modes.

MOVING WITHIN A DOCUMENT

Press Ctrl+Home and Ctrl+End to move to the beginning and end of a document, respectively. These shortcuts work not just in Word, but in any other Windows application, and are worth remembering as they allow your hands to remain on the keyboard as you type.

STEP 5: Save the Changes

➤ It is very, very important to save your work repeatedly during a session so that you do not lose it all in the event of a power failure or other unforeseen event.

➤ Pull down the **File menu** and click **Save,** or click the **Save button** on the Standard toolbar. You will not see the Save As dialog box because the document is saved automatically under the existing name (My First Document).

KEEP DUPLICATE COPIES OF IMPORTANT FILES

It is absolutely critical to maintain duplicate copies of important files on a separate disk stored away from the computer. In addition, you should print each new document at the end of every session, saving it before printing (power failures happen when least expected—for example, during the print operation). Hard copy is not as good as a duplicate disk, but it is better than nothing.

STEP 6: Selecting Text

➤ Point to the first letter in the first sentence. Press and hold the left mouse button as you drag the mouse over the first sentence. Release the mouse.

➤ The sentence should remain selected as shown in Figure 1.8d. The selected text is the text that will be affected by the next command. Click anywhere else in the document to deselect the text.

➤ Point to any word in the first sentence, then press and hold the **Ctrl key** as you click the mouse, to select the entire sentence. Press the **Del key** to delete the selected text (the first sentence) from the document.

Click and drag over the
first sentence to select it

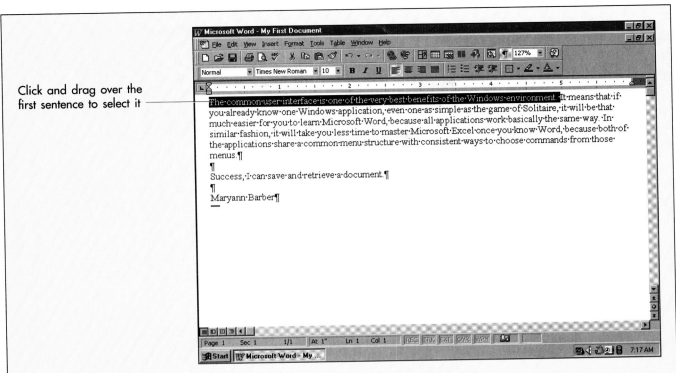

(d) Selecting Text (step 6)

FIGURE 1.8 Hands-on Exercise 2 (continued)

PICK UP THE MOUSE

It seems that you always run out of room on your real desk, just when
you need to move the mouse a little further. The solution is to pick up
the mouse and move it closer to you—the pointer will stay in its present
position on the screen, but when you put the mouse down, you will have
more room on your desk in which to work.

STEP 7: The Undo Command

➤ Pull down the **Edit menu** as shown in Figure 1.8e. Click **Undo** to reverse
(undo) the last command.

---

100 LEVELS OF UNDO

The *Undo command* is present in Word as it is in every Windows application. Incredible as it sounds, however, Word enables you to undo the
last 100 changes to a document. Click the drop-down arrow next to the
Undo button to produce a list of your previous actions. (The most recent
command is listed first.) Click the action you want to undo, which also
undoes all of the preceding commands. Undoing the fifth command in the
list, for example, will also undo the preceding four commands.

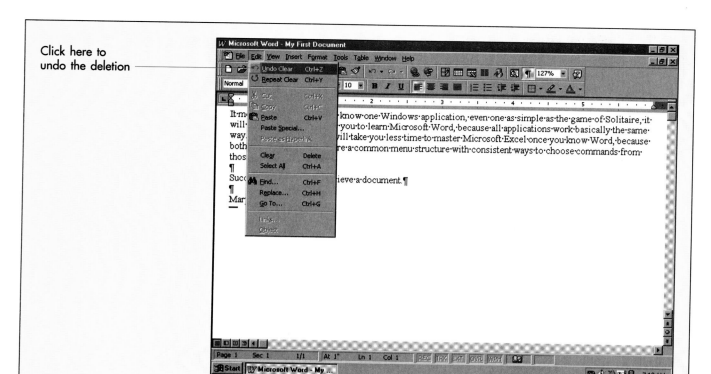

Click here to undo the deletion

(e) The Undo Command (step 7)

FIGURE 1.8   Hands-on Exercise 2 (continued)

➤ The deleted text should be returned to your document. The Undo command is a tremendous safety net and can be used at almost any time.

➤ Click anywhere outside the selected text to deselect the sentence.

STEP 8: The Help Menu

➤ Pull down the **Help menu.** Click **Contents and Index** to display the Help topics window in Figure 1.8f.

➤ Click the **Index tab.** Type **Undo** (the topic you wish to look up). The Undo topic is automatically selected.

➤ Click **Display** to show a second help screen with detailed information.

➤ Click the **Close button** to close the Help window.

TIPS FROM THE OFFICE ASSISTANT

The Office Assistant indicates it has a suggestion by displaying a lightbulb. Click the lightbulb to display the tip, then click the Back or Next button as appropriate to view additional tips. The Assistant will not, however, repeat a tip from an earlier session unless you reset it at the start of a new session. This is especially important to remember in a laboratory situation where you are sharing a computer with other students. To reset the tips, click the Assistant to display a balloon asking what you want to do, click the Options button in the balloon, click Options, then click the button to Reset My Tips.

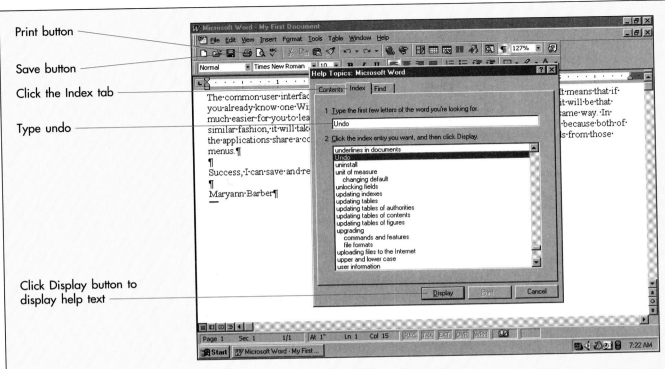

Print button

Save button

Click the Index tab

Type undo

Click Display button to
display help text

(f) The Help Menu (step 8)

FIGURE 1.8   Hands-on Exercise 2 (continued)

STEP 9: Print the Revised Document

➤ Click the **Save button** on the Standard toolbar to save the revised document
a final time.

➤ Click the **Print button** to print the document. Submit the printed document
to your instructor as proof you did Hands-on Exercises 1 and 2.

➤ Pull down the **File menu.** Click **Close** to close the document and remain in
Word. Click **Exit** if you do not want to continue with the next exercise at this
time.

DOCUMENT PROPERTIES

Prove to your instructor how hard you've worked by printing various statistics about your document, including the number of revisions and the
total editing time. Pull down the File menu, click the Print command to
display the Print dialog box, click the drop down arrow in the Print What
list box, select Document properties, then click OK. You can view the
information (without printing) by pulling down the File menu, clicking the
Properties command, then selecting the Statistics tab from the resulting
dialog box.

There is simply no excuse to misspell a word, since the **spell check** is an integral part of Microsoft Word. (The spell check is also available for every other application in the Microsoft Office.) Spelling errors make your work look sloppy and discourage the reader before he or she has read what you had to say. They can cost you a job, a grade, a lucrative contract, or an award you deserve.

The spell check can be set to automatically check a document as text is entered, or it can be called explicitly by clicking the Spelling and Grammar button on the Standard toolbar. The spell check compares each word in a document to the entries in a built-in dictionary, then flags any word that is in the document, but not in the built-in dictionary, as an error.

The dictionary included with Microsoft Office is limited to standard English and does not include many proper names, acronyms, abbreviations, or specialized terms, and hence, the use of any such item is considered a misspelling. You can, however, add such words to a **custom dictionary** so that they will not be flagged in the future. The spell check will inform you of repeated words and irregular capitalization. It cannot, however, flag properly spelled words that are used improperly, and thus cannot tell you that *Two bee or knot too be* is not the answer.

The capabilities of the spell check are illustrated in conjunction with Figure 1.9a. The spell check goes through the document and returns the errors one at a time, offering several options for each mistake. You can change the misspelled word to one of the alternatives suggested by Word, leave the word as is, or add the word to a custom dictionary.

The first error is the word *embarassing,* with Word's suggestion(s) for correction displayed in the list box in Figure 1.9b. To accept the highlighted suggestion, click the Change command button and the substitution will be made automatically in the document. To accept an alternative suggestion, click the desired word, then click the Change command button. Alternatively, you can click the AutoCorrect button to correct the mistake in the current document, and, in addition, automatically correct the same mistake in any future document.

The spell check detects both irregular capitalization and duplicated words, as shown in Figures 1.9c and 1.9d, respectively. The error in Figure 1.9e, *Grauer,* is not a misspelling per se, but a proper noun not found in the standard dictionary. No correction is required and the appropriate action is to ignore the word (taking no further action)—or better yet, add it to the custom dictionary so that it will not be flagged in future sessions. And finally, we could not resist including the example in Figure 1.9f, which shows another use of the spell check. (It's included for devotees of crossword puzzles who need a five-letter word beginning with *s* and ending with *n.*)

Flagged errors

A spelling checker will catch embarassing mistakes, iRregular capitalization, and duplicate words words. It will also flag proper nouns, for example, Robert Grauer, but you can add these terms to an auxiliary dictionary so that they will not be flagged in the future. It will not, however, notice properly spelled words that are used incorrectly; for example, Two bee or knot too be is not the answer.

(a) The Text

FIGURE 1.9 The Spell Check

Word not found in the dictionary

Selected suggestion

Click here to substitute
selected suggestion

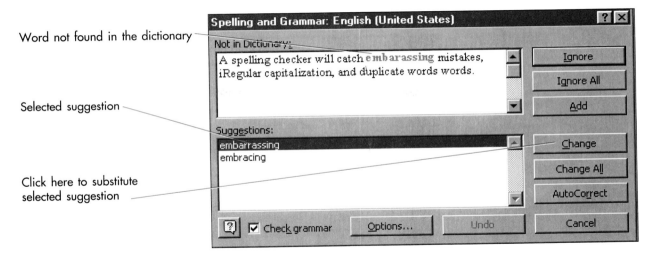

(b) Ordinary Misspelling

Irregular capitalization
is flagged as an error

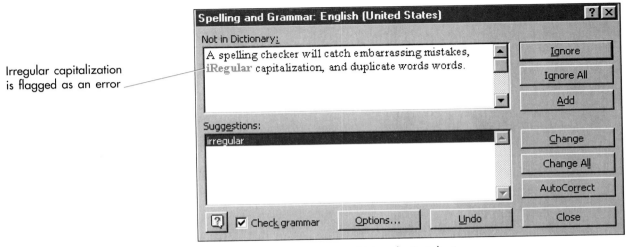

(c) Irregular Capitalization

Click here to delete
duplicated word

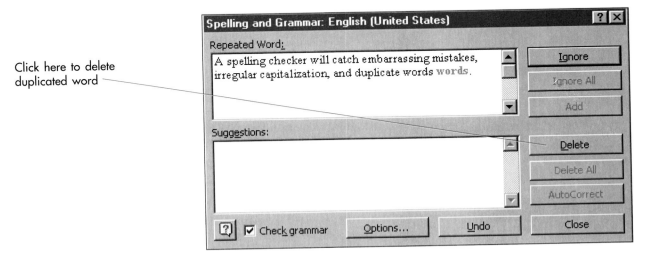

(d) Duplicated Word

FIGURE 1.9   The Spell Check (continued)

Click here to ignore word
as no correction is necessary

Click here to add word to
the custom dictionary

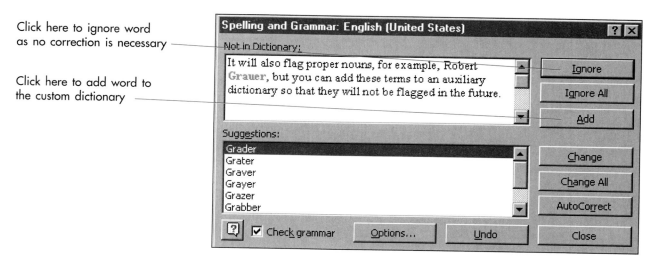

(e) Proper Noun

? represents unknown character

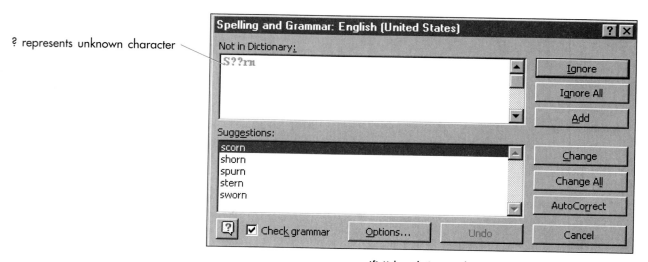

(f) Help with Crosswords

FIGURE 1.9   The Spell Check (continued)

AutoCorrect

The **AutoCorrect** feature corrects mistakes as they are made without any effort on your part. It makes you a better typist. If, for example, you typed *teh* instead of *the,* Word would change the spelling without even telling you. Word will also change *adn* to *and, i* to *I,* and *occurence* to *occurrence.*

Microsoft Word includes a predefined table of common mistakes and uses that table to make substitutions whenever it encounters an error it recognizes. You can add additional items to the table to include the frequent errors you make. You can also use the feature to define your own shorthand—for example, cis for Computer Information Systems as shown in Figure 1.10.

The AutoCorrect will also correct mistakes in capitalization; for example, it will capitalize the first letter in a sentence, recognize that MIami should be Miami, and capitalize the days of the week. It's even smart enough to correct the accidental use of the Caps Lock key, and it will toggle the key off!

Enter additions to table
of common mistakes

Table of common mistakes
and their corrections

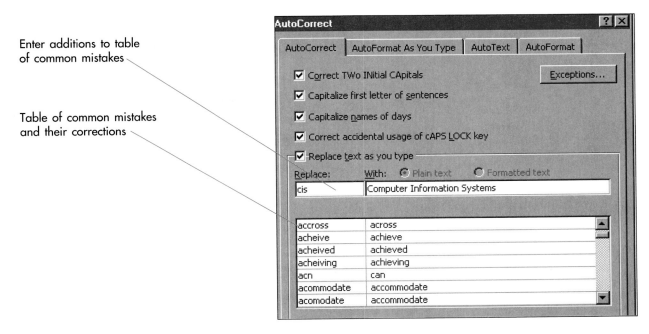

FIGURE 1.10   AutoCorrect

THESAURUS

Mark Twain said the difference between the right word and almost the right word is the difference between a lightning bug and lightning. The *thesaurus* is an important tool in any word processor and is both fun and educational. It helps you to avoid repetition, and it will polish your writing.

The thesaurus is called from the Language command in the Tools menu. You position the cursor at the appropriate word within the document, then invoke the thesaurus and follow your instincts. The thesaurus recognizes multiple meanings and forms of a word (for example, adjective, noun, and verb) as in Figure 1.11a, and (by double clicking) allows you to look up any listed meaning to produce additional choices as in Figure 1.11b. You can explore further alternatives by selecting a synonym and clicking the Look Up button. The thesaurus also provides a list of antonyms for most entries, as in Figure 1.11c.

Synonyms for selected meaning

Meanings and forms of selected
word (double click to look up
meaning, for additional choices)

Click here to replace word
with selected synonym

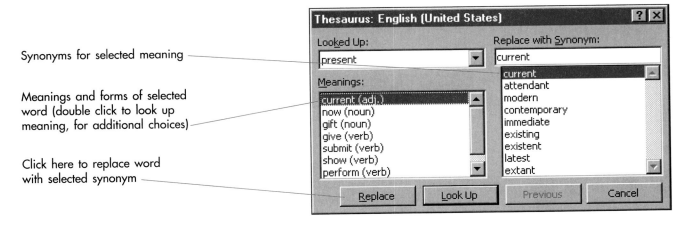

(a) Initial Word

FIGURE 1.11   The Thesaurus

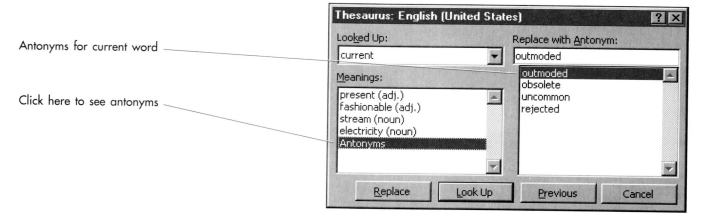

Additional choices produced by double clicking selected meaning

(b) Additional Choices

Antonyms for current word

Click here to see antonyms

(c) Antonyms

FIGURE 1.11   The Thesaurus (continued)

GRAMMAR CHECK

The **grammar check** attempts to catch mistakes in punctuation, writing style, and word usage by comparing strings of text within a document to a series of predefined rules. As with the spell check, errors are brought to the screen where you can accept the suggested correction and make the replacement automatically, or more often, edit the selected text and make your own changes.

You can also ask the grammar check to explain the rule it is attempting to enforce. Unlike the spell check, the grammar check is subjective, and what seems appropriate to you may be objectionable to someone else. Indeed, the grammar check is quite flexible, and can be set to check for different writing styles; that is, you can implement one set of rules to check a business letter and a different set of rules for casual writing. Many times, however, you will find that the English language is just too complex for the grammar check to detect every error, although it will find many errors.

The grammar check caught the inconsistency between subject and verb in Figure 1.12a and suggested the appropriate correction (am instead of are). In Figure 1.12b, it suggested the elimination of the superfluous comma. These examples show the grammar check at its best, but it is often more subjective and less capable. It detected the error in Figure 1.12c, for example, but suggested an inappropriate correction, "to complicate" as opposed to "too complicated". Suffice it to say, that there is no substitute for carefully proofreading every document.

Suggested correction is appropriate

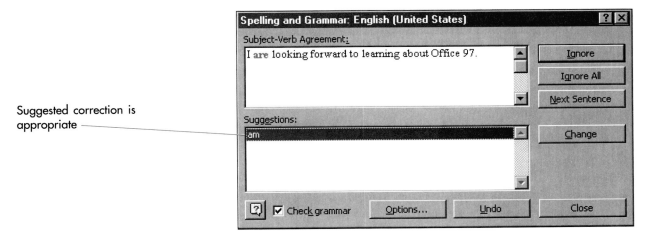

(a) Inconsistent Verb

Double punctuation is deleted

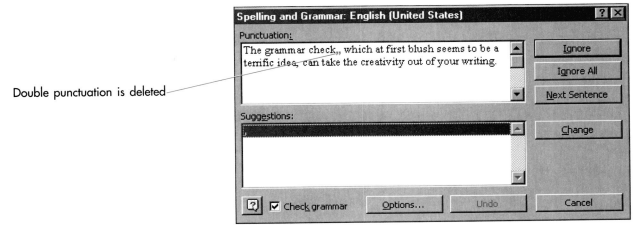

(b) Doubled Punctuation

Suggested correction is not appropriate

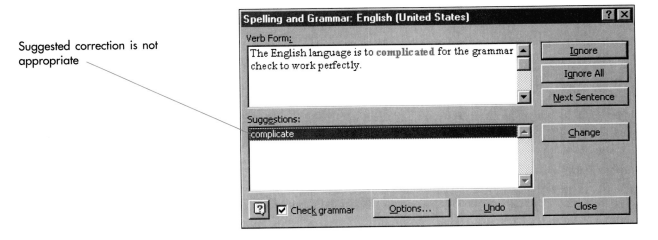

(c) Limitations

FIGURE 1.12   The Grammar Check

The Save command was used in the first two exercises. The Save As command will be introduced in the next exercise as a very useful alternative. We also introduce you to different backup options. We believe that now, when you are first starting to learn about word processing, is the time to develop good working habits.

You already know that the Save command copies the document currently being edited (the document in memory) to disk. The initial execution of the command requires you to assign a file name and to specify the drive and folder in which the file is to be stored. All subsequent executions of the Save command save the document under the original name, replacing the previously saved version with the new one.

The ***Save As command*** saves another copy of a document under a different name (and/or a different file type), and is useful when you want to retain a copy of the original document. The Save As command provides you with two copies of a document. The original document is kept on disk under its original name. A copy of the document is saved on disk under a new name and remains in memory. All subsequent editing is done on the new document.

We cannot overemphasize the importance of periodically saving a document, so that if something does go wrong, you won't lose all of your work. Nothing is more frustrating than to lose two hours of effort, due to an unexpected program crash or to a temporary loss of power. Save your work frequently, at least once every 15 minutes. Pull down the File menu and click Save, or click the Save button on the Standard toolbar. Do it!

QUIT WITHOUT SAVING

There will be times when you do not want to save the changes to a document, such as when you have edited it beyond recognition and wish you had never started. Pull down the File menu and click the Close command, then click No in response to the message asking whether you want to save the changes to the document. Pull down the File menu and reopen the file (it should be the first file in the list of most recently edited documents), then start over from the beginning.

Backup Options

Microsoft Word offers several different ***backup*** options. We believe the two most important options are to create a backup copy in conjunction with every save command, and to periodically (and automatically) save a document. Both options are implemented in step 3 in the next hands-on exercise.

Figure 1.13 illustrates the option to create a backup copy of the document every time a Save command is executed. Assume, for example, that you have created the simple document, *The fox jumped over the fence* and saved it under the name "Fox". Assume further that you edit the document to read, *The quick brown fox jumped over the fence,* and that you saved it a second time. The second save command changes the name of the original document from "Fox" to "Backup of Fox", then saves the current contents of memory as "Fox". In other words, the disk now contains two versions of the document: the current version "Fox" and the most recent previous version "Backup of Fox".

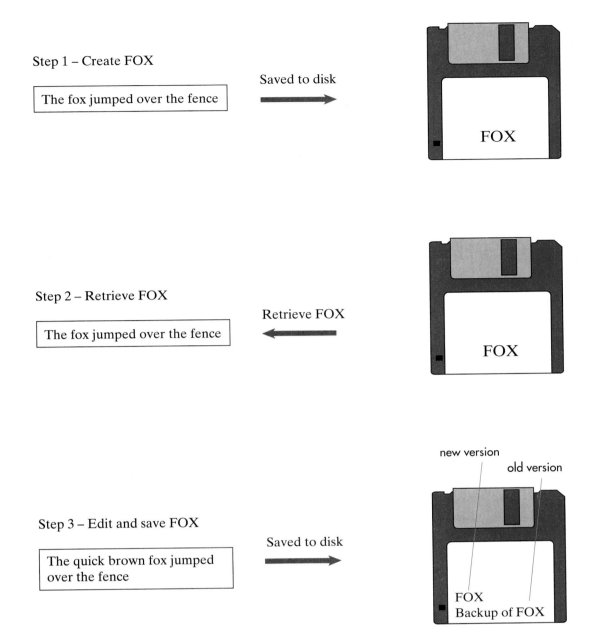

Step 1 – Create FOX

| The fox jumped over the fence |

Saved to disk →

FOX

Step 2 – Retrieve FOX

| The fox jumped over the fence |

Retrieve FOX ←

FOX

Step 3 – Edit and save FOX

| The quick brown fox jumped over the fence |

Saved to disk →

new version
old version

FOX
Backup of FOX

FIGURE 1.13   Backup Procedures

The cycle goes on indefinitely, with "Fox" always containing the current version, and "Backup of Fox" the most recent previous version. Thus if you revise and save the document a third time, "Fox" will contain the latest revision while "Backup of Fox" would contain the previous version alluding to the quick brown fox. The original (first) version of the document disappears entirely since only two versions are kept.

The contents of "Fox" and "Backup of Fox" are different, but the existence of the latter enables you to retrieve the previous version if you inadvertently edit beyond repair or accidentally erase the current "Fox" version. Should this occur (and it will), you can always retrieve its predecessor and at least salvage your work prior to the last save operation.

The Spell Check

Objective: To open an existing document, check it for spelling, then use the Save As command to save the document under a different file name. Use Figure 1.14 as a guide in the exercise.

STEP 1: Preview a Document

➤ Start Microsoft Word. Pull down the **File menu** and click **Open** (or click the **Open button** on the Standard toolbar). You should see a dialog box similar to the one in Figure 1.14a.

➤ Select the appropriate drive, drive C or drive A, depending on the location of your data. Double click the **Exploring Word folder** to make it the active folder (the folder in which you will save the document).

➤ Scroll in the Name list box until you can select (click) the **Try the Spell Check** document. Click the **Preview button** on the toolbar to preview the document as shown in Figure 1.14a.

➤ Click the **Open command button** to open the file. Your document should appear on the screen.

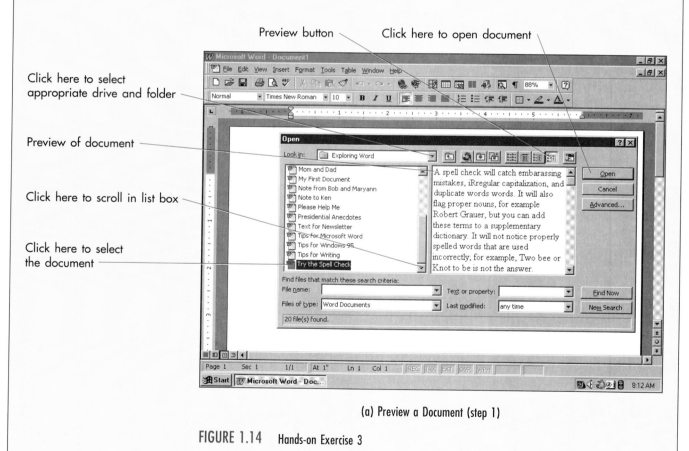

(a) Preview a Document (step 1)

FIGURE 1.14   Hands-on Exercise 3

STEP 2: The Save As Command

➤ Pull down the **File menu.** Click **Save As** to produce a dialog box in Figure 1.14b.

➤ Enter **Modified Spell Check** as the name of the new document. (A file name may contain up to 255 characters, and blanks are permitted.) Click the **Save command button.**

➤ There are now two identical copies of the file on disk: Try the Spell Check, which we supplied, and Modified Spell Check, which you just created. The title bar of the document window shows the latter name.

Click here to save the document under the new name

Enter new name for the document

Change file type for compatibility with Word 95

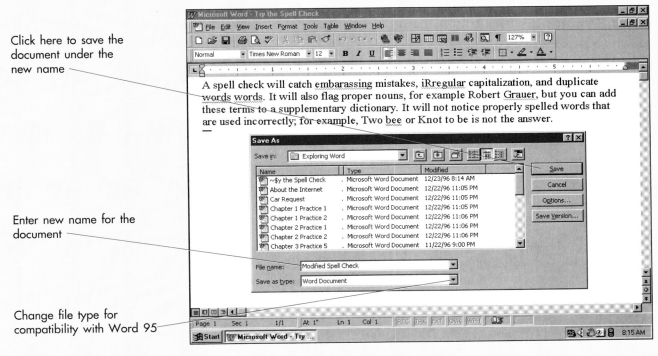

(b) The Save As Command (step 2)

FIGURE 1.14   Hands-on Exercise 3 (continued)

DIFFERENT FILE TYPES

The file format for Word 97 is incompatible with the format for Word 95. The newer release (Word 97) can open a document created in its predecessor (Word 95), but the reverse is not possible; that is, you cannot open a document created in Word 97 in Word 95. You can, however, use the Save As command in Word 97 to specify the Word 6.0/95 file type, enabling you to create a document in the new release and read it in the old (although you will lose any formatting unique to Word 97).

STEP 3: Establish Automatic Backup

➤ Pull down the **Tools menu.** Click **Options.** Click the **Save tab** to display the dialog box of Figure 1.14c.

➤ Click the first check box to choose **Always Create Backup Copy.**

➤ Set the other options as you see fit; for example, you can specify that the document be saved automatically every 10–15 minutes. Click **OK.**

Title bar reflects the new document

Click the Save tab

Click desired options

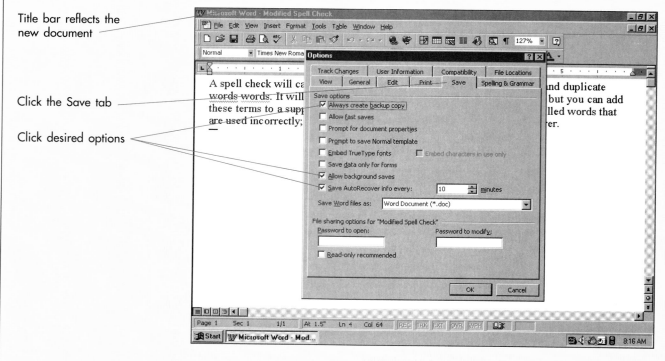

(c) Create a Backup (step 3)

FIGURE 1.14   Hands-on Exercise 3 (continued)

STEP 4: The Spell Check

➤ If necessary, press **Ctrl+Home** to move to the beginning of the document. Click the **Spelling and Grammar button** on the Standard toolbar to check the document.

➤ "Embarassing" is flagged as the first misspelling as shown in Figure 1.14d. Click the **Change button** to accept the suggested spelling.

➤ "iRregular" is flagged as an example of irregular capitalization. Click the **Change button** to accept the suggested correction.

➤ Continue checking the document, which displays misspellings and other irregularities one at a time. Click the appropriate command button as each mistake is found.

• Click the **Delete button** to remove the duplicated word.

• Click the **Ignore button** to accept Grauer (or click the **Add button** to add Grauer to the custom dictionary).

➤ The grammar check is illustrated in step 5.

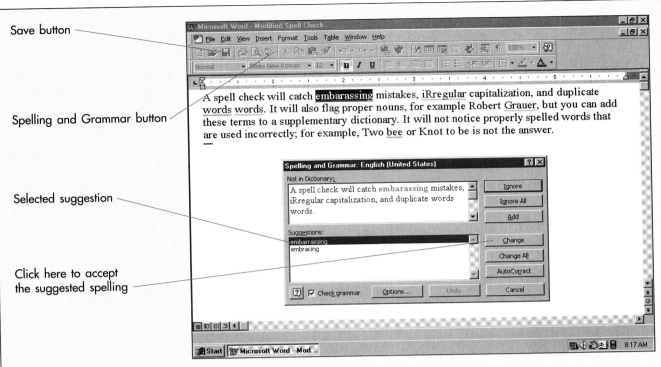

Save button

Spelling and Grammar button

Selected suggestion

Click here to accept
the suggested spelling

(d) The Spell Check (step 4)

FIGURE 1.14   Hands-on Exercise 3 (continued)

AUTOMATIC SPELLING AND GRAMMAR CHECKING

Red and green wavy lines may appear throughout a document to indicate spelling and grammatical errors, respectively. Point to any underlined word, then click the right mouse button to display a context-sensitive help menu with suggested corrections. To enable (disable) these options, pull down the Tools menu, click the Options command, click the Spelling and Grammar tab, and check (clear) the options to check spelling (or grammar) as you type.

STEP 5: The Grammar Check

➤ The last sentence, "Two bee or knot to be is not the answer", should be flagged as an error, as shown in Figure 1.14e. If this is not the case:

- Pull down the **Tools menu,** click **Options,** then click the **Spelling and Grammar tab.**
- Check the box to **Check Grammar with Spelling,** then click the button to **Recheck document.** Click **Yes** when told that the spelling and grammar check will be reset, then click **OK** to close the Options dialog box.
- Press **Ctrl+Home** to return to the beginning of the document, then click the **Spelling and Grammar button** to recheck the document.

➤ Click the **Assistant button** in the Spelling and Grammar dialog box for an explanation of the error. The Office Assistant will appear, indicating that

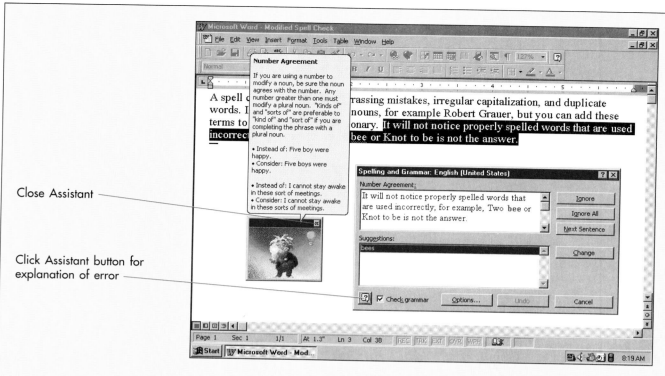

Close Assistant

Click Assistant button for
explanation of error

(e) The Grammar Check (step 5)

FIGURE 1.14   Hands-on Exercise 3 (continued)

there needs to be number agreement between subject and verb. Close the
Office Assistant after you have read the explanation.

➤ Click **Ignore** to reject the suggestion. Click **OK** when you see the dialog box,
indicating the spelling and grammar check is complete.

CHECK SPELLING ONLY

The grammar check is invoked by default in conjunction with the spell
check. You can, however, check the spelling of a document without checking its grammar. Pull down the Tools menu, click Options to display the
Options dialog box, then click the Spelling and Grammar tab. Clear the
box to check grammar with spelling, then click OK to accept the change
and close the dialog box.

STEP 6: The Thesaurus

➤ Select (click) the word *incorrectly,* which appears on the last line of your document as shown in Figure 1.14f.

➤ Pull down the **Tools menu,** click **Language,** then click **Thesaurus** to display
synonyms for the word you selected.

➤ Select (click) *inaccurately,* the synonym you will use in place of the original
word. Click the **Replace button** to make the change automatically.

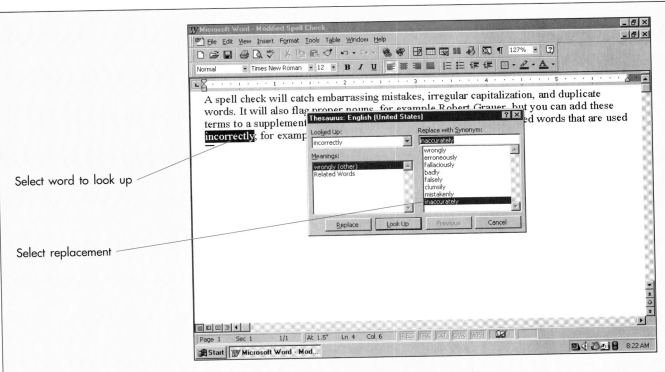

Select word to look up

Select replacement

(f) The Thesaurus (step 6)

FIGURE 1.14   Hands-on Exercise 3 (continued)

STEP 7: AutoCorrect

➤ Press **Ctrl+Home** to move to the beginning of the document.

➤ Type the *misspelled* phrase **Teh Spell Check was used to check this document.** Try to look at the monitor as you type to see the AutoCorrect feature in action; Word will correct the misspelling and change *Teh* to *The.*

➤ If you did not see the correction being made, click the arrow next to the Undo command on the Standard toolbar and undo the last several actions. Click the arrow next to the Redo command and redo the corrections.

➤ Save the document.

CREATE YOUR OWN SHORTHAND

Use AutoCorrect to expand abbreviations such as "usa" for United States of America. Pull down the Tools menu, click AutoCorrect, type the abbreviation in the Replace text box and the expanded entry in the With text box. Click the Add command button, then click OK to exit the dialog box and return to the document. The next time you type usa in a document, it will automatically be expanded to United States of America.

STEP 8: Exit Word

➤ Pull down the **File menu.** Click **Exit** to exit Word.

The chapter provided a broad-based introduction to word processing in general and to Microsoft Word in particular. Help is available from many sources. You can use the Help menu or the Office Assistant as you can in any Office application. You can also go to the Microsoft Web site to obtain more recent, and often more detailed, information.

Microsoft Word is always in one of two modes, insert or overtype; the choice between the two depends on the desired editing. The insertion point marks the place within a document where text is added or replaced.

The enter key is pressed at the end of a paragraph, but not at the end of a line because Word automatically wraps text from one line to the next. A hard return is created by the user when he or she presses the enter key; a soft return is created by Word as it wraps text and begins a new line.

The Save and Open commands work in conjunction with one another. The Save command copies the document in memory to disk under its existing name. The Open command retrieves a previously saved document. The Save As command saves the document under a different name and is useful when you want to retain a copy of the current document prior to all changes.

A spell check compares the words in a document to those in a standard and/or custom dictionary and offers suggestions to correct the mistakes it finds. It will detect misspellings, duplicated phrases, and/or irregular capitalization, but will not flag properly spelled words that are used incorrectly.

The AutoCorrect feature corrects predefined spelling errors and/or mistakes in capitalization, automatically, as the words are entered. The feature can also be used to create a personal shorthand as it will expand abbreviations as they are typed.

The thesaurus suggests synonyms and/or antonyms. It can also recognize multiple forms of a word (noun, verb, and adjective) and offer suggestions for each. The grammar check searches for mistakes in punctuation, writing style, and word usage by comparing strings of text within a document to a series of predefined rules.

KEY WORDS AND CONCEPTS

AutoCorrect	Office Assistant	Status bar
Backup	Open command	Text box
Custom dictionary	Overtype mode	Thesaurus
File menu	Page Layout view	Toggle switch
Formatting toolbar	Save As command	Toolbar
Grammar check	Save command	Undo command
Hard return	ScreenTip	Vertical ruler
Horizontal ruler	Show/Hide ¶ button	View menu
Insert mode	Soft return	Word wrap
Insertion point	Spell check	
Normal view	Standard toolbar	

MULTIPLE CHOICE

1. When entering text within a document, the enter key is normally pressed at the end of every:
   (a) Line
   (b) Sentence
   (c) Paragraph
   (d) All of the above

2. Which menu contains the commands to save the current document, or to open a previously saved document?
   (a) The Tools menu
   (b) The File menu
   (c) The View menu
   (d) The Edit menu

3. How do you execute the Print command?
   (a) Click the Print button on the standard toolbar
   (b) Pull down the File menu, then click the Print command
   (c) Use the appropriate keyboard shortcut
   (d) All of the above

4. The Open command:
   (a) Brings a document from disk into memory
   (b) Brings a document from disk into memory, then erases the document on disk
   (c) Stores the document in memory on disk
   (d) Stores the document in memory on disk, then erases the document from memory

5. The Save command:
   (a) Brings a document from disk into memory
   (b) Brings a document from disk into memory, then erases the document on disk
   (c) Stores the document in memory on disk
   (d) Stores the document in memory on disk, then erases the document from memory

6. What is the easiest way to change the phrase, *revenues, profits, gross margin,* to read *revenues, profits, and gross margin?*
   (a) Use the insert mode, position the cursor before the *g* in *gross,* then type the word *and* followed by a space
   (b) Use the insert mode, position the cursor after the *g* in *gross,* then type the word *and* followed by a space
   (c) Use the overtype mode, position the cursor before the *g* in *gross,* then type the word *and* followed by a space
   (d) Use the overtype mode, position the cursor after the *g* in *gross,* then type the word *and* followed by a space

7. A document has been entered into Word with a given set of margins, which are subsequently changed. What can you say about the number of hard and soft returns before and after the change in margins?
   (a) The number of hard returns is the same, but the number and/or position of the soft returns is different
   (b) The number of soft returns is the same, but the number and/or position of the hard returns is different
   (c) The number and position of both hard and soft returns is unchanged
   (d) The number and position of both hard and soft returns is different

8. Which of the following will be detected by the spell check?
   (a) Duplicate words
   (b) Irregular capitalization
   (c) Both (a) and (b)
   (d) Neither (a) nor (b)

9. Which of the following is likely to be found in a custom dictionary?
   (a) Proper names
   (b) Words related to the user's particular application
   (c) Acronyms created by the user for his or her application
   (d) All of the above

10. Ted and Sally both use Word but on different computers. Both have written a letter to Dr. Joel Stutz and have run a spell check on their respective documents. Ted's program flags *Stutz* as a misspelling, whereas Sally's accepts it as written. Why?
   (a) The situation is impossible; that is, if they use identical word processing programs they should get identical results
   (b) Ted has added *Stutz* to his custom dictionary
   (c) Sally has added *Stutz* to her custom dictionary
   (d) All of the above reasons are equally likely as a cause of the problem

11. The spell check will do all of the following *except:*
   (a) Flag properly spelled words used incorrectly
   (b) Identify misspelled words
   (c) Accept (as correctly spelled) words found in the custom dictionary
   (d) Suggest alternatives to misspellings it identifies

12. The AutoCorrect feature will:
   (a) Correct errors in capitalization as they occur during typing
   (b) Expand user-defined abbreviations as the entries are typed
   (c) Both (a) and (b)
   (d) Neither (a) nor (b)

13. When does the Save As dialog box appear?
   (a) The first time a file is saved using either the Save or Save As commands
   (b) Every time a file is saved by clicking the Save button on the Standard toolbar
   (c) Both (a) and (b)
   (d) Neither (a) nor (b)

14. Which of the following is true about the thesaurus?
   (a) It recognizes different forms of a word; for example, a noun and a verb
   (b) It provides antonyms as well as synonyms
   (c) Both (a) and (b)
   (d) Neither (a) nor (b)

15. The grammar check:
   (a) Implements different rules for casual and business writing
   (b) Will detect all subtleties in the English language
   (c) Is always run in conjunction with a spell check
   (d) All of the above

ANSWERS

1. c	**6.** a	**11.** a
2. b	**7.** a	**12.** c
3. d	**8.** c	**13.** a
4. a	**9.** d	**14.** c
5. c	**10.** c	**15.** a

PRACTICE WITH MICROSOFT WORD

1. Retrieve the *Chapter1 Practice 1* document shown in Figure 1.15 from the Exploring Word folder, then make the following changes:
   a. Select the text *Your name* and replace it with your name.
   b. Replace *May 31, 1995* with the current date.
   c. Insert the phrase *one or* in line 2 so that the text reads . . . *one or more characters than currently exist.*
   d. Delete the word *And* from sentence four in line 5, then change the w in *when* to a capital letter to begin the sentence.
   e. Change the phrase *most efficient* to *best*.
   f. Place the insertion point at the end of sentence 2, make sure you are in the insert mode, then add the following sentence: *The insert mode adds characters at the insertion point while moving existing text to the right in order to make room for the new text.*
   g. Place the insertion point at the end of the last sentence, press the enter key twice in a row, then enter the following text: *There are several keys that function as toggle switches of which you should be aware. The Caps Lock key toggles between upper- and lowercase letters, and the Num Lock key alternates between typing numbers and using the arrow keys.*
   h. Save the revised document, then print it and submit it to your instructor.

2. Select-then-do: Formatting is not covered until Chapter 2, but we think you are ready to try your hand at basic formatting now. Most formatting operations are done in the context of select-then-do as described in the document in Figure 1.16. You select the text you want to format, then you execute the appropriate formatting command, most easily by clicking the appropriate button on the Formatting toolbar. The function of each button should be apparent from its icon, but you can simply point to a button to display a ScreenTip that is indicative of the button's function.

To: Your Name

From: Robert Grauer and Maryann Barber

Subject: Microsoft Word for Windows

Date: May 31, 1997

This is just a short note to help you get acquainted with the insertion and replacement modes in Word for Windows. When the editing to be done results in more characters than currently exist, you want to be in the insertion mode when making the change. On the other hand, when the editing to be done contains the same or fewer characters, the replacement mode is best. And when replacing characters, it is most efficient to use the mouse to select the characters to be deleted and then just type the new characters; the selected characters are automatically deleted and the new characters typed take their place.

FIGURE 1.15   Document for Practice Exercise 1

An unformatted version of the document in Figure 1.16 exists on the data disk as *Chapter1 Practice 2*. Open the document, then format it to match the completed version in Figure 1.16. Just select the text to format, then click the appropriate button. We changed type size in the original document to 24 points for the title and 12 points for text in the document itself. Be sure to add your name and date as shown in the figure, then submit the completed document to your instructor.

3. Your background: Write a short description of your computer background similar to the document in Figure 1.17. The document should be in the form of a note from student to instructor that describes your background and should mention any previous knowledge of computers you have, prior computer courses you have taken, your objectives for this course, and so on. Indicate whether you own a PC, whether you have access to one at work, and/or whether you are considering purchase. Include any other information about yourself and/or your computer-related background.

Place your name somewhere in the document in boldface italics. We would also like you to use boldface and italics to emphasize the components of any computer system you describe. Use any font or point size you like. Note, too, the last paragraph, which asks you to print the summary statistics for the document when you submit the assignment to your instructor. (Use the tip on Document Properties on page 25 to print the total editing time and other information about your document.)

4. The cover page: Create a cover page that you can use for your assignments this semester. Your cover page should be similar to the one in Figure 1.18 with respect to content and should include the title of the assignment, your name, course information, and date. The formatting is up to you. Print the completed cover page and submit it to your instructor for inclusion in a class contest to judge the most innovative design.

Select-Then-Do

Many operations in Word are executed as select-then-do operations. You first select a block of text, then you issue a command that will affect the selected text. You may select the text in many different ways, the most basic of which is to click and drag over the desired characters. You may also take one of many shortcuts, which include double clicking on a word, pressing Ctrl as you click a sentence, and triple clicking on a paragraph.

Once text is selected, you may then delete it, **boldface** or *italicize* it, or even change its color. You may move it or copy it to another location, in the same or a different document. You can highlight it, underline, or even check its spelling. Then, depending on whether or not you like what you have done, you may undo it, redo it, and/or repeat it on subsequently selected text.

Jessica Kinzer
September 1, 1997

FIGURE 1.16   Document for Practice Exercise 2

The Computer and Me

My name is Jessica Kinzer and I am a complete novice when it comes to computers. I did not take a computer course in high school and this is my first semester at the University of Miami. My family does not own a computer, nor have I had the opportunity to use one at work. So when it comes to beginners, I am a beginner's beginner. I am looking forward to taking this course, as I have heard that it will truly make me computer literate. I know that I desperately need computer skills not only when I enter the job market, but to survive my four years here as well. I am looking forward to learning Word, Excel, and PowerPoint and I hope that I can pick up some Internet skills as well.

I did not buy a computer before I came to school as I wanted to see what type of system I would be using for my classes. After my first few weeks in class, I think that I would like to buy a ***200 Mz Pentium*** machine with ***32Mb RAM*** and a ***3 Gb hard drive.*** I would like a ***12X speed CD-ROM*** and a ***sound card*** (with ***speakers,*** of course). I also would like to get a ***laser printer.*** Now, if only I had the money.

This document did not take long at all to create as you can see by the summary statistics that are printed on the next page. I think I will really enjoy this class.

Jessica Kinzer
March 2, 1997

FIGURE 1.17   Document for Practice Exercise 3

Exploring Word Assignment

Jessica Kinzer
CIS 120
September 1, 1997

FIGURE 1.18   Document for Practice Exercise 4

5. Figure 1.19 contains the draft version of the *Chapter 1 Practice 5* document contained on the data disk.

   a. Proofread the document and circle any mistakes in spelling, grammar, capitalization, or punctuation.

   b. Open the document in Word and run the spell check. Did Word catch any mistakes you missed? Did you find any errors that were missed by the program?

   c. Use the thesaurus to come up with alternative words for *document,* which appears entirely too often within the paragraph.

   d. Run the grammar check on the revised document. Did the program catch any grammatical errors you missed? Did you find any mistakes that were missed by the program?

   e. Add your name to the revised document, save it, print it, and submit the completed document to your instructor.

6. The document in Figure 1.20 illustrates a new feature in Office 97 in which all applications automatically detect any hyperlinks that are embedded in a document. All you need to do is enter the link, and the application automatically converts it to a hyperlink. You can then click on the link to open Internet Explorer and display the associated Web page, provided you have an Internet connection. See for yourself by creating the document in Figure 1.20 and submitting it to your instructor.

As indicated, Word will, by default, convert any Internet path (e.g., any text beginning with http:// or www) to a hyperlink. If this is not the case, pull down the Tools menu, click AutoCorrect, then click the AutoFormat-as-you-Type tab. Check the box in the Replace-as-you-Type area for Internet and Network paths. Click OK. The next time you enter a Web or e-mail address, it will be converted automatically to a hyperlink.

The Grammar Check

All documents should be thoroughly proofed before they be printed and distributed. This means that documents, at a minimum should be spell cheked,, grammar cheked, and proof read by the author. A documents that has spelling errors and/or grammatical errors makes the Author look unprofessional and illiterate and their is nothing worse than allowing a first impression too be won that makes you appear slopy and disinterested, and a document full or of misteakes will do exactly that. Alot of people do not not realize how damaging a bad first impression could be, and documents full of misteakes has cost people oppurtunities that they trained and prepared many years for.

Microsoft Word includes an automated grammar check that will detect many, but certainly not all, errors as the previous paragraph demonstrates. Unlike the spell check, the grammar check is subjective, and what seems appropriate to you may be objectionable to someone else. The English language is just to complicated for the grammar check to detect every error, or even most errors. Hence there is no substitute for carefully proof reading a document your self. Hence there is no substitute for carefully proof reading a document your self.

FIGURE 1.19   Document for Practice Exercise 5

It's Web-Enabled

Perhaps the most significant change in Office 97 is that every document is Web-enabled, meaning that the application will automatically detect and highlight any hyperlinks that appear in a document. This sentence, for example, contains the Web address, www.microsoft.com, which is highlighted in blue just as it might appear in a regular Web document. We did not do anything special to create the hyperlink; that is, we simply typed the address, and Word in turn created the hyperlink.

You can click the link from within Word, and provided you have an Internet connection, your Web browser will display the associated page. Note, too, that once you click the link, its color will change (e.g., from blue to magenta) just as it would if you were viewing the page in Netscape or the Internet Explorer. Prove to your instructor that you have done this exercise by creating this document, then adding a paragraph or two that reference your favorite Web pages.

FIGURE 1.20   Document for Practice Exercise 6

7. Webster Online: Figure 1.21 shows our favorite online dictionary, which is accessed most easily by clicking the Search button in Internet Explorer, then clicking the link to Definitions and Quotes. Enter the word you want to look up (*oxymoron,* for example), then press the Look Up Word button to display the definition in Figure 1.21. This is truly an interactive dictionary because most words in it are created as hyperlinks, which in turn will lead you to other definitions. Use the dictionary to look up the meaning of the word *palindrome.* How many examples of oxymorons and palindromes can you think of?

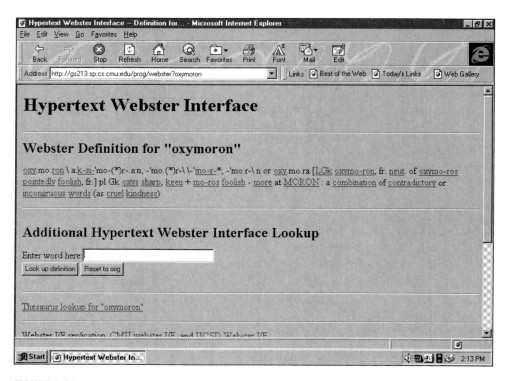

FIGURE 1.21   Screen for Practice Exercise 7

Case Studies

It's a Mess

Newcomers to word processing quickly learn the concept of word wrap and the distinction between hard and soft returns. This lesson was lost, however, on your friend who created the *Please Help Me* document on the data disk. The first several sentences were entered without any hard returns at all, whereas the opposite problem exists toward the end of the document. This is a good friend, and her paper is due in one hour. Please help.

Planning for Disaster

Do you have a backup strategy? Do you even know what a backup strategy is? You should learn, because sooner or later you will wish you had one. You will erase a file, be unable to read from a floppy disk, or worse yet suffer a hardware failure in which you are unable to access the hard drive. The problem always seems to occur the night before an assignment is due. The ultimate disaster is the disappearance of your computer, by theft or natural disaster (e.g., Hurricane Andrew). Describe in 250 words or less the backup strategy you plan to implement in conjunction with your work in this class.

A Letter Home

You really like this course and want very much to have your own computer, but you're strapped for cash and have decided to ask your parents for help. Write a one-page letter describing the advantages of having your own system and how it will help you in school. Tell your parents what the system will cost, and that you can save money by buying through the mail. Describe the configuration you intend to buy (don't forget to include the price of software) and then provide prices from at least three different companies. Cut out the advertisements and include them in your letter. Bring your material to class and compare your research with that of your classmates.

Computer Magazines

A subscription to a computer magazine should be given serious consideration if you intend to stay abreast in a rapidly changing field. The reviews on new products are especially helpful and you will appreciate the advertisements should you need to buy. Go to the library or a newsstand and obtain a magazine that appeals to you, then write a brief review of the magazine for class. Devote at least one paragraph to an article or other item you found useful.

A Junior Year Abroad

How lucky can you get? You are spending the second half of your junior year in Paris. The problem is you will have to submit your work in French, and the English version of Microsoft Word won't do. Is there a foreign-language version available? What about the dictionary and thesaurus? How do you enter the accented characters, which occur so frequently? You are leaving in two months, so you'd better get busy. What are your options? *Bon voyage!*

The Writer's Reference

The chapter discussed the use of a spell check, thesaurus, and grammar check, but many other resources are available. The Web contains a host of sites with additional resources that are invaluable to the writer. You can find Shakespeare online, as well as Bartlett's quotations. You can also find Webster's dictionary as well as a dictionary of acronyms. One way to find these resources is to click the Search button in Internet Explorer, then scroll down the page to the Writer's Reference section. You can also go to the address directly (home.microsoft.com/access.allinone.asp). Explore one or more of these resources, then write a short note to your instructor to summarize your findings.

Microsoft Online

Help for Microsoft Word is available from a variety of sources. You can consult the Office Assistant, or you can pull down the Help menu to display the Help Contents and Index. Both techniques were illustrated in the chapter. In addition, you can go to the Microsoft Web site to obtain more recent, and often more detailed, information. You will find the answers to the most frequently asked questions and you can access the same knowledge base used by Microsoft support engineers. Experiment with various sources of help, then submit a summary of your findings to your instructor. Try to differentiate among the various techniques and suggest the most appropriate use for each.

Microsoft Bookshelf

Bookshelf Basics is contained on the CD-ROM version of Microsoft Office and provides access to three frequently used reference books: *The American Heritage Dictionary, The Original Roget's Thesaurus,* and *The Columbia Dictionary of Quotations.* Examine each of these references and determine how useful they are to you as a student. Bookshelf Basics is free with Office 97, but the rest of Microsoft Bookshelf is not. What additional books are found in the complete version of Microsoft Bookshelf? How much does it cost? Is it worth the price, or can you find the equivalent information for free on the Web? Summarize your findings in a short note to your instructor.

GAINING PROFICIENCY: EDITING AND FORMATTING

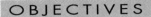

2

OBJECTIVES

After reading this chapter you will be able to:

1. Define the select-then-do methodology; describe several shortcuts with the mouse and/or the keyboard to select text.
2. Use the clipboard and/or the drag-and-drop capability to move and copy text within a document.
3. Use the Find, Replace, and Go To commands to substitute one character string for another.
4. Define scrolling; scroll to the beginning and end of a document.
5. Distinguish between the Normal and Page Layout views; state how to change the view and/or magnification of a document.
6. Define typography; distinguish between a serif and a sans serif typeface; use the Format Font command to change the font and/or type size.
7. Use the Format Paragraph command to change line spacing, alignment, tabs, and indents, and to control pagination.
8. Use the Borders and Shading command to box and shade text.
9. Describe the Undo and Redo commands and how they are related to one another.
10. Use the Page Setup command to change the margins and/or orientation; differentiate between a soft and a hard page break.

OVERVIEW

The previous chapter taught you the basics of Microsoft Word and enabled you to create and print a simple document. The present chapter significantly extends your capabilities, by presenting a variety of commands to change the contents and appearance of a document. These operations are known as editing and formatting, respectively.

You will learn how to move and copy text within a document and how to find and replace one character string with another. You will also learn the basics of typography and be able to switch between the different fonts included within Windows. You will be able to change alignment, indentation, line spacing, margins, and page orientation. All of these commands are used in three hands-on exercises, which require your participation at the computer, and which are the very essence of the chapter.

As you read the chapter, realize that there are many different ways to accomplish the same task and that it would be impossible to cover them all. Our approach is to present the overall concepts and suggest the ways we think are most appropriate at the time we introduce the material. We also offer numerous shortcuts in the form of boxed tips that appear throughout the chapter and urge you to explore further on your own. It is not necessary for you to memorize anything as online help is always available. Be flexible and willing to experiment.

WRITE NOW, EDIT LATER

You write a sentence, then change it, and change it again, and one hour later you've produced a single paragraph. It happens to every writer—you stare at a blank screen and flashing cursor and are unable to write. The best solution is to brainstorm and write down anything that pops into your head, and to keep on writing. Don't worry about typos or spelling errors because you can fix them later. Above all, resist the temptation to continually edit the few words you've written because overediting will drain the life out of what you are writing. The important thing is to get your ideas on paper.

SELECT-THEN-DO

Many operations in Word take place within the context of a *select-then-do* methodology; that is, you select a block of text, then you execute the command to operate on that text. The most basic way to select text is by dragging the mouse; that is, click at the beginning of the selection, press and hold the left mouse button as you move to the end of the selection, then release the mouse.

There are, however, a variety of shortcuts to facilitate the process; for example, double click anywhere within a word to select the word, or press the Ctrl key and click the mouse anywhere within a sentence to select the sentence. Additional shortcuts are presented in each of the hands-on exercises, at which point you will have many opportunities to practice selecting text.

Selected text is affected by any subsequent operation; for example, clicking the Bold or Italic button changes the selected text to boldface or italics, respectively. You can also drag the selected text to a new location, press the Del key to erase the selected text, or execute any other editing or formatting command. The text continues to be selected until you click elsewhere in the document.

THE RIGHT MOUSE BUTTON

Point anywhere within a document, then click the right mouse button to display a shortcut menu. Shortcut menus contain commands appropriate to the item you have selected. Click in the menu to execute a command, or click outside the menu to close the menu without executing a command.

MOVING AND COPYING TEXT

The ability to move and/or copy text is essential in order to develop any degree of proficiency in editing. A move operation removes the text from its current location and places it elsewhere in the same (or even a different) document; a copy operation retains the text in its present location and places a duplicate elsewhere. Either operation can be accomplished using the Windows clipboard and a combination of the *Cut, Copy,* and *Paste commands.* (A shortcut, using the mouse to *drag-and-drop* text from one location to another, is described in step 8 in the first hands-on exercise.)

The *clipboard* is a temporary storage area available to any Windows application. Selected text is cut or copied from a document and placed onto the clipboard from where it can be pasted to a new location(s). A move requires that you select the text and execute a Cut command to remove the text from the document and place it on the clipboard. You then move the insertion point to the new location and paste the text from the clipboard into that location. A copy operation necessitates the same steps except that a Copy command is executed rather than a cut, leaving the selected text in its original location as well as placing a copy on the clipboard.

The Cut, Copy, and Paste commands are found in the Edit menu, or alternatively, can be executed by clicking the appropriate buttons on the Standard toolbar. The contents of the clipboard are replaced by each subsequent Cut or Copy command, but are unaffected by the Paste command; that is, the contents of the clipboard can be pasted into multiple locations in the same or different documents.

DELETE WITH CAUTION

You work too hard developing your thoughts to see them disappear in a flash. Hence, instead of deleting large blocks of text, try moving them to the end of your document (or even a new document) from where they can be recalled later if you change your mind. A related practice is to remain in the insert mode (as opposed to overtype) to prevent the inadvertent deletion of existing text as new ideas are added.

UNDO AND REDO COMMANDS

The *Undo command* was introduced in Chapter 1, but it is repeated here because it is so valuable. The command is executed from the Edit menu or by clicking the Undo button on the Standard toolbar. Word enables you to undo up to the last 100 changes to a document. You just click the arrow next to the Undo button on the Standard toolbar to display a reverse-order list of your previous commands, then you click the command you want to undo, which also undoes all of the preceding commands. Undoing the fifth command in the list, for example, will also undo the preceding four commands.

The *Redo command* redoes (reverses) the last command that was undone. As with the Undo command, the Redo command redoes all of the previous commands prior to the command you select. Redoing the fifth command in the list, for example, will also redo the preceding four commands. The Undo and Redo commands work in conjunction with one another; that is, every time a command is undone it can be redone at a later time.

The Find, Replace, and Go To commands share a common dialog box with different tabs for each command as shown in Figure 2.1. The **Find command** locates one or more occurrences of specific text (e.g., a word or phrase). The **Replace command** goes one step further in that it locates the text, and then enables you to optionally replace (one or more occurrences of) that text with different text. The **Go To command** goes directly to a specific place (e.g., a specific page) in the document.

Search text

Search will be case-sensitive
(will not find *There* or *THERE*)

Search will find whole words only
(will not find *therefore* or *thereby*)

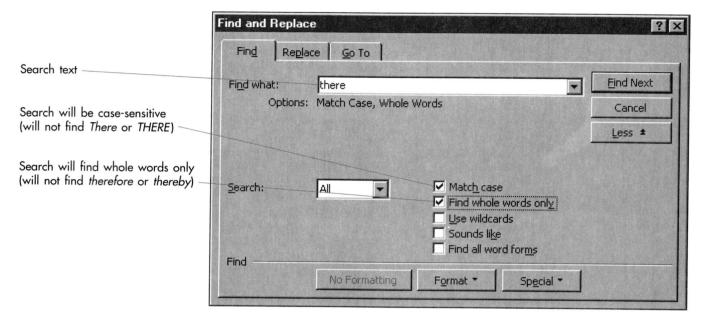

(a) Find Command

Search text

Replacement text

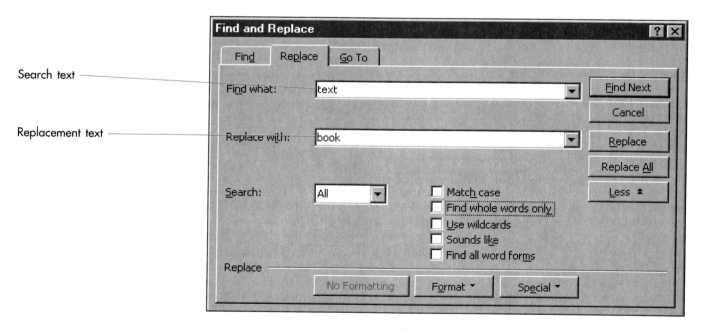

(b) Replace Command

FIGURE 2.1   The Find, Replace, and Go To Commands

Page to go to

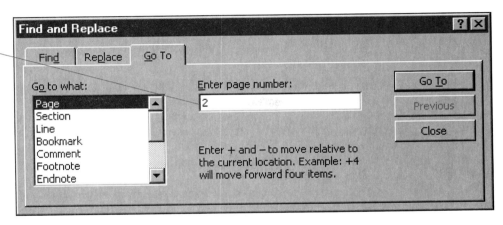

(c) Go To Command

FIGURE 2.1   The Find, Replace, and Go To Commands (continued)

The search in both the Find and Replace commands is case-sensitive or case-insensitive. A ***case-sensitive search*** (where Match Case is selected as in Figure 2.1a) matches not only the text, but also the use of upper- and lowercase letters. Thus, *There* is different from *there,* and a search on one will not identify the other. A ***case-sensitive search*** (where Match Case is *not* as selected in Figure 2.1b) is just the opposite and finds both *There* and *there.* A search may also specify ***whole words only*** to identify *there,* but not *therefore* or *thereby.* And finally, the search and replacement text can also specify different numbers of characters; for example, you could replace *16* with *sixteen.*

The Replace command in Figure 2.1b implements either ***selective replacement,*** which lets you examine each occurrence of the character string in context and decide whether to replace it, or ***automatic replacement,*** where the substitution is made automatically. Selective replacement is implemented by clicking the Find Next command button, then clicking (or not clicking) the Replace button to make the substitution. Automatic replacement (through the entire document) is implemented by clicking the Replace All button. This often produces unintended consequences and is not recommended; for example, if you substitute the word *text* for *book,* the phrase *text book* would become *text text,* which is not what you had in mind.

The Find and Replace commands can include formatting and/or special characters. You can, for example, change all italicized text to boldface, or you can change five consecutive spaces to a tab character. You can also use ***wild cards*** in the character string. For example, to find all four-letter words that begin with "f" and end with "l" (such as *fall, fill,* or *fail*), search for f??l. (The question mark stands for any character, just like a wild card in a card game.) You can also search for all forms of a word; for example, if you specify *am,* it will also find *is* and *are.* You can even search for a word based on how it sounds. When searching for *Marion,* for example, check the Sounds Like check box, and the search will find both *Marion* and *Marian.*

SCROLLING

Scrolling occurs when a document is too large to be seen in its entirety. Figure 2.2a displays a large printed document, only part of which is visible on the screen as illustrated in Figure 2.2b. In order to see a different portion of the document, you need to scroll, whereby new lines will be brought into view as the old lines disappear.

To: Our Students
From: Robert Grauer and Maryann Barber

Welcome to the wonderful world of word processing. Over the next several chapters we will build a foundation in the basics of Microsoft Word, then teach you to format specialized documents, create professional looking tables and charts, and produce well-designed newsletters. Before you know it, you will be a word processing and desktop publishing wizard!

The first chapter presented the basics of word processing and showed you how to create a simple document. You learned how to insert, replace, and/or delete text. This chapter will teach you about fonts and special effects (such as boldfacing and italicizing) and how to use them effectively — how too little is better than too much.

You will go on to experiment with margins, tab stops, line spacing, and justification, learning first to format simple documents and then going on to longer, more complex ones. It is with the latter that we explore headers and footers, page numbering, widows and orphans (yes, we really did mean widows and orphans). It is here that we bring in graphics, working with newspaper-type columns, and the elements of a good page design. And without question, we will introduce the tools that make life so much easier (and your writing so much more impressive) — the Speller, Grammar Checker, Thesaurus, Glossaries, and Styles.

If you are wondering what all these things are, read on in the text and proceed with the hands-on exercises. Create a simple newsletter, then really knock their socks off by adding graphics, fonts, and WordArt. Create a simple calendar and then create more intricate forms that no one will believe were done by little old you. Create a resume with your beginner's skills, and then make it look like so much more with your intermediate (even advanced) skills. Last, but not least, run a mail merge to produce the cover letters that will accompany your resume as it is mailed to companies across the United States (and even the world).

It is up to you to practice, for it is only through working at the computer that you will learn what you need to know. Experiment and don't be afraid to make mistakes. Practice and practice some more.

Our goal is for you to learn and to enjoy what you are learning. We have great confidence in you, and in our ability to help you discover what you can do. You can visit the home page for the *Exploring Windows* series at www.prenhall.com/grauer. You can also send us e-mail. Bob's address is rgrauer@umiami.miami.edu. Maryann's address is mbarber@homer.bus.miami.edu. As you read the last sentence, notice that Word 97 is Web-enabled and that the Internet and e-mail references appear as hyperlinks in this document. You can click the address of our home page from within Word and your browser will display the page, provided you have an Internet connection. You can also click the e-mail address to open your mail program, provided it has been configured correctly.

We look forward to hearing from you and hope that you will like our textbook. You are about to embark on a wonderful journey toward computer literacy. Be patient and inquisitive.

(a) Printed Document

FIGURE 2.2 Scrolling

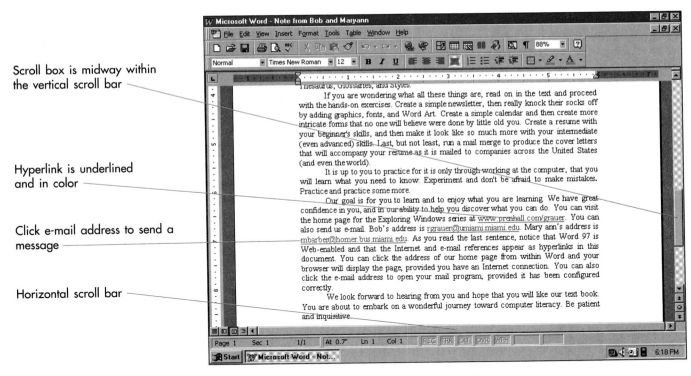

Scroll box is midway within the vertical scroll bar

Hyperlink is underlined and in color

Click e-mail address to send a message

Horizontal scroll bar

(b) Screen Display

FIGURE 2.2   Scrolling (continued)

Scrolling comes about automatically as you reach the bottom of the screen. Entering a new line of text, clicking on the down arrow within the scroll bar, or pressing the down arrow key brings a new line into view at the bottom of the screen and simultaneously removes a line at the top. (The process is reversed at the top of the screen.)

Scrolling can be done with either the mouse or the keyboard. Scrolling with the mouse (e.g., clicking the down arrow in the scroll bar) changes what is displayed on the screen, but does not move the insertion point, so that you must click the mouse after scrolling prior to entering the text at the new location. Scrolling with the keyboard, however (e.g., pressing Ctrl+Home or Ctrl+End to move to the beginning or end of a document, respectively), changes what is displayed on the screen as well as the location of the insertion point, and you can begin typing immediately.

Scrolling occurs most often in a vertical direction as shown in Figure 2.2. It can also occur horizontally, when the length of a line in a document exceeds the number of characters that can be displayed horizontally on the screen.

IT'S WEB ENABLED

Every document in Office 97 is Web-enabled, which means that Internet and e-mail references appear as hyperlinks within a document. Thus you can click the address of any Web page from within Word and your browser will display the page, provided you have an Internet connection. You can also click the e-mail address to open your mail program, provided it has been configured correctly.

The ***View menu*** provides different views of a document. Each view can be displayed at different magnifications, which in turn determine the amount of scrolling necessary to see remote parts of a document.

The ***Normal view*** is the default view and it provides the fastest way to enter text. The ***Page Layout*** view more closely resembles the printed document and displays the top and bottom margins, headers and footers, page numbers, graphics, and other features that do not appear in the Normal view. The Normal view tends to be faster because Word spends less time formatting the display.

The ***Zoom command*** displays the document on the screen at different magnifications; for example, 75%, 100%, or 200%. (The Zoom command does not affect the size of the text on the printed page.) A Zoom percentage (magnification) of 100% displays the document in the approximate size of the text on the printed page. You can increase the percentage to 200% to make the characters appear larger. You can also decrease the magnification to 75% to see more of the document at one time.

Word will automatically determine the magnification if you select one of three additional Zoom options—Page Width, Whole Page, or Many Pages (Whole Page and Many Pages are available only in the Page Layout view). Figure 2.3a, for example, displays a two-page document in Page Layout view. Figure 2.3b shows the corresponding settings in the Zoom command. (The 37% magnification is determined automatically once you specify the number of pages as shown in the figure.)

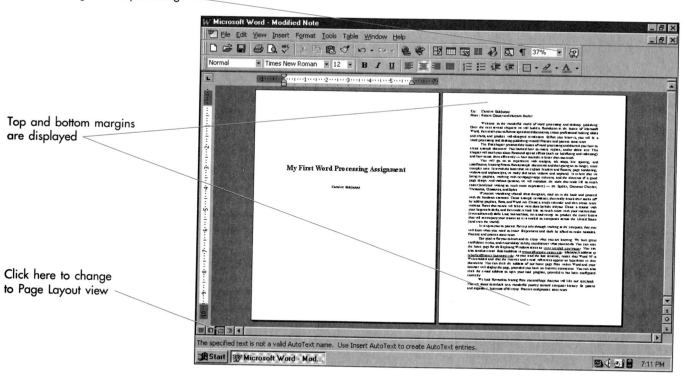

Click to change Zoom percentage

Top and bottom margins are displayed

Click here to change to Page Layout view

My First Word Processing Assignment

(a) Page Layout View

FIGURE 2.3   View Menu and Zoom Command

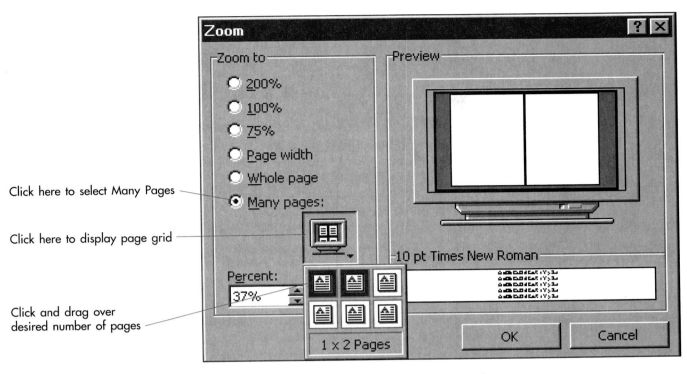

Click here to select Many Pages

Click here to display page grid

Click and drag over
desired number of pages

(b) Zoom Command

FIGURE 2.3   View Menu and Zoom Command (continued)

HANDS-ON EXERCISE 1

Editing a Document

Objective: To edit an existing document; to change the view and magnification of a document; to scroll through a document. To use the Find and Replace commands; to move and copy text using the clipboard and the drag-and-drop facility. Use Figure 2.4 as a guide in the exercise.

STEP 1: View Menu and Zoom Command

➤ Start Word as described in the hands-on exercises from Chapter 1. Pull down the **File menu** and click **Open** (or click the **Open button** on the toolbar).

• Click the **drop-down arrow** on the Look In list box. Click the appropriate drive, drive C or drive A, depending on the location of your data.

• Double click the **Exploring Word folder** to make it the active folder (the folder in which you will save the document).

• Scroll in the Name list box (if necessary) until you can click the **Note from Bob and Maryann** to select this document. Double click the **document icon** or click the **Open command button** to open the file.

➤ The document should appear on the screen as shown in Figure 2.4a.

➤ Change to the Page Layout view at Page Width magnification:

• Pull down the **View menu** and click **Page Layout** (or click the **Page Layout button** above the status bar) as shown in Figure 2.4a.

• Click the **down arrow** in the Zoom box to change to **Page Width.**

Enter your name ─────

Click down arrow to
change magnification

Click the Page Layout
button to change the view

To: Our Students
From: Robert Grauer and Mary Ann Barber

Welcome to the wonderful world of word processing. Over the next several chapters we will build a foundation in the basics of Microsoft Word, then teach you to format specialized documents, create professional looking tables and charts, and produce well-designed newsletters. Before you know it, you will be a word processing and desktop publishing wizard!

The first chapter presented the basics of word processing and showed you how to create a simple document. You learned how to insert, replace, and/or delete text. This chapter will teach you about fonts and special effects (such as boldfacing and italicizing) and how to use them effectively — how too little is better than too much.

You will go on to experiment with margins, tab stops, line spacing, and justification, learning first to format simple documents and then going on to longer, more complex ones. It is with the latter that we explore headers and footers, page numbering, widows and orphans (yes, we really did mean widows and orphans). It is here that we bring in graphics, working with newspaper-type columns, and the elements of a good page design. And without question, we will introduce the tools that make life so much

(a) The View Menu and Zoom Command (step 1)

FIGURE 2.4   Hands-on Exercise 1

➤ Click and drag the mouse to select the phrase **Our Students,** which appears at the beginning of the document. Type your name to replace the selected text.

➤ Pull down the **File menu,** click the **Save As** command, then save the document as **Modified Note.** (This creates a second copy of the document and leaves the original unchanged.)

CREATE A BACKUP COPY

The Options button in the Save As dialog box enables you to specify the backup options in effect. Click the Options command button, then check the box to Always Create Backup Copy. The next time you save the document, the previous version on disk becomes a backup copy while the document in memory becomes the current version on disk.

STEP 2: Scrolling

➤ Click and drag the **scroll box** within the vertical scroll bar to scroll to the end of the document as shown in Figure 2.4b. Click immediately before the period at the end of the last sentence.

➤ Type a **comma,** then insert the phrase **but most of all, enjoy.**

➤ Drag the **scroll box** to the top of the scroll bar to get back to the beginning of the document. Click immediately before the period ending the first sentence, press the **space bar,** then add the phrase **and desktop publishing.**

➤ Save the document.

Drag scroll box to scroll more quickly

Insert this phrase at the end of the document

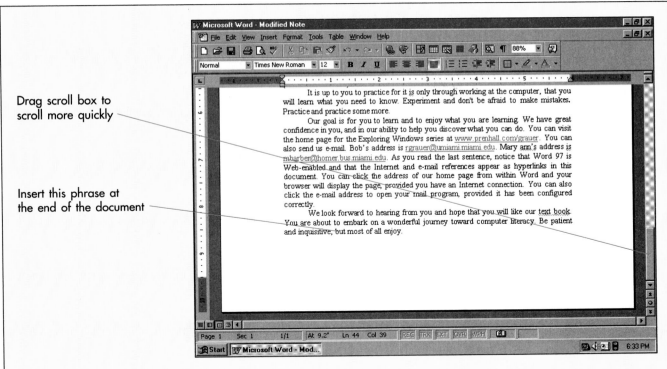

FIGURE 2.4   Hands-on Exercise 1 (continued)

THE MOUSE AND THE SCROLL BAR

Scroll quickly through a document by clicking above or below the scroll box to scroll up or down an entire screen. Move to the top, bottom, or an approximate position within a document by dragging the scroll box to the corresponding position in the scroll bar; for example, dragging the scroll box to the middle of the bar moves the mouse pointer to the middle of the document. Scrolling with the mouse does not change the location of the insertion point, however, and thus you must click the mouse at the new location prior to entering text at that location.

STEP 3: The Replace Command

➤ Press **Ctrl+Home** to move to the beginning of the document. Pull down the **Edit menu.** Click **Replace** to produce the dialog box of Figure 2.4c. Click the **More button** to display the available options.

- Type **text** in the Find what text box.
- Press the **Tab key.** Type **book** in the Replace with text box.

➤ Click the **Find Next button** to find the first occurrence of the word *text*. The dialog box remains on the screen and the first occurrence of *text* is selected. This is *not* an appropriate substitution; that is, you should not substitute *book* for *text* at this point.

➤ Click the **Find Next button** to move to the next occurrence without making the replacement. This time the substitution is appropriate.

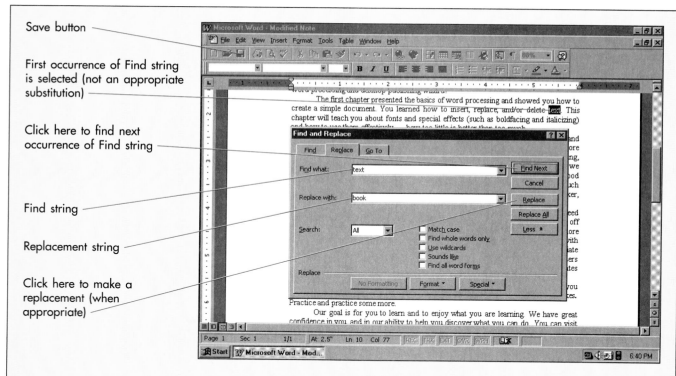

Save button

First occurrence of Find string is selected (not an appropriate substitution)

Click here to find next occurrence of Find string

Find string

Replacement string

Click here to make a replacement (when appropriate)

(c) Replace Command (step 3)

FIGURE 2.4   Hands-on Exercise 1 (continued)

➤ Click **Replace** to make the change and automatically move to the next occurrence where the substitution is again inappropriate. Click **Find Next** a final time. Word will indicate that it has finished searching the document. Click **OK.**

➤ Change the Find and Replace strings to **Mary Ann** and **Maryann,** respectively. Click the **Replace All** button to make the substitution globally without confirmation. Word will indicate that it has finished searching and that two replacements were made. Click **OK.**

➤ Click the **Close command button** to close the dialog box. Click the **Save button** to save the document. Scroll through the document to review your changes.

SCROLLING WITH THE KEYBOARD

Press Ctrl+Home and Ctrl+End to move to the beginning and end of a document, respectively. Press Home and End to move to the beginning and end of a line. Press PgUp or PgDn to scroll one screen in the indicated direction. The advantage of scrolling via the keyboard (instead of the mouse) is that the location of the insertion point changes automatically and you can begin typing immediately.

STEP 4: The Clipboard

➤ Press **PgDn** to scroll toward the end of the document until you come to the paragraph beginning **It is up to you.** Select the sentence **Practice and practice some more** by dragging the mouse over the sentence. (Be sure to include the period.) The sentence will be selected as shown in Figure 2.4d.

➤ Pull down the **Edit menu** and click the **Copy command** or click the **Copy button** on the Standard toolbar.

➤ Press **Ctrl+End** to scroll to the end of the document. Press the **space bar.** Pull down the **Edit menu** and click the **Paste command** (or click the **Paste button** on the Standard toolbar).

➤ Move the insertion point to the end of the first paragraph (following the exclamation point after the word *Wizard*). Press the **space bar.** Click the **Paste button** on the Standard toolbar to paste the sentence a second time.

Click here to copy the selected sentence to the clipboard

Click and drag to select the sentence

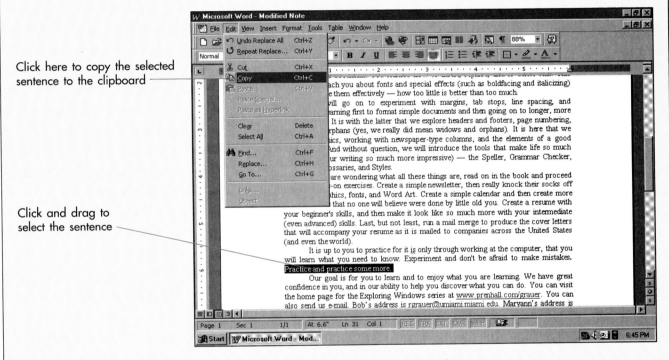

(d) Copy Command (step 4)

FIGURE 2.4   Hands-on Exercise 1 (continued)

CUT, COPY, AND PASTE

Ctrl+X, Ctrl+C, and **Ctrl+V** are keyboard shortcuts to cut, copy, and paste, respectively. (The shortcuts are easier to remember when you realize that the operative letters X, C, and V are next to each other at the bottom left side of the keyboard.) You can also use the Cut, Copy, and Paste buttons on the Standard toolbar.

STEP 5: Undo and Redo Commands

➤ Click the **drop-down arrow** next to the Undo button to display the previously executed actions as in Figure 2.4e. The list of actions corresponds to the editing commands you have issued since the start of the exercise. (Your list will be different from ours if you deviated from any instructions in the hands-on exercise.)

➤ Click **Paste** (the first command on the list) to undo the last editing command; the sentence, Practice and practice some more, disappears from the end of the first paragraph.

➤ Click the remaining steps on the undo list to retrace your steps through the exercise one command at a time. Alternatively, you can scroll to the bottom of the list and click the last command, which automatically undoes all of the preceding commands.

➤ Either way, when the undo list is empty, you will have the document as it existed at the start of the exercise.

➤ Click the **drop-down arrow** for the Redo command to display the list of commands you have undone; click each command in sequence (or click the command at the bottom of the list) and you will restore the document.

➤ Save the document.

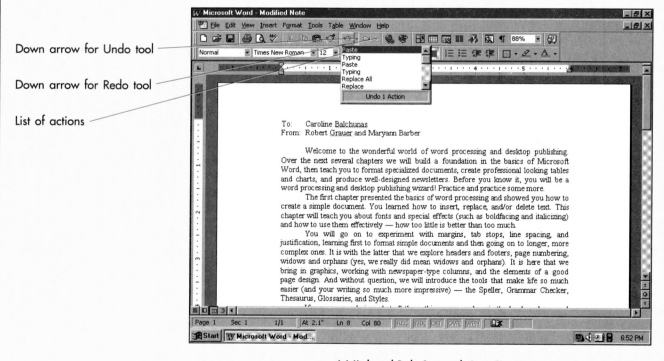

Down arrow for Undo tool

Down arrow for Redo tool

List of actions

(e) Undo and Redo Commands (step 5)

FIGURE 2.4   Hands-on Exercise 1 (continued)

STEP 6: Drag and Drop

➤ Click and drag to select the phrase **format specialized documents** (including the comma and space) as shown in Figure 2.4f, then drag the phrase to its new location immediately before the word *and*. (A dotted vertical bar appears as you drag the text, to indicate its new location.)

➤ Release the mouse button to complete the move.

➤ Click the **drop-down arrow** for the Undo command; click **Move** to undo the move.

➤ To copy the selected text to the same location (instead of moving it), press and hold the **Ctrl key** as you drag the text to its new location. (A plus sign appears as you drag the text, to indicate it is being copied rather than moved.)

➤ Practice the drag-and-drop procedure several times until you are confident you can move and copy with precision.

➤ Click anywhere in the document to deselect the text. Save the document.

Click and drag phrase to new location

Dotted vertical bar shows where phrase will be placed

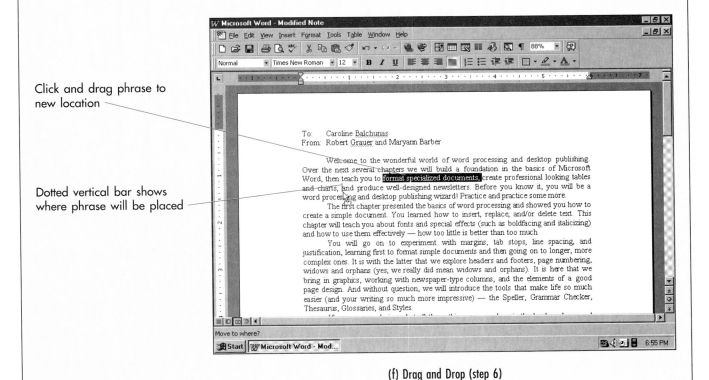

(f) Drag and Drop (step 6)

FIGURE 2.4   Hands-on Exercise 1 (continued)

STEP 7: The Print Preview Command

➤ Pull down the **File menu** and click **Print Preview** (or clock the **Print Preview button** on the Standard toolbar). You should see your entire document as shown in Figure 2.4g.

➤ Check that the entire document fits on one page—that is, check that you can see all three lines in the last paragraph. If not, click the **Shrink to Fit button** on the toolbar to automatically change the font sizes in the document to force it on one page.

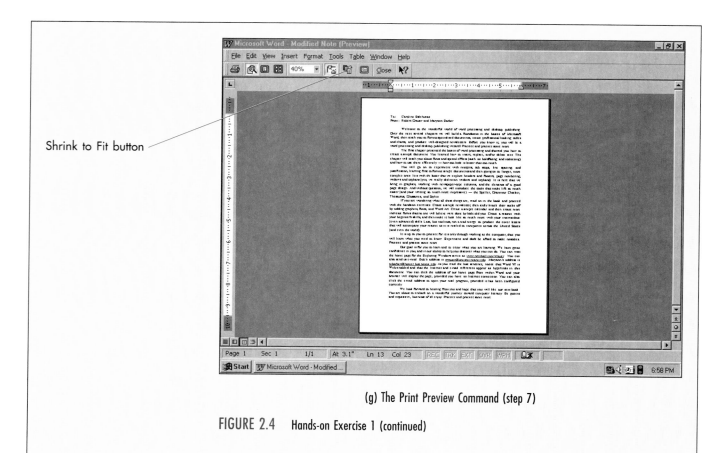

Shrink to Fit button

(g) The Print Preview Command (step 7)

FIGURE 2.4   Hands-on Exercise 1 (continued)

➤ Click the **Print button** to print the document so that you can submit it to your instructor. Click the **Close button** to exit Print Preview and return to your document.

➤ Close the document. Exit Word if you do not want to continue with the next exercise at this time.

TYPOGRAPHY

Typography is the process of selecting typefaces, type styles, and type sizes. The importance of these decisions is obvious, for the ultimate success of any document depends greatly on its appearance. Type should reinforce the message without calling attention to itself and should be consistent with the information you want to convey.

Typeface

A **typeface** is a complete set of characters (upper- and lowercase letters, numbers, punctuation marks, and special symbols). Figure 2.5 illustrates three typefaces—**Times New Roman, Arial,** and **Courier New**—that are supplied with Windows, and which in turn are accessible from any Windows application.

One definitive characteristic of any typeface is the presence or absence of tiny cross lines that end the main strokes of each letter. A **serif** typeface has these lines. A **sans serif** typeface (*sans* from the French for *without*) does not. Times New Roman and Courier New are examples of a serif typeface. Arial is a sans serif typeface.

Typography is the process of selecting typefaces, type styles, and type sizes. A serif typeface has tiny cross strokes that end the main strokes of each letter. A sans serif typeface does not have these strokes. Serif typefaces are typically used with large amounts of text. Sans serif typefaces are used for headings and limited amounts of text. A proportional typeface allocates space in accordance with the width of each character and is what you are used to seeing. A monospaced typeface uses the same amount of space for every character. A well-designed document will limit the number of typefaces so as not to overwhelm the reader.

(a) Times New Roman (serif and proportional)

Typography is the process of selecting typefaces, type styles, and type sizes. A serif typeface has tiny cross strokes that end the main strokes of each letter. A sans serif typeface does not have these strokes. Serif typefaces are typically used with large amounts of text. Sans serif typefaces are used for headings and limited amounts of text. A proportional typeface allocates space in accordance with the width of each character and is what you are used to seeing. A monospaced typeface uses the same amount of space for every character. A well-designed document will limit the number of typefaces so as not to overwhelm the reader.

(b) Arial (sans serif and proportional)

```
Typography is the process of selecting typefaces, type styles,
and type sizes. A serif typeface has tiny cross strokes that end
the main strokes of each letter. A sans serif typeface does not
have these strokes. Serif typefaces are typically used with large
amounts of text. Sans serif typefaces are used for headings and
limited amounts of text. A proportional typeface allocates space
in accordance with the width of each character and is what you
are used to seeing. A monospaced typeface uses the same amount of
space for every character. A well-designed document will limit
the number of typefaces so as not to overwhelm the reader.
```

(c) Courier New (serif and monospaced)

FIGURE 2.5   Typefaces

Serifs help the eye to connect one letter with the next and are generally used with large amounts of text. This book, for example, is set in a serif typeface. A sans serif typeface is more effective with smaller amounts of text and appears in headlines, corporate logos, airport signs, and so on.

A second characteristic of a typeface is whether it is monospaced or proportional. A ***monospaced typeface*** (e.g., Courier New) uses the same amount of space for every character regardless of its width. A ***proportional typeface*** (e.g., Times New Roman or Arial) allocates space according to the width of the character. Monospaced fonts are used in tables and financial projections where text must be precisely lined up, one character underneath the other. Proportional typefaces create a more professional appearance and are appropriate for most documents.

Any typeface can be set in different ***type styles*** (e.g., regular, **bold**, or *italic*). A ***font*** (as the term is used in Windows) is a specific typeface in a specific style; for example, *Times New Roman Italic*, Arial Bold, or **`Courier New Bold Italic.`**

TYPOGRAPHY TIP—USE RESTRAINT

More is not better, especially in the case of too many typefaces and styles, which produce cluttered documents that impress no one. Try to limit yourself to a maximum of two typefaces per document, but choose multiple sizes and/or styles within those typefaces. Use boldface or italics for emphasis; but do so in moderation, because if you emphasize too many elements, the effect is lost.

Type Size

Type size is a vertical measurement and is specified in points, where one ***point*** is equal to $\frac{1}{72}$ of an inch; that is, there are 72 points to the inch. The measurement is made from the top of the tallest letter in a character set (for example, an uppercase T) to the bottom of the lowest letter (for example, a lowercase y). Most documents are set in 10 or 12 point type. Newspaper columns may be set as small as 8 point type. Type sizes of 14 points or higher are ineffective for large amounts of text. Figure 2.6 shows the same phrase set in varying type sizes.

Some typefaces appear larger (smaller) than others even though they may be set in the same point size. The type in Figure 2.6a, for example, looks smaller than the corresponding type in Figure 2.6b even though both are set in the same point size.

Format Font Command

The ***Format Font command*** gives you complete control over the typeface, size, and style of the text in a document. Executing the command before entering text will set the format of the text you type from that point on. You can also use the command to change the font of existing text by selecting the text, then executing the command. Either way, you will see the dialog box in Figure 2.7, in which you specify the font (typeface), style, and point size.

You can choose any of the special effects (e.g., ~~strikethrough~~ or SMALL CAPS) and/or change the underline options (whether or not spaces are to be underlined). You can even change the color of the text on the monitor, but you need a color printer for the printed document. (The Character Spacing and Animation tabs produce different sets of options in which you control the spacing and appearance of the characters and are beyond the scope of our discussion.)

This is Arial 8 point type

This is Arial 10 point type

This is Arial 12 point type

This is Arial 18 point type

This is Arial 24 point type

This is Arial 30 point type

(a) Sans Serif Typeface

This is Times New Roman 8 point type

This is Times New Roman 10 point type

This is Times New Roman 12 point type

This is Times New Roman 18 point type

This is Times New Roman 24 point type

This is Times New Roman 30 point

(b) Serif Typeface

FIGURE 2.6   Type Size

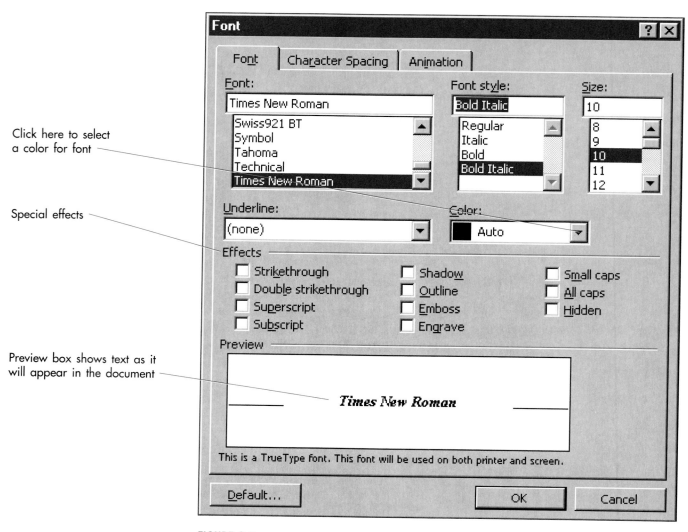

Click here to select a color for font

Special effects

Preview box shows text as it will appear in the document

FIGURE 2.7   Format Font Command

The Preview box shows the text as it will appear in the document. The message at the bottom of the dialog box indicates that Times New Roman is a TrueType font and that the same font will be used on both the screen and the monitor. TrueType fonts ensure that your document is truly WYSIWYG (What You See Is What You Get) because the fonts you see on the monitor will be identical to those in the printed document.

PAGE SETUP COMMAND

The *Page Setup command* in the File menu lets you change margins, paper size, orientation, paper source, and/or layout. All parameters are accessed from the dialog box in Figure 2.8 by clicking the appropriate tab within the dialog box.

The default margins are indicated in Figure 2.8a and are one inch on the top and bottom of the page, and one and a quarter inches on the left and right. You can change any (or all) of these settings by entering a new value in the appropriate text box, either by typing it explicitly or clicking the up/down arrow. All of the settings in the Page Setup command apply to the whole document regardless of the position of the insertion point. (Different settings can be established for different parts of a document by creating sections, which is beyond the scope of our present discussion.)

Margin tab is selected

Type a new value

Click to change value

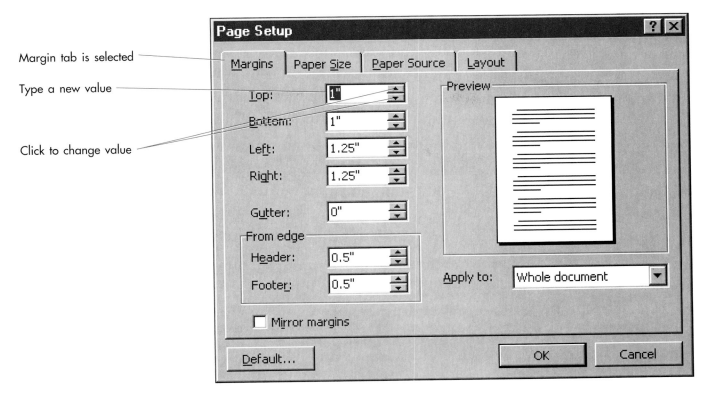

(a) Margins

Paper Size tab is selected

Click either Portrait or Landscape orientation (Landscape is currently selected)

Preview box shows sample document, which corresponds to current settings

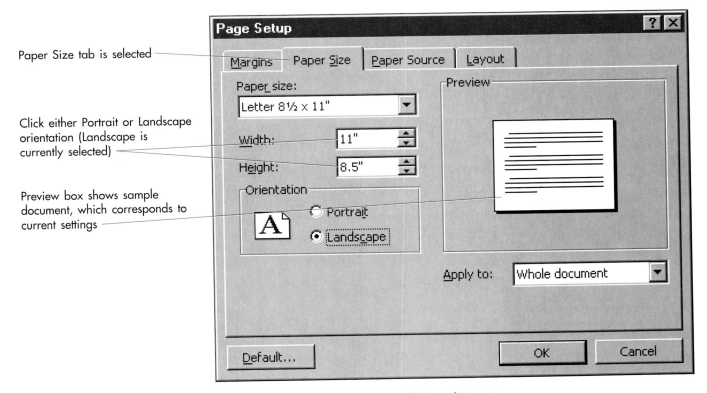

(b) Size and Orientation

FIGURE 2.8   Page Setup Command

The Paper Size tab within the Page Setup command enables you to change the orientation of a page as shown in Figure 2.8b. ***Portrait orientation*** is the default. ***Landscape orientation*** flips the page 90 degrees so that its dimensions are 11 × 8½ rather than the other way around. Note, too, the Preview area in both Figures 2.8a and 2.8b, which shows how the document will appear with the selected parameters.

The Paper Source tab is used to specify which tray should be used on printers with multiple trays, and is helpful when you want to load different types of paper simultaneously. The Layout tab is used to specify options for headers and footers (text that appears at the top or bottom of each page in a document).

Page Breaks

One of the first concepts you learned was that of word wrap, whereby Word inserts a soft return at the end of a line in order to begin a new line. The number and/or location of the soft returns change automatically as you add or delete text within a document. Soft returns are very different from the hard returns inserted by the user, whose number and location remain constant.

In much the same way, Word creates a ***soft page break*** to go to the top of a new page when text no longer fits on the current page. And just as you can insert a hard return to start a new paragraph, you can insert a ***hard page break*** to force any part of a document to begin on a new page. A hard page break is inserted into a document using the Break command in the Insert menu or through the Ctrl+enter keyboard shortcut. (You can prevent the occurrence of awkward page breaks through the Format Paragraph command as described later in the chapter.

AN EXERCISE IN DESIGN

The following exercise has you retrieve an existing document from the set of practice files, then experiment with various typefaces, type styles, and point sizes. The original document uses a monospaced (typewriter style) font, without boldface or italics, and you are asked to improve its appearance. The first step directs you to save the document under a new name so that you can always return to the original if necessary.

There is no right and wrong with respect to design, and you are free to choose any combination of fonts that appeals to you. The exercise takes you through various formatting options but lets you make the final decision. It does, however, ask you to print the final document and submit it to your instructor.

IMPOSE A TIME LIMIT

A word processor is supposed to save time and make you more productive. It will do exactly that, provided you use the word processor for its primary purpose—writing and editing. It is all too easy, however, to lose sight of that objective and spend too much time formatting the document. Concentrate on the content of your document rather than its appearance. Impose a time limit on the amount of time you will spend on formatting. End the session when the limit is reached.

Character Formatting

Objective: To experiment with character formatting; to change fonts and to use boldface and italics; to copy formatting with the format painter; to insert a page break and see different views of a document. Use Figure 2.9 as a guide in the exercise.

STEP 1: Open the Existing Document

➤ Start Word. Pull down the **File menu** and click **Open** (or click the **Open button** on the toolbar). To open a file:

- Click the **drop-down arrow** on the Look In list box. Click the appropriate drive, drive C or drive A, depending on the location of your data.
- Double click the **Exploring Word folder** to make it the active folder (the folder in which you will open and save the document).
- Scroll in the **Open list box** (if necessary) until you can click **Tips for Writing** to select this document. Double click the **document icon** or click the **Open command button** to open the file.

➤ Pull down the **File menu.** Click the **Save As command** to save the document as **Modified Tips.**

➤ Pull down the **View menu** and click **Normal** (or click the **Normal View button** above the status bar).

➤ Set the magnification (zoom) to **Page Width.**

SELECTING TEXT

The *selection bar,* a blank column at the far left of the document window, makes it easy to select a line, paragraph, or the entire document. To select a line, move the mouse pointer to the selection bar, point to the line and click the left mouse button. To select a paragraph, move the mouse pointer to the selection bar, point to any line in the paragraph, and double click the mouse. To select the entire document, move the mouse pointer to the selection bar and press the Ctrl key while you click the mouse.

STEP 2: The Right Mouse Button

➤ Select the first tip as shown in Figure 2.9a. Point to the selected text and click the **right mouse button** to display the shortcut menu.

➤ Click outside the menu to close the menu without executing a command.

➤ Press the **Ctrl key** as you click the selection bar to select the entire document, then click the **right mouse button** to display the shortcut menu.

➤ Click **Font** to execute the Format Font command.

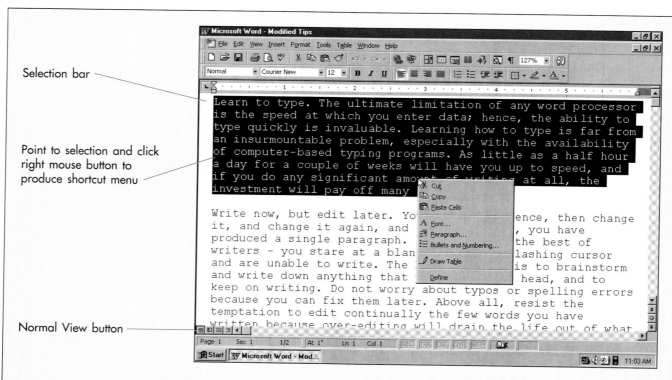

Selection bar

Point to selection and click
right mouse button to
produce shortcut menu

Normal View button

(a) Shortcut Menu (step 2)

FIGURE 2.9   Hands-on Exercise 2

STEP 3: Changing Fonts

➤ Click the **down arrow** on the Font list box of Figure 2.9b to scroll through the available fonts. Select a different font, such as Times New Roman.

➤ Click the **down arrow** in the Font Size list box to choose a point size.

➤ Click **OK** to change the font and point size for the selected text.

➤ Pull down the **Edit menu** and click **Undo** (or click the **Undo button** on the Standard toolbar) to return to the original font.

➤ Experiment with different fonts and/or different point sizes until you are satisfied with the selection. We chose 12 point Times New Roman.

FIND AND REPLACE FORMATTING

The Replace command enables you to replace formatting as well as text. To replace any text set in bold with the same text in italics, pull down the Edit menu, and click the Replace command. Click the Find what text box, but do *not* enter any text. Click the More button to expand the dialog box. Click the Format command button, click Font, click Bold in the Font Style list, and click OK. Click the Replace with text box and again do *not* enter any text. Click the Format command button, click Font, click Italic in the Font Style list, and click OK. Click the Find Next or Replace All command button to do selective or automatic replacement. Use a similar technique to replace one font with another.

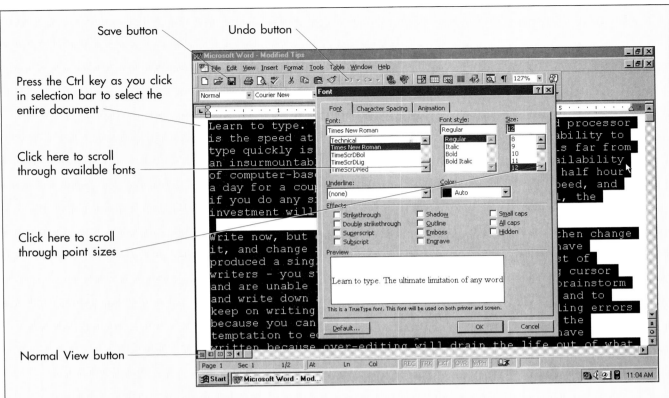

Save button

Undo button

Press the Ctrl key as you click in selection bar to select the entire document

Click here to scroll through available fonts

Click here to scroll through point sizes

Normal View button

(b) Format Font Command (step 3)

FIGURE 2.9   Hands-on Exercise 2 (continued)

STEP 4: Boldface and Italics

➤ Drag the mouse over the sentence **Learn to type** at the beginning of the document.

➤ Click the **Italic button** on the Formatting toolbar to italicize the selected phrase, which will remain selected after the italics take effect.

➤ Click the **Bold button** to boldface the selected text. The text is now in bold italic.

➤ Experiment with different styles (bold, italics, underlining, or bold italic) until you are satisfied. The Italic, Bold, and Underline buttons function as toggle switches; that is, clicking the Italic button when text is already italicized returns the text to normal.

➤ Save the document

THE "WHAT'S THIS" BUTTON

Pull down the Help menu and click the What's This button command (or press Shift+F1). Point to any button on any toolbar (the mouse pointer changes to an arrow with a question mark), then click the button to display a Help balloon to explain the function of that button. Press the Esc key to close the balloon and return the mouse pointer to normal.

STEP 5: The Format Painter

➤ Click anywhere within the sentence Learn to Type. **Double click** the **Format Painter button** on the Standard toolbar. The mouse pointer changes to a paintbrush as shown in Figure 2.9c.

➤ Drag the mouse pointer over the next title, **Write now, edit later,** and release the mouse. The formatting from the original sentence (bold italic as shown in Figure 2.9c) has been applied to this sentence as well.

➤ Drag the mouse pointer (in the shape of a paintbrush) over the remaining titles (the first sentence in each paragraph) to copy the formatting.

➤ Click the **Format Painter button** after you have painted the title of the last tip to turn the feature off.

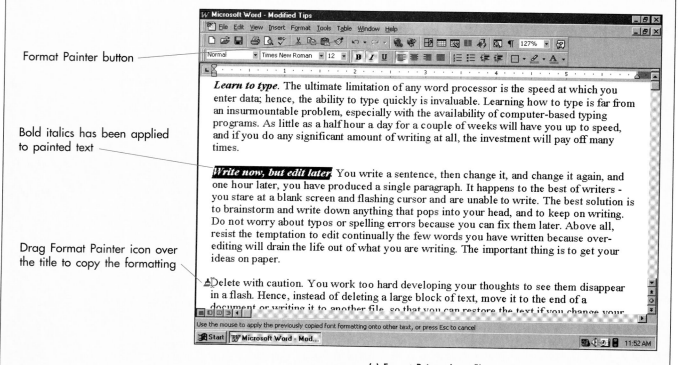

Format Painter button

Bold italics has been applied to painted text

Drag Format Painter icon over the title to copy the formatting

(c) Format Painter (step 5)

FIGURE 2.9   Hands-on Exercise 2 (continued)

THE FORMAT PAINTER

The *Format Painter* copies the formatting of the selected text to other places in a document. Select the text with the formatting you want to copy, then click or double click the Format Painter button on the Standard toolbar. Clicking the button will paint only one selection. Double clicking the button will paint multiple selections until the feature is turned off by again clicking the Format Painter button. Either way, the mouse pointer changes to a paintbrush, which you can drag over text to give it the identical formatting characteristics as the original selection.

STEP 6: Change Margins

➤ Press **Ctrl+End** to move to the end of the document as shown in Figure 2.9d. You will see a dotted line indicating a soft page break. (If you do not see the page break, it means that your document fits on one page because you used a different font and/or a smaller point size. We used 12 point Times New Roman.)

➤ Pull down the **File menu.** Click **Page Setup.** Click the **Margins tab** if necessary. Change the bottom margin to **.75** inch. Check that these settings apply to the **Whole Document.** Click **OK.** The page break disappears because more text fits on the page.

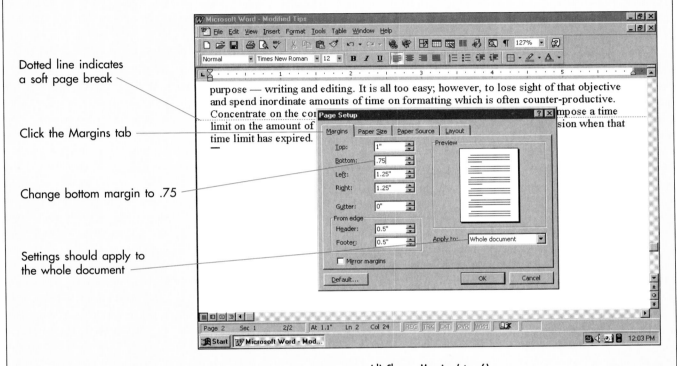

(d) Change Margins (step 6)

FIGURE 2.9   Hands-on Exercise 2 (continued)

DIALOG BOX SHORTCUTS

You can use keyboard shortcuts to select options in a dialog box. Press Tab (Shift+Tab) to move forward (backward) from one field or command button to the next. Press Alt plus the underlined letter to move directly to a field or command button. Press enter to activate the selected command button. Press Esc to exit the dialog box without taking action. Press the space bar to toggle check boxes on or off. Press the down arrow to open a drop-down list box once the list has been accessed, then press the up or down arrow to move between options in a list box.

STEP 7: Create a Title Page

➤ Press **Ctrl+Home** to move to the beginning of the document. Press **enter** three or four times to add a few blank lines.

➤ Press **Ctrl+enter** to insert a hard page break. You will see the words "Page Break" in the middle of a dotted line as shown in Figure 2.9e.

➤ Press the **up arrow key** three times. Enter the title **Tips for Writing.** Select the title, and format it in a larger point size, such as 24 points.

➤ Enter your name on the next line and format it in a different point size, such as 14 points. Select both the title and your name as shown in the figure. Click the **Center button** on the Formatting toolbar. Save the document.

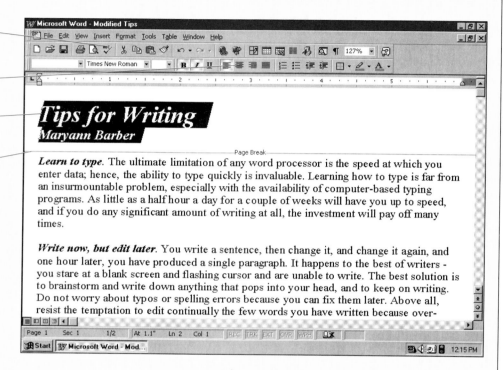

Spelling and Grammar button

Center button

Click and drag to select both lines

Press Ctrl+enter to insert a hard page break

(e) Create the Title Page (step 7)

FIGURE 2.9   Hands-on Exercise 2 (continued)

THE SPELL CHECK

Use the spell check prior to saving a document for the last time, even if the document is just a sentence or two. Spelling errors make your work look sloppy and discourage the reader before he or she has read what you had to say. Spelling errors can cost you a job, a grade, or a lucrative contract. The spell check requires but a single click, so why not use it?

STEP 8: The Completed Document

➤ Pull down the **View menu** and click **Page Layout** (or click the **Page Layout button** above the status bar).

➤ Click the **Zoom Control arrow** on the Standard toolbar and select **Two Pages.** Release the mouse to view the completed document in Figure 2.9f. You may want to add additional blank lines at the top of the title page to move the title further down on the page.

➤ Save the document a final time. Exit Word if you do not want to continue with the next exercise at this time.

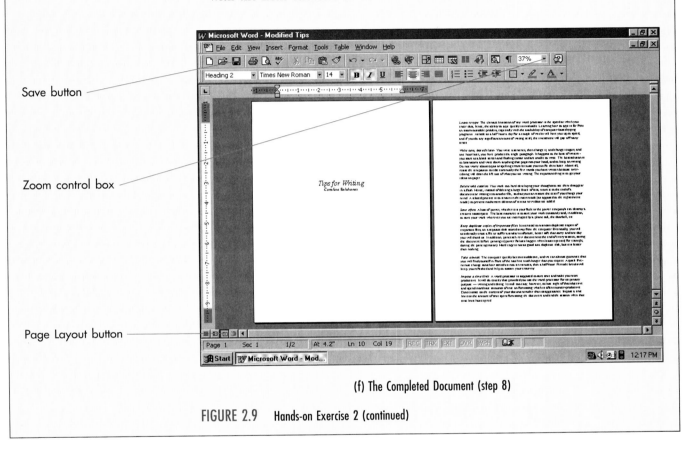

Save button

Zoom control box

Page Layout button

(f) The Completed Document (step 8)

FIGURE 2.9   Hands-on Exercise 2 (continued)

PARAGRAPH FORMATTING

A change in typography is only one way to alter the appearance of a document. You can also change the alignment, indentation, tab stops, or line spacing for any paragraph(s) within the document. You can control the pagination and prevent the occurrence of awkward page breaks by specifying that an entire paragraph has to appear on the same page, or that a one-line paragraph (e.g., a heading) should appear on the same page as the next paragraph. You can include borders or shading for added emphasis around selected paragraphs.

All of these features are implemented at the paragraph level and affect all selected paragraphs. If no paragraphs are selected, the commands affect the entire current paragraph (the paragraph containing the insertion point), regardless of the position of the insertion point when the command is executed.

Alignment

Text can be aligned in four different ways as shown in Figure 2.10. It may be justified (flush left/flush right), left aligned (flush left with a ragged right margin), right aligned (flush right with a ragged left margin), or centered within the margins (ragged left and right).

Left aligned text is perhaps the easiest to read. The first letters of each line align with each other, helping the eye to find the beginning of each line. The lines themselves are of irregular length. There is uniform spacing between words, and the ragged margin on the right adds white space to the text, giving it a lighter and more informal look.

Justified text produces lines of equal length, with the spacing between words adjusted to align at the margins. It may be more difficult to read than text that is left aligned because of the uneven (sometimes excessive) word spacing and/or the greater number of hyphenated words needed to justify the lines.

Type that is centered or right aligned is restricted to limited amounts of text where the effect is more important than the ease of reading. Centered text, for example, appears frequently on wedding invitations, poems, or formal announcements. Right aligned text is used with figure captions and short headlines.

Indents

Individual paragraphs can be indented so that they appear to have different margins from the rest of a document. Indentation is established at the paragraph level; thus different indentation can be in effect for different paragraphs. One paragraph may be indented from the left margin only, another from the right margin only, and a third from both the left and right margins. The first line of any paragraph may be indented differently from the rest of the paragraph. And finally, a paragraph may be set with no indentation at all, so that it aligns on the left and right margins.

The indentation of a paragraph is determined by three settings: the *left indent,* the *right indent,* and a *special indent* (if any). There are two types of special indentation, first line and hanging, as will be explained shortly. The left and right indents are set to zero by default, as is the special indent, and produce a paragraph with no indentation at all as shown in Figure 2.11a. Positive values for the left and right indents offset the paragraph from both margins as shown in Figure 2.11b.

The *first line indent* (Figure 2.11c) affects only the first line in the paragraph and is implemented by pressing the Tab key at the beginning of the paragraph. A *hanging indent* (Figure 2.11d) sets the first line of a paragraph at the left indent and indents the remaining lines according to the amount specified. Hanging indents are often used with bulleted or numbered lists.

INDENTS VERSUS MARGINS

Indents measure the distance between the text and the margins. *Margins* mark the distance from the text to the edge of the page. Indents are determined at the paragraph level, whereas margins are established at the section (document) level. The left and right margins are set (by default) to 1.25 inches each; the left and right indents default to zero. The first line indent is measured from the setting of the left indent.

We, the people of the United States, in order to form a more perfect Union, establish justice, insure domestic tranquillity, provide for the common defense, promote the general welfare, and secure the blessings of liberty to ourselves and our posterity, do ordain and establish this Constitution for the United States of America.

(a) Justified (flush left/flush right)

We, the people of the United States, in order to form a more perfect Union, establish justice, insure domestic tranquillity, provide for the common defense, promote the general welfare, and secure the blessings of liberty to ourselves and our posterity, do ordain and establish this Constitution for the United States of America.

(b) Left Aligned (flush left/ragged right)

We, the people of the United States, in order to form a more perfect Union, establish justice, insure domestic tranquillity, provide for the common defense, promote the general welfare, and secure the blessings of liberty to ourselves and our posterity, do ordain and establish this Constitution for the United States of America.

(c) Right Aligned (ragged left/flush right)

We, the people of the United States, in order to form a more perfect Union, establish justice, insure domestic tranquillity, provide for the common defense, promote the general welfare, and secure the blessings of liberty to ourselves and our posterity, do ordain and establish this Constitution for the United States of America.

(d) Centered (ragged left/ragged right)

FIGURE 2.10   Alignment

The left and right indents are defined as the distance between the text and the left and right margins, respectively. Both parameters are set to zero in this paragraph and so the text aligns on both margins. Different indentation can be applied to different paragraphs in the same document.

(a) No Indents

Positive values for the left and right indents offset a paragraph from the rest of a document and are often used for long quotations. This paragraph has left and right indents of one-half inch each. Different indentation can be applied to different paragraphs in the same document.

(b) Left and Right Indents

A first line indent affects only the first line in the paragraph and is implemented by pressing the Tab key at the beginning of the paragraph. The remainder of the paragraph is aligned at the left margin (or the left indent if it differs from the left margin) as can be seen from this example. Different indentation can be applied to different paragraphs in the same document.

(c) First Line Indent

A hanging indent sets the first line of a paragraph at the left indent and indents the remaining lines according to the amount specified. Hanging indents are often used with bulleted or numbered lists. Different indentation can be applied to different paragraphs in the same document.

(d) Hanging (Special) Indent

FIGURE 2.11   Indents

Tabs

Anyone who has used a typewriter is familiar with the function of the Tab key; that is, press Tab and the insertion point moves to the next **tab stop** (a measured position to align text at a specific place). The Tab key is much more powerful in Word as you can choose from four different types of tab stops (left, center, right, and decimal). You can also specify a **leader character,** typically dots or hyphens, to draw the reader's eye across the page. Tabs are often used to create tables within a document.

The default tab stops are set every ½ inch and are left aligned, but you can change the **alignment** and/or position with the Format Tabs command. Figure 2.12 illustrates a dot leader in combination with a right tab to produce a Table of Contents. The default tab stops have been cleared in Figure 2.12a, in favor of a single right tab at 5.5 inches. The option button for a dot leader has also been checked. The resulting document is shown in Figure 2.12b.

Tab set at 5.5"

Right tab is selected

Dot leader is selected

Click here to clear all tabs

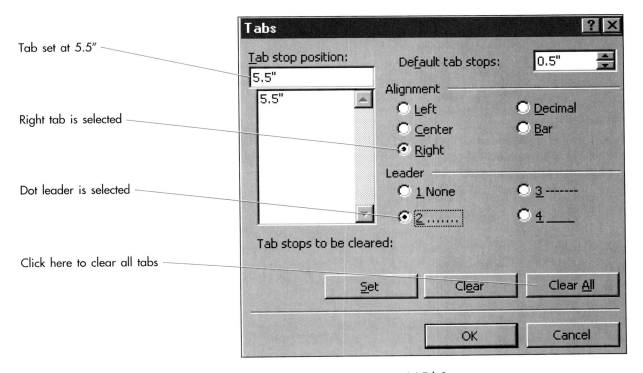

(a) Tab Stops

Right tab with dot leader

(b) Table of Contents

FIGURE 2.12 Tabs

The Format Tabs command is quite powerful, so it is useful to repeat the different alignments:

- Left alignment, where the text *begins* at the tab stop, corresponds to the Tab key on a typewriter.
- Right alignment, where the text *ends* at the tab stop, is used to align page numbers in a table of contents or to align text at the right margin.
- Center alignment, where text centers over the tab stop, is used infrequently for special effect.
- Decimal alignment, which lines up numeric values in a column on the decimal point, is helpful with statistical text.

Line Spacing

Line spacing determines the space between the lines in a paragraph. Word provides complete flexibility and enables you to select any multiple of line spacing (single, double, line and a half, and so on). You can also specify line spacing in terms of points (there are 72 points per inch).

Line spacing is set at the paragraph level through the Format Paragraph command, which sets the spacing within a paragraph. The command also enables you to add extra spacing before the first line in a paragraph or after the last line. (Either technique is preferable to the common practice of single spacing the paragraphs within a document, then adding a blank line between paragraphs.)

FORMAT PARAGRAPH COMMAND

The *Format Paragraph command* is where you specify the alignment, indentation, line spacing, and pagination for the selected paragraph(s). As indicated, all of these features are implemented at the paragraph level and affect all selected paragraphs. If no paragraphs are selected, the command affects the entire current paragraph (the paragraph containing the insertion point), regardless of the position of the insertion point when the command is executed.

The Format Paragraph command is illustrated in Figure 2.13. The Indents and Spacing tab in Figure 2.13a calls for a hanging indent, line spacing of 1.5 lines, and justified alignment. The preview area within the dialog box enables you to see how the paragraph will appear within the document.

The Line and Page Breaks tab in Figure 2.13b illustrates an entirely different set of parameters in which you control the pagination within a document. You are already familiar with the concept of page breaks, and the distinction between soft page breaks (inserted by Word) versus hard page breaks (inserted by the user). The check boxes in Figure 2.13b enable you to prevent the occurrence of awkward soft page breaks that detract from the appearance of a document.

You might, for example, want to prevent widows and orphans, terms used to describe isolated lines that seem out of place. A *widow* refers to the last line of a paragraph appearing by itself at the top of a page. An *orphan* is the first line of a paragraph appearing by itself at the bottom of a page.

You can also impose additional controls by clicking one or more check boxes. Use the Keep Lines Together option to prevent a soft page break from occurring within a paragraph and ensure that the entire paragraph appears on the same page. (The paragraph is moved to the top of the next page if it doesn't fit on the bottom of the current page.) Use the Keep with Next option to prevent a soft page break between the two paragraphs. This option is typically used to keep a heading (a one-line paragraph) with its associated text in the next paragraph.

Full justification is selected ──────

Hanging indent is selected ──────

Line spacing is set at 1.5 lines ──────

Preview box displays
a sample paragraph ──────

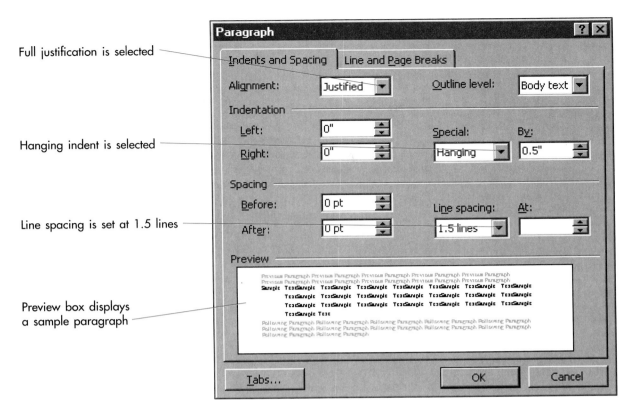

(a) Indents and Spacing

Line and Page Breaks tab
is selected ──────

Pagination options prevent
awkward soft page breaks ──────

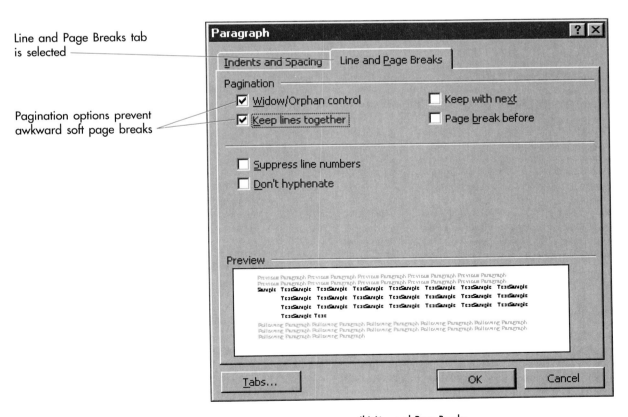

(b) Line and Page Breaks

FIGURE 2.13   Format Paragraph Command

Borders and Shading

The ***Borders and Shading command*** puts the finishing touches on a document and is illustrated in Figure 2.14. It lets you create boxed and/or shaded text as well as place horizontal or vertical lines around a paragraph. You can choose from several different line styles in any color (assuming you have a color printer). You can place a uniform border around a paragraph (choose Box), or you can choose a shadow effect with thicker lines at the right and bottom. You can also apply lines to selected sides of a paragraph(s) by selecting a line style, then clicking the desired sides as apprpriate.

Shading is implemented independently of the border. Clear (no shading) is the default. Solid (100%) shading creates a solid box where the text is turned white so you can read it. Shading of 10 or 20 percent is generally most effective to add emphasis to the selected paragraph. The Borders and Shading command is implemented on the paragraph level and affects the entire paragraph—either the current or selected paragraph(s).

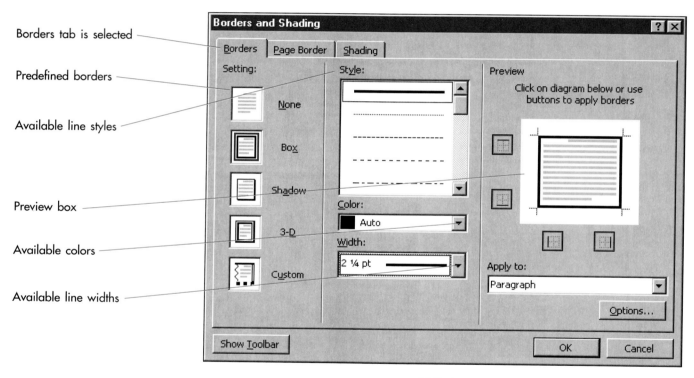

(a) Borders

FIGURE 2.14   Paragraph Borders and Shading

FORMATTING AND THE PARAGRAPH MARK

The paragraph mark ¶ at the end of a paragraph does more than just indicate the presence of a hard return. It also stores all of the formatting in effect for the paragraph. Hence in order to preserve the formatting when you move or copy a paragraph, you must include the paragraph mark in the selected text. Click the Show/Hide ¶ button on the toolbar to display the paragraph mark and make sure it has been selected.

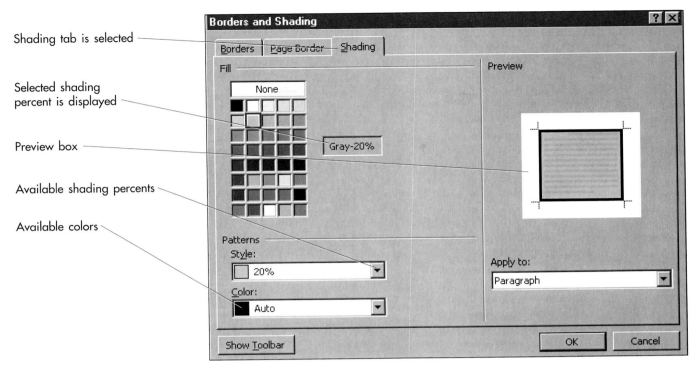

Shading tab is selected

Selected shading percent is displayed

Preview box

Available shading percents

Available colors

(b) Shading

FIGURE 2.14   Paragraph Borders and Shading (continued)

PARAGRAPH FORMATTING AND THE INSERTION POINT

Indents, tab stops, line spacing, alignment, pagination, borders, and shading are all set at the paragraph level and affect all selected paragraphs and/or the current paragraph (the paragraph containing the insertion point). The position of the insertion point within the paragraph does not matter as the insertion point can be anywhere within the paragraph when the Format Paragraph command is executed. Keep the concept of paragraph formatting in mind as you do the following hands-on exercise.

HANDS-ON EXERCISE 3

Paragraph Formatting

Objective: To implement line spacing, alignment, and indents; to implement widow and orphan protection; to box and shade a selected paragraph.

STEP 1: Load the Practice Document

➤ Open the **Modified Tips** document from the previous exercise. If necessary, change to the Page Layout view. Click the **Zoom drop-down arrow** and click **Two Pages** to match the view in Figure 2.15a.

➤ Select the entire second page as shown in the figure. Click the **right mouse button** to produce the shortcut menu. Click **Paragraph.**

Point to selected text and click right mouse button to produce shortcut menu

Click Page Layout button

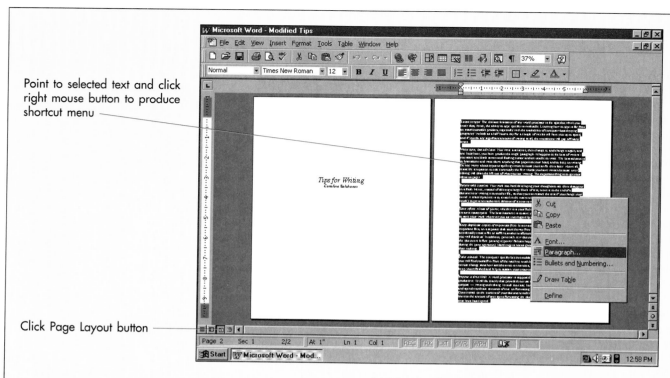

(a) Select-then-do (step 1)

FIGURE 2.15   Hands-on Exercise 3

SELECT TEXT WITH THE F8 EXTEND KEY

Move to the beginning of the text you want to select, then press the F8 (extend) key. The letters EXT will appear in the status bar. Use the arrow keys to extend the selection in the indicated direction; for example, press the down arrow key to select the line. You can also press any character—for example, a letter, space, or period—to extend the selection to the first occurrence of that character. Press Esc to cancel the selection mode.

STEP 2: Line Spacing, Justification, and Pagination

➤ If necessary, click the **Indents and Spacing tab** to view the options in Figure 2.15b.

- Click the **down arrow** on the list box for Line Spacing and select **1.5 Lines.**
- Click the **down arrow** on the Alignment list box and select **Justified** as shown in Figure 2.15b.
- The Preview area shows the effect of these settings.

➤ Click the tab for **Line and Page Breaks.**

- Check the box for **Keep Lines Together.** If necessary, check the box for **Widow/Orphan Control.**

➤ Click **OK** to accept all of the settings in the dialog box.

Click the Indents
and Spacing tab

Click the drop-down arrow
to select the alignment

Click the drop-down arrow
to select the line spacing

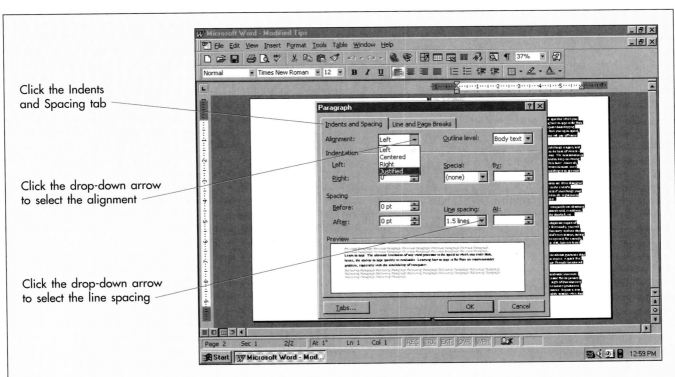

(b) Format Paragraph Command (step 2)

FIGURE 2.15   Hands-on Exercise 3 (continued)

➤ Click anywhere in the document to deselect the text and see the effects of the formatting changes:

- The document is fully justified and the line spacing has increased.
- The document now extends to three pages, with all of the fifth paragraph appearing on the last page.
- There is a large bottom margin on the second page as a consequence of keeping the lines together in paragraph five.

➤ Save the document.

CUSTOMIZE THE TOOLBAR

Customize the Formatting toolbar to display the buttons for line spacing. Point to any toolbar, click the right mouse button to display a shortcut menu, and click Customize to display the Customize dialog box. Click the Commands tab, select Format from the Categories list box, then scroll in the Commands list box until you click and drag the line spacing buttons to the end of the Formatting toolbar. You must drag the button within the Formatting toolbar (the mouse pointer will change to a + from an ×, indicating that you can copy the button). Close the Customize dialog box. The next time you want to change line spacing, just click the appropriate button on the Formatting toolbar.

STEP 3: Indents

➤ Select the second paragraph as shown in Figure 2.15c. (The second paragraph will not yet be indented.)

➤ Pull down the **Format menu** and click **Paragraph** (or press the **right mouse button** to produce the shortcut menu and click **Paragraph**).

➤ If necessary, click the **Indents and Spacing tab** in the Paragraph dialog box. Click the **up arrow** on the Left Indentation text box to set the **Left Indent** to **.5** inch. Set the **Right indent** to **.5** inch. Click **OK.** Your document should match Figure 2.15c.

➤ Save the document.

Drag to change first line indent

Drag to change left indent

Drag to change first line and left indents

Drag to change right indent

Select second paragraph and set left and right indents to .5" each

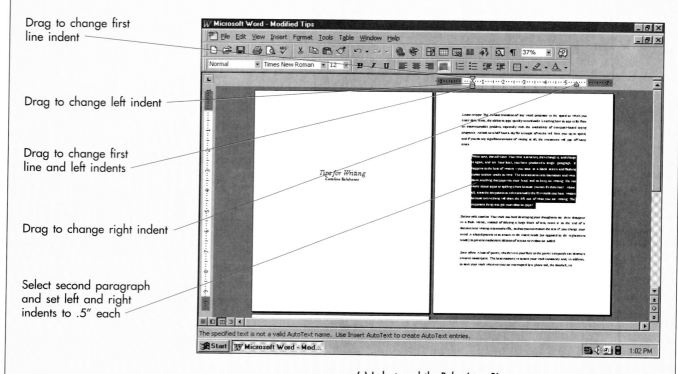

(c) Indents and the Ruler (step 3)

FIGURE 2.15 Hands-on Exercise 3 (continued)

INDENTS AND THE RULER

Use the ruler to change the special, left, and/or right indents. Select the paragraph (or paragraphs) in which you want to change indents, then drag the appropriate indent markers to the new location(s). If you get a hanging indent when you wanted to change the left indent, it means you dragged the bottom triangle instead of the box. Click the Undo button and try again. (You can always use the Format Paragraph command rather than the ruler if you continue to have difficulty.)

STEP 4: Borders and Shading

➤ Pull down the **Format menu.** Click **Borders and Shading** to produce the dialog box in Figure 2.15d.

➤ If necessary, click the **Borders tab.** Select a style and width for the line around the box. Click the rectangle labeled **Box** under Settings.

➤ Click the **Shading Tab.** Click the **down arrow** on the Style list box. Click **10%.**

➤ Click **OK** to accept the settings for both Borders and Shading.

➤ Save the document.

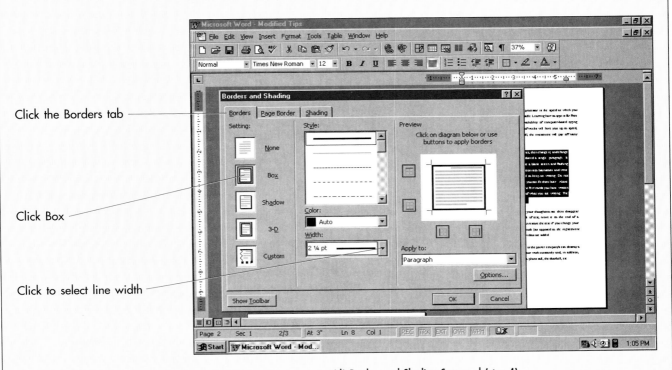

Click the Borders tab

Click Box

Click to select line width

(d) Borders and Shading Command (step 4)

FIGURE 2.15   Hands-on Exercise 3 (continued)

THE PAGE BORDER COMMAND

You can apply a border to the title page of your document, to every page except the title page, or to every page including the title page. Pull down the Format menu, click Borders and Shading, and click the Page Borders tab. First design the border by selecting a style, color, width, and art (if any). Then choose the page(s) to which you want to apply the border by clicking the drop-down arrow in the Apply to list box. Close the Borders and Shading dialog box. See practice exercise 5 at the end of the chapter.

STEP 5: Help with Formatting

➤ Pull down the **Help menu** and click the **What's This command** (or press **Shift+F1**). The mouse pointer changes to an arrow with a question mark.

➤ Click anywhere inside the boxed paragraph to display the formatting information shown in Figure 2.15e.

➤ Click in a different paragraph to see its formatting. Press the **Esc key** to return the pointer to normal.

DISPLAY THE HARD RETURNS

Many formattting commands are implemented at the paragraph level, and thus it helps to know where a paragraph ends. Click the Show/Hide ¶ button on the Standard toolbar to display the hard returns (paragraph marks) and other nonprinting characters (such as tab characters or blank spaces) contained within a document. The Show/Hide ¶ functions as a toggle switch; the first time you click it the hard returns are displayed, the second time you press it the returns are hidden, and so on.

STEP 6: The Zoom Command

➤ Pull down the **View menu.** Click **Zoom** to produce the dialog box in Figure 2.15f.

➤ Click the **Many Pages** option button. Click the **monitor icon** to display a sample selection box, then click and drag to display three pages across as shown in the figure. Release the mouse. Click **OK.**

STEP 7: Advice from the Office Assistant

➤ Click the **Office Assistant button** on the Standard toolbar or press the **F1 key** to display the Assistant. Click the lightbulb (assuming the Assistant has a suggestion) to display the tip. Click the **Back** or **Next** buttons as appropriate to view additional tips.

➤ The Assistant will not, however, repeat a tip from an earlier session unless you reset it at the start of a new session. To reset the tips, click the Assistant to display a balloon asking what you want to do, click the **Options button** in the balloon, click **Options,** then click the button to **Reset My Tips.**

HELP FOR MICROSOFT WORD

Microsoft Word offers help from a variety of sources. You can pull down the Help menu as you can with any Windows application and/or you can click the Office Assisant button on the Standard toolbar. You can also go to the Microsoft Web site to obtain more recent, and often more detailed, information. Pull down the Help menu, click Microsoft on the Web, then click Online Support to go to the Microsoft Web site, provided you have an Internet connection.

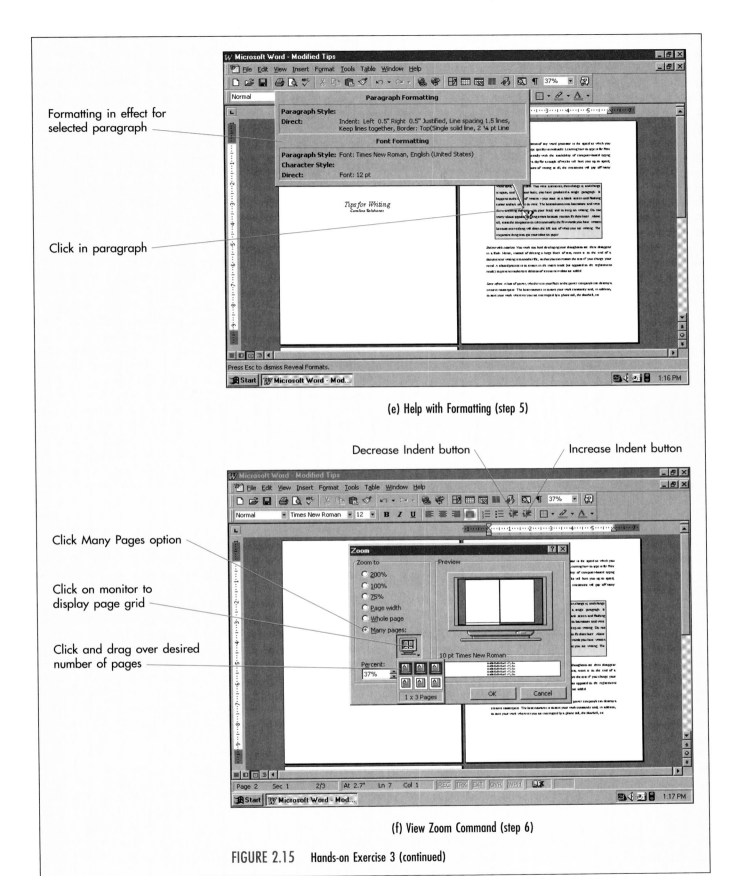

Formatting in effect for
selected paragraph

Click in paragraph

(e) Help with Formatting (step 5)

Decrease Indent button   Increase Indent button

Click Many Pages option

Click on monitor to
display page grid

Click and drag over desired
number of pages

(f) View Zoom Command (step 6)

FIGURE 2.15   Hands-on Exercise 3 (continued)

STEP 8: The Completed Document

➤ Your screen should match the one in Figure 2.15g, which displays all three pages of the document.

➤ The Page Layout view displays both a vertical and a horizontal ruler. The boxed and indented paragraph is clearly shown in the second page.

➤ The soft page break between pages two and three occurs between tips rather than within a tip; that is, the text of each tip is kept together on the same page.

➤ Save the document a final time. Print the completed document and submit it to your instructor. Exit Word.

Horizontal ruler ⎯

Vertical ruler ⎯

Page break occurs
between tips ⎯

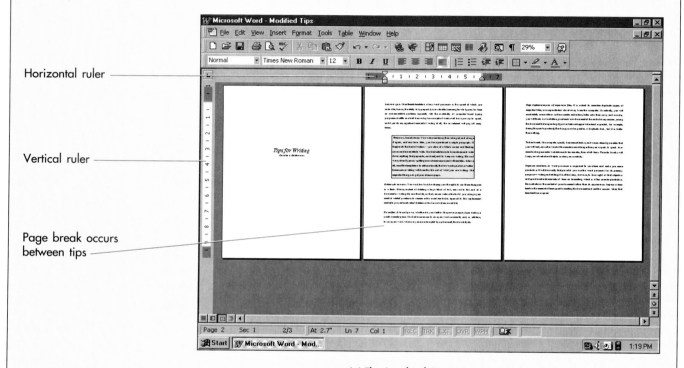

(g) The Completed Document (step 8)

FIGURE 2.15   Hands-on Exercise 3 (continued)

PRINT SELECTED PAGES

Why print an entire document if you want only a few pages? Pull down the File menu and click Print as you usually do to initiate the printing process. Click the Pages option button, then enter the page numbers and/or page ranges you want; for example, 3, 6–8 will print page three and pages six through eight.

Many operations in Word are done within the context of select-then-do; that is, select the text, then execute the necessary command. Text may be selected by dragging the mouse, by using the selection bar to the left of the document, or by using the keyboard. Text is deselected by clicking anywhere within the document.

The Find and Replace commands locate a designated character string and optionally replace one or more occurrences of that string with a different character string. The search may be case-sensitive and/or restricted to whole words as necessary.

Text is moved or copied through a combination of the Cut, Copy, and Paste commands and/or the drag-and-drop facility. The contents of the clipboard are replaced by any subsequent Cut or Copy command, but are unaffected by the Paste command; that is, the same text can be pasted into multiple locations.

The Undo command reverses the effect of previous commands. The Undo and Redo commands work in conjunction with one another; that is, every command that is undone can be redone at a later time.

Scrolling occurs when a document is too large to be seen in its entirety. Scrolling with the mouse changes what is displayed on the screen, but does not move the insertion point; that is, you must click the mouse to move the insertion point. Scrolling via the keyboard (for example, PgUp and PgDn) changes what is seen on the screen as well as the location of the insertion point.

The Page Layout view displays top and bottom margins, headers and footers, and other elements not seen in the Normal view. The Normal view is faster because Word spends less time formatting the display. Both views can be seen at different magnifications.

TrueType fonts are scaleable and accessible from any Windows application. The Format Font command enables you to choose the typeface (e.g., Times New Roman or Arial), style (e.g., bold or italic), point size, and color of text.

The Format Paragraph command determines the line spacing, alignment, indents, and text flow, all of which are set at the paragraph level. Borders and shading are also set at the paragraph level. Margins, page size, and orientation, are set in the Page Setup command and affect the entire document (or section).

KEY WORDS AND CONCEPTS

Alignment	First line indent	Monospaced typeface
Arial	Font	Normal view
Automatic replacement	Format Font command	Page break
Borders and Shading command	Format Painter	Page Layout view
Case-insensitive replacement	Format Paragraph command	Page Setup command
Case-sensitive replacement	Go To command	Paste command
Clipboard	Hanging indent	Point size
Copy command	Hard page break	Portrait orientation
Courier New	Indents	Proportional typeface
Cut command	Landscape orientation	Redo command
Drag and drop	Leader character	Replace command
Find command	Left indent	Right indent
	Line spacing	Sans serif typeface
	Margins	Scrolling
		Select-then-do

Selection bar
Selective replacement
Serif typeface
Shortcut menu
Soft page break
Special indent
Tab stop

Times New Roman
Typeface
Type size
Type style
Typography
Undo command
View menu

Whole word
  replacement
Widows and orphans
Wild card
Zoom command

MULTIPLE CHOICE

1. Which of the following commands does *not* place data onto the clipboard?
   (a) Cut
   (b) Copy
   (c) Paste
   (d) All of the above

2. What happens if you select a block of text, copy it, move to the beginning of the document, paste it, move to the end of the document, and paste the text again?
   (a) The selected text will appear in three places: at the original location, and at the beginning and end of the document
   (b) The selected text will appear in two places: at the beginning and end of the document
   (c) The selected text will appear in just the original location
   (d) The situation is not possible; that is, you cannot paste twice in a row without an intervening cut or copy operation

3. What happens if you select a block of text, cut it, move to the beginning of the document, paste it, move to the end of the document, and paste the text again?
   (a) The selected text will appear in three places: at the original location and at the beginning and end of the document
   (b) The selected text will appear in two places: at the beginning and end of the document
   (c) The selected text will appear in just the original location
   (d) The situation is not possible; that is, you cannot paste twice in a row without an intervening cut or copy operation

4. Which of the following are set at the paragraph level?
   (a) Alignment
   (b) Tabs and indents
   (c) Line spacing
   (d) All of the above

5. How do you change the font for *existing* text within a document?
   (a) Select the text, then choose the new font
   (b) Choose the new font, then select the text
   (c) Either (a) or (b)
   (d) Neither (a) nor (b)

6. The Page Setup command can be used to change:
   (a) The margins in a document
   (b) The orientation of a document
   (c) Both (a) and (b)
   (d) Neither (a) nor (b)

7. Which of the following is a true statement regarding indents?
   (a) Indents are measured from the edge of the page rather than from the margin
   (b) The left, right, and first line indents must be set to the same value
   (c) The insertion point can be anywhere in the paragraph when indents are set
   (d) Indents must be set with the Format Paragraph command

8. The spacing in an existing multipage document is changed from single spacing to double spacing throughout the document. What can you say about the number of hard and soft page breaks before and after the formatting change?
   (a) The number of soft page breaks is the same, but the number and/or position of the hard page breaks is different
   (b) The number of hard page breaks is the same, but the number and/or position of the soft page breaks is different
   (c) The number and position of both hard and soft page breaks is the same
   (d) The number and position of both hard and soft page breaks is different

9. The default tab stops are set to:
   (a) Left indents every ½ inch
   (b) Left indents every ¼ inch
   (c) Right indents every ½ inch
   (d) Right indents every ¼ inch

10. Which of the following describes the Arial and Times New Roman fonts?
   (a) Arial is a sans serif font, Times New Roman is a serif font
   (b) Arial is a serif font, Times New Roman is a sans serif font
   (c) Both are serif fonts
   (d) Both are sans serif fonts

11. The find and replacement strings must be
   (a) The same length
   (b) The same case, either upper or lower
   (c) The same length and the same case
   (d) None of the above

12. Assume that you are in the middle of a multipage document. How do you scroll to the beginning of the document and simultaneously change the insertion point?
   (a) Press Ctrl+Home
   (b) Drag the scroll bar to the top of the scroll box
   (c) Both (a) and (b)
   (d) Neither (a) nor (b)

13. Which of the following substitutions can be accomplished by the Find and Replace command?
    (a) All occurrences of the words "Times New Roman" can be replaced with the word "Arial"
    (b) All text set in the Times New Roman font can be replaced by the Arial font
    (c) Both (a) and (b)
    (d) Neither (a) nor (b)

14. Which of the following deselects a selected block of text?
    (a) Clicking anywhere outside the selected text
    (b) Clicking any alignment button on the toolbar
    (c) Clicking the Bold, Italic, or Underline button
    (d) All of the above

15. Which view, and which magnification, lets you see the whole page, including top and bottom margins?
    (a) Page Layout view at 100% magnification
    (b) Page Layout view at Whole Page magnification
    (c) Normal view at 100% magnification
    (d) Normal view at Whole Page magnification

ANSWERS

1. c	**6.** c	**11.** d
2. a	**7.** c	**12.** a
3. b	**8.** b	**13.** c
4. d	**9.** a	**14.** a
5. a	**10.** a	**15.** b

PRACTICE WITH MICROSOFT WORD

1. Open the *Chapter 2 Practice 1* document that is displayed in Figure 2.16 and make the following changes.
    a. Copy the sentence *Discretion is the better part of valor* to the beginning of the first paragraph.
    b. Move the second paragraph to the end of the document.
    c. Change the typeface of the entire document to 12 point Arial.
    d. Change all whole word occurrences of *feel* to *think*.
    e. Change the spacing of the entire document from single spacing to 1.5. Change the alignment of the entire document to justified.
    f. Set the phrases *Format Font command* and *Format Paragraph command* in italics.
    g. Indent the second paragraph .25 inch on both the left and right.
    h. Box and shade the last paragraph.
    i. Create a title page that precedes the document. Set the title, *Discretion in Design,* in 24 point Arial bold and center it approximately two inches from the top of the page. Right align your name toward the bottom of the title page in 12 point Arial regular.
    j. Print the revised document and submit it to your instructor.

It is not difficult, especially with practice, to learn to format a document. It is not long before the mouse goes automatically to the Format Font command to change the selected text to a sans-serif font, to increase the font size, or to apply a boldface or italic style. Nor is it long before you go directly to the Format Paragraph command to change the alignment or line spacing for selected paragraphs.

What is not easy, however, is to teach discretion in applying formats. Too many different formats on one page can be distracting, and in almost all cases, less is better. Be conservative and never feel that you have to demonstrate everything you know how to do in each and every document that you create. Discretion is the better part of valor. No more than two different typefaces should be used in a single document, although each can be used in a variety of different styles and sizes.

It is always a good idea to stay on the lookout for what you feel are good designs and then determine exactly what you like and don't like about each. In that way, you are constantly building ideas for your own future designs.

FIGURE 2.16   Document for Practice Exercise 1

2. Figure 2.17 displays a completed version of the *Chapter 2 Practice 2* document that exists on the data disk. We want you to retrieve the original document from the data disk, then change the document so that it matches Figure 2.17. No editing is required as the text in the original document is identical to the finished document.

   The only changes are in formatting, but you will have to compare the documents in order to determine the nature of the changes. Color is a nice touch (which depends on the availability of a color printer) and is not required. Add your name somewhere in the document, then print the revised document and submit it to your instructor.

3. Create a simple document containing the text of the Preamble to the Constitution as shown in Figure 2.18.
   a. Set the Preamble in 12 point Times New Roman.
   b. Use single spacing and left alignment.
   c. Copy the Preamble to a new page, then change to a larger point size and more interesting typeface.
   d. Create a title page for your assignment, containing your name, course name, and appropriate title.
   e. Use a different typeface for the title page than in the rest of the document, and set the title in at least 24 points.
   f. Submit all three pages (the title page and both versions of the Preamble) to your instructor.

TYPOGRAPHY

The art of formatting a document is more than just knowing definitions, but knowing the definitions is definitely a starting point. A *typeface* is a complete set of characters with the same general appearance, and can be *serif* (cross lines at the end of the main strokes of each letter) or *sans serif* (without the cross lines). A *type size* is a vertical measurement, made from the top of the tallest letter in the character set to the bottom of the lowest letter in the character set. *Type style* refers to variations in the typeface, such as boldface and italics.

Several typefaces are shipped with Windows, including *Times New Roman,* a serif typeface, and **Arial**, a sans serif typeface. Times New Roman should be used for large amounts of text, whereas Arial is best used for titles and subtitles. It is best not to use too many different typefaces in the same document, but rather to use only one or two and then make the document interesting by varying their size and style.

FIGURE 2.17   Document for Practice Exercise 2

We, the people of the United States, in order to form a more perfect Union, establish justice, insure domestic tranquillity, provide for the common defense, promote the general welfare, and secure the blessings of liberty to ourselves and our posterity, do ordain and establish this Constitution for the United States of America.

FIGURE 2.18   Document for Practice Exercise 3

4. As indicated in the chapter, anyone who has used a typewriter is familiar with the function of the Tab key; that is, press Tab and the insertion point moves to the next tab stop (a measured position to align text at a specific place). The Tab key is more powerful in Word because you can choose from four different types of tab stops (left, center, right, and decimal). You can also specify a leader character, typically dots or hyphens, to draw the reader's eye across the page.

Create the document in Figure 2.19 and add your name in the indicated position. (Use the Help facility to discover how to work with tab stops.) Submit the completed document to your instructor as proof that you have mastered the Tab key.

EXAMPLES OF TAB STOPS

Example 1 - Right tab at 6":

CIS 120   **Maryann Barber**
FALL 1997   **September 21, 1997**

Example 2 - Right tab with a dot leader at 6":

Chapter 1 1
Chapter 2 31
Chapter 3   56

Example 3 - Right tab at 1" and left tab at 1.25":

To:	Maryann Barber
From:	Joel Stutz
Department:	Computer Information Systems
Subject:	Exams

Example 4 - Left tab at 2" and a decimal tab at 3.5":

Rent	$375.38
Utilities	$125.59
Phone	$56.92
Cable	$42.45

FIGURE 2.19   Document for Practice Exercise 4

5. The Page Borders Command: Figure 2.20 illustrates a hypothetical title page for a paper describing the capabilities of borders and shading. The Borders and Shading command is applied at the paragraph level as indicated in the chapter. You can, however, select the Page Border tab within the Borders and Shading dialog box to create an unusual and attractive document. Experiment with the command to create a title page similar to Figure 2.20. Submit the document to your instructor as proof you did the exercise.

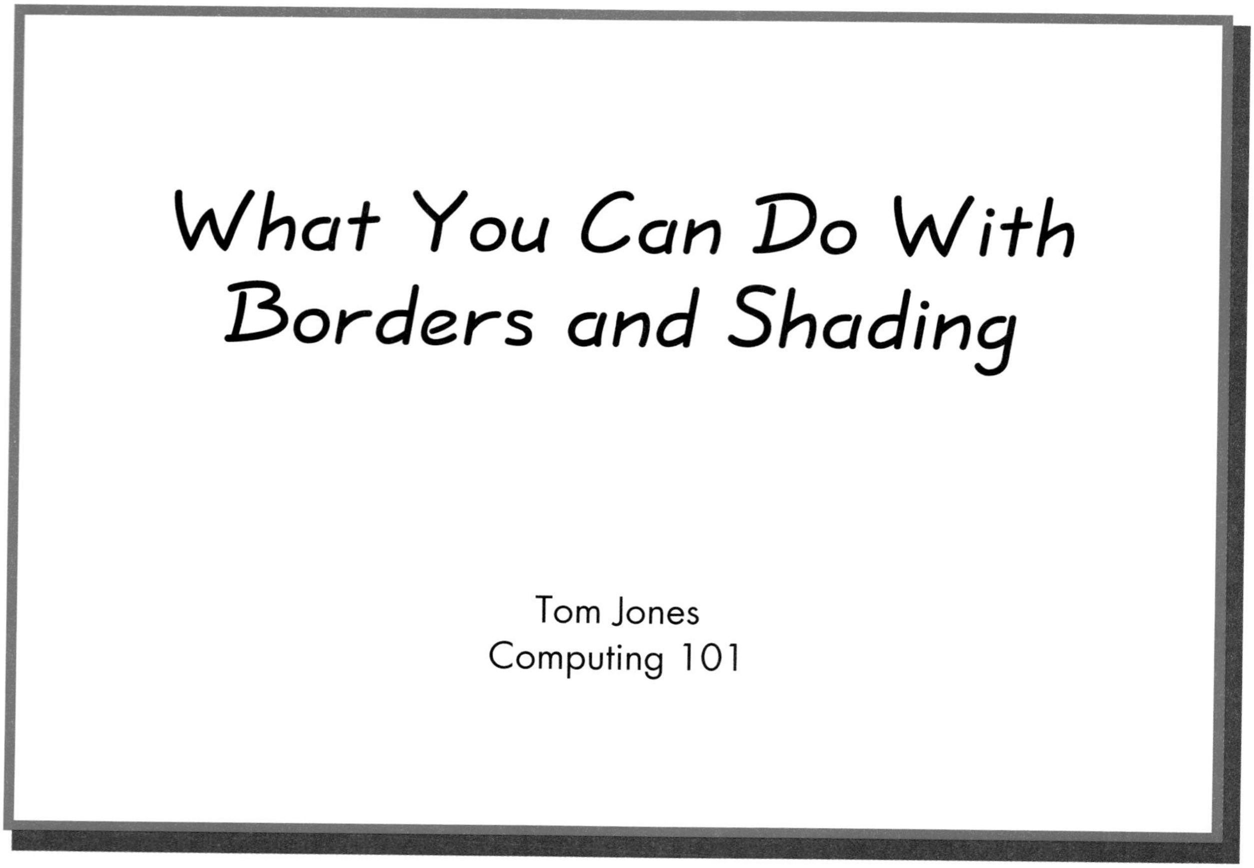

What You Can Do With Borders and Shading

Tom Jones
Computing 101

FIGURE 2.20   Document for Practice Exercise 5

6. Exploring Fonts: The Font Folder within the Control Panel displays the names of the fonts available on a system and enables you to obtain a printed sample of any specific font. Click the Start button, click (or point to) the Settings command, click (or point to) Control Panel, then click the Fonts command to open the font folder and display the fonts on your system.

a. Double click a font you want to view (e.g., Contemporary Brush in Figure 2.21), then click the Print button to print a sample of the selected font.

b. Click the Fonts button on the Taskbar to return to the Fonts window and open a different font. Print a sample page of this font as well.

c. Start Word. Create a title page containing your name, class, date, and the title of this assignment (My Favorite Fonts). Center the title. Use boldface or italics as you see fit. Be sure to use appropriate type sizes.

d. Staple the three pages together (the title page and two font samples), then submit them to your instructor.

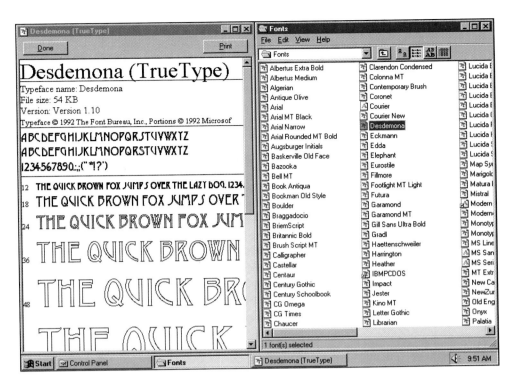

FIGURE 2.21 Screen for Practice Exercise 6

CASE STUDIES

Computers Past and Present

The ENIAC was the scientific marvel of its day and the world's first operational electronic computer. It could perform 5,000 additions per second, weighed 30 tons, and took 1,500 square feet of floor space. The price was a modest $486,000 in 1946 dollars. The story of the ENIAC and other influential computers of the author's choosing is found in the file *History of Computers,* which we forgot to format, so we are asking you to do it for us.

Be sure to use appropriate emphasis for the names of the various computers. Create a title page in front of the document, then submit the completed assignment to your instructor. If you are ambitious, you can enhance this assignment by using your favorite search engine to look for computer museums on the Web. Visit one or two sites, and include this information on a separate page at the end of the document. One last task, and that is to update the description of Today's PC (the last computer in the document).

Your First Consultant's Job

Go to a real installation, such as a doctor's or an attorney's office, the company where you work, or the computer lab at school. Determine the backup procedures that are in effect, then write a one-page report indicating whether the policy is adequate and, if necessary, offering suggestions for improvement. Your report should be addressed to the individual in charge of the business, and it should cover all aspects of the backup strategy—that is, which files are backed up and how often, and what software is used for the backup operation. Use appropriate emphasis (for example, bold italics) to identify any potential problems. This is a professional document (it is your first consultant's job), and its appearance must be perfect in every way.

Paper Makes a Difference

Most of us take paper for granted, but the right paper can make a significant difference in the effectiveness of the document. Reports and formal correspondence are usually printed on white paper, but you would be surprised how many different shades of white there are. Other types of documents lend themselves to colored paper for additional impact. In short, which paper you use is far from an automatic decision. Walk into a local copy store and see if they have any specialty papers available. Our favorite source for paper is a company called *Paper Direct* (1-800-APAPERS). Ask for a catalog, then consider the use of a specialty paper the next time you have an important project.

The Invitation

Choose an event and produce the perfect invitation. The possibilities are endless and limited only by your imagination. You can invite people to your wedding or to a fraternity party. Your laser printer and abundance of fancy fonts enable you to do anything a professional printer can do. Clip art and/or special paper will add the finishing touch. Go to it—this assignment is a lot of fun.

One Space After a Period

Touch typing classes typically teach the student to place two spaces after a period. The technique worked well in the days of the typewriter and monospaced fonts, but it creates an artificially large space when used with proportional fonts and a word processor. Select any document that is at least several paragraphs in length and print the document with the current spacing. Use the Find and Replace commands to change to the alternate spacing, then print the document a second time. Which spacing looks better to you? Submit both versions of the document to your instructor with a brief note summarizing your findings.

The Contest

Almost everyone enjoys some form of competition. Ask your instructor to choose a specific type of document, such as a flyer or résumé, and declare a contest in the class to produce the "best" document. Submit your entry, but write your name on the back of the document so that it can be judged anonymously. Your instructor may want to select a set of semifinalists and then distribute copies of those documents so that the class can vote on the winner.

3

ENHANCING A DOCUMENT: THE WEB AND OTHER RESOURCES

OBJECTIVES

After reading this chapter you will be able to:

1. Describe object linking and embedding; explain how it is used to create a compound document.
2. Describe the resources in the Microsoft Clip Gallery; insert clip art and/or a photograph into a document.
3. Use the Format Picture command to wrap text around a clip art image; describe various tools on the Picture toolbar.
4. Use WordArt to insert decorative text into a document.
5. Describe the Internet and World Wide Web; explain how to display the Web toolbar within Microsoft Word.
6. Define a Web-enabled document; download resources from the Web for inclusion in a Word document.
7. Insert a footnote or endnote into a document to cite a reference.
8. Use wizards and templates to create a document; list several wizards provided with Microsoft Word.

OVERVIEW

This chapter describes how to enhance a document using resources within Microsoft Office as well as resources on the Internet and World Wide Web. We begin with the Microsoft Clip Gallery, a collection of clip art, photographs, sounds, and video clips that can be inserted into any Office document. We also introduce Microsoft WordArt to create special effects with text.

The clip art and photographs included within the Microsoft Clip Gallery pale in comparison to the resources on the Internet. Accordingly, we present a brief introduction to the Internet, then show you how to download a picture from the Web and insert it into a document. We also show you how to add footnotes to give appropriate credit to your sources.

The chapter also describes the various wizards and templates that are built into Microsoft Word to help you create professionally formatted documents. We believe this to be a very enjoyable chapter that will add significantly to your capability in Microsoft Word. As always, learning is best accomplished by doing, and the hands-on exercises are essential to master the material.

A COMPOUND DOCUMENT

The applications in Microsoft Office are thoroughly integrated with one another. Equally important, they share information through a technology known as *Object Linking and Embedding (OLE),* which enables you to create a *compound document* containing data (objects) from multiple applications.

Consider, for example, the compound document in Figure 3.1, which was created in Microsoft Word but contains objects (data) from other applications. The *clip art* (a graphic as opposed to a photograph) was taken from the Microsoft Clip Gallery. The title of the document was created using Microsoft WordArt. The document also illustrates the Insert Symbol command to insert special characters such as the Windows logo.

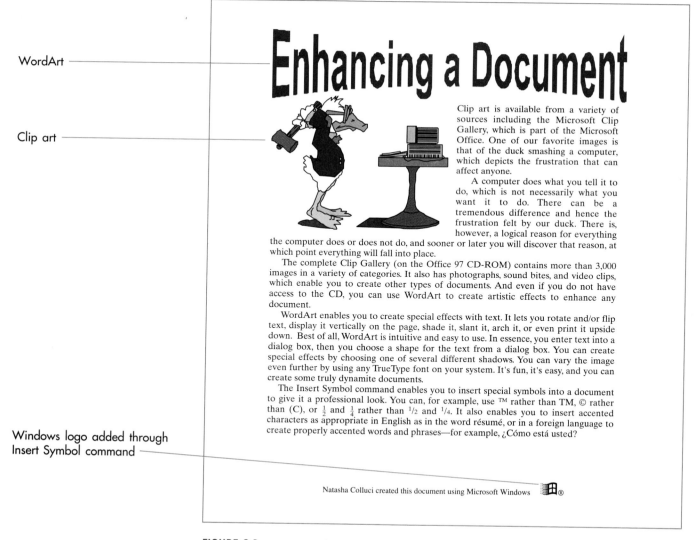

FIGURE 3.1   A Compound Document

Microsoft Clip Gallery

The *Microsoft Clip Gallery* contains more than 3,000 clip art images and almost 150 photographs. It also contains sound files and video clips, although these objects are more common in PowerPoint presentations than in Word documents. The Clip Gallery can be accessed in a variety of ways, most easily through the *Insert Picture command,* which is available in every Office application.

To use the Clip Gallery, you choose the type of object by clicking the appropriate tab—for example, clip art in Figure 3.2a. Next you select the category, such as Science and Technology in Figure 3.2b, and an image within that category, such as the astronaut walking in space. And finally, you click the Insert button to insert the object (the clip art or photograph) into the document.

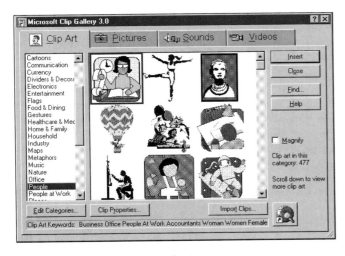

(a) Clip Art

(b) Photographs

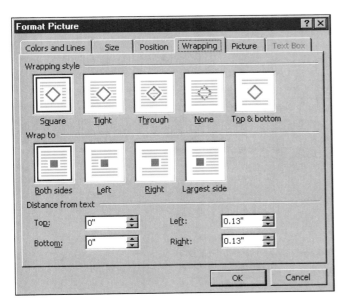

(c) Format Picture Command

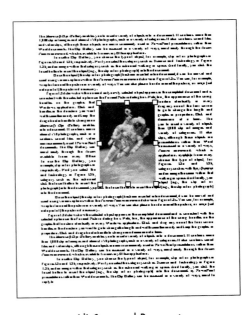

(d) Compound Document

FIGURE 3.2   Microsoft Clip Gallery

Once the object has been inserted into a document, it can be moved and sized using various options within the **Format Picture command** shown in Figure 3.2c. You can, for example, wrap text around the picture, place a border around the picture, or even **crop** (cut out a part of) the picture if necessary. Figure 3.2d shows how the selected object appears in the completed document and is consistent with the selected options in the Format Picture dialog box. Note, too, the **sizing handles** on the graphic, which enable you to move and size the figure within the document.

The Insert Symbol Command

One characteristic of a professional document is the use of typographic symbols in place of ordinary typing—for example, ® rather than (R), © rather than (C), or ½ and ¼ rather than 1/2 and 1/4. Much of this formatting is implemented automatically by Word through substitutions built into the **AutoCorrect command.** Other characters, especially accented characters such as the "é" in résumé, or those in a foreign language (e.g., ¿Cómo está usted?), have to be inserted manually into a document.

Look carefully at the last line of Figure 3.1, and notice the Windows 95 logo at the end of the sentence. The latter was created through the **Insert Symbol command,** as shown in Figure 3.3. You select the font containing the desired character (e.g., Wingdings in Figure 3.3), then you select the character, and finally you click the Insert command button to place the character in the document.

Selected font

Select the character

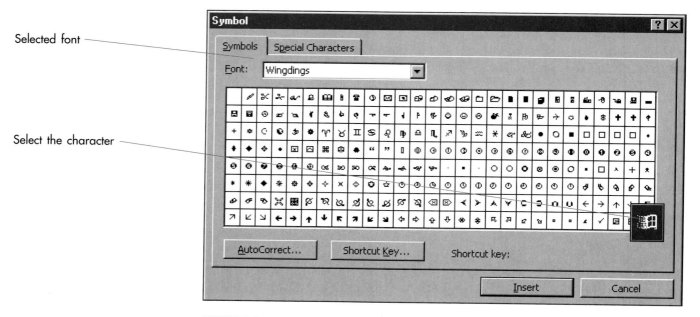

FIGURE 3.3   The Insert Symbol Command

THE WINGDINGS AND SYMBOLS FONTS

The Wingdings and Symbols fonts are two of the best-kept secrets in Windows 95. Both fonts contain a variety of special characters that can be inserted into a document through the Insert Symbol command. These fonts are scaleable to any point size, enabling you to create some truly unusual documents. (See practice exercise 3 at the end of the chapter.)

Microsoft WordArt

Microsoft WordArt is an application within Microsoft Office that creates decorative text to add interest to a document. You can use WordArt in addition to clip art, as was done in Figure 3.1, or in place of clip art if the right image is not available. You're limited only by your imagination, as you can rotate text in any direction, add three-dimensional effects, display the text vertically down the page, shade it, slant it, arch it, or even print it upside down.

WordArt is intuitive and easy to use. In essence, you choose a style for the text from among the selections in the dialog box of Figure 3.4a, then you enter your specific text as shown in Figure 3.4b. You can modify the style through various special effects, you can use any TrueType font on your system, and you can change the color or shading. Figure 3.4c shows the completed WordArt object. It's fun, it's easy, and you can create some truly dynamite documents.

Select WordArt style

Enter text

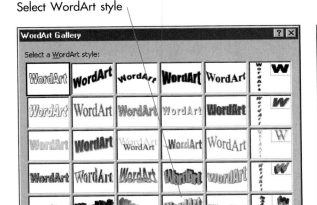

(a) Choose the Style

(b) Enter the Text

(c) Completed WordArt

FIGURE 3.4   Microsoft WordArt

Object Linking and Embedding

Objective: To create a compound document containing clip art and WordArt. To illustrate the Insert Symbol command to place typographical symbols into a document. Use Figure 3.5 as a guide in the exercise.

STEP 1: The Microsoft Clip Gallery

➤ Start Word. Open the **Clipart and WordArt** document in the Exploring Word folder. Save the document as **Modified Clip Art and WordArt.**

➤ Check that the insertion point is at the beginning of the document. Pull down the **Insert menu,** click **Picture,** then click **ClipArt** to display the Microsoft Clip Gallery as shown in Figure 3.5a. Click **OK** if you see a dialog box reminding you that additional clip art is available on a CD-ROM.

➤ If necessary, click the **ClipArt tab** and select (click) the **Cartoons category.** Select the **Duck and Computer** (or a different image if you prefer), then click the **Insert button** to place the clip art into your document.

➤ The Microsoft Clip Gallery dialog box will close and the picture will be inserted into your document, where it can be moved and sized as described in the next several steps.

Select Duck and Computer

Select Cartoons

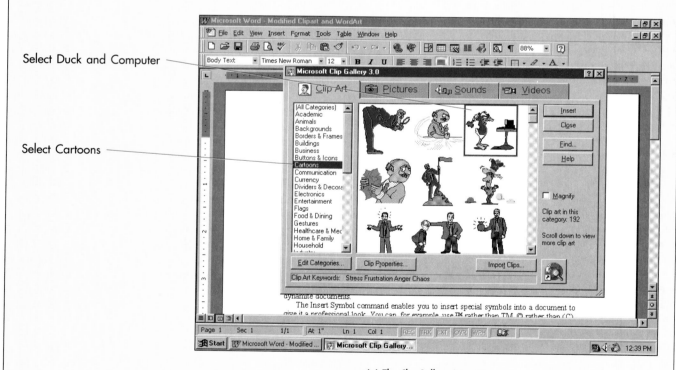

(a) The Clip Gallery (step 1)

FIGURE 3.5   Hands-on Exercise 1

ADDITIONAL CLIP IMAGES

The Microsoft Clip Gallery contains over 100MB of data consisting of more than 3,000 clip art images, 144 photographs, 28 sounds, and 20 video clips. Only a fraction of these are installed with Microsoft Office, but you can access the additional objects from the Office CD at any time. You can also install some or all of the objects on your hard disk, provided you have sufficient space. Start the Windows Explorer, then open the ClipArt folder on the Office CD. Double click the Setup icon to start the Setup Wizard, then follow the on-screen instructions to install the additional components you want.

STEP 2: Move and Size the Picture

➤ Word automatically selects the duck and changes to the Page Layout view in Figure 3.5b. Move and size the duck as described below.

➤ To move an object:

- Click the object (e.g., the duck) to display the sizing handles.
- Point to any part of the duck except a sizing handle (the mouse pointer changes to a four-sided arrow), then click and drag to move the duck elsewhere in the document. You can position the duck anywhere in the document, but you cannot wrap text around the duck until you execute the Format Picture command in step 3.

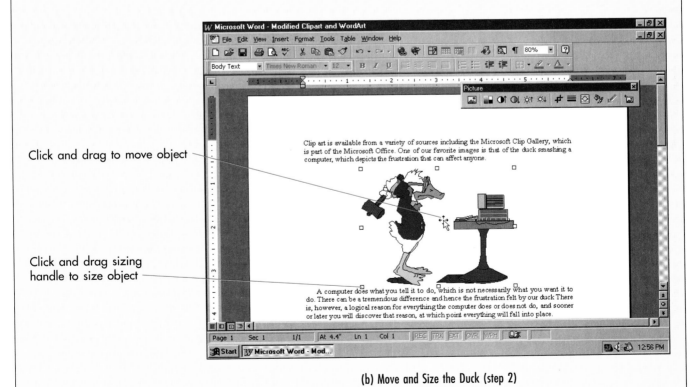

Click and drag to move object

Click and drag sizing handle to size object

(b) Move and Size the Duck (step 2)

FIGURE 3.5   Hands-on Exercise 1 (continued)

➤ To size an object:
  • Click the object (e.g., the duck) to display the sizing handles.
  • Drag a corner handle (the mouse pointer changes to a double arrow) to change the length and width of the picture simultaneously; this keeps the graphic in proportion as it sizes it.
  • Drag a handle on the horizontal or vertical border to change one dimension only; this distorts the picture.
➤ Save the document.

TO CLICK OR DOUBLE CLICK

Clicking an object selects the object and displays the sizing handles, allowing you to move and/or size the object. Double clicking an object starts the application that created it and enables you to modify the object using that application. Double click the duck, for example, and you display the Microsoft Clip Gallery dialog box, in which you can select a different picture and insert it into the document in place of the original.

STEP 3: Format the Picture
➤ Be sure the duck is still selected, then pull down the **Format menu** and select the **Picture command** to display the Format Picture dialog box in Figure 3.5c.

Click Wrapping tab

Click Square style

Click Right as
Wrap to position

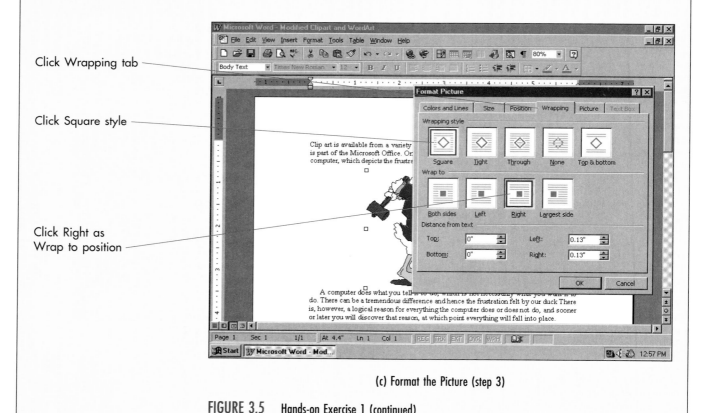

(c) Format the Picture (step 3)

FIGURE 3.5   Hands-on Exercise 1 (continued)

- Click the **Wrapping tab,** select **Square** as the Wrapping style, and click **right** as the Wrap to position. Click **OK** to close the Format Picture dialog box and implement these selections.
- The text should be wrapped to the right of the duck. Move and size the duck until you are satisfied with its position. Note, however, that the duck will always be positioned (wrapped) according to the settings in the Format Picture command.
- Save the document.

THE PICTURE TOOLBAR

The Picture toolbar offers the easiest way to execute various commands associated with a picture or clip art image. It is displayed automatically when a picture is selected; otherwise it is suppressed. As with any toolbar, you can point to a button to display a ScreenTip containing the name of the button, which indicates its function. You will find buttons for wrapping and formatting a picture, a Line Styles button to place a border around a picture, and a cropping button to crop (erase) part of a picture.

STEP 4: WordArt

- Press **Ctrl+Home** to move to the beginning of the document. Pull down the **Insert menu,** click **Picture,** then click **WordArt** to display the WordArt Gallery dialog box.
- Select the WordArt style you like (you can change it later). Click **OK.** You will see a second dialog box in which you enter the text. Enter **Enhancing a Document.** Click **OK.**
- The WordArt object appears in your document in the style you selected. Point to the WordArt object and click the **right mouse button** to display the shortcut menu in Figure 3.5d. Click **Format WordArt** to display the Format WordArt dialog box.
- Click the **Wrapping tab,** then select **Top & Bottom** as the Wrapping style. Click **OK.** It is important to select this wrapping option to facilitate placing the WordArt at the top of the document. Save the document.

FORMATTING WORDART

The WordArt toolbar offers the easiest way to execute various commands associated with a WordArt object. It is displayed automatically when a WordArt object is selected; otherwise it is suppressed. As with any toolbar, you can point to a button to display a ScreenTip containing the name of the button, which indicates its function. You will find buttons to display the text vertically, change the style or shape, and/or edit the text.

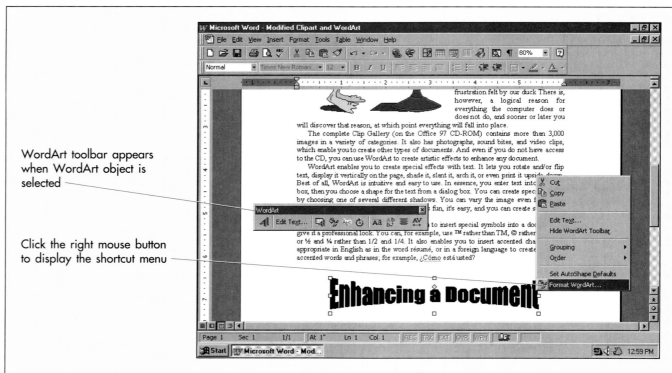

WordArt toolbar appears when WordArt object is selected

Click the right mouse button to display the shortcut menu

(d) WordArt (step 4)

FIGURE 3.5   Hands-on Exercise 1 (continued)

STEP 5: WordArt (continued)

➤ Click and drag the WordArt object to move it to the top of the document, as shown in Figure 3.5e. (The Format WordArt dialog box is not yet visible.)

➤ Point to the WordArt object, click the **right mouse button** to display a shortcut menu, then click **Format WordArt** to display the Format WordArt dialog box.

➤ Click the **Colors and Lines tab,** then click the **Fill Color drop-down arrow** to display the available colors. Select a different color (e.g., blue).

➤ Move and/or size the WordArt object as necessary. Save the document.

THE THIRD DIMENSION

You can make your WordArt images even more dramatic by adding 3-D effects. You can tilt the text up or down, right or left, increase or decrease the depth, and change the shading. Pull down the View menu, click Toolbars, click Customize to display the complete list of available toolbars, then check the box to display the 3-D Settings toolbar. Select the WordArt object, then experiment with various tools and special effects. The results are even better if you have a color printer.

Click Colors and Lines tab

Click Fill Color
drop-down arrow

Select a color

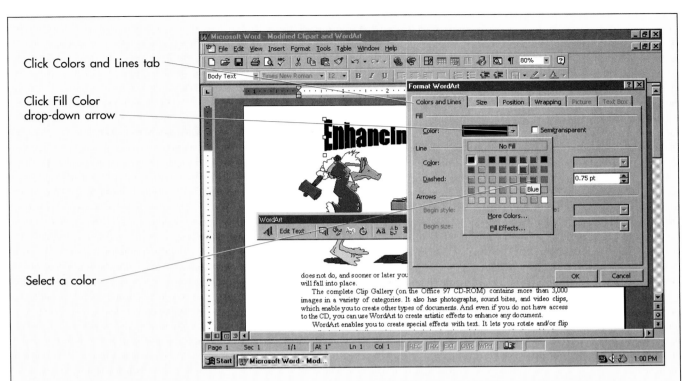

(e) WordArt Continued (step 5)

FIGURE 3.5   Hands-on Exercise 1 (continued)

STEP 6: The Insert Symbol Command

➤ Press **Ctrl+End** to move to the end of the document, as shown in Figure 3.5f. (The Symbol dialog box is not yet visible.) Press the **enter key** to insert a blank line at the end of the document.

➤ Type the sentence, **John Smith created this document using Microsoft Windows,** substituting your name for John Smith. Click the **Center button** on the Formatting toolbar to center the sentence.

➤ Pull down the **Insert menu,** click **Symbol,** then choose **Wingdings** from the Font list box. Click the **Windows logo** (the last character in the last line), click **Insert,** then close the Symbol dialog box.

➤ Click and drag to select the newly inserted symbol, click the **drop-down arrow** on the **Font Size box,** then change the font to **24** points. Press the **right arrow key** to deselect the symbol.

➤ Click the **drop-down arrow** on the **Font Size box** and change to **10 point type** so that subsequent text is entered in this size.

➤ Type **(r)** after the Windows logo and try to watch the monitor as you enter the text. The (r) will be converted automatically to ® because of the Auto-Format command, as described in the boxed tip on page 116.

➤ Save the document.

Font size box ——————

Center button ——————

Click Font drop-down arrow
to display available fonts ——————

Select Windows logo ——————

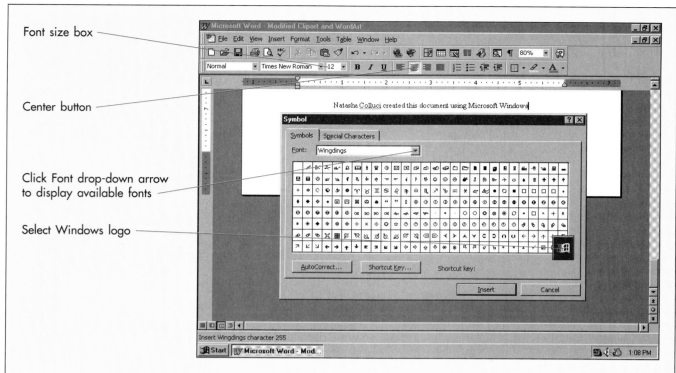

(f) Insert Symbol Command (step 6)

FIGURE 3.5   Hands-on Exercise 1 (continued)

AUTOCORRECT AND AUTOFORMAT

The AutoCorrect feature not only corrects mistakes as you type by substituting one character string for another (e.g., *the* for *teh*), but it will also substitute symbols for typewritten equivalents such as © for (c), provided the entries are included in the table of substitutions. The AutoFormat feature is similar in concept and replaces common fractions such as 1/2 or 1/4 with ½ or ¼. It also converts ordinal numbers such as 1st or 2nd to 1st or 2nd. See practice exercise 3 for additional examples. If either feature is not working, pull down the Tools menu, click the AutoCorrect command, then choose the appropriate settings within the AutoCorrect dialog box.

STEP 7: The Completed Document

➤ Click the **drop-down arrow** on the Zoom box and select **Whole Page** to preview the completed document as shown in Figure 3.5g.

➤ Print the document and submit it to your instructor as proof that you did the exercise. Close the document. Exit Word if you do not want to continue with the next exercise at this time.

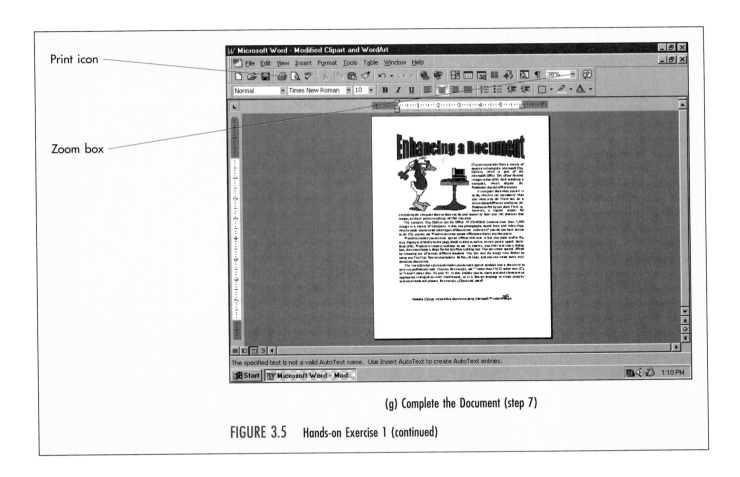

Print icon

Zoom box

(g) Complete the Document (step 7)

FIGURE 3.5   Hands-on Exercise 1 (continued)

RESOURCES FROM THE INTERNET AND WORLD WIDE WEB

The resources in the Microsoft Clip Gallery in Office 97 are impressive when compared to previous versions of Microsoft Office, but pale in comparison to what is available on the Internet and World Wide Web. Hence, any discussion of enhancing a document through clip art and/or photographs must also include the Internet. We begin with a brief description of the Internet and World Wide Web and then describe how to incorporate these resources into a Word document.

The ***Internet*** is a network of networks that connects computers across the country and around the world. It grew out of a U.S. Department of Defense (DOD) experimental project begun in 1969 to test the feasibility of a wide area (long distance) computer network over which scientists and military personnel could share messages and data.

The ***World Wide Web*** (***WWW,*** or simply, the Web) is a very large subset of the Internet, consisting of those computers containing hypertext and/or hypermedia documents. A ***hypertext document*** is a document that contains a link (reference) to another document, which may be on the same computer, or even on a different computer, with the latter located anywhere in the world. ***Hypermedia*** is similar in concept, except that it provides links to graphic, sound, and video files in addition to text files.

Either type of document enables you to move effortlessly from one document (or computer) to another. And therein lies the fascination of the Web: By simply clicking link after link you move smoothly from one document to the next.

You can start your journey at your professor's home page in New York, for example, which may contain a reference to the Library of Congress, which in turn may take you to a different document, and on. So, off you go to Washington D.C., and from there to a different document on a computer across the country or perhaps around the world.

Every document in Office 97 is **Web-enabled,** meaning that the application (e.g., Microsoft Word) will automatically detect and highlight any **hyperlinks** that are entered into a document. The Word document in Figure 3.6, for example, displays the Web address www.microsoft.com in underlined blue text just as it would appear in a regular Web (hypertext) document. This is not merely a change in formatting, but an actual hyperlink to a document on the Web (or corporate intranet).

You can click the link from within Word and, provided you have an Internet connection, your Web browser will display the associated page. Note, too, that once you click the link, its color will change (e.g., from blue to magenta) just as it would if you were viewing the page in Netscape or the Internet Explorer. We did not do anything special to create the hyperlink; we simply typed the address as we were creating the document, and Word in turn created the hyperlink.

Look carefully at the screen in Figure 3.6, noting the presence of the **Web toolbar,** which appears immediately under the Formatting toolbar. (The Web toolbar is displayed by executing the Toolbars command from the View menu.) The Web toolbar contains buttons similar to those on the toolbar in Internet Explorer. You can, for example, enter the address (URL) of a Web page (or a local document) to activate your browser and access the page. You can use the Favorites button to add a page to your list of favorites and/or open a previously added page. You can click the Back and Forward buttons to move between previously displayed pages. And, as with any toolbar, ScreenTips are displayed when you point to a button whose name indicates its function.

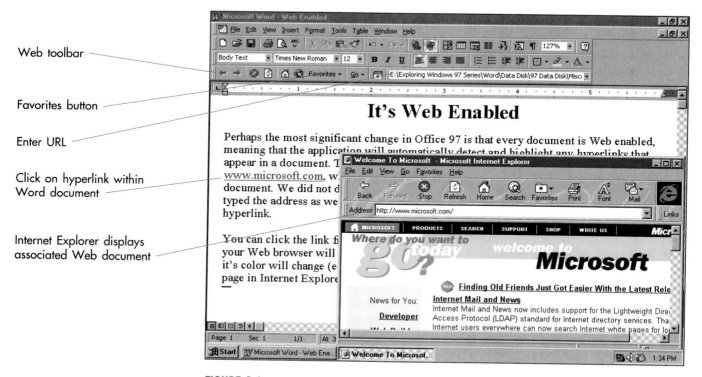

FIGURE 3.6 Internet Enhancements

Copyright Protection

A *copyright* provides legal protection for a written or artistic work, giving the author exclusive rights to its use and reproduction, except as governed under the fair use exclusion as explained below. Anything on the Internet or World Wide Web should be considered copyrighted unless the document specifically says it is in the *public domain,* in which case the author is giving everyone the right to freely reproduce and distribute the material.

Does copyright protection mean you cannot quote in your term papers statistics and other facts you find while browsing the Web? Does it mean you cannot download an image to include in your report? The answer to both questions depends on the amount of the material and on your intended use of the information. It is considered *fair use,* and thus not an infringement of copyright, to use a portion of the work for educational, nonprofit purposes, or for the purpose of critical review or commentary. In other words, you can use a quote, downloaded image, or other information from the Web *if* you cite the original work in your footnotes and/or bibliography. Facts themselves are not covered by copyright, so you can use statistical and other data without fear of infringement. You should, however, cite the original source in your document.

Footnotes and Endnotes

A *footnote* provides additional information about an item, such as its source, and appears at the bottom of the page where the reference occurs. An *endnote* is similar in concept but appears at the end of a document. A horizontal line separates the notes from the rest of the document.

The ***Insert Footnote command*** inserts a note into a document, and automatically assigns the next sequential number to that note. To create a note, position the insertion point where you want the reference, pull down the Insert menu, click Footnote to display the dialog box in Figure 3.7a, then choose either the

Choose Footnote or Endnote

Click to start numbering from a number other than 1

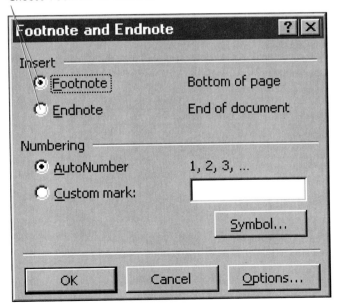

(a) Footnotes and Endnotes

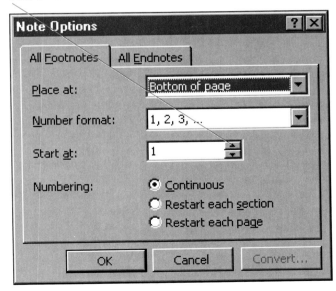

(b) Options

FIGURE 3.7   Footnotes and Endnotes

Footnote or Endnote option button. A superscript reference is inserted into the document, and you will be positioned at the bottom of the page (a footnote) or at the end of the document (an endnote) where you enter the text of the note.

The Options command button in the Footnote and Endnote dialog box enables you to modify the formatting of either type of note as shown in Figure 3.7b. You can change the numbering format (e.g., to Roman numerals) and/or start numbering from a number other than 1. You can also convert footnotes to endnotes or vice versa.

The Insert Footnote command adjusts for last-minute changes, either in your writing or in your professor's requirements. It will, for example, renumber all existing notes to accommodate the addition or deletion of a footnote or endnote. Existing notes are moved (or deleted) within a document by moving (deleting) the reference mark rather than the text of the footnote.

HANDS-ON EXERCISE 2

The Internet as a Resource

Objective: To download a picture from the Internet and use it in a Word document. Use Figure 3.8 as a guide in the exercise. The exercise requires that you have an Internet connection.

STEP 1: The Web Toolbar

➤ Start Word. Point to any toolbar, then click the **right mouse button** to display a context-sensitive menu, which lists the available toolbars in Word.

➤ Click **Web** to display the Web toolbar, as shown in Figure 3.8a. Do not be concerned if the position of your toolbars is different from ours.

➤ Click the **Address box.** Enter **www.whitehouse.gov** (the http:// is assumed), then press the **enter key** to connect to this site. Your Web browser (e.g., Internet Explorer) will open automatically and connect you to the White House home page.

➤ If the Internet Explorer window does not open on your desktop, point to its button on the Windows 95 taskbar, click the **right mouse button** to display a context-sensitive menu, then click the **Restore command** to display the window. Click the **Maximize button** so that your browser takes up the entire screen.

DOCKED VERSUS FLOATING TOOLBARS

A toolbar is either docked along an edge of a window or floating within the window. To move a docked toolbar, click and drag the move handle (the parallel lines that appear at the left of the toolbar) to a new position. To move a floating toolbar, click and drag its title bar—if you drag a floating toolbar to the edge of the window, it becomes a docked toolbar and vice versa. You can also change the shape of a floating toolbar by dragging any border in the direction you want to go. And finally, you can double click the background of any toolbar to toggle between a floating toolbar and a docked (fixed) toolbar.

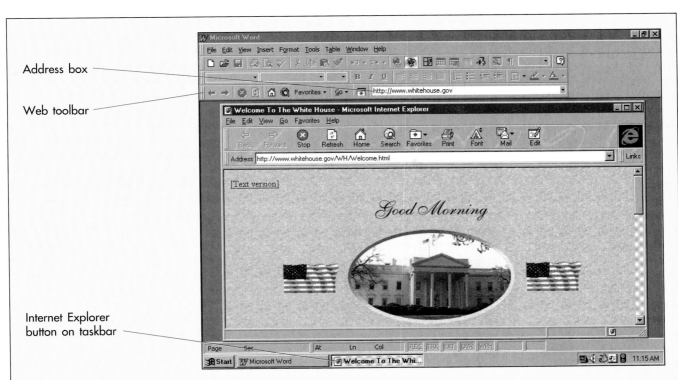

Address box

Web toolbar

Internet Explorer
button on taskbar

(a) The Web Toolbar (step 1)

FIGURE 3.8   Hands-on Exercise 2

STEP 2: Save the Picture

➤ You should be connected to the White House Web site. Click the **down arrow** on the vertical scroll bar until you can click the link to **White House History and Tours.**

➤ Click the link to **The Presidents of the United States** (or a similar link if the site has changed since our last visit), then click the link to your favorite president, e.g., **John F. Kennedy.** You should see the screen in Figure 3.8b (the Save As dialog box is not yet visible).

➤ Point to the picture of President Kennedy, click the **right mouse button** to display a shortcut menu, then click the **Save Picture as command** to display the Save As dialog box.

• Click the **drop-down arrow** in the Save in list box to specify the drive and folder in which you want to save the graphic (e.g., the Exploring Word folder on drive C).

• The file name and file type are entered automatically by Internet Explorer. (You may change the name, but don't change the file type.) Click the **Save button** to download the image. Remember the file name and location because you will need to access the file in the next step.

➤ The Save As dialog box will close automatically as soon as the picture has been downloaded to your PC. Click the link to the **Inaugural Address** after the dialog box closes.

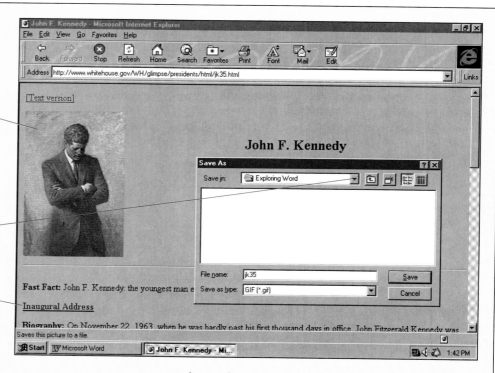

Point to the picture and click right mouse button

Click drop-down arrow in Save in list box to specify drive and folder

Click this link after downloading graphic

(b) Save the Picture (step 2)

FIGURE 3.8   Hands-on Exercise 2 (continued)

MULTITASKING

Multitasking—the ability to run multiple applications at the same time—is one of the primary advantages of the Windows environment. Minimizing an application is different from closing it, and you want to minimize, rather than close, an application to take advantage of multitasking. Closing an application removes it from memory so that you have to restart the application if you want to return to it later in the session. Minimizing, however, leaves the application open in memory, but shrinks its window to a button on the Windows 95 taskbar.

STEP 3: Copy the Quotation

➤ You should see the text of President Kennedy's address as shown in Figure 3.8c. Scroll down in the document until you can select the sentence beginning with **"And so, my fellow Americans . . ."**

➤ Point to the selected sentence, then click the **right mouse button** to display the shortcut menu. Click **Copy** to copy the selected text to the clipboard.

➤ Click the button for Microsoft Word on the taskbar, then open a new document. Pull down the **Edit menu** and click the **Paste command** (or click the **Paste button** on the Standard toolbar) to paste the contents of the clipboard (the quotation from President Kennedy) into the Word document.

➤ Save the document as **President Kennedy.** Close the Internet Explorer.

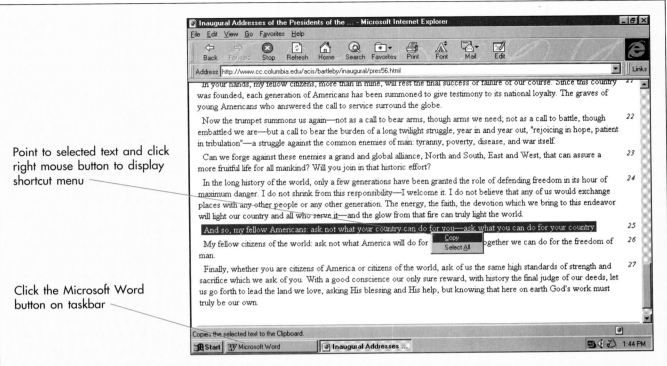

Point to selected text and click right mouse button to display shortcut menu

Click the Microsoft Word button on taskbar

(c) Copy the Quotation (step 3)

FIGURE 3.8   Hands-on Exercise 2 (continued)

THE CLIPBOARD

The clipboard is a temporary storage area that is available to all Windows applications. Selected text is cut or copied from a document and placed on the clipboard from where it can be pasted to a new location(s). You can use the clipboard (with the appropriate combination of Cut, Copy, and Paste commands) to move and copy text within a document. You can also use it to move and copy text from one document to another or from one application to another, e.g., from Internet Explorer to Microsoft Word.

STEP 4: Insert a Footnote

➤ Add quotation marks as shown in Figure 3.8d. Change the font to **28 point Times New Roman.** Click at the end of the quotation.

➤ Pull down the **Insert menu.** Click **Footnote** to display the Footnote and Endnote dialog box. Check that the option buttons for **Footnote** and **AutoNumber** are selected, then click **OK.**

➤ The insertion point moves to the bottom of the page, where you can add the text of the footnote. Enter **Inaugural Address, John F. Kennedy, January 20, 1961.** Click the **Close button** on the Footnote toolbar.

➤ Save the document.

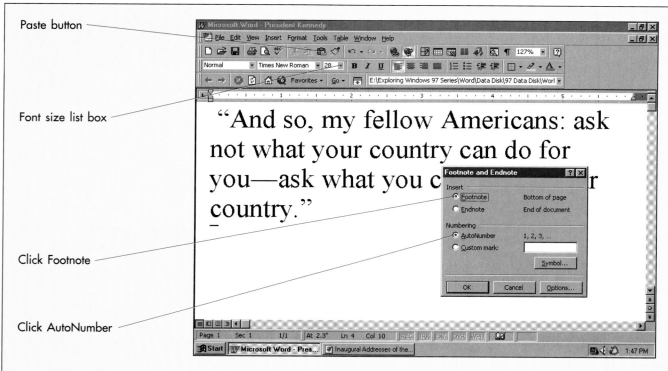

Paste button

Font size list box

Click Footnote

Click AutoNumber

(d) Add a Footnote (step 4)

FIGURE 3.8 Hands-on Exercise 2 (continued)

STEP 5: Insert the Picture

➤ Press **Ctrl+Home** to move to the beginning of the document. Pull down the **Insert menu,** point to (or click) **Picture,** then click **From File** to display the Insert Picture dialog box shown in Figure 3.8e.

➤ Click the **drop-down arrow** on the Look in text box to select the drive and folder where you previously saved the picture (e.g., the Exploring Word folder on drive C).

➤ Select (click) **jk35,** which is the file containing the picture of President Kennedy. Click the **Preview button** (if necessary) to display the picture before inserting it into the document.

➤ Click **Insert,** and the picture of President Kennedy will appear in your document. Do not worry about its size or position at this time.

CROPPING A PICTURE

Select (click) a picture and Word automatically displays the Picture toolbar, which lets you modify the picture in subtle ways. The Crop tool is one of the most useful as it enables you to eliminate (crop) part of a picture. Select the picture to display the Picture toolbar and display the sizing handles. Click the Crop tool (the ScreenTip will display the name of the tool), then click and drag a sizing handle to crop the part of the picture you want to eliminate.

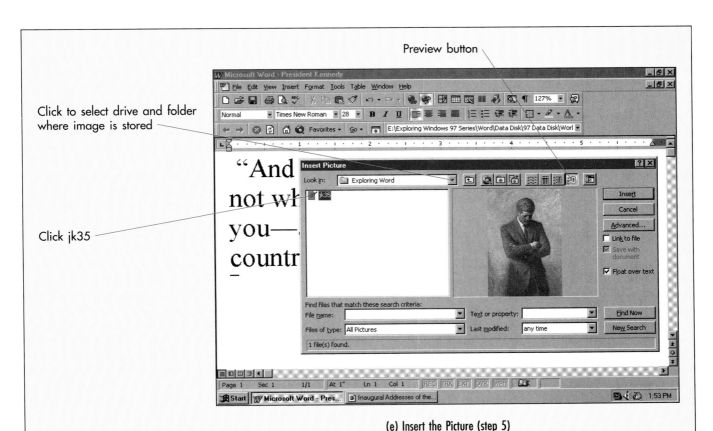

Preview button

Click to select drive and folder where image is stored

Click jk35

(e) Insert the Picture (step 5)

FIGURE 3.8   Hands-on Exercise 2 (continued)

STEP 6: Move and Size the Picture

➤ Word automatically changes to the Page Layout View when you insert a picture. Zoom to **Whole Page** to view the document as shown in Figure 3.8f (the line styles are not yet visible).

➤ Move and size the picture until it is positioned as shown. Alternatively, you can experiment with a different layout for your document.

➤ Check that the picture is still selected. Click the **Line Styles button** on the Picture toolbar to display the styles in Figure 3.8f. Click the **1 pt line** to place a 1 point border around the picture.

➤ Center the quotation as a finishing touch. Save the document.

MISSING HYPERLINK

Word will, by default, convert any Internet path (e.g., any text beginning with http:// or www) to a hyperlink. If this is not the case, pull down the Tools menu, click AutoCorrect, then click the AutoFormat As You Type tab. Check the box in the Replace as you type area for Internet and Network paths. Click OK. The next time you enter a Web or e-mail address, it will be converted automatically to a hyperlink.

STEP 7: Insert a Second Footnote

➤ Click the **drop-down arrow** on the Zoom box to return to **Page Width.** Click below the picture. Press **enter** to add a blank line.

➤ Select the blank line and change the point size to 12, then add the text **Photograph is from the White House Web page** as shown in Figure 3.8g. Do not press the enter key.

➤ The insertion point should be immediately after the sentence you just entered. Pull down the **Insert menu,** click **Footnote** to display the Footnote and Endnote dialog box, then check that the option buttons for **Footnote** and **AutoNumber** are selected. Click **OK.**

➤ Word inserts a new footnote and simultaneously positions you at the bottom of the page to add the actual note. (If both footnotes do not fit on the bottom of the page, zoom back to the Whole Page and resize the picture.) The existing footnote has been changed to note number 2 (since it comes after the new footnote).

➤ Enter the complete reference **www.whitehouse.gov/WH/glimpse/presidents/ html/jk35.html** as well as today's date. Word recognizes the Web address and automatically converts it to a hyperlink, enabling you to click on the link and return to the Web page from where you obtained the picture.

➤ Save the document, then print the document to submit to your instructor as proof you did the exercise.

➤ Exit Word if you do not want to continue with the next exercise at this time.

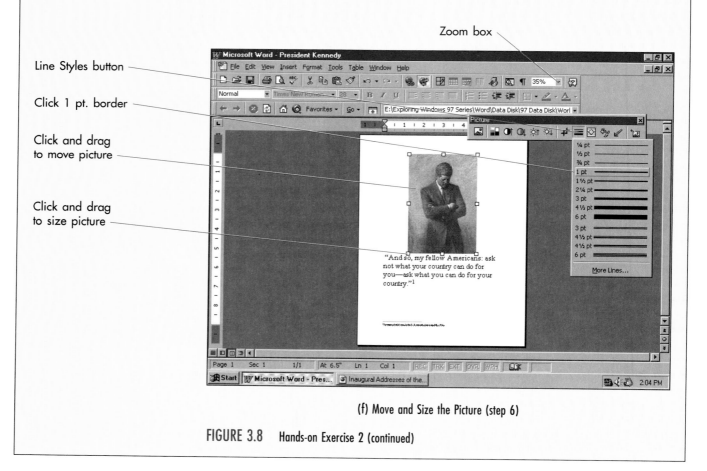

(f) Move and Size the Picture (step 6)

FIGURE 3.8   Hands-on Exercise 2 (continued)

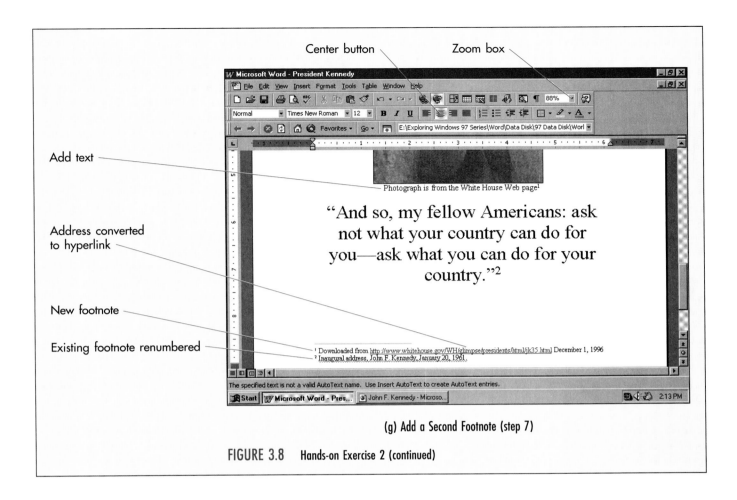

Center button   Zoom box

Add text

Address converted
to hyperlink

New footnote

Existing footnote renumbered

Photograph is from the White House Web page[1]

"And so, my fellow Americans: ask not what your country can do for you—ask what you can do for your country."[2]

[1] Downloaded from http://www.whitehouse.gov/WH/glimpse/presidents/html/jk35.html December 1, 1996
[2] Inaugural address, John F. Kennedy, January 20, 1961.

The specified text is not a valid AutoText name. Use Insert AutoText to create AutoText entries.

(g) Add a Second Footnote (step 7)

FIGURE 3.8   Hands-on Exercise 2 (continued)

WIZARDS AND TEMPLATES

We have created some very interesting documents throughout the text, but in every instance we have formatted the document entirely on our own. It is time now to see what is available to "jump start" the process by borrowing professional designs from others. Accordingly, we discuss the wizards and templates that are built into Microsoft Word.

A *template* is a partially completed document that contains formatting, text, and/or graphics. It may be as simple as a memo or as complex as a résumé or newsletter. Microsoft Word provides a variety of templates for common documents including a résumé, agenda, and fax cover sheet. You simply open the template, then modify the existing text as necessary, while retaining the formatting in the template. A *wizard* makes the process even easier by asking a series of questions, then creating a customized template based on your answers.

Figure 3.9 illustrates the use of wizards and templates in conjunction with a résumé. You can choose from one of three existing templates (contemporary, elegant, and professional) to which you add personal information. Alternatively, you can select the *Résumé Wizard* to create a customized template, as was done in Figure 3.9a.

After the Résumé Wizard is selected, it prompts you for the information it needs to create a basic résumé. You specify the style in Figure 3.9b, enter the requested information in Figure 3.9c, and choose the categories in Figure 3.9d. The wizard continues to ask additional questions (not shown in Figure 3.9), after which it displays the (partially) completed résumé based on your responses. You then complete the résumé by entering the specifics of your employment and/or

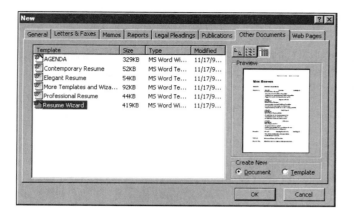

(a) Résumé Wizard

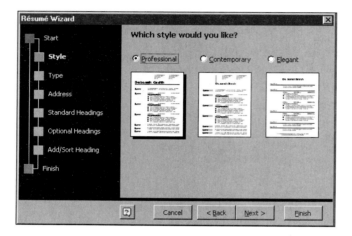

(b) Choose the Style

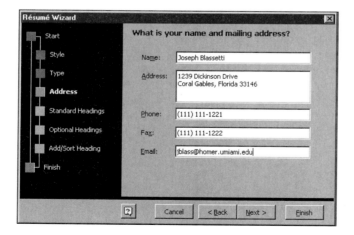

(c) Supply the Information

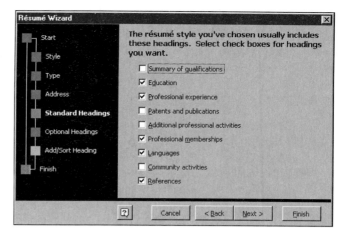

(d) Choose the Headings

(e) The Completed Résumé

FIGURE 3.9 Creating a Résumé

additional information. As you edit the document, you can copy and paste information within the résumé, just as you would with a regular document. It takes a little practice, but the end result is a professionally formatted résumé in a minimum of time.

Microsoft Word contains templates and wizards for a variety of other documents. (Look carefully at the tabs within the dialog box of Figure 3.9a and you can infer that Word will help you to create letters, faxes, memos, reports, legal pleadings, publications, and even Web pages.) Consider, too, Figure 3.10, which displays four attractive documents that were created using the respective wizards. Realize, however, that while wizards and templates will help you to create professionally designed documents, they are only a beginning. *The content is still up to you.*

THIRTY SECONDS IS ALL YOU HAVE

Thirty seconds is the average amount of time a personnel manager spends skimming your résumé and deciding whether or not to call you for an interview. It doesn't matter how much training you have had or how good you are if your résumé and cover letter fail to project a professional image. Know your audience and use the vocabulary of your targeted field. Be positive and describe your experience from an accomplishment point of view. Maintain a separate list of references and have it available on request. Be sure that all information is accurate. Be conscientious about the design of your résumé, and proofread the final documents very carefully.

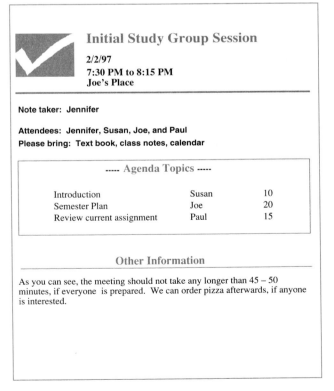

(a) Calendar

(b) Agenda

FIGURE 3.10   What You Can Do with Wizards

Fax

277 Rivera Drive
Coral Gables, FL 33146
Phone (111) 111-8897
Fax: (111) 111-9822

Fax

To:	Jennifer	From:	Susan Peterson
Fax:	(305) 222-8977	**Date:**	January 27, 1997
Phone:	(305) 222-3009	**Pages:**	2
Re:	Initial Study Group Session	**CC:**	

☐**Urgent** ☐**For Review** ☐**Please Comment** ☐**Please Reply** ☐**Please Recycle**

Comments: Attached you should find the agenda for our initial study group session. Please let me know if you have any questions. I look forward to seeing you on Friday 2 nd .

(c) Fax Cover Sheet

Interoffice Memo

Date:	12/22/96
To:	Dr. Robert Plant
	Dr. John Stewart
From:	Maryann M. Barber
RE:	CIS 120 Final Exam

The meeting to prepare the final exam for CIS 120 will be on Friday, April 18, 1997 at 3:00 PM in my office. I have attached a copy of last semester's final, which I would like for you to review prior to the meeting. In addition, if you could take a few minutes and create approxiumated 20 new questions for this semester's test, it would make our job at the meeitng a lot easier. The meeting should last no longer than an hour, provided that we all do our homework before the meeting. If you have any questions before that time, please let me know.

Attachments

12/22/96	Confidential	1

(d) Memo

FIGURE 3.10   What You Can Do with Wizards (continued)

The following exercise introduces you to the Agenda and Fax wizards. We ask you to create an agenda, then optionally fax the agenda to a classmate. As you do the exercise you will notice that the two wizards have several features in common, and that once you master one wizard, you intuitively know how to use the others. Note, too, that you can use the *Fax Wizard* to create a cover sheet, even if you do not send an actual fax.

Our next exercise directs you in the use of the *Agenda Wizard* to create an agenda for a hypothetical meeting. To add realism to the exercise, we suggest that you form a study group consisting of three or four members of this class, then create an agenda for the first meeting of your group. Not only will it help you in this exercise, but you will have a study group for the semester.

MISSING WIZARDS

The Agenda Wizard is not installed in a typical setup and hence you may not see it initially. To install the Wizard, just copy the file from the ValuePack\Template\Word folder on the Office 97 CD-ROM to the Program Files\Microsoft Office\Templates\Other Documents folder on your hard drive. Alternatively, you can download the Agenda Wizard from the Microsoft Web site. Pull down the Help menu, click Microsoft on the Web, then click Free Stuff to connect to the site. Follow the directions on the Web page to download the Wizard.

Wizards and Templates

Objective: To use the Agenda Wizard to create an agenda for a study group, then use the Fax Wizard to fax the agenda to your group. You can do the exercise even if you do not send an actual fax. Use Figure 3.11 as a guide in the exercise.

STEP 1: The File New Command

➤ Start Word. Pull down the **File menu.** Click **New** to display the New dialog box shown in Figure 3.11a. Click the **Other Documents tab** to display the documents shown in Figure 3.11a.

➤ Click the **Details button** to switch to the Details view to see the file name, type, size, and date of last modification. Click and drag the vertical line between the Template and Size columns, to increase the size of the Template column, so that you can see the complete document name.

➤ Select (click) **Agenda.** (See boxed tip on page 130 if you cannot find the Agenda Wizard.) If necessary, click the option button to **Create New Document** (as opposed to a template). Click **OK** to start the **Agenda Wizard.**

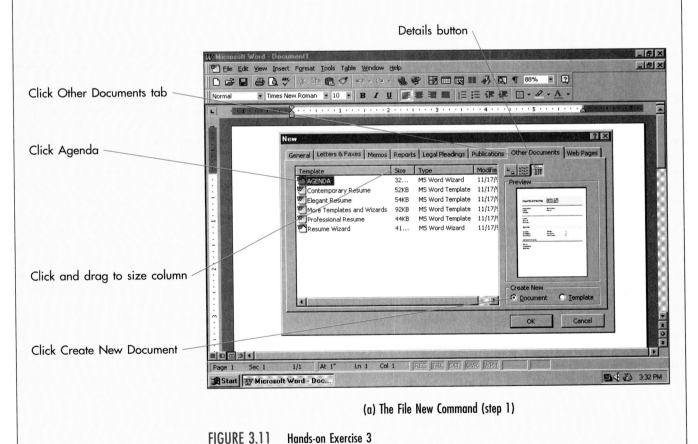

(a) The File New Command (step 1)

FIGURE 3.11 Hands-on Exercise 3

STEP 2: The Agenda Wizard

➤ You should see the main screen of the Agenda Wizard as shown in Figure 3.11b. Click **Next** to begin. The Wizard will take you through a series of questions, from start to finish. To create the desired agenda:

- Click **Boxes** as the style of the agenda. Click **Next.**

- Enter the date and time of your meeting. Enter **Initial Study Group Session** as the title. Enter **Joe's Place** as the location. Click **Next.**

- The Wizard asks which headings you want and supplies a check box next to each heading. The check boxes function as toggle switches to select (deselect) each heading. We suggest you clear all entries except **Please bring.** Click **Next.**

- The Wizard asks which names you want in the agenda. Clear all headings except **Note Taker** and **Attendees.** Click **Next.**

- Enter at least three topics for the agenda. Press the **Tab key** to move from one text box to the next (e.g., from Agenda topic, to Person, to Minutes). Click the **Add** button when you have completed the information for one topic.

- If necessary, reorder the topics by clicking the desired topic, then clicking the **Move Up** or **Move Down** command button. Click **Next** when you are satisfied with the agenda.

- Click **No** when asked whether you want a form to record the minutes of the meeting. Click **Next.**

➤ The final screen of the Agenda Wizard indicates that the Wizard has all the information it needs. Click the **Finish button.**

Click Next

(b) The Agenda Wizard (step 2)

FIGURE 3.11   Hands-on Exercise 3 (continued)

STEP 3: Complete the Agenda

➤ You should see an initial agenda similar to the document in Figure 3.11c. Close the Office Assistant if it appears (or you can leave it open and request help as necessary).

➤ Save the agenda as **Initial Study Group Session** in the **Exploring Word** folder. If necessary, change to the **Normal view** and zoom to **Page Width** so that your document more closely matches ours.

➤ Complete the Agenda by entering the additional information, such as the names of the note taker and attendees as well as the specifics of what to read or bring, as shown in the figure. Click at the indicated position on the figure prior to entering the text, so that your entries align properly.

➤ Click the **Spelling and Grammar button** to check the agenda for spelling.

➤ Save the document but do not close it.

➤ Click the **Print button** on the Standard toolbar to print the completed document and submit it to your instructor.

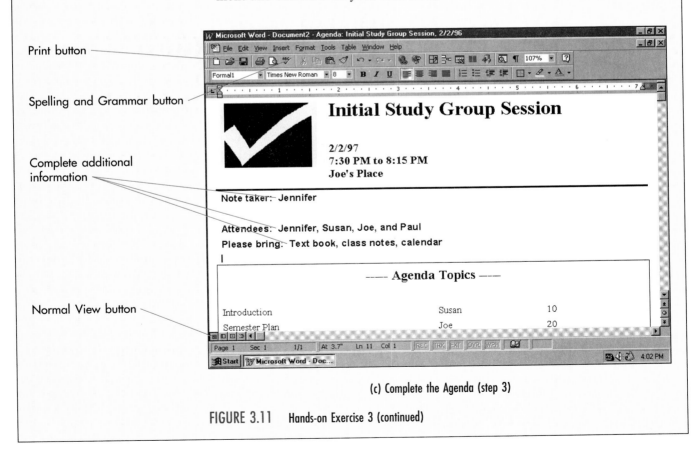

(c) Complete the Agenda (step 3)

FIGURE 3.11 Hands-on Exercise 3 (continued)

CHANGING THE VIEW

Word provides different views of a document and different magnifications of each view. The choice depends on your preference and need. (We switch all the time.) The Normal view suppresses the margins, giving you more room in which to work. The Page Layout view, on the other hand, displays the margins, so that what you see on the monitor more closely resembles the printed page. The easiest way to change from one view to the other is by clicking the appropriate icon above the status bar. The easiest way to change the magnification is to click the drop-down arrow in the Zoom box on the Standard toolbar.

STEP 4: The Fax Wizard

➤ Pull down the **File menu** and click **New** to display the New dialog box. Click the **Letters & Faxes tab** to display the indicated wizards and templates. Check that the **Document option button** is selected. Double click the **Fax Wizard** to start it.

➤ You should see the main screen of the Fax Wizard. Click **Next** to begin. The Wizard will take you through a series of questions, from start to finish, as shown in Figure 3.11d:

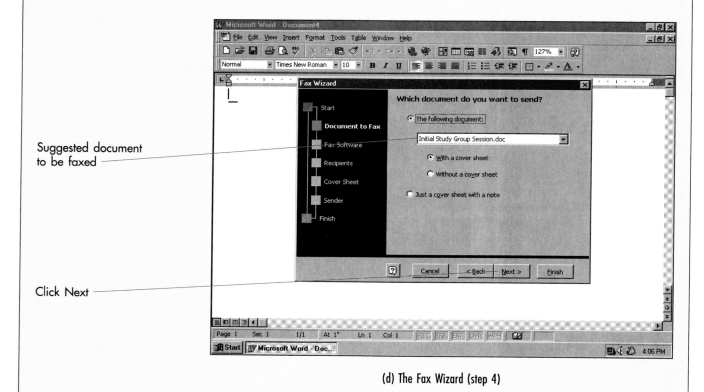

(d) The Fax Wizard (step 4)

FIGURE 3.11   Hands-on Exercise 3 (continued)

- The Fax Wizard suggests Initial Study Group as the name of the document you want to fax (because the document is still open). The option button **With a Cover Sheet** is selected. Click **Next.**
- **Microsoft Fax** is selected as the software to use. Click **Next.**
- Enter the name and fax number of one person in your group. Complete this entry even if you do not intend to send an actual fax. Click **Next.**
- Choose the style of the cover sheet. We selected **Professional.** Click **Next.**
- If necessary, complete and/or modify the information about the sender so that it reflects your name and telephone number. Click **Next.**
- Read the last screen reminding you about how to list phone numbers correctly. Click **Finish.**

STEP 5: Complete the Fax

➤ You should see a fax cover sheet similar to the document in Figure 3.11e. Close the Office Assistant if it appears, or request help as you see fit. Do *not* click the button to Send Fax Now.

➤ Save the cover sheet as **Fax Cover Sheet** in the **Exploring Word** folder. If necessary, change to the **Normal view** and zoom to **Page Width** so that your document more closely matches ours.

➤ Complete the cover sheet by entering the additional information as appropriate. Click at the indicated position in Figure 3.11e prior to entering the text, so that your entries align properly.

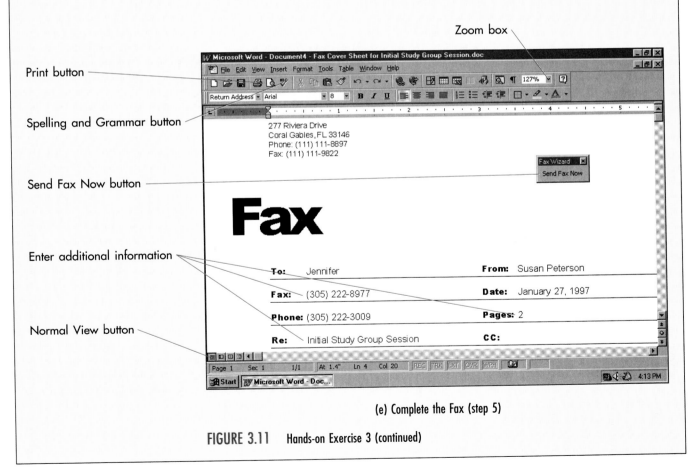

(e) Complete the Fax (step 5)

FIGURE 3.11   Hands-on Exercise 3 (continued)

➤ Click the **Spelling and Grammar button** to check the agenda for spelling. Save the document.

➤ Save the document a final time. Click the **Print button** on the Standard toolbar to print the completed document, and submit it to your instructor as proof that you did the exercise.

STEP 6: Send the Fax

➤ Do this step only if you want to send the fax. You cannot do this from your lab at school! Click the **Send Fax Now** button to begin sending the fax.

➤ Just sit back and relax and watch the Fax Wizard as it goes through the steps of sending the fax as shown in Figure 3.11f. Check with the recipient to be sure he or she received the fax. Click **OK** to return to the document.

➤ Exit Word. Congratulations on a job well done.

TROUBLESHOOTING

If you're having difficulty sending a fax it could be because the dialing properties of your modem are set improperly. Click the Start menu, click Settings, click Control Panel, then double click the Modems icon to display the Modems Properties dialog box. If necessary, click the General tab, click the Dialing Properties button, verify that your settings are correct, then click OK to close the Dialing Properties dialog box.

Fax status

Click OK

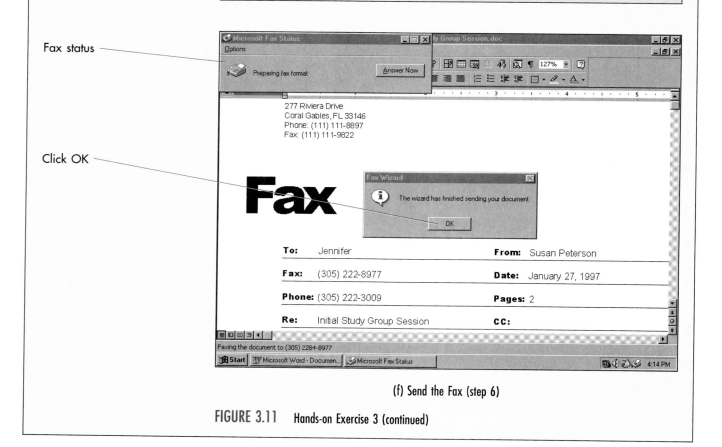

(f) Send the Fax (step 6)

FIGURE 3.11   Hands-on Exercise 3 (continued)

The applications in Microsoft Office are thoroughly integrated with one another. They look alike and work alike. Equally important, they share information through a technology known as Object Linking and Embedding (OLE), which enables you to create a compound document containing data (objects) from multiple applications.

The Microsoft Clip Gallery contains more than 3,000 clip art images and almost 150 photographs, each in a variety of categories. It also contains sound files and video clips, although these objects are more commonly used in PowerPoint presentations than in Word documents. Microsoft WordArt is an application within Microsoft Office that creates decorative text, which can be used to add interest to a document.

The Insert Symbol command provides access to special characters, making it easy to place typographic characters into a document. The symbols can be taken from any TrueType font and can be displayed in any point size.

The Internet is a network of networks. The World Wide Web (WWW, or simply the Web) is a very large subset of the Internet, consisting of those computers containing hypertext and/or hypermedia documents. Resources (e.g., clip art or photographs) can be downloaded from the Web for inclusion in a Word document.

Every document in Office 97 is Web-enabled, meaning that the application will automatically detect and highlight any hyperlinks that are entered in a document. You can click a hyperlink from within Word and, provided you have an Internet connection, your Web browser will display the associated page. Each Office application also contains a Web toolbar with icons similar to those found on the toolbar in Internet Explorer.

A copyright provides legal protection to a written or artistic work, giving the author exclusive rights to its use and reproduction except as governed under the fair use exclusion. Anything on the Internet or World Wide Web should be considered copyrighted unless the document specifically says it is in the public domain. The fair use exclusion enables you to use a portion of the work for educational, nonprofit purposes, or for the purpose of critical review or commentary.

A footnote provides additional information about an item, such as its source, and appears at the bottom of the page where the reference occurs. The Insert Footnote command inserts a footnote into a document and automatically assigns the next sequential number to that note.

Wizards and templates help create professionally designed documents with a minimum of time and effort. A template is a partially completed document that contains formatting and other information. A wizard is an interactive program that creates a customized template based on the answers you supply.

OBJECT LINKING AND EMBEDDING

Object Linking and Embedding (OLE) enables you to create a compound document containing objects (data) from multiple Windows applications. Each of the techniques, linking and embedding, can be implemented in various ways. Althogh OLE is one of the major benefits of working in the Windows environment, it would be impossible to illustrate all of the techniques in a single exercise. Accordingly, we have created the icon at the left to help you identify the many OLE examples that appear throughout the *Exploring Windows* series.

OLE

Agenda Wizard
AutoCorrect
AutoFormat
Clip art
Clipboard
Compound document
Copyright
Crop
Endnote
Fair use exclusion
Fax Wizard
Footnote
Format Picture
   command

Hyperlink
Hypermedia
Hypertext
Insert Footnote
   command
Insert Picture command
Insert Symbol
   command
Internet
Microsoft Clip Gallery
Microsoft WordArt
Object Linking and
   Embedding (OLE)
Picture toolbar

Public domain
Résumé Wizard
Sizing handle
Template
Web-enabled
Web toolbar
Wizard
WordArt
WordArt toolbar
World Wide Web

MULTIPLE CHOICE

1. How do you change the size of a selected object so that the height and width change in proportion to one another?
   - (a) Click and drag any of the four corner handles in the direction you want to go
   - (b) Click and drag the sizing handle on the top border, then click and drag the sizing handle on the left side
   - (c) Click and drag the sizing handle on the bottom border, then click and drag the sizing handle on the right side
   - (d) All of the above

2. The Microsoft Clip Galley:
   - (a) Is accessed through the Insert Picture command
   - (b) Is available to every application in the Microsoft Office
   - (c) Enables you to search for a specific piece of clip art by specifying a key word in the description of the clip art
   - (d) All of the above

3. Which view, and which magnification, offers the most convenient way to position a graphic within a document?
   - (a) Page Width in the Page Layout view
   - (b) Full Page in the Page Layout view
   - (c) Page Width in the Normal view
   - (d) Full Page in the Normal view

4. Which of the following objects can be inserted from the Microsoft Clip Gallery?
   - (a) Clip art
   - (b) Photographs
   - (c) Sound and video files
   - (d) All of the above

5. Which of the following is the most likely explanation of why photographs do not appear in the Microsoft Clip Gallery dialog box?

(a) The user executed the Insert Picture Clip Art command, rather than the Insert Picture Photograph command

(b) Photographs are not accessible through the Clip Gallery regardless of which command is executed

(c) The photographs are not included in the default installation of Office and hence are available only with the Office CD-ROM

(d) None of the above

6. What is the difference between clicking and double clicking an object within a compound document?

(a) Clicking selects the object; double clicking opens the application that created the object

(b) Double clicking selects the object; clicking opens the application that created the object

(c) Clicking changes to Normal view; double clicking changes to Page Layout view

(d) Double clicking changes to Normal view; clicking changes to Page Layout view

7. Which of the following is true about footnotes or endnotes?

(a) The addition of a footnote or endnote automatically renumbers the notes that follow

(b) The deletion of a footnote or endnote automatically renumbers the notes that follow

(c) Both (a) and (b)

(d) Neither (a) nor (b)

8. Which of the following is true about the Insert Symbol command?

(a) It can insert a symbol in different type sizes

(b) It can access any TrueType font installed on the system

(c) Both (a) and (b)

(d) Neither (a) nor (b)

9. Which of the following is true regarding objects and the associated toolbars?

(a) Clicking on a WordArt object displays the WordArt toolbar

(b) Clicking on a Picture displays the Picture Toolbar

(c) Both (a) and (b)

(d) Neither (a) nor (b)

10. Which of the following objects can be downloaded from the Web for inclusion in a Word document?

(a) Clip art

(b) Photographs

(c) Sound and video files

(d) All of the above

11. Which of the following is true regarding the Web toolbar?

(a) It enables you to enter the address of a Web page from within a Word document

(b) It enables you to add a Web page to a list of favorite pages

(c) It contains a button to return to previous Web pages

(d) All of the above

12. What happens if you enter the text *www.intel.com* into a document?
    (a) The entry is converted to a hyperlink, and the text will be underlined and displayed in a different color
    (b) The associated page will be opened, provided your computer has access to the Internet
    (c) Both (a) and (b)
    (d) Neither (a) nor (b)

13. Which of the following is a true statement about wizards?
    (a) They are accessed through the New command in the File menu
    (b) They always produce a finished document
    (c) Both (a) and (b)
    (d) Neither (a) nor (b)

14. How do you access the wizards built into Microsoft Word?
    (a) Pull down the Wizards and Templates menu
    (b) Pull down the Insert menu and choose the Wizards and Templates command
    (c) Pull down the File menu and choose the New command
    (d) None of the above

15. Which of the following is true regarding wizards and templates?
    (a) A wizard may create a template
    (b) A template may create a wizard
    (c) Both (a) and (b)
    (d) Neither (a) nor (b)

ANSWERS

1. a	**6.** a	**11.** d
2. d	**7.** c	**12.** a
3. b	**8.** c	**13.** a
4. d	**9.** c	**14.** c
5. c	**10.** d	**15.** a

PRACTICE WITH MICROSOFT WORD

1. Inserting Objects: Figure 3.12 illustrates a flyer that we created for a hypothetical computer sale. We embedded clip art and WordArt and created what we believe is an attractive flyer. Try to duplicate our advertisement, or better yet, create your own. Include your name somewhere in the document as a sales associate. Be sure to spell check your ad, then print the completed flyer and submit it to your instructor.

2. Exploring TrueType: Installing Windows 95 also installs several TrueType fonts, which in turn are accessible from any application. Two of the fonts, Symbols and Wingdings, contain a variety of special characters that can be used to create some unusual documents. Use the Insert Symbol command, your imagination, and the fact that TrueType fonts are scaleable to any point size to re-create the documents in Figure 3.13. Better yet, use your imagination to create your own documents.

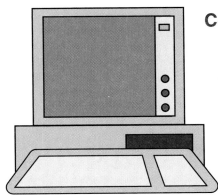

Computer World's Annual Pre-Inventory Sale

When: Saturday, June 21, 1997
          8:00AM - 10:00PM

Where: 13640 South Dixie Highway

Computer World

Computers
Printers
Fax/Modems
CD-ROM drives
Sound Systems
Software
Etc.

Pre-Inventory Sale

Sales Associate: Bianca Costo

FIGURE 3.12   Document for Practice Exercise 1

Valentine's Day
We'll serenade your sweetheart
Call 284-LOVE

STUDENT COMPUTER LAB
Fall Semester Hours

FIGURE 3.13   Documents for Practice Exercise 2

3. It's Easier Than It Looks: The document in Figure 3.14 was created to illustrate the automatic formatting and correction facilities that are built into Microsoft Word. We want you to create the document, include your name at the bottom, then submit the completed document to your instructor as proof that you did the exercise. All you have to do is follow the instructions within the document and let Word do the formatting and correcting for you.

The only potential difficulty is that the options on your system may be set to negate some of the features to which we refer. Accordingly, you need to pull down the Tools menu, click the AutoCorrect command, and click the AutoFormat As You Type tab. Verify that the options referenced in the document are in effect. You also need to review the table of predefined substitutions on the AutoCorrect tab to learn the typewritten characters that will trigger the smiley faces, copyright, and registered trademark substitutions.

It's Easier Than It Looks

This document was created to demonstrate the AutoCorrect and AutoFormat features that are built into Microsoft Word. In essence, you type as you always did and enter traditional characters, then let Word perform its "magic" by substituting symbols and other formatting for you. Among the many features included in these powerful commands are the:

1. Automatic creation of numbered lists by typing a number followed by a period, tab, or right parenthesis. Just remember to press the return key twice to turn off this feature.
2. Symbols for common fractions such as ½ or ¼.
3. Ordinal numbers with superscripts created automatically such as 1st, 2nd, or 3rd.
4. Copyright © and Registered trademark ® symbols.

AutoFormat will even add a border to a paragraph any time you type three or more hyphens, equal signs, or underscores on a line by itself.

==

_____

And finally, the AutoCorrect feature has built-in substitution for smiley faces that look best when set in a larger point size such as 72 points.

FIGURE 3.14   Document for Practice Exercise 3

4. What You Can Do with Clip Art: We are not artistic by nature, and there is no way that we could have created the original clip art image of the duck smashing the computer. We did, however, create the variation shown in Figure 3.15 by using various tools on the Drawing toolbar. All it took was a little imagination and a sense of what can be done.

Start by inserting the clip art image into a new document and displaying the Drawing toolbar. Select the clip art image, click the drop-down arrow on the Draw button on the Drawing toolbar, and click the Ungroup command. The duck and the computer are now separate objects, each of which can be selected and manipulated separately.

Click anywhere in the document to deselect both the duck and the computer, then select just the duck. Click the Copy button to copy the duck to the clipboard, then click the Paste button to duplicate the duck. Click and drag the second duck to the right side of the document. Click the drop-down arrow on the Draw button on the Drawing toolbar, click the Rotate or Flip command, then click Flip Horizontal to turn the duck around. To change the color and design of the duck's jacket, you need to ungroup the duck itself, then select the jacket and execute the appropriate command(s).

The rest is up to you. Use the ScreenTips and online help to learn about the different tools. Create one or more variations of the duck or any other clip art image and submit them to your instructor.

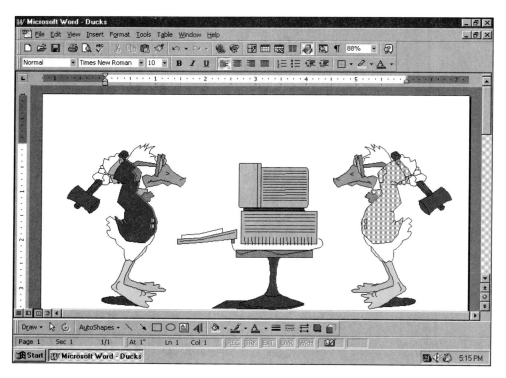

FIGURE 3.15 Screen for Practice Exercise 4

5. Presidential Anecdotes: Figure 3.16 displays the finished version of a document containing 10 presidential anecdotes. The anecdotes were taken from the book *Presidential Anecdotes,* by Paul F. Boller, Jr., published by Penguin Books (New York, NY, 1981). Open the *Chapter 3 Practice 5* document that is found on the data disk, then make the following changes:

a. Add a footnote after Mr. Boller's name, which appears at the end of the second sentence, citing the information about the book. This, in turn, renumbers all existing footnotes in the document.

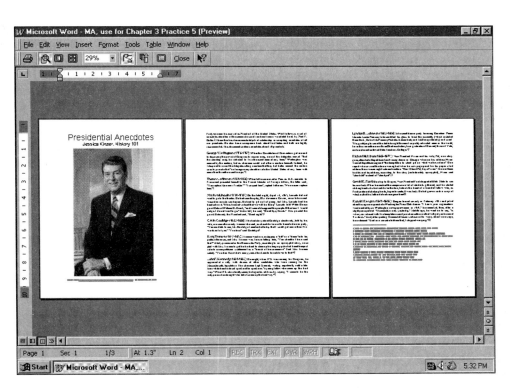

FIGURE 3.16   Screen for Practice Exercise 5

b. Switch the order of the anecdotes for Lincoln and Jefferson so that the presidents appear in order. The footnotes for these references are changed automatically.

c. Convert all of the footnotes to endnotes, as shown in the figure.

d. Go to the White House Web site and download a picture of any of the 10 presidents, then incorporate that picture into a cover page. Remember to cite the reference with an appropriate footnote.

e. Submit the completed document to your instructor.

6. Photographs Online: The Smithsonian Institution is a priceless resource for all Americans. Go to the home page of the Smithsonian (*www.si.edu*) and click the link to Resources, which in turn takes you to the Photographs online page (*photo2.si.edu*) shown in Figure 3.17. Click the link to search the photo database, then choose one or two photographs on any subject that you find especially interesting.

Use the technique described in the chapter to download those photographs to your PC, then use the Insert Picture command to incorporate those pictures into a Word document. Write a short paper (250 to 500 words) describing those photographs and submit the paper to your professor as proof you did this exercise. Be sure to include an appropriate footnote to cite the source of the photographs.

7. Music on the Web: The World Wide Web is a source of infinite variety, including music from your favorite rock group. You can find biographical information and/or photographs such as the one in Figure 3.18. You can even find music, which you can download and play, provided you have the necessary hardware. It's fun, it's easy, so go to it. Use any search engine to find documents about your favorite rock group. Try to find biographical information as well as a picture, then incorporate the results of your research into a short paper to submit to your instructor.

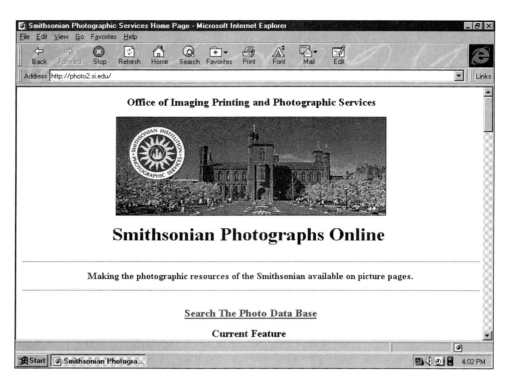

FIGURE 3.17   Screen for Practice Exercise 6

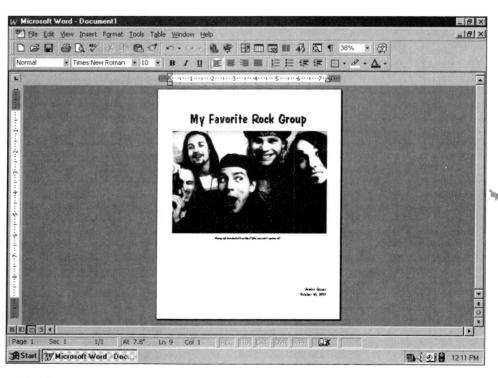

FIGURE 3.18   Screen for Practice Exercise 7

8. The iCOMP index was developed by Intel to compare the speeds of various microprocessors. We want you to search the Web and find a chart showing values in the current iCOMP index. (The chart you find need not be the same as the one in Figure 3.19.) Once you find the chart, download the graphic and incorporate it into a memo to your instructor. Add a paragraph or two describing the purpose of the index as shown in Figure 3.19.

A Comparison of Microcomputers

John Doe, CIS 120
(http://pentium.intel.com/procs/perf/icomp/index.htm)

The capability of a PC depends on the microprocessor on which it is based. Intel microprocessors are currently in their sixth generation, with each generation giving rise to increasingly powerful personal computers. All generations are upward compatible; that is, software written for one generation will automatically run on the next. This upward compatibility is crucial because it protects your investment in software when you upgrade to a faster computer.

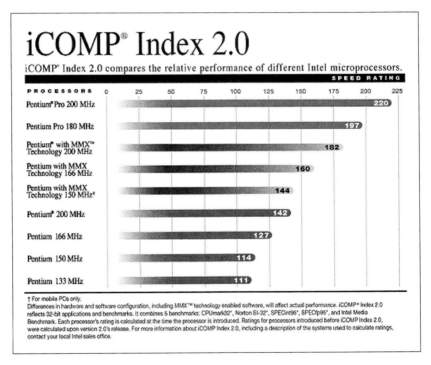

Each generation has multiple microprocessors that are differentiated by *clock speed*, an indication of how fast instructions are executed. Clock speed is measured in *megahertz* (MHz). The higher the clock speed, the faster the machine. Thus, all Pentiums are not created equal, because they operate at different clock speeds. The *Intel CPU Performance Index* (see chart) was created to compare the performance of one microprocessor to another. The index consists of a single number to indicate the relative performance of the microprocessor; the higher the number, the faster the processor.

FIGURE 3.19 Document for Practice Exercise 8

The Letterhead

A well-designed letterhead adds impact to your correspondence. Collect samples of professional stationery, then design your own letterhead, which includes your name, address, phone, and any other information you deem relevant. Include a fax number and/or e-mail address as appropriate. Using your imagination, design the letterhead for your planned career. Try different fonts and/or the Format Border command to add horizontal line(s) under the text. Consider a graphic logo, but keep it simple. You might also want to decrease the top margin so that the letterhead prints closer to the top of the page.

An Ad for Travel

The Clip Gallery includes the maps and flags of many foreign countries. It also has maps of all 50 states as well as pictures of many landmarks. Design a one-page flyer for a place you want to visit, either in the United States or abroad. Collect the assignments, then ask your instructor to hold a contest to decide the most appealing document. It's fun, it's easy, and it's educational. Bon voyage!

The Cover Page

Use WordArt and/or the Clip Gallery to create a truly original cover page that you can use with all of your assignments. The cover page should include the title of the assignment, your name, course information, and date. (Use the Insert Date and Time command to insert the date as a field so that it will be updated automatically every time you retrieve the document.) The formatting is up to you. Print the completed cover page and submit it to your instructor, then use the cover page for all future assignments.

The Résumé

Use your imagination to create a résumé for Benjamin Franklin or Leonardo da Vinci, two acknowledged geniuses. The résumé is limited to one page and will be judged for content (yes, you have to do a little research on the Web) as well as appearance. You can intersperse fact and fiction as appropriate; for example, you may want to leave space for a telephone and/or a fax number, but could indicate that these devices have not yet been invented. You can choose a format for the résumé using the Résumé Wizard, or better yet, design your own.

File Compression

Photographs add significantly to the appearance of a document, but they also add to its size. Accordingly, you might want to consider acquiring a file compression program to facilitate copying large documents to a floppy disk in order to transport your documents to and from school, home, or work. You can download an evaluation copy of the popular WinZip program at *www.winzip.com*. Investigate the subject of file compression, then submit a summary of your findings to your instructor.

Copyright Infringement

It's fun to download images from the Web for inclusion in a document, but is it legal? Copyright protection (infringement) is one of the most pressing legal issues on the Web. Search the Web for sites that provide information on current copyright law. One excellent site is the copyright page at the Institute for Learning Technologies at *www.ilt.columbia.edu/projects/copyright.* Another excellent reference is the page at *www.benedict.com.* Research these and other sites, then summarize your findings in a short note to your instructor.

Macros

The Insert Symbol command can be used to insert foreign characters into a document, but this technique is too slow if you use these characters with any frequency. It is much more efficient to develop a series of macros (keyboard shortcuts) that will insert the characters for you. You could, for example, create a macro to insert an accented *e,* then invoke that macro through the Ctrl+e keyboard shortcut. Parallel macros could be developed for the other vowels or special characters that you use frequently. Use the Help menu to learn about macros, then summarize your findings in a short note to your instructor.

ADVANCED FEATURES: OUTLINES, TABLES, STYLES, AND SECTIONS

4

OBJECTIVES

After reading this chapter you will be able to:

1. Create a bulleted or numbered list; create an outline using a multilevel list.
2. Describe the Outline view; explain how this view facilitates moving text within a document.
3. Describe the tables feature; create a table and insert it into a document.
4. Explain how styles automate the formatting process and provide a consistent appearance to common elements in a document.
5. Use the AutoFormat command to apply styles to an existing document; create, modify, and apply a style to selected elements of a document.
6. Define a section; explain how section formatting differs from character and paragraph formatting.
7. Create a header and/or a footer; establish different headers or footers for the first, odd, or even pages in the same document.
8. Insert page numbers into a document; use the Edit menu's Go To command to move directly to a specific page in a document.
9. Create and update a table of contents.

OVERVIEW

This chapter presents a series of advanced features that will be especially useful the next time you have to write a term paper with specific formatting requirements. We show you how to create a bulleted or numbered list to emphasize important items within a term paper, and how to create an outline for that paper. We also introduce the tables feature, which is one of the most powerful features in Microsoft Word as it provides an easy way to arrange text, numbers, and/or graphics.

The second half of the chapter develops the use of styles, or sets of formatting instructions that provide a consistent appearance to similar elements in a document. We describe the AutoFormat command that assigns styles to an existing document and greatly simplifies the formatting process. We show you how to create a new style, how to modify an existing style, and how to apply those styles to text within a document. We introduce the Outline view, which is used in conjunction with styles to provide a condensed view of a document. We also discuss several items associated with longer documents, such as page numbers, headers and footers, and a table of contents.

The chapter contains four hands-on exercises to apply the material at the computer. This is one more exercise than in our earlier chapters, but we think you will appreciate the practical application of these very important capabilities within Microsoft Word.

BULLETS AND LISTS

A list helps you organize information by highlighting important topics. A *bulleted list* emphasizes (and separates) the items. A *numbered list* sequences (and prioritizes) the items and is automatically updated to accommodate additions or deletions. An *outline* (or multilevel numbered list) extends a numbered list to several levels, and it too is updated automatically when topics are added or deleted. Each of these lists is created through the *Bullets and Numbering command* in the Format menu, which displays the Bullets and Numbering dialog box in Figure 4.1.

The tabs within the Bullets and Numbering dialog box are used to choose the type of list and customize its appearance. The Bulleted tab selected in Figure 4.1a enables you to specify one of several predefined symbols for the bullet. Typically, that is all you do, although you can use the Customize button to change the default spacing (of ¼ inch) of the text from the bullet and/or to choose a different symbol for the bullet.

The Numbered tab in Figure 4.1b lets you choose Arabic or Roman numerals, or upper- or lowercase letters, for a Numbered list. As with a bulleted list, the Customize button lets you change the default spacing, the numbering style, and/or the punctuation before or after the number or letter. Note, too, the option buttons to restart or continue numbering, which become important if a list appears in multiple places within a document. In other words, each occurrence of a list can start numbering anew, or it can continue from where the previous list left off.

The Outline Numbered tab in Figure 4.1c enables you to create an outline to organize your thoughts. As with the other types of lists, you can choose one of several default styles, and/or modify a style through the Customize command button. You can also specify whether each outline within a document is to restart its numbering, or whether it is to continue numbering from the previous outline.

CREATING AN OUTLINE

The following exercise explores the Bullets and Numbering command in conjunction with creating an outline for a hypothetical paper on the United States Constitution. The exercise begins by having you create a bulleted list, then asking you to convert it to a numbered list, and finally to an outline. The end result is the type of outline your professor may ask you to create prior to writing a term paper.

As you do the exercise, remember that a conventional outline is created as a multilevel list within the Bullets and Numbering command. Text for the outline is entered in the Page Layout or Normal view, *not* the Outline view. The latter provides a completely different capability—a condensed view of a document that is used in conjunction with styles and is discussed later in the chapter. We mention this to avoid confusion should you stumble into the Outline view.

Choose the type of bullet

Click Customize to choose additional bullet symbols

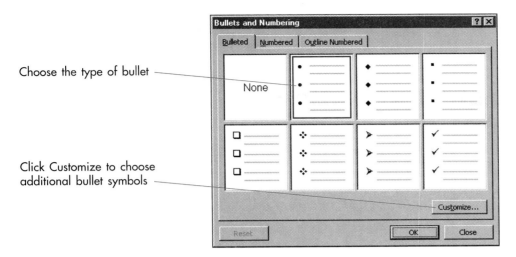

(a) Bulleted List

Click to select numbering style

A numbered list can use letters rather than numbers

Restarts numbering for each list within document

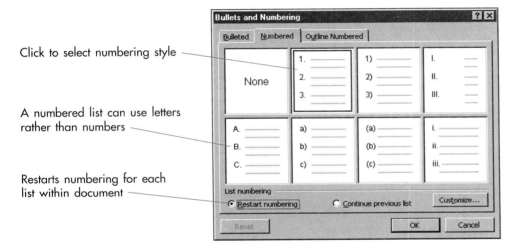

(b) Numbered List

Choose the Outline style

Click Customize to change the formatting

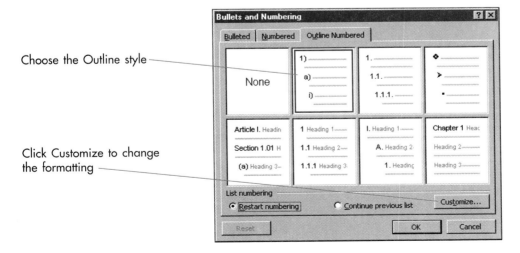

(c) Outline

FIGURE 4.1   Bullets and Numbering

Bullets, Lists, and Outlines

Objective: To use the Bullets and Numbering command to create a bulleted list, a numbered list, and an outline. Use Figure 4.2 as a guide in doing the exercise.

STEP 1: Create a Bulleted List

➤ Start Word and begin a new document. Type **Preamble,** the first topic in our list, and press **enter.**

➤ Type the three remaining topics, **Article I—Legislative Branch, Article II—Executive Branch,** and **Article III—Judicial Branch.** Do not press enter after the last item.

➤ Click and drag to select all four topics as shown in Figure 4.2a. Pull down the **Format menu** and click the **Bullets and Numbering command** to display the Bullets and Numbering dialog box.

➤ If necessary, click the **Bulleted tab,** select the type of bullet you want, then click **OK** to accept this setting and close the dialog box. Bullets have been added to the list.

➤ Click after the words **Judicial Branch** to deselect the list and also to position the insertion point at the end of the list. Press **enter** to begin a new line. A bullet appears automatically since Word copies the formatting from one paragraph to the next.

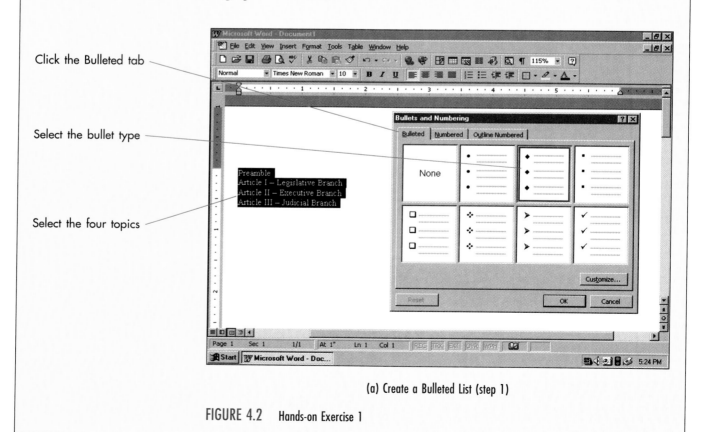

Click the Bulleted tab

Select the bullet type

Select the four topics

(a) Create a Bulleted List (step 1)

FIGURE 4.2 Hands-on Exercise 1

➤ Type **Amendments.** Press **enter** to end this line and begin the next, which already has a bullet. Press **enter** a second time to terminate the bulleted list.

➤ Save the document as **US Constitution** in the **Exploring Word folder.**

THE BULLETS AND NUMBERING BUTTONS

Select the items for which you want to create a list, then click the Numbering or Bullets button on the Formatting toolbar to create a numbered or bulleted list, respectively. The buttons function as toggle switches; that is, click the button once (when the items are selected) and the list formatting is in effect. Click the button a second time and the bullets or numbers disappear. The buttons also enable you to switch from one type of list to another; that is, selecting a bulleted list and clicking the Numbering button changes the list to a numbered list, and vice versa.

STEP 2: Modify a Numbered List

➤ Click and drag to select the five items in the bulleted list, then click the **Numbering button** on the Standard toolbar.

➤ The bulleted list has been converted to a numbered list as shown in Figure 4.2b. (The last two items have not yet been added to the list.)

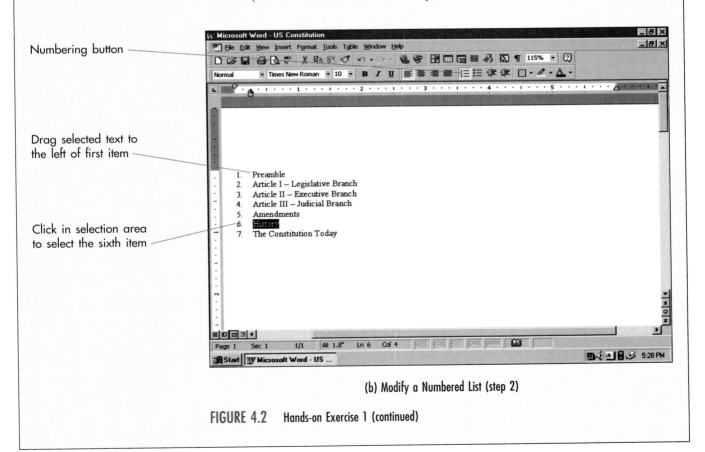

Numbering button

Drag selected text to the left of first item

Click in selection area to select the sixth item

(b) Modify a Numbered List (step 2)

FIGURE 4.2   Hands-on Exercise 1 (continued)

➤ Click immediately after the last item in the list and press **enter** to begin a new line. Word automatically adds the next sequential number to the list. Type **History** and press **enter.** Type **The Constitution Today** as the seventh item.

➤ Click in the selection area to select the sixth item, **History** (only the text is selected). Now drag the selected text to the beginning of the list, in front of *Preamble.* Release the mouse.

➤ The list is automatically renumbered. *History* is now the first item, *Preamble* is the second item, and so on. Save the document.

AUTOMATIC CREATION OF A NUMBERED LIST

Word automatically creates a numbered list whenever you begin a paragraph with a number or letter, followed by a period, tab, or right parenthesis. Once the list is started, press the enter key at the end of a line, and Word generates the next sequential number or letter in the list. To end the list, press the backspace key once, or press the enter key twice. To turn the autonumbering feature on or off, pull down the Tools menu, click AutoCorrect to display the AutoCorrect dialog box, click the AutoFormat as you Type tab, then check (clear) the box for Automatic Numbered lists.

STEP 3: Convert to an Outline

➤ Click and drag to select the entire list, click the **right mouse button** to display a context-sensitive menu, then click the **Bullets and Numbering command** to display the Bullets and Numbering dialog box in Figure 4.2c.

➤ Click the **Outline Numbered tab,** then select the type of outline you want. (Do not be concerned if the selected formatting does not display Roman numerals as we customize the outline later in the exercise.)

➤ Click **OK** to accept the formatting and close the dialog box. The numbered list has been converted to an outline, although that is difficult to see at this point.

➤ Click at the end of the third item, **Article I—Legislative Branch.** Press **enter.** The number 4 is generated automatically for the next item in the list.

➤ Press the **Tab key** to indent this item and automatically move to the next level of numbering (a lowercase *a*). Type **House of Representatives.**

➤ Press **enter.** The next sequential number (a lowercase *b*) is generated automatically. Type **Senate.**

➤ Save the document.

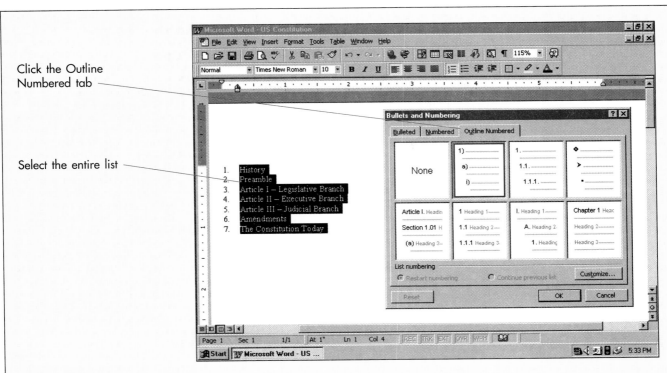

Click the Outline
Numbered tab

Select the entire list

(c) Convert to an Outline (step 3)

FIGURE 4.2   Hands-on Exercise 1 (continued)

THE TAB AND SHIFT+TAB KEYS

The easiest way to enter text into an outline is to type continually from one line to the next, using the Tab and Shift+Tab keys as necessary. Press the enter key after completing an item to move to the next item, which is automatically created at the same level, then continue typing if the item is to remain at this level. To change the level, press the Tab key to demote the item (move it to the next lower level), or the Shift+Tab combination to promote the item (move it to the next higher level).

STEP 4: Complete the Text of the Outline

➤ Your outline should be similar in appearance to Figure 4.2d, except that you have not yet entered most of the text. Click at the end of the line containing *House of Representatives.*

➤ Press **enter** to start a new item (which begins with a lowercase *b*). Press **Tab** to indent one level, changing the number to a lowercase *i*. Type **Length of term.** Press **enter.** Type **Requirements for office.** Enter these two items for the Senate as well.

➤ Enter the remaining text as shown in Figure 4.2.d, using the **Tab** and **Shift+Tab** keys to demote and promote the items. Save the document.

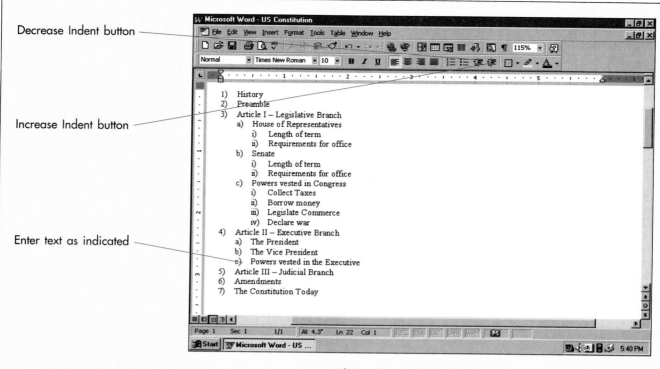

Decrease Indent button

Increase Indent button

Enter text as indicated

(d) Enter Text into the Outline (step 4)

FIGURE 4.2   Hands-on Exercise 1 (continued)

THE INCREASE AND DECREASE INDENT BUTTONS

The Increase and Decrease Indent buttons on the Standard toolbar are another way to change the level within an outline. Click anywhere within an item, then click the appropriate button to change the level within the outline. Indentation is implemented at the paragraph level, and hence you can click the button without selecting the entire item. You can also click and drag to select multiple item(s), then click the desired button.

STEP 5: Customize the Outline

➤ Select the entire outline, pull down the **Format menu,** then click **Bullets and Numbering** to display the Bullets and Numbering dialog box.

➤ Click **Customize** to display the Customize dialog box as shown in Figure 4.2e. Level **1** should be selected in the Level list box.

• Click the **drop-down arrow** in the Number style list box and select **I, II, III** as the style.

• Click in the Number format text box, which now contains the Roman numeral I followed by a right parenthesis. Click and drag to select the parenthesis and replace it with a period.

• Click the **drop-down arrow** in the Number position list box. Click **right** to right-align the Roman numerals that will appear in your outline.

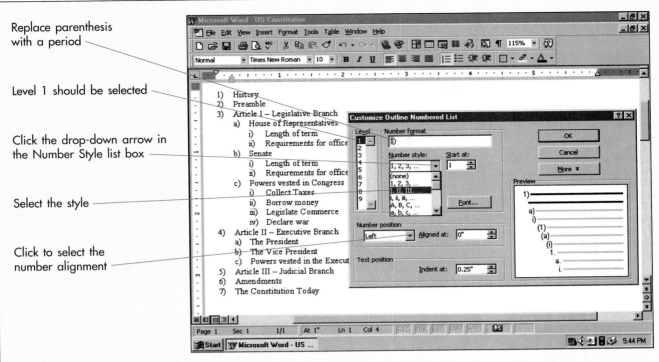

Replace parenthesis with a period

Level 1 should be selected

Click the drop-down arrow in the Number Style list box

Select the style

Click to select the number alignment

(e) Customize the Outline (step 5)

FIGURE 4.2 Hands-on Exercise 1 (continued)

➤ Click the number **2** in the Level list box and select **A, B, C** as the Number style. Click in the Number format text box and replace the right parenthesis with a period.

➤ Click the number **3** in the Level list box and select **1, 2, 3** as the Number style. Click in the Number format text box and replace the right parenthesis with a period.

➤ Click **OK** to accept these settings and close the dialog box. The formatting of your outline has changed to match the customization in this step.

CHANGE THE FORMATTING

Word provides several types of default formatting for an outline. Surprisingly, however, Roman numerals are not provided as the default and hence you may want to change the formatting to meet your exact requirements. The formats are changed one level at a time by selecting the style for a level, then changing the punctuation (e.g., by substituting a period for a right parenthesis). If you make a mistake, you can return to the default format by closing the Custom Outline Numbered List dialog box, then clicking the Reset button from within the Bullets and Numbering dialog box.

STEP 6: The Completed Outline

➤ Your outline should reflect the style in Figure 4.2f. The major headings begin with Roman numerals, the second level headings with uppercase letters, and so on.

➤ Press **Ctrl+Home** to move to the beginning of the outline. The insertion point is after Roman numeral I, in front of the word *History*. Type **The United States Constitution.** Press **enter.**

➤ The new text appears as Roman numeral I and all existing entries have been renumbered appropriately.

➤ The insertion point is immediately before the word *History*. Press **enter** to create a blank line (for your name).

➤ The blank line is now Roman numeral II and *History* has been moved to Roman numeral III.

➤ Press the **Tab** key so that the blank line (which will contain your name) is item A. This also renumbers *History* as Roman numeral II.

➤ Enter your name as shown in Figure 4.2f. Save the document, then print the outline and submit it to your instructor as proof you did this exercise.

➤ Close the document. Exit Word if you do not want to continue with the next exercise at this time.

Enter new major heading

Press Tab key to renumber as item A

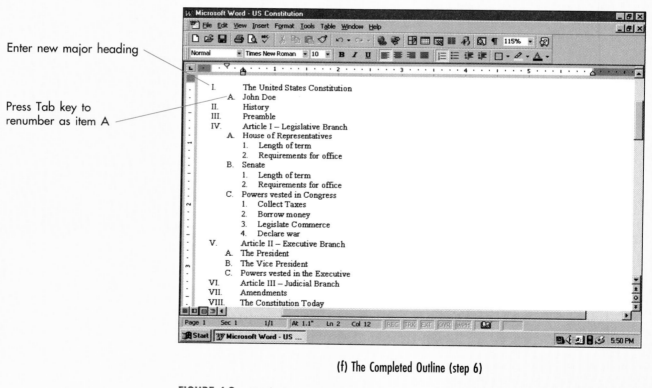

(f) The Completed Outline (step 6)

FIGURE 4.2 Hands-on Exercise 1 (continued)

The *tables feature* is one of the most powerful in Word and is the basis for an almost limitless variety of documents. The study schedule in Figure 4.3a, for example, is actually a 12 × 8 (12 rows and 8 columns) table as can be seen from the underlying structure in Figure 4.3b. The completed table looks quite impressive, but it is very easy to create once you understand how a table works. (See the practice exercises at the end of the chapter for other examples.)

The rows and columns in a table intersect to form *cells.* Each cell is formatted independently of every other cell and may contain text, numbers and/or graphics. Commands operate on one or more cells. Individual cells can be joined together to form a larger cell as was done in the first and last rows of Figure 4.3a. The rows within a table can be different heights, just as each column can be a different width. You can specify the height or width explicitly, or you can let Word determine it for you.

A cell can contain anything, even clip art as in the bottom right corner of Figure 4.3a. Just click in the cell where you want the clip art to go, then use the Insert Picture command as you have throughout the text. Use the sizing handles once the clip art has been inserted to move and/or position it within the cell.

A table is created through the *Insert Table command* in the *Table menu.* The command produces a dialog box in which you enter the number of rows and columns. Once the table has been defined, you enter text in individual cells. Text wraps as it is entered within a cell, so that you can add or delete text in a cell without affecting the entries in other cells. You can format the contents of an individual cell the same way you format an ordinary paragraph; that is, you can change the font, use boldface or italics, change the alignment, or apply any other formatting command. You can select multiple cells and apply the formatting to all selected cells at once.

You can also modify the structure of a table after it has been created. The Insert and Delete commands in the Table menu enable you to add new rows or columns, or delete existing rows or columns. You can invoke other commands to shade and/or border selected cells or the entire table.

You can work with a table using commands in the Table menu, or you can use the various tools on the Tables and Borders toolbar. (Just point to a button to display a ScreenTip indicative of its function.) Some of the buttons are simply shortcuts for commands within the Table menu. Other buttons offer new and intriguing possibilities, such as the button to Change Text Direction.

It's easy, and as you might have guessed, it's time for another hands-on exercise in which you create the table in Figure 4.3.

LEFT	CENTER	RIGHT

Many documents call for left, centered, and/or right aligned text on the same line, an effect that is achieved through setting tabs, or more easily through a table. To achieve the effect shown in the heading of this box, create a 1 × 3 table (one row and three columns), type the text in the three cells as needed, then use the buttons on the Formatting toolbar to left-align, center, and right-align the respective cells. Select the table, pull down the Format menu, click Borders and Shading, then specify None as the Border setting.

Weekly Class and Study Schedule

	Monday	Tuesday	Wednesday	Thursday	Friday	Saturday	Sunday
8:00AM							
9:00AM							
10:00AM							
11:00AM							
12:00PM							
1:00PM							
2:00PM							
3:00PM							
4:00PM							
Notes:							

(a) Completed Table

(b) Underlying Structure

FIGURE 4.3   The Tables Feature

Tables

Objective: To create a table; to change row heights and column widths; to join cells together; to apply borders and shading to selected cells. Use Figure 4.4 as a guide in the exercise.

STEP 1: The Page Setup Command

➤ Start Word. Click the **Tables and Borders button** on the Standard toolbar to display the Tables and Borders toolbar as shown in Figure 4.4a. The button functions as a toggle switch—click it once and the toolbar is displayed. Click the button a second time and the toolbar is suppressed.

➤ Pull down the **File menu.** Click **Page Setup.** Click the **Paper Size tab** to display the dialog box in Figure 4.4a. Click the **Landscape option button.**

➤ Click the **Margins tab.** Change the top and bottom margins to **.75** inch. Change the left and right margins to **.5** inch each. Click **OK** to accept the settings and close the dialog box.

➤ Change to the **Page Layout** view. Zoom to **Page Width.**

➤ Save the document as **My Study Schedule** in the Exploring Word folder.

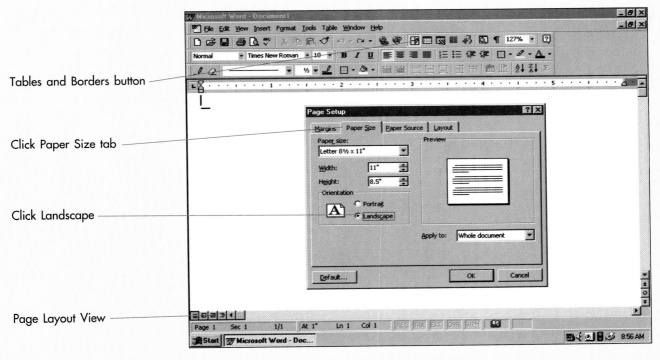

Tables and Borders button

Click Paper Size tab

Click Landscape

Page Layout View

(a) The Page Setup Command (step 1)

FIGURE 4.4 Hands-on Exercise 2

THE TABLES AND BORDERS TOOLBAR

The Tables and Borders toolbar contains a variety of tools for use in creating and/or modifying a table. Some of the buttons are simply shortcuts for commands within the Table menu. Other buttons offer new and intriguing possibilities, such as the button to Change Text Direction. You can point to any button to display a ScreenTip to show the name of the button, which is indicative of its function. You can also use the Help command for additional information.

STEP 2: Create the Table

➤ Pull down the **Table menu.** Click **Insert Table** to display the dialog box in Figure 4.4b.

➤ Enter **8** as the number of columns. Enter **12** as the number of rows. Click **OK** and the table will be inserted into the document.

Insert Table button

Enter 8 for the number of columns

Enter 12 for the number of rows

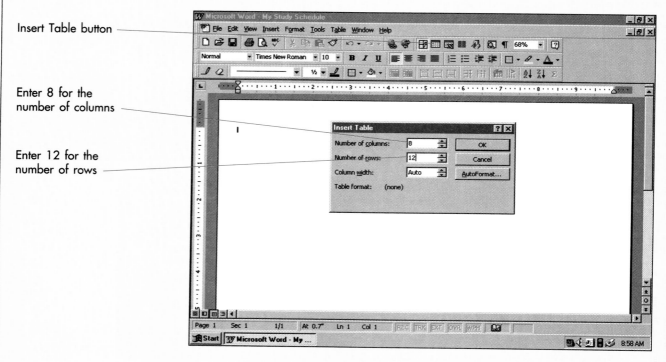

(b) Create the Table (step 2)

FIGURE 4.4   Hands-on Exercise 2 (continued)

THE INSERT TABLE BUTTON

The fastest way to create a table is to use the Insert Table button on the Standard toolbar. Click the Insert Table button to display a grid, then drag the mouse across and down the grid until you have the desired number of rows and columns. Release the mouse to create the table.

STEP 3: Table Basics

➤ Practice moving within the table:

- If the cells in the table are empty (as they are now), press the **left** and **right arrow keys** to move from cell to cell.

➤ If the cells contain text (as they will later in the exercise), you must press **Tab** and **Shift+Tab** to move from cell to cell.

- Press the **up** and **down arrow keys** to move from row to row. This works for both empty cells and cells with text.

➤ Select a cell row, column, or block of contiguous cells:

- To select a single cell, click immediately to the right of the left cell border (the pointer changes to an arrow when you are in the proper position).
- To select an entire row, click outside the table to the left of the first cell in that row.
- To select a column, click just above the top of the column (the pointer changes to a small black arrow).
- To select adjacent cells, drag the mouse over the cells.
- To select the entire table, drag the mouse over the table (or use the **Select Table** command from the Table menu).

TABS AND TABLES

The Tab key functions differently in a table than in a regular document. Press the Tab key to move to the next cell in the current row (or to the first cell in the next row if you are at the end of a row). Press Tab when you are in the last cell of a table to add a new blank row to the bottom of the table. Press Shift+Tab to move to the previous cell in the current row (or to the last cell in the previous row). You must press Ctrl+Tab to insert a regular tab character within a cell.

STEP 4: Merge the Cells

➤ Click outside the table to the left of the first cell in the first row to select the entire first row as shown in Figure 4.4c.

➤ Pull down the **Table menu** and click **Merge Cells** (or click the **Merge Cells button** on the Tables and Borders toolbar).

➤ Type **Weekly Class and Study Schedule** and format the text in 24 point Arial bold. Center the text within the cell.

➤ Click outside the table to the left of the first cell in the last row to select the entire row. Click the **Merge Cells button** to join the cells into a single cell.

➤ Type **Notes:** and format the entry in 12 point Arial bold.

➤ Save the table.

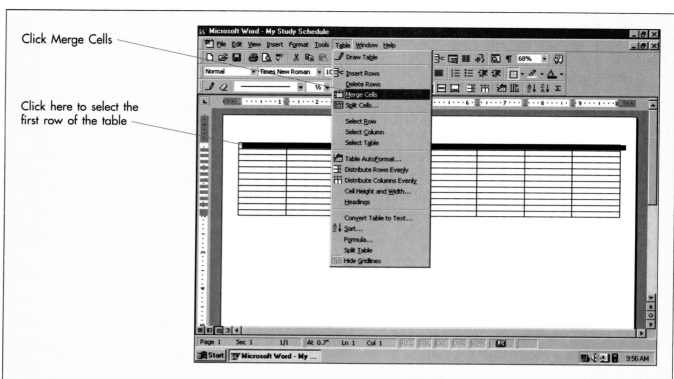

Click Merge Cells

Click here to select the first row of the table

(c) Merge the Cells (step 4)

FIGURE 4.4   Hands-on Exercise 2 (continued)

TABLES AND THE SHOW/HIDE ¶ BUTTON

The Show/Hide ¶ button can be toggled on (off) to display (hide) the non-printing characters associated with a table. The □ symbol indicates the end-of-cell (or end-of-row) marker and is analogous to the ¶ symbol at the end of a paragraph in a regular document.

STEP 5: Enter the Days and Hours

➤ Click the second cell in the second row. Type **Monday.**

➤ Press the **Tab** (or **right arrow**) **key** to move to the next cell. Type **Tuesday.** Continue until the days of the week have been entered.

➤ Use the Formatting Toolbar to change the font and alignment for the days of the week:

  • Select the entire row. Click the **Bold button.**

  • Click the **Font List box** to choose an appropriate font such as **Arial.**

  • Click the **Font Size List box** to choose an appropriate size such as **10** point.

  • Click the **Center button** on the Formatting toolbar.

➤ Click anywhere in the table to deselect the text and see the effect of the formatting change.

➤ Click the first cell in the third row. Type **8:00AM.** Press the **down arrow key** to move to the first cell in the fourth row. Type **9:00AM.**

➤ Continue in this fashion until you have entered the hourly periods up to **4:00PM.** Format as appropriate. (We right aligned the time periods and changed the font to Arial bold.) Your table should match Figure 4.4d. Save the table.

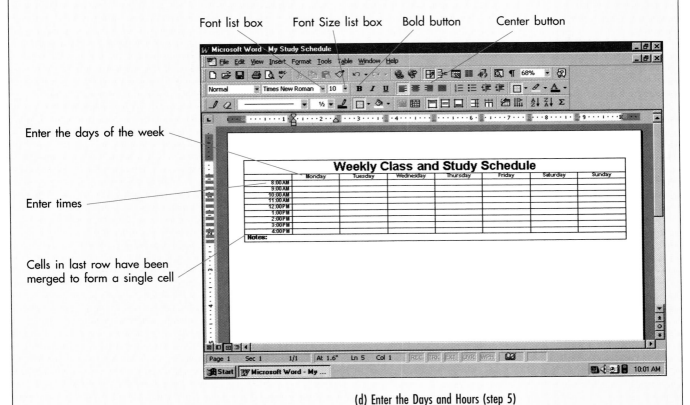

(d) Enter the Days and Hours (step 5)

FIGURE 4.4   Hands-on Exercise 2 (continued)

STEP 6: Change the Row Heights

➤ Click immediately after the word *notes.* Press the **enter key** five times. The height of the cell increases automatically to accommodate the blank lines.

➤ Select the cells containing the hours of the day. Pull down the **Table menu.** Click **Cell Height and Width** to display the dialog box in Figure 4.4e.

➤ If necessary, click the **Row tab.** Click the arrow for the Height of Rows list box. Click **Exactly,** then enter **36** (36 points is equal to ½ inch) in the At text box. Click **OK.**

➤ Click the **Center Vertically button** on the Tables and Borders toolbar to center the times vertically within their respective cells.

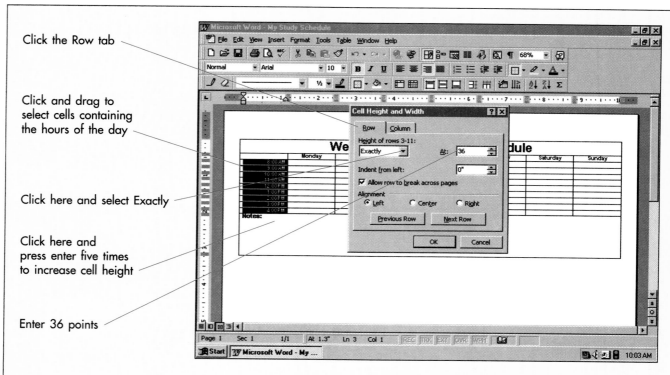

Click the Row tab

Click and drag to
select cells containing
the hours of the day

Click here and select Exactly

Click here and
press enter five times
to increase cell height

Enter 36 points

(e) Change the Row Height (step 6)

FIGURE 4.4   Hands-on Exercise 2 (continued)

STEP 7: Borders and Shading

➤ Click outside the first row (the cell containing the title of the table) to select the cell. Pull down the **Format menu,** click the **Borders and Shading** command to display the Borders and Shading dialog box as shown in Figure 4.4f.

➤ Click the **Shading tab.** Click the **drop-down arrow** on the Style list box, then select **100%** as the Style pattern. Click **OK.**

➤ Click outside the cell to see the effect of this command. You should see white letters on a solid black background. Save the document.

USE COLOR REVERSES FOR EMPHASIS

White letters on a solid background (technically called a reverse) is a favorite technique of desktop publishers. It looks even better in color. Select the text, click the Shading button on the Tables and Borders toolbar, then click the desired background color (e.g., red) to create the solid background. Next, click the drop-down arrow on the Font Color list box, click white for the text color, and click the Bold button to emphasize the white text. Click elsewhere in the document to see the result.

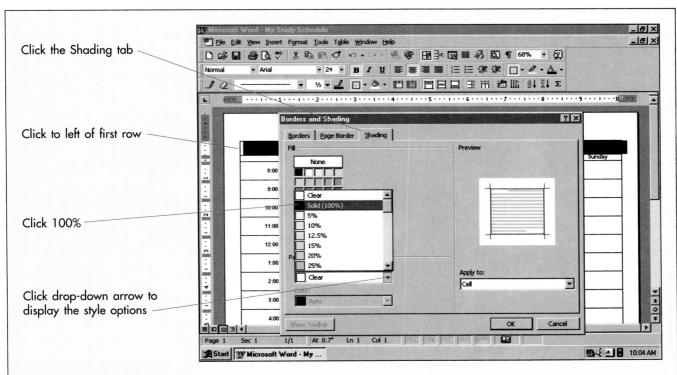

Click the Shading tab

Click to left of first row

Click 100%

Click drop-down arrow to display the style options

(f) Borders and Shading (step 7)

FIGURE 4.4   Hands-on Exercise 2 (continued)

STEP 8: Insert the Clip Art

➤ Click the **drop-down arrow** on the Zoom list box and zoom to **Whole Page.** Click in the last cell in the table, the cell for your notes.

➤ Pull down the **Insert menu,** click **Picture,** then click **ClipArt** to display the Microsoft Clip Gallery as shown in Figure 4.4g. Click **OK** if you see a dialog box reminding you that additional clip art is available on the Office CD.

➤ If necessary, click the **Clip Art tab** and select (click) the **Academic category.** Select the Professor lecturing the class (or a different image if you prefer), then click the **Insert button.**

➤ The Microsoft Clip Gallery dialog box will close and the picture will be inserted into the table, where it can be moved and sized as described in step 9. Do not be concerned if the clip art is too large for your table or if it spills to a second page.

ADDITIONAL CLIP IMAGES

Only a fraction of the more than 3,000 clip art images are installed with the default installation of Office 97, but you can access the additional images from the Office CD at any time. You can also install some or all of the images on your hard disk, provided you have sufficient space. Start Windows Explorer, then open the ClipArt folder on the Office CD. Double click the Setup icon to start the Setup Wizard, then follow the onscreen instructions to install the additional components you want.

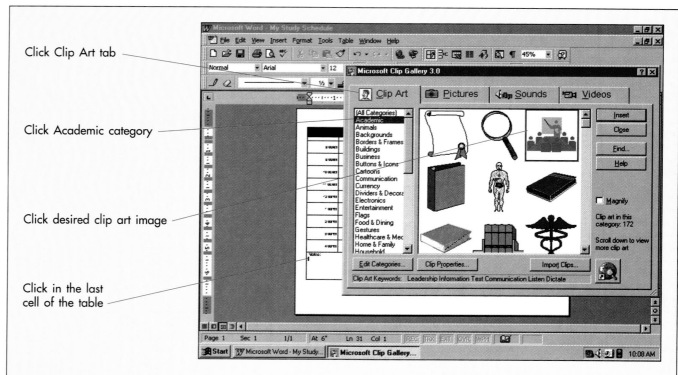

Click Clip Art tab

Click Academic category

Click desired clip art image

Click in the last cell of the table

(g) Insert Clip Art (step 8)

FIGURE 4.4 Hands-on Exercise 2 (continued)

STEP 9: Complete the Table

➤ Point to the clip art, click the **right mouse button** to display a shortcut menu, then click the **Format Picture command** to display the Format Picture dialog box. Click the **Wrapping tab,** select **None** as the Wrapping style, and click **OK** to close the Format Picture dialog box.

➤ The clip art should still be selected as indicated by the sizing handles in Figure 4.4h. Move and size the clip art until you are satisfied with its position within the table.

➤ Add your name somewhere in the table. Add other finishing touches (especially color if you have a color printer) to further personalize your table. Save the document.

➤ Print the completed table and submit it to your instructor as proof you did this exercise.

➤ Close the document. Exit Word if you do not want to continue with the next exercise at this time.

THE PICTURE TOOLBAR

The Picture toolbar is displayed automatically when a picture is selected; otherwise it is suppressed. As with any toolbar, you can point to a button to display a ScreenTip containing the name of the button, which is indicative of its function. You will find buttons for wrapping and formatting a picture, a Line Styles tool to place a border around the picture, and a Cropping tool to crop (erase) part of a picture.

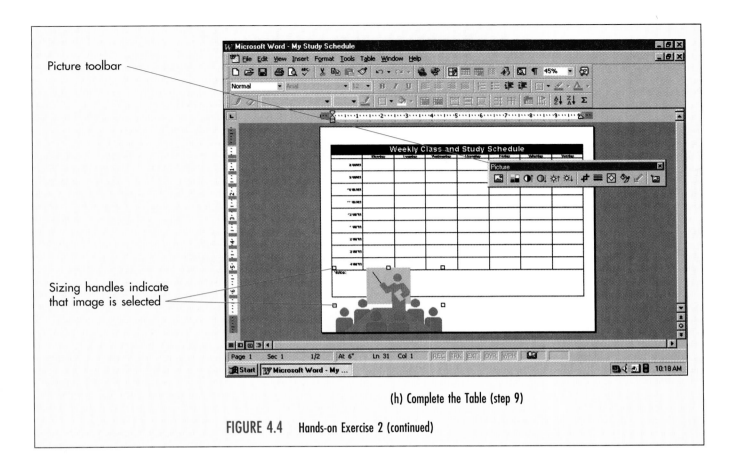

Picture toolbar

Sizing handles indicate
that image is selected

(h) Complete the Table (step 9)

FIGURE 4.4   Hands-on Exercise 2 (continued)

STYLES

A characteristic of professional documents is the use of uniform formatting for each element. Different elements can have different formatting; for example, headings may be set in one font and the text under those headings in a different font. You may want the headings centered and the text fully justified.

If you are like most people, you will change your mind several times before arriving at a satisfactory design, after which you will want consistent formatting for each element in the document. You can use the Format Painter on the Standard toolbar to copy the formatting from one occurrence of an element to another, but it still requires you to select the individual elements and paint each one whenever formatting changes.

A much easier way to achieve uniformity is to store the formatting information as a *style,* then apply that style to multiple occurrences of the same element within the document. Change the style and you automatically change all text defined by that style.

Styles are created on the character or paragraph level. A ***character style*** stores character formatting (font, size, and style) and affects only the selected text. A ***paragraph style*** stores paragraph formatting (alignment, line spacing, indents, tabs, text flow, and borders and shading, as well as the font, size, and style of the text in the paragraph). A paragraph style affects the current paragraph or multiple paragraphs if several paragraphs are selected. The ***Style command*** in the Format menu is used to create and/or modify either type of style, then enables you to apply that style within a document.

Execution of the Style command displays the dialog box shown in Figure 4.5, which lists the styles in use within a document. The ***Normal style*** contains the

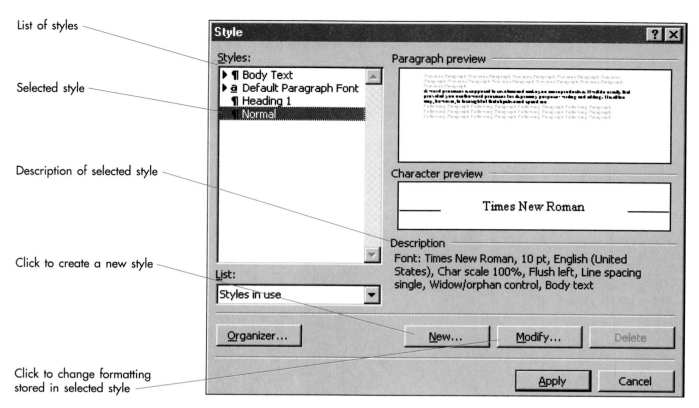

Labels pointing to the dialog box (left to right / top to bottom):

- List of styles
- Selected style
- Description of selected style
- Click to create a new style
- Click to change formatting stored in selected style

Style dialog box contents:

Styles:
- ▶ ¶ Body Text
- ▶ a Default Paragraph Font
- ¶ Heading 1
- ¶ Normal

List: Styles in use

Paragraph preview

Character preview

Times New Roman

Description
Font: Times New Roman, 10 pt, English (United States), Char scale 100%, Flush left, Line spacing single, Widow/orphan control, Body text

Buttons: Organizer... New... Modify... Delete Apply Cancel

FIGURE 4.5   The Normal Style

default paragraph settings (left aligned, single spacing, and the default font) and is automatically assigned to every paragraph unless a different style is specified. The *Heading 1* and *Body Text* styles are used in conjunction with the AutoFormat command, which applies these styles throughout a document. (The AutoFormat command is illustrated in the next hands-on exercise.) The *Default Paragraph Font* is a character style that specifies the (default) font for new text.

The Description box displays the style definition; for example, Times New Roman, 10 point, flush left, single spacing, and widow/orphan control. The Paragraph Preview box shows how paragraphs formatted in that style will appear. The Modify command button provides access to the Format Paragraph and Format Font commands to change the characteristics of the selected style. The Apply command button applies the style to all selected paragraphs or to the current paragraph. The New command button enables you to define a new style.

Styles automate the formatting process and provide a consistent appearance to a document. Any type of character or paragraph formatting can be stored within a style, and once a style has been defined, it can be applied to multiple occurrences of the same element within a document to produce identical formatting.

STYLES AND PARAGRAPHS

A paragraph style affects the entire paragraph; that is, you cannot apply a paragraph style to only part of a paragraph. To apply a style to an existing paragraph, place the insertion point anywhere within the paragraph, pull down the Style list box on the Formatting toolbar, then click the name of the style you want

One additional advantage of styles is that they enable you to view a document in the *Outline view.* The Outline view does not display a conventional outline (such as the multilevel list created earlier in the chapter), but rather a structural view of a document that can be collapsed or expanded as necessary. Consider, for example, Figure 4.6, which displays the Outline view of a document that will be the basis of the next hands-on exercise. The document consists of a series of tips for Word 97. The heading for each tip is formatted according to the Heading 1 style. The text of each tip is formatted according to the Body Text style.

The advantage of the Outline view is that you can collapse or expand portions of a document to provide varying amounts of detail. We have, for example, collapsed almost the entire document in Figure 4.6, displaying the headings while suppressing the body text. We also expanded the text for two tips (Download the Practice Files and Moving Within a Document) for purposes of illustration.

Now assume that you want to move the latter tip from its present position to immediately below the first tip. Without the Outline view, the text would stretch over two pages, making it difficult to see the text of both tips at the same time. Using the Outline view, however, you can collapse what you don't need to see, then simply click and drag the headings to rearrange the text within the document.

Outline toolbar appears automatically in the Outline view —

This text has been expanded —

The text for these tips has been collapsed —

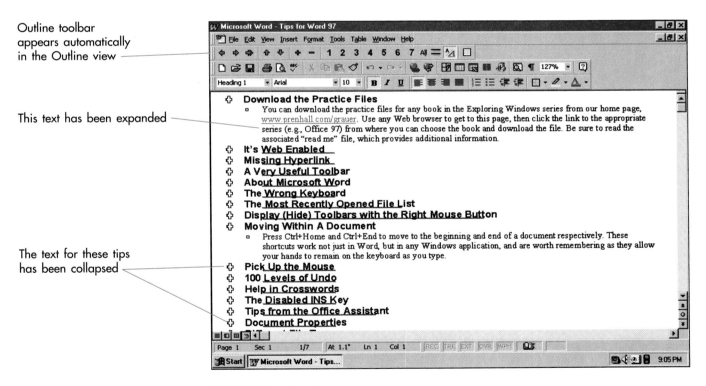

FIGURE 4.6   The Outline View

THE OUTLINE VERSUS THE OUTLINE VIEW

A conventional outline is created as a multilevel list within the Bullets and Numbering command. Text for the outline is entered in the Page Layout or Normal view, *not* the Outline view. The latter provides a condensed view of a document that is used in conjunction with styles.

The AutoFormat Command

Styles are extremely powerful. They enable you to impose uniform formatting within a document and they let you take advantage of the Outline view. What if, however, you have an existing and/or lengthy document that does not contain any styles (other than the default Normal style, which is applied to every paragraph)? Do you have to manually go through every paragraph in order to apply the appropriate style? The AutoFormat command provides a quick solution.

The **AutoFormat command** enables you to format lengthy documents quickly, easily, and in a consistent fashion. In essence, the command analyzes a document and formats it for you. Its most important capability is the application of styles to individual paragraphs; that is, the command goes through an entire document, determines how each paragraph is used, then applies an appropriate style to each paragraph. The formatting process assumes that one-line paragraphs are headings and applies the predefined Heading 1 style to those paragraphs. It applies the Body Text style to ordinary paragraphs and can also detect lists and apply a numbered or bullet style to those lists.

The AutoFormat command will also add special touches to a document if you request those options. It can replace "ordinary quotation marks" with "smart quotation marks" that curl and face each other. It will replace ordinal numbers (1st, 2nd, or 3rd) with the corresponding superscripts (1st, 2nd, or 3rd), or common fractions (1/2 or 1/4) with typographical symbols (½ or ¼).

The AutoFormat command will also replace Internet references (Web addresses and e-mail addresses) with hyperlinks. It will recognize, for example, any entry beginning with http: or www. as a hyperlink and display the entry as underlined blue text (www.microsoft.com). This is not merely a change in formatting, but an actual hyperlink to a document on the Web or corporate Intranet. It also converts entries containing an @ sign, such as rgrauer@umiami.miami.edu to a hyperlink as well. All Office 97 documents are Web-enabled. Thus, clicking on a hyperlink or e-mail address within a Word document opens your Web browser or e-mail program, respectively.

The options for the AutoFormat command are controlled through the Auto-Correct command in the Tools menu as shown in Figure 4.7. Once the options have been set, all formatting is done automatically by selecting the AutoFormat command from the Format menu. The changes are not final, however, as the command gives you the opportunity to review each formatting change individually, then accept the change or reject it as appropriate. (You can also format text automatically as it is entered according to the options specified under the AutoFormat As You Type tab.)

AUTOMATIC BORDERS AND LISTS

The AutoFormat As You Type option applies sophisticated formatting as text is entered. It automatically creates a numbered list any time a number is followed by a period, tab, or right parenthesis (press enter twice in a row to turn off the feature). It will also add a border to a paragraph any time you type three or more hyphens, equal signs, or underscores followed by the enter key. Pull down the Tools menu, click Options, click the AutoFormat tab, then click the AutoFormat As You Type option button to select the desired features.

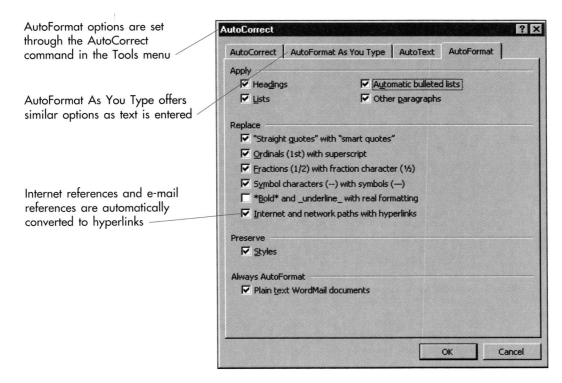

AutoFormat options are set through the AutoCorrect command in the Tools menu

AutoFormat As You Type offers similar options as text is entered

Internet references and e-mail references are automatically converted to hyperlinks

FIGURE 4.7 The AutoFormat Command

HANDS-ON EXERCISE 3

Styles

Objective: To use the AutoFormat command on an existing document; to modify existing styles; to create a new style. Use Figure 4.8 as a guide for the exercise.

STEP 1: Load the Practice Document

➤ Start Word. Pull down the **File menu.** Open the document **Tips for Word 97** from the Exploring Word folder. (This document contains 50 tips that appear throughout the text.)

➤ Pull down the **File menu** a second time. Save the document as **Modified Tips for Word 97** so that you can return to the original if necessary.

➤ If necessary, pull down the **View menu** and click **Normal** (or click the **Normal View button** above the status bar). Pull down the **View menu** a second time, click **Zoom,** click **Page Width,** and click **OK** (or click the **arrow** on the **Zoom Control box** on the Standard toolbar and select **Page Width**).

STEP 2: The AutoFormat Command

➤ Press **Ctrl+Home** to move to the beginning of the document. Pull down the **Format menu.** Click **AutoFormat** to display the AutoFormat dialog box in Figure 4.8a.

➤ Click the **Options command button** to display the AutoCorrect dialog box. Be sure that every check box is selected to implement the maximum amount of automatic formatting. Click **OK.**

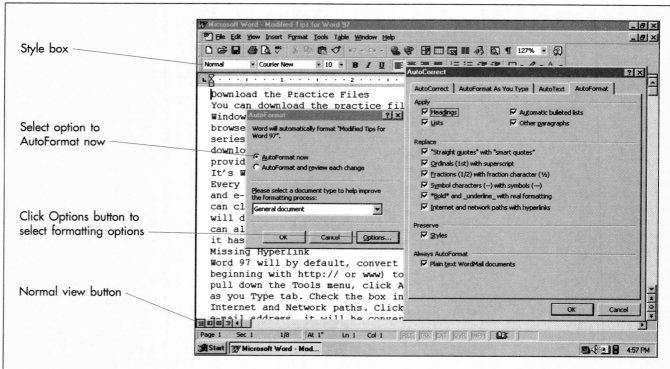

Style box

Select option to AutoFormat now

Click Options button to select formatting options

Normal view button

(a) AutoFormat Command (step 2)

FIGURE 4.8 Hands-on Exercise 3

> Click the **OK command button** in the AutoFormat dialog box to format the document. You will see a message at the left side of the status bar as the formatting is taking place, then you will see the newly formatted document.

> Save the document.

STEP 3: Style Assignments

> Click anywhere in the heading of the first tip. The Style box on the Formatting toolbar displays Heading 1 to indicate that this style has been applied to the title of the tip.

> Click anywhere in the text of the first tip (except on the hyperlink). The Style box on the Formatting toolbar displays Body Text to indicate that this style has been applied to the current paragraph.

> Click the title of any tip and you will see the Heading 1 style in the Style box. Click the text of any tip and you will see the Body Text style in the Style box.

STEP 4: Modify the Body Text Style

> Press **Ctrl+Home** to move to the beginning of the document. Click anywhere in the text of the first tip (except within the hyperlink).

> Pull down the **Format menu.** Click **Style.** The Body Text style is automatically selected, and its characteristics are displayed within the description box.

> Click the **Modify command button** to display the Modify Style dialog box in Figure 4.8b.

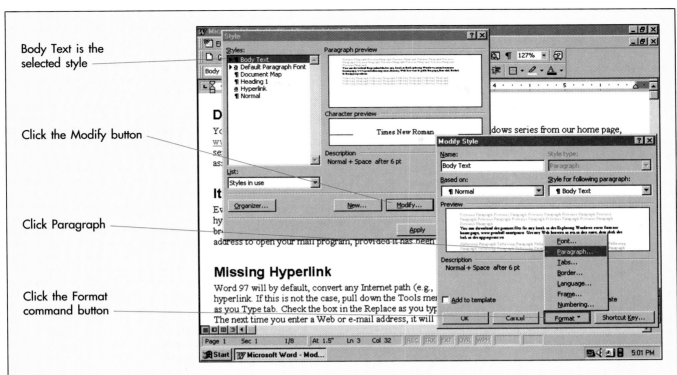

Body Text is the
selected style

Click the Modify button

Click Paragraph

Click the Format
command button

(b) Modify the Body Text Style (step 4)

FIGURE 4.8   Hands-on Exercise 3 (continued)

> Click the **Format command button.**
> - Click **Paragraph** to produce the Paragraph dialog box.
> - Click the **Indents and Spacing** tab.
> - Click the **arrow** on the **Alignment list box.** Click **Justified.**
> - Change the **Spacing After** to **12.**
> - Click the **Line and Page Breaks tab** on the Paragraph dialog box.
> - Click the **Keep Lines Together** check box so an individual tip will not be broken over two pages. Click **OK** to close the Paragraph dialog box.
> Click **OK** to close the Modify Style dialog box. Click the **Close command button** to return to the document.
> All paragraphs in the document change automatically to reflect the new definition of the Body Text style.

SPACE BEFORE AND AFTER

It's common practice to press the enter key twice at the end of a paragraph (once to end the paragraph, and a second time to insert a blank line before the next paragraph). The same effect can be achieved by setting the spacing before or after the paragraph using the Spacing Before or After list boxes in the Format Paragraph command. The latter technique gives you greater flexibility in that you can specify any amount of spacing (e.g., 6 points to leave only half a line) before or after a paragraph. It also enables you to change the spacing between paragraphs more easily because the information is stored within the paragraph style.

STEP 5: Review the Formatting

➤ Pull down the **Help menu** and click the **What's This command** (or press **Shift+F1**). The mouse pointer changes to a large question mark.

➤ Click in any paragraph to display the formatting in effect for that paragraph as shown in Figure 4.8c.

➤ You will see formatting specifications for the Body Text style (Indent: Left 0″, Justified, Space After 12 pt, Keep Lines Together, Font Times New Roman, 10pt, and English (US)).

➤ Click in any other paragraph to see the formatting in effect for that paragraph. Press **Esc** to return to normal editing.

Formatting in effect

Click in the paragraph to display formatting in effect

Pointer changes to large question mark

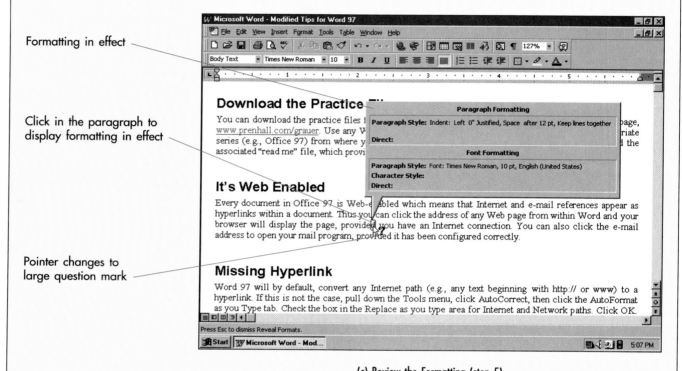

(c) Review the Formatting (step 5)

FIGURE 4.8   Hands-on Exercise 3 (continued)

STEP 6: Modify the Heading 1 Style

➤ Click anywhere in the title of the first tip. The Style box on the Formatting toolbar contains Heading 1 to indicate that this style has been applied to the current paragraph.

➤ Pull down the **Format menu.** Click **Style.** The Heading 1 style is automatically selected, and its characteristics are displayed within the description box.

➤ Click the **Modify command button** to display the Modify Style dialog box.

➤ Click the **Format command button.**

• Click **Paragraph** to display the Paragraph dialog box. Click the **Indents and Spacing tab.**

• Change the **Spacing After** to **0** (there should be no space separating the heading and the paragraph).

- Change the **Spacing Before** to **0** (since there are already 12 points after the Body Text style as per the settings in step 4). Click **OK.**
- Click the **Format command button** a second time.
- Click **Font** to display the Font dialog box.
- Click **10** in the Font size box. Click **OK.**

➤ Click **OK** to close the Modify Style dialog box. Click the **Close command button** to return to the document and view the changes.

➤ Save the document.

MODIFY STYLES BY EXAMPLE

The Modify command button in the Format Style command is one way to change a style, but it prevents the use of the toolbar buttons. Thus it's easier to modify an existing style by example. Select any text that is defined by the style you want to modify, then reformat that text using the Formatting toolbar, shortcut keys, or pull-down menus. Click the Style box on the Formatting toolbar, make sure the selected style is the correct one, press enter, then click OK when asked if you want to update the style to reflect recent changes.

STEP 7: The Outline View

➤ Pull down the **View menu** and click **Outline** (or click the **Outline view button** above the status bar) to display the document in the Outline view.

➤ Pull down the **Edit menu** and click **Select All** (or press **Ctrl+A**) to select the entire document. Click the **Collapse button** on the Outlining toolbar to collapse the entire document so that only the headings are visible.

➤ Click in the heading of the first tip (Download the Practice Files) as shown in Figure 4.7d. Click the **Expand button** on the Outlining toolbar to see the subordinate items under this heading.

➤ Experiment with the Collapse and Expand buttons to display different levels of information in the outline.

HELP WITH THE OUTLINING TOOLBAR

The Outlining toolbar is displayed automatically in the Outline view and suppressed otherwise. Press Shift+F1 to change the mouse pointer to a large arrow next to a question mark, then click any button on the Outlining toolbar to learn its function. You will find buttons to promote and demote items, to display or suppress formatting, and/or to collapse and expand the outline.

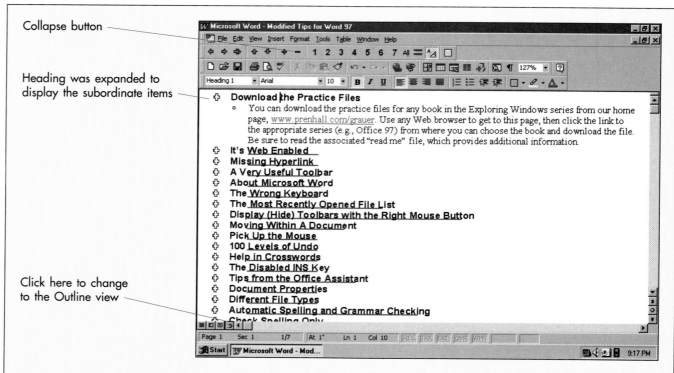

Collapse button

Heading was expanded to display the subordinate items

Click here to change to the Outline view

(d) The Outline View (step 7)

FIGURE 4.8   Hands-on Exercise 3 (continued)

STEP 8: Moving Text

➤ The advantage of the Outline view is that it facilitates moving text in a large document. You can move either an expanded or collapsed item, but the latter is generally easier as you see the overall structure of the document.

➤ Click the **down arrow** on the vertical scroll bar until you see the tip, **Create Your Own Shorthand.** Click and drag to select the tip as shown in Figure 4.7e.

➤ Point to the **plus sign** next to the selected tip (the mouse pointer changes to a double arrow), then click and drag to move the tip below the **Different File Types** as shown in Figure 4.7e. Release the mouse.

➤ Change back to the Page Layout view. Save the document.

THE DOCUMENT MAP

The Document Map is a new feature in Word 97 that helps you to navigate within a large document. Click the Document Map button on the Standard toolbar to divide the screen into two panes. The headings in a document are displayed in the left pane and the text of the document is visible in the right pane. To go to a specific point in a document, click its heading in the left pane, and the insertion point is moved automatically to that point in the document, which is visible in the right pane. Click the Map button a second time to turn the feature off.

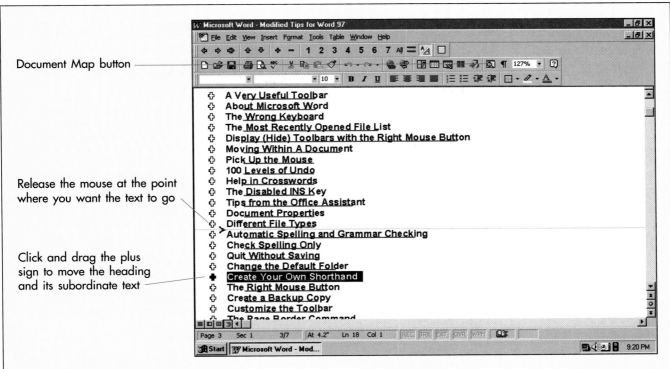

Document Map button

Release the mouse at the point where you want the text to go

Click and drag the plus sign to move the heading and its subordinate text

(e) Moving Text (step 8)

FIGURE 4.8   Hands-on Exercise 3 (continued)

STEP 9: Create a New Style

➤ Press **Ctrl+Home** to move to the beginning of the document. Press **Ctrl+enter** to create a page break for a title page.

➤ Move the insertion point on to the page break. Press the **enter key** five to ten times to move to an appropriate position for the title.

➤ Click the **Show/Hide ¶ button** on the Standard toolbar to display the non-printing characters. Select the paragraph marks, pull down the **Style list** on the Formatting toolbar, and click **Normal.**

➤ Deselect the paragraph marks to continue editing.

➤ Place the insertion point immediately to the left of the last hard return above the page break.

➤ Enter the title, **50 Tips in Microsoft Word,** and format it in 28 Point Arial Bold as shown in Figure 4.8f.

➤ Click the **Center button** on the Formatting toolbar.

➤ Check that the title is still selected, then click in the **Styles List box** on the Formatting toolbar. The style name, Normal, is selected.

➤ Type **My Style** (the name of the new style). Press **enter.** You have just created a new style that we will use in the next exercise.

➤ Save the document.

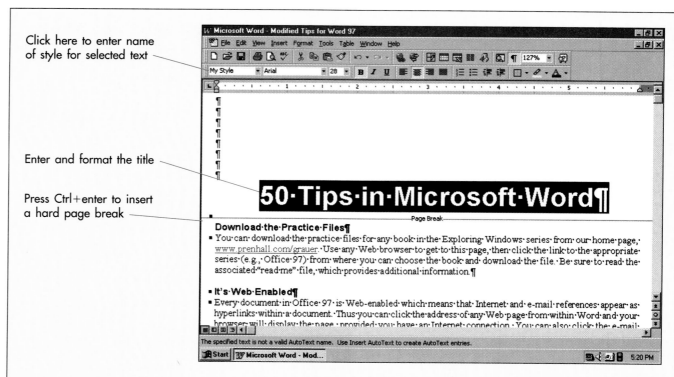

Click here to enter name of style for selected text

Enter and format the title

Press Ctrl+enter to insert a hard page break

(f) Create a New Style (step 9)

FIGURE 4.8   Hands-on Exercise 3 (continued)

STEP 10: Complete the Title Page

➤ Click the **Page Layout View button** above the status bar. Click the **arrow** on the **Zoom box** on the Standard toolbar. Click **Two Pages.**

➤ Scroll through the document to see the effects of your formatting.

➤ Press **Ctrl+Home** to return to the beginning of the document, then change to **Page Width** so that you can read what you are typing. Complete the title page as shown in Figure 4.8g.

➤ Click immediately to the left of the ¶ after the title. Press **enter** once or twice.

➤ Click the **arrow** on the **Font Size box** on the Formatting toolbar. Click **12.** Type **by Robert Grauer and Maryann Barber.** Press **enter.**

➤ Save the document. Exit Word if you do not want to continue with the next exercise at this time.

MORE FONTS

We have restricted our design to the Arial and Times New Roman fonts because they are supplied with Office 97 and hence are always available. In all likelihood, you will have several additional fonts available, in which case you can modify the fonts in the Heading 1 and/or Body Text styles to create a completely different design.

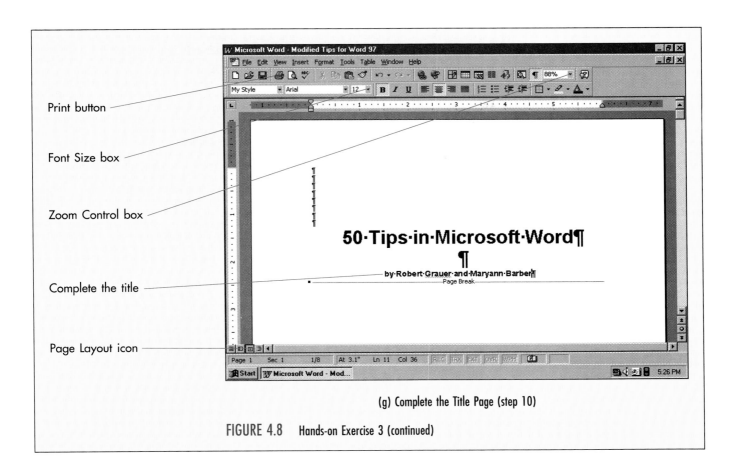

Print button

Font Size box

Zoom Control box

Complete the title

Page Layout icon

(g) Complete the Title Page (step 10)

FIGURE 4.8   Hands-on Exercise 3 (continued)

WORKING IN LONG DOCUMENTS

Long documents, such as term papers or reports, require additional formatting for better organization. These documents typically contain page numbers, headers and/or footers, and a table of contents. Each of these elements is discussed in turn and will be illustrated in a hands-on exercise.

Page Numbers

The **Insert Page Numbers command** is the easiest way to place *page numbers* into a document and is illustrated in Figure 4.9. The page numbers can appear at the top or bottom of a page, and can be left, centered, or right-aligned. Additional flexibility is provided as shown in Figure 4.9b; you can use Roman rather than Arabic numerals, and you need not start at page number one.

The Insert Page Number command is limited in two ways. It does not provide for additional text next to the page number, nor does it allow for alternating left and right placements on the odd and even pages of a document as in a book or newsletter. Both restrictions are overcome by creating a header or footer which contains the page number.

Headers and Footers

Headers and footers give a professional appearance to a document. A **header** consists of one or more lines that are printed at the top of every page. A **footer** is

Click to display available
positions for the page numbers

Click here to display available
alignments for the page numbers

Click here to format
the page numbers

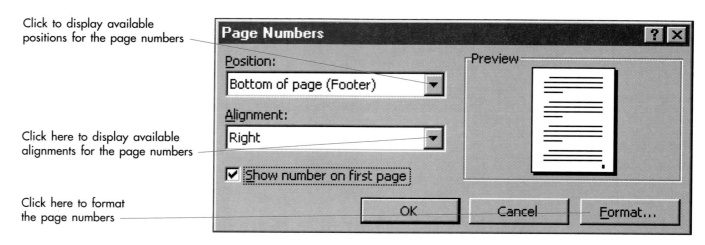

(a) Placement

Click to display available
formats for the page numbers

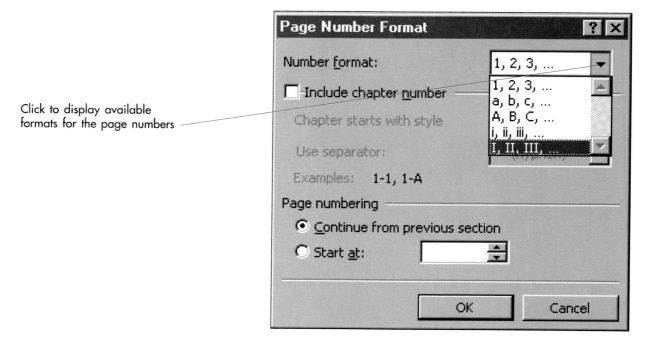

(b) Format

FIGURE 4.9   Page Numbers

printed at the bottom of the page. A document may contain headers but not footers, footers but not headers, or both headers and footers.

Headers and footers are created from the View menu. (A simple header or footer is also created automatically by the Insert Page Number command, depending on whether the page number is at the top or bottom of a page.) Headers and footers are formatted like any other paragraph and can be centered, left- or right-aligned. They can be formatted in any typeface or point size and can include special codes to automatically insert the page number, date, and/or time a document is printed.

The advantage of using a header or footer (over typing the text yourself at the top or bottom of every page) is that you type the text only once, after which it appears automatically according to your specifications. In addition, the placement of the headers and footers is adjusted for changes in page breaks caused by the insertion or deletion of text in the body of the document.

Headers and footers can change continually throughout a document. The Page Setup dialog box (in the File menu) enables you to specify a different header or footer for the first page, and/or different headers and footers for the odd and even pages. If, however, you wanted to change the header (or footer) midway through a document, you would need to insert a section break at the point where the new header (or footer) is to begin.

Sections

Formatting in Word occurs on three levels. You are already familiar with formatting at the character and paragraph levels that have been used throughout the text. Formatting at the section level controls headers and footers, page numbering, page size and orientation, margins, and columns. All of the documents in the text so far have consisted of a single *section,* and thus any section formatting applied to the entire document. You can, however, divide a document into sections and format each section independently.

Formatting at the section level may appear complicated initially, but it gives you the ability to create more sophisticated documents. You can use section formatting to:

> ➤ Change the margins within a multipage letter where the first page (the letterhead) requires a larger top margin than the other pages in the letter.

> ➤ Change the orientation from portrait to landscape to accommodate a wide table at the end of the document. (See practice exercise 2 at the end of the chapter.)

> ➤ Change the page numbering, for example to use Roman numerals at the beginning of the document for a table of contents and Arabic numerals thereafter.

> ➤ Change the number of columns in a newsletter, which may contain a single column at the top of a page for the masthead, then two or three columns in the body of the newsletter.

In all instances, you determine where one section ends and another begins by using the ***Insert menu*** to create a ***section break.*** You also have the option of deciding how the section break will be implemented on the printed page; that is, you can specify that the new section continue on the same page, that it begin on a new page, or that it begin on the next odd or even page even if a blank page has to be inserted.

Word stores the formatting characteristics of each section in the section break at the end of a section. Thus, deleting a section break also deletes the section formatting, causing the text above the break to assume the formatting characteristics of the next section.

Figure 4.10 displays a multipage view of a ten-page document. The document has been divided into two sections, and the insertion point is currently on the fourth page of the document (page four of ten), which is also the first page of the second section. Note the corresponding indications on the status bar and the position of the headers and footers throughout the document.

Figure 4.10 also displays the Headers and Footers toolbar, which contains various icons associated with these elements. As indicated, a header or footer may contain text and/or special codes—for example, the word "page" followed by a code for the page number. The latter is inserted into the header by clicking the appropriate button on the Headers and Footers toolbar.

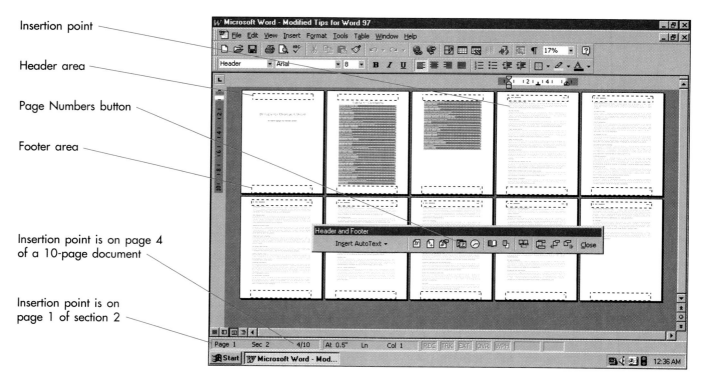

Insertion point

Header area

Page Numbers button

Footer area

Insertion point is on page 4
of a 10-page document

Insertion point is on
page 1 of section 2

FIGURE 4.10   Headers and Footers

THE SECTION VERSUS THE PARAGRAPH

Line spacing, alignment, tabs, and indents are implemented at the paragraph level. Change any of these parameters anywhere within the current (or selected) paragraph(s) and you change *only* those paragraph(s). Margins, headers and footers, page numbering, page size and orientation, and newspaper columns are implemented at the section level. Change these parameters anywhere within a section, and you change those characteristics for every page within that section.

Table of Contents

A *table of contents* lists headings in the order they appear in a document and the page numbers where the entries begin. Word will create the table of contents automatically, provided you have identified each heading in the document with a built-in heading style (Heading 1 through Heading 9). Word will also update the table automatically to accommodate the addition or deletion of headings and/or changes in page numbers brought about through changes in the document.

The table of contents is created through the ***Index and Tables command*** from the Insert menu as shown in Figure 4.11. You have your choice of several predefined formats and the number of levels within each format; the latter correspond to the heading styles used within the document. You can also choose the ***leader character*** and whether or not to right align the page numbers.

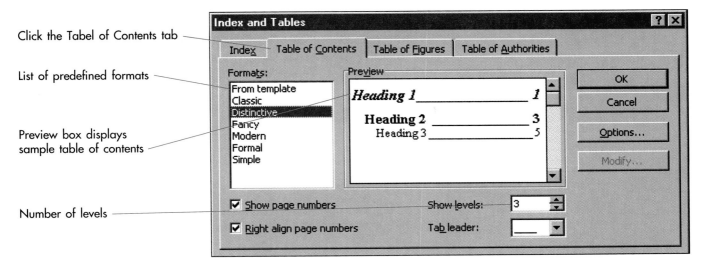

Click the Tabel of Contents tab

List of predefined formats

Preview box displays
sample table of contents

Number of levels

FIGURE 4.11   Index and Tables Command

The Go To Command

The *Go To command* moves the insertion point to the top of a designated page. The command is accessed from the Edit menu, or by pressing the F5 function key, or by double clicking the Page number on the status bar. After the command has been executed, you are presented with a dialog box in which you enter the desired page number. You can also specify a relative page number—for example, P+2 to move forward two pages, or P-1 to move back one page.

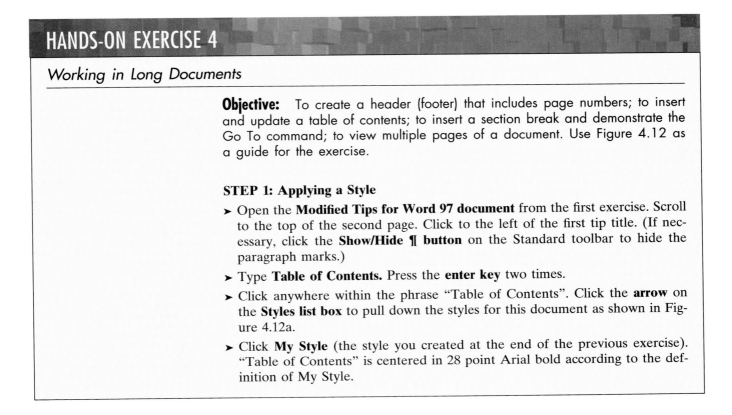

HANDS-ON EXERCISE 4

Working in Long Documents

Objective: To create a header (footer) that includes page numbers; to insert and update a table of contents; to insert a section break and demonstrate the Go To command; to view multiple pages of a document. Use Figure 4.12 as a guide for the exercise.

STEP 1: Applying a Style

➤ Open the **Modified Tips for Word 97 document** from the first exercise. Scroll to the top of the second page. Click to the left of the first tip title. (If necessary, click the **Show/Hide ¶ button** on the Standard toolbar to hide the paragraph marks.)

➤ Type **Table of Contents.** Press the **enter key** two times.

➤ Click anywhere within the phrase "Table of Contents". Click the **arrow** on the **Styles list box** to pull down the styles for this document as shown in Figure 4.12a.

➤ Click **My Style** (the style you created at the end of the previous exercise). "Table of Contents" is centered in 28 point Arial bold according to the definition of My Style.

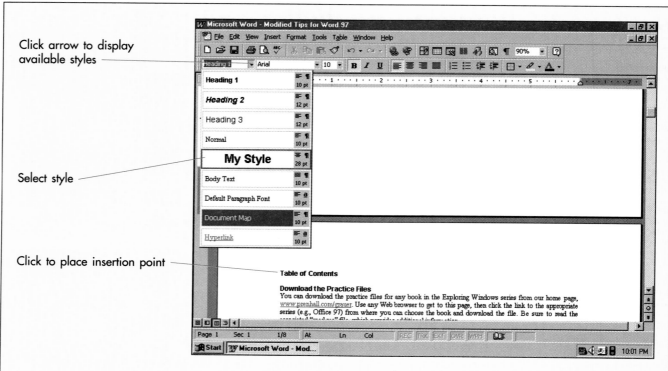

Click arrow to display available styles

Select style

Click to place insertion point

(a) Applying a Style (step 1)

FIGURE 4.12   Hands-on Exercise 4

STEP 2: View Many Pages

➤ Click the line immediately under the heading for the table of contents. Pull down the **View menu.** Click **Zoom** to display the dialog box in Figure 4.12b.

➤ Click the **monitor icon.** Click and drag the **page icons** to display two pages down by five pages across as shown in the figure. Release the mouse.

➤ Click **OK.** The display changes to show all eight pages in the document.

STEP 3: Create the Table of Contents

➤ Pull down the **Insert menu.** Click **Index and Tables.** If necessary, click the **Table of Contents tab** to display the dialog box in Figure 4.12c.

➤ Check the boxes to **Show Page Numbers** and to **Right Align Page Numbers.**

➤ Click **Distinctive** in the **Formats list box.** Click the **arrow** in the **Tab Leader list box.** Choose a dot leader. Click **OK.** Word takes a moment to create the table of contents, which extends to two pages.

AUTOFORMAT AND THE TABLE OF CONTENTS

Word will create a table of contents automatically, provided you use the built-in heading styles to define the items for inclusion. If you have not applied the heading styles to the document, the AutoFormat command will do it for you. Once the heading styles are in the document, pull down the Insert command, click Index and Tables, then click the Table of Contents command.

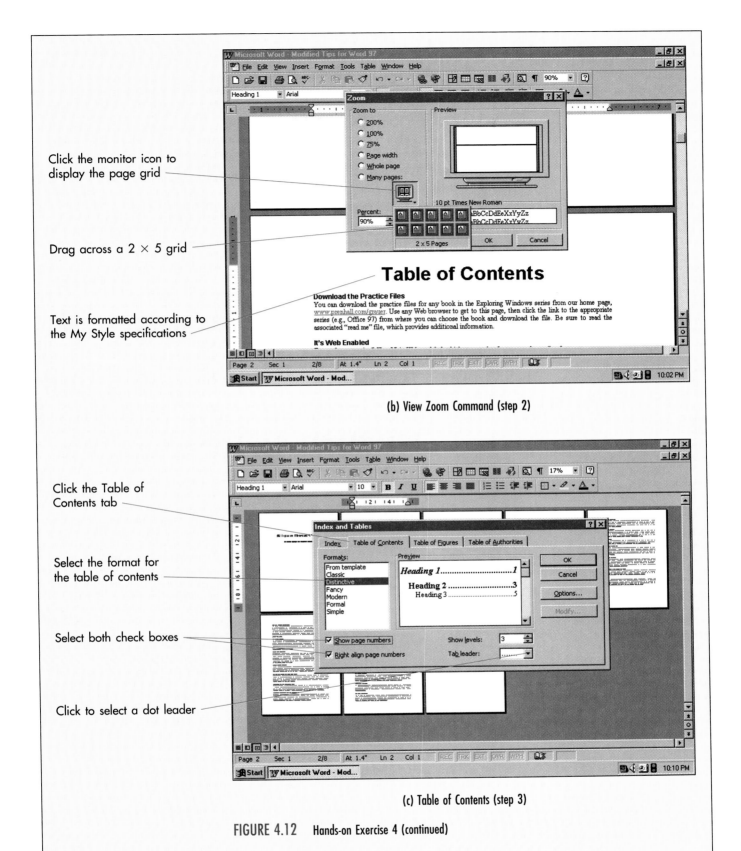

Click the monitor icon to display the page grid

Drag across a 2 × 5 grid

Text is formatted according to the My Style specifications

(b) View Zoom Command (step 2)

Click the Table of Contents tab

Select the format for the table of contents

Select both check boxes

Click to select a dot leader

(c) Table of Contents (step 3)

FIGURE 4.12   Hands-on Exercise 4 (continued)

STEP 4: Field Codes versus Field Text

➤ Click the **arrow** on the **Zoom Control box** on the Standard toolbar. Click **Page Width** in order to read the table of contents as in Figure 4.12d.

➤ Use the **up arrow key** to scroll to the beginning of the table of contents. Click in the first entry in the table of contents, then press **Shift+F9.** The entire table of contents is replaced by an entry similar to {TOC \o "1-3"} to indicate a field code; the exact code depends on your selections in step 4.

➤ Press **Shift+F9** a second time. The field code for the table of contents is replaced by text.

➤ Pull down the **Edit menu.** Click **Go To** to display the dialog box in Figure 4.12d.

➤ Type **3** and press the **enter key** to go to page 3, which contains the bottom portion of the table of contents. Click **Close.**

Zoom Control box ————

Click in the Table of Contents to select it ————

Enter 3 to move to page 3 ————

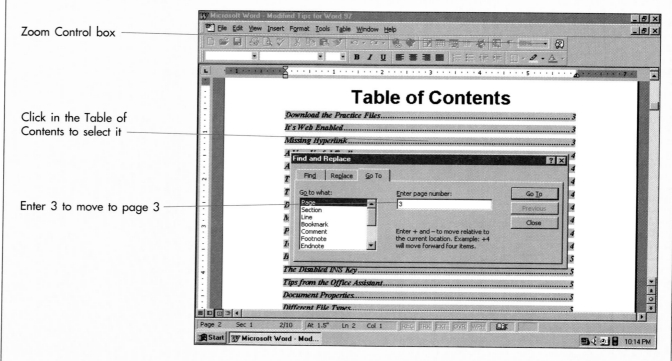

(d) Field Codes versus Field Text (step 4)

FIGURE 4.12   Hands-on Exercise 4 (continued)

THE GO TO AND GO BACK COMMANDS

The F5 key is the shortcut equivalent of the Edit Go To command and produces a dialog box to move to a specific location (a page or section) within a document. The Shift+F5 combination executes the Go Back command and returns to a previous location of the insertion point; press Shift+F5 repeatedly to cycle through the last three locations of the insertion point.

STEP 5: Insert a Section Break

➤ Scroll down page three until you are at the end of the table of contents. Click to the left of the first tip heading as shown in Figure 4.12e.

➤ Pull down the **Insert menu.** Click **Break** to display the Break dialog box. Click the **Next Page button** under Section Breaks. Click **OK** to create a section break, simultaneously forcing the first tip to begin on a new page.

➤ The status bar displays Page 1 Sec 2 to indicate you are on page one in the second section. (See the boxed tip on page numbering if the status bar indicates Page 4 Sec 2.) The entry 4/10 indicates that you are physically on the fourth page of a ten-page document.

Select a Next Page
section break

Click OK to insert
the section break

Insertion point is to the left
of the first tip heading

Double click to
go to this item

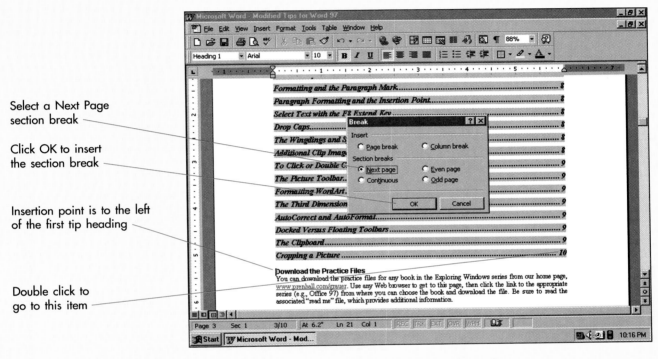

(e) Inserting a Section Break (step 5)

FIGURE 4.12   Hands-on Exercise 4 (continued)

SECTIONS AND PAGE NUMBERING

Word gives you the option of numbering pages consecutively from one section to the next, or alternatively, of starting each section from page one. To view (change) the page numbering options in effect, pull down the Insert menu, click Page Numbers, click the Format command button, then click the option button for the page numbering you want. To start each section at page one, click the Start At option button, type 1 as the beginning page number, then click OK.

MOVING WITHIN LONG DOCUMENTS

Double click the page indicator on the status bar to display the dialog box for the *Edit Go To command.* You can also double click a page number in the table of contents (created through the Index and Tables command in the Insert menu) to go directly to the associated entry.

STEP 6: Create the Header

➤ Pull down the **File menu.** Click **Page Setup.** If necessary, click the **Layout tab** to display the dialog box in Figure 4.12f.

➤ If necessary, clear the box for Different Odd and Even Pages and for Different First Page, as all pages in this section (section two) are to have the same header. Click **OK.**

Click the Layout tab

Clear these check boxes

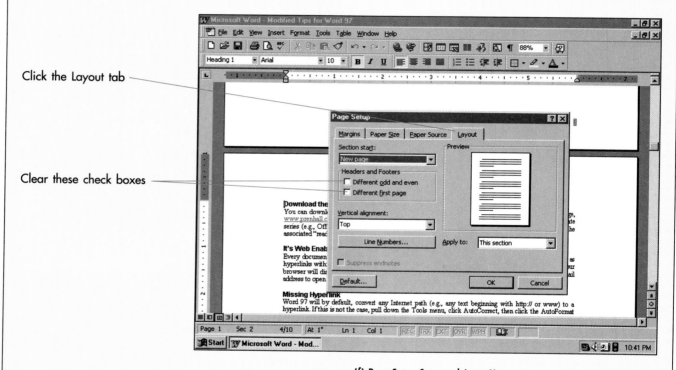

(f) Page Setup Command (step 6)

FIGURE 4.12   Hands-on Exercise 4 (continued)

HEADERS AND FOOTERS

If you do not see a header or footer, it is most likely because you are in the wrong view. Headers and footers are displayed in the Page Layout view but not in the Normal view. (Click the Page Layout button on the status bar to change the view.) Even in the Page Layout view the header (footer) is faded, indicating that it cannot be edited unless it is selected (opened) by double clicking.

STEP 7: Create the Header (continued)

➤ Pull down the **View menu.** Click **Header and Footer** to produce the screen in Figure 4.12g. The text in the document is faded to indicate that you are editing the header, as opposed to the document.

➤ The "Same as Previous" indicator is on since Word automatically uses the header from the previous section. Click the **Same as Previous button** on the Header and Footer toolbar to toggle the indicator off and to create a different header for this section. The indicator disappears from the header.

➤ If necessary, click in the header. Click the **arrow** on the **Font list box** on the Formatting toolbar. Click **Arial.** Click the **arrow** on the Font size box. Click **8.** Type **50 Tips In Microsoft Word.**

➤ Press the **Tab key** twice. Type **PAGE.** Press the **space bar.** Click the **Insert Page Number button** on the Header and Footer toolbar to insert a code for the page number.

➤ Click the **Close button.** The header is faded, and the document text is available for editing.

➤ Save the document.

Font list box

Enter header text

Close button

Same As Previous button

Insert Page Numbers button

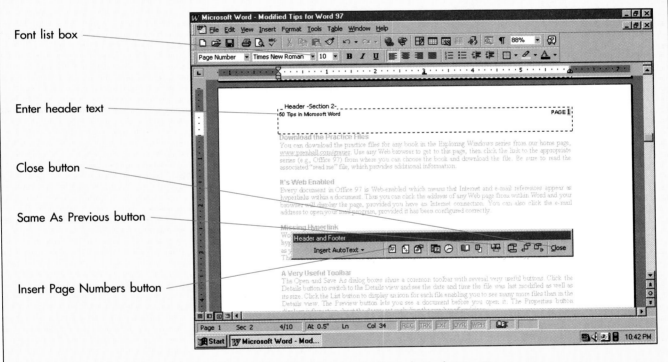

(g) Create the Header (step 7)

FIGURE 4.12   Hands-on Exercise 4 (continued)

STEP 8: Update the Table of Contents

➤ Press **Ctrl+Home** to move to the beginning of the document. The status bar indicates Page 1, Sec 1.

➤ Click the **Select Browse Object button** on the Vertical scroll bar, then click the **Browse by Page** icon.

➤ Click the **Next button** on the vertical scroll bar (or press **Ctrl+PgDn**) to move to the page containing the table of contents.

➤ Click in the table of contents. Press the **F9 key** to update the table of contents. If necessary, click the **Update Entire Table** button as shown in Figure 4.12h, then click **OK.**

➤ The pages are renumbered to reflect the actual page numbers in the second section.

Page numbers will change

Select Update entire table

Click the Select Browse Object button

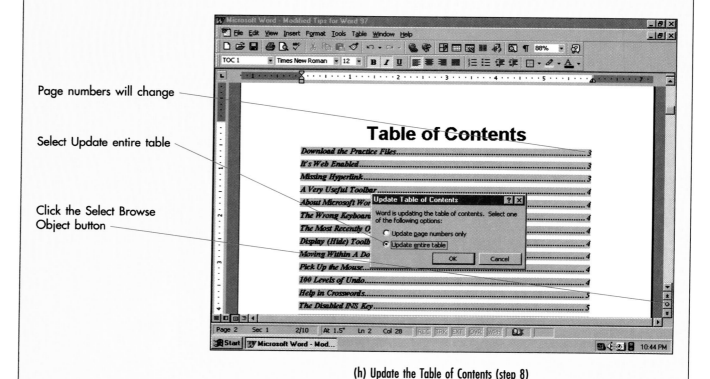

(h) Update the Table of Contents (step 8)

FIGURE 4.12   Hands-on Exercise 4 (continued)

SELECT BROWSE OBJECT

Click the Select Browse Object button toward the bottom of the vertical scroll bar to display a menu in which you specify how to browse through a document. Typically you browse from one page to the next, but you can browse by footnote, section, graphic, table, or any of the other objects listed. Once you select the object, click the Next or Previous buttons on the vertical scroll bar (or press Ctrl+PgDn or Ctrl+PgUp) to move to the next or previous occurrence of the selected object.

STEP 9: The Completed Document

➤ Pull down the **View menu.** Click **Zoom.** Click **Many Pages.** Click the **monitor icon.**

➤ Click and drag across the **page icons** to display two pages down by five pages. Release the mouse. Click **OK.**

➤ The completed document is shown in Figure 4.12i.

➤ Press **Ctrl+End** to move to the last page in the document.

➤ The status bar displays Page 7, Sec 2, 10/10 to indicate the seventh page in the second section, which is also the tenth page in the ten-page document.

➤ Save the document. Print the entire document. Exit Word.

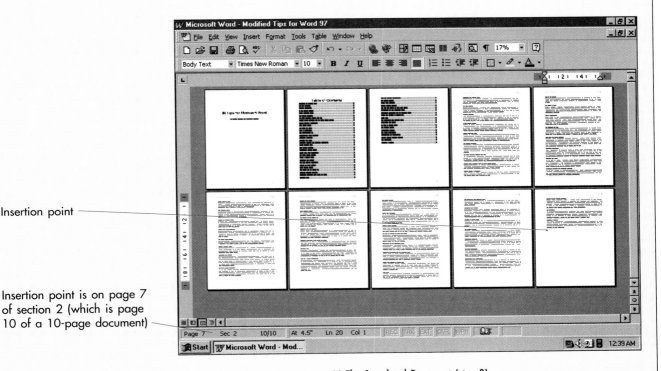

Insertion point

Insertion point is on page 7 of section 2 (which is page 10 of a 10-page document)

(i) The Completed Document (step 9)

FIGURE 4.12   Hands-on Exercise 4 (continued)

UPDATING THE TABLE OF CONTENTS

Use a shortcut menu to update the table of contents. Point anywhere in the table of contents, then press the right mouse button, to display a shortcut menu. Click Update Field, click the Update Entire Table command button, and click OK. The table of contents will be adjusted automatically to reflect page number changes as well as the addition or deletion of any items defined by any built-in heading style.

A list helps to organize information by emphasizing important topics. A bulleted or numbered list can be created by clicking the appropriate button on the Formatting toolbar or by executing the Bullets and Numbering command in the Format menu. An outline extends a numbered list to several levels.

Tables represent a very powerful capability within Word and are created through the Insert Table command in the Table menu or by using the Insert Table button on the Standard toolbar. Each cell in a table is formatted independently and may contain text, numbers, and/or graphics.

A style is a set of formatting instructions that has been saved under a distinct name. Styles are created at the character or paragraph level and provide a consistent appearance to similar elements throughout a document. Existing styles can be modified to change the formatting of all text defined by that style.

The Outline view displays a condensed view of a document based on styles within the document. Text may be collapsed or expanded as necessary to facilitate moving text within long documents.

The AutoFormat command analyzes a document and formats it for you. The command goes through an entire document, determines how each paragraph is used, then applies an appropriate style to each paragraph.

Formatting occurs at the character, paragraph, or section level. Section formatting controls margins, columns, page orientation and size, page numbering, and headers and footers. A header consists of one or more lines that are printed at the top of every (designated) page in a document. A footer is text that is printed at the bottom of designated pages. Page numbers may be added to either a header or footer.

A table of contents lists headings in the order they appear in a document with their respective page numbers. It can be created automatically, provided the built-in heading styles were previously applied to the items for inclusion. The Edit Go To command enables you to move directly to a specific page, section, or bookmark within a document.

KEY WORDS AND CONCEPTS

AutoFormat command
Body Text style
Bookmark
Bulleted list
Bullets and Numbering
  command
Cell
Character style
Default Paragraph Font
  style
Footer
Format Style command
Go To command

Header
Heading 1 style
Index and Tables
  command
Insert menu
Insert Page Numbers
  command
Insert Table command
Leader character
Multilevel numbered
  list
Normal style
Numbered list

Outline
Outline view
Page numbers
Paragraph style
Section
Section break
Style
Style command
Table menu
Table of contents
Tables feature

MULTIPLE CHOICE

1. Which of the following can be stored within a paragraph style?
   (a) Tabs and indents
   (b) Line spacing and alignment
   (c) Shading and borders
   (d) All of the above

2. What is the easiest way to change the alignment of five paragraphs scattered throughout a document, each of which has been formatted with the same style?
   (a) Select the paragraphs individually, then click the appropriate alignment button on the Formatting toolbar
   (b) Select the paragraphs at the same time, then click the appropriate alignment button on the Formatting toolbar
   (c) Change the format of the existing style, which changes the paragraphs
   (d) Retype the paragraphs according to the new specifications

3. The AutoFormat command will do all of the following except:
   (a) Apply styles to individual paragraphs
   (b) Apply boldface italics to terms that require additional emphasis
   (c) Replace ordinary quotes with smart quotes
   (d) Substitute typographic symbols for ordinary letters—such as © for (C)

4. Which of the following is used to create a conventional outline?
   (a) The Bullets and Numbering command
   (b) The Outline view
   (c) Both (a) and (b)
   (d) Neither (a) nor (b)

5. In which view do you see headers and/or footers?
   (a) Page Layout view
   (b) Normal view
   (c) Both (a) and (b)
   (d) Neither (a) nor (b)

6. Which of the following numbering schemes can be used with page numbers?
   (a) Roman numerals (I, II, III . . . or i, ii, iii)
   (b) Regular numbers (1, 2, 3, . . .)
   (c) Letters (A, B, C . . . or a, b, c)
   (d) All of the above

7. Which of the following is true regarding headers and footers?
   (a) Every document must have at least one header
   (b) Every document must have at least one footer
   (c) Both (a) and (b)
   (d) Neither (a) nor (b)

8. Which of the following is a *false* statement regarding lists?
   (a) A bulleted list can be changed to a numbered list and vice versa
   (b) The symbol for the bulleted list can be changed to a different character
   (c) The numbers in a numbered list can be changed to letters or roman numerals
   (d) The bullets or numbers cannot be removed

9. Page numbers can be specified in:
   (a) A header but not a footer
   (b) A footer but not a header
   (c) A header or a footer
   (d) Neither a header nor a footer

10. Which of the following is true regarding the formatting within a document?
    (a) Line spacing and alignment are implemented at the section level
    (b) Margins, headers, and footers are implemented at the paragraph level
    (c) Both (a) and (b)
    (d) Neither (a) nor (b)

11. What happens when you press the Tab key from within a table?
    (a) A Tab character is inserted just as it would be for ordinary text
    (b) The insertion point moves to the next column in the same row or the first column in the next row if you are at the end of the row
    (c) Both (a) and (b)
    (d) Neither (a) nor (b)

12. Which of the following is true, given that the status bar displays Page 1, Section 3, followed by 7/9?
    (a) The document has a maximum of three sections
    (b) The third section begins on page 7
    (c) The insertion point is on the very first page of the document
    (d) All of the above

13. The Edit Go To command enables you to move the insertion point to:
    (a) A specific page
    (b) A relative page forward or backward from the current page
    (c) A specific section
    (d) Any of the above

14. Once a table of contents has been created and inserted into a document:
    (a) Any subsequent page changes arising from the insertion or deletion of text to existing paragraphs must be entered manually
    (b) Any additions to the entries in the table arising due to the insertion of new paragraphs defined by a heading style must be entered manually
    (c) Both (a) and (b)
    (d) Neither (a) nor (b)

15. Which of the following is *false* about the Outline view?
    (a) It can be collapsed to display only headings
    (b) It can be expanded to show the entire document
    (c) It requires the application of styles
    (d) It is used to create a conventional outline

ANSWERS

1. d	**6.** d	**11.** b
2. c	**7.** d	**12.** b
3. b	**8.** d	**13.** d
4. a	**9.** c	**14.** d
5. a	**10.** d	**15.** d

PRACTICE WITH MICROSOFT WORD

1. Use your favorite search engine to locate the text of the United States Constitution. There are many available sites and associated documents, one of which is displayed in Figure 4.13. We erased the address, however; otherwise the problem would be too easy. Once you locate the text of the Constitution, expand the outline created in the first hands-on exercise to include information about the other provisions of the Constitution (Articles IV through VII, the Bill of Rights, and the other amendments). Submit the completed outline to your professor as proof you did this exercise.

2. Sections and Page Orientation: Formatting in Word takes place at the character, paragraph, or section level. The latter controls the margins and page orientation within a document and is illustrated in Figure 4.14. Create the study schedule as described in the second hands-on exercise, then insert a title page in front of the table. Note, however, that the title page and table must appear in different sections so that you can use the portrait and landscape orientations, respectively. Print the two-page document, consisting of the title page and table, and submit it to your instructor.

3. For the health conscious: Figure 4.15 displays the first five tips in a document describing tips for healthier living. Retrieve the document *Chapter 4 Practice 3* from the Exploring Word folder, then modify it as follows:

   a. Use the AutoFormat command to apply the Heading 1 and Body Text styles throughout the document.

   b. Change the specifications for the Body Text and Heading 1 styles so that your document matches the document in the figure. The Heading 1 style calls for 12 point Arial bold with a blue top border (which requires a color printer). The Body Text style is 12 point Times New Roman, justified, with a ¼ inch left indent.

   c. Create a title page for the document consisting of the title, *Tips for Healthy Living,* the author, *Marion B. Grauer,* and an additional line, indicating that the document was prepared for you.

   d. Create a header for the document consisting of the title, *Tips for Healthy Living,* and a page number. The header is not to appear on the title page.

4. Sports fans: The tables feature is perfect to display the standings of any league, be it amateur or professional. Figure 4.16, for example, shows standings in baseball and was a breeze. Pick any sport or league that you like and create a table with the standings as of today. You can use a newspaper, but it's more fun to use the Web.

   Use Figure 4.16 as a guide, but feel free to improve on our design, perhaps through the inclusion of clip art. Color is a nice touch, but it is definitely not required. White text on a black background is also very effective. Experiment freely, but set a time limit for yourself.

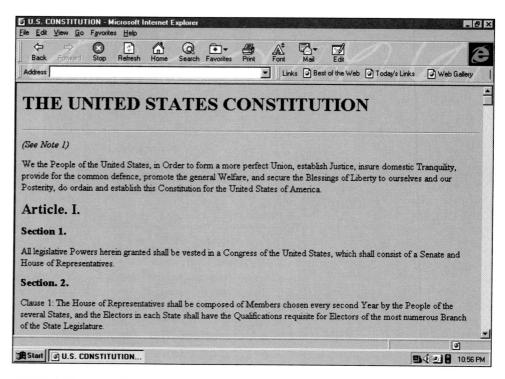

FIGURE 4.13 Screen for Practice Exercise 1

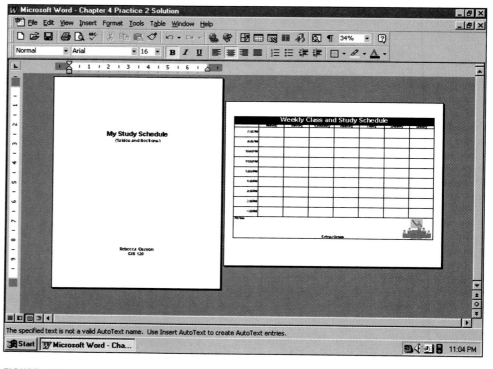

FIGURE 4.14 Screen for Practice Exercise 2

Start a Diet Journal

Keep a daily record of your weight and the foods you've eaten. Study your journal to become aware of your eating behavior. It will tell you when you're eating too much or if you're eating the wrong foods.

Why Do You Want to Lose Weight?

Write a list of reasons in your diet journal and refer to it often to sustain your motivation. Good health, good looks, more self-confidence, and new romantic possibilities are only the beginning.

Fighting Fatigue

Paradoxically, the more you do, the less tired you'll feel. Regular balanced exercise will speed up your metabolism, burn calories more efficiently, raise your energy level, and lift your spirits.

You Are What You Eat

Foods laden with fat, salt, and sugar leave you feeling lethargic and depressed. They set you up for more overeating. A nutritious low-fat diet has the opposite effect. You feel energized, revitalized, and happier.

"Water is the only drink for a wise man." —Thoreau

Water is the perfect weight-loss beverage. It fills your stomach, curbs your appetite, and cleanses your entire system. Add a twist of lemon or lime to improve the taste, and drink eight glasses every day.

FIGURE 4.15   Document for Practice Exercise 3

American League
Standings as of May 2, 1997

East	Wins	Losses	Percent
Baltimore Orioles	17	7	.708
Boston Red Sox	13	12	.520
New York Yankees	14	13	.519
Toronto Blue Jays	11	13	.458
Detroit Tigers	11	16	.407
Central	**Wins**	**Losses**	**Percent**
Milwaukee Brewers	12	11	.522
Cleveland Indians	13	13	.500
Kansas City Royals	12	12	.500
Minnesota Twins	11	16	.407
Chicago White Sox	8	17	.320
West	**Wins**	**Losses**	**Percent**
Seattle Mariners	16	11	.593
Texas Rangers	14	10	.583
California Angels	12	12	.500
Oakland A's	13	14	.481

FIGURE 4.16   Document for Practice Exercise 4

5. Form design: The tables feature is ideal to create forms as shown by the document in Figure 4.17, which displays an employment application. Reproduce the document shown in the figure or design your own application. Submit the completed document to your instructor.

Computer Consultants, Inc.
Employee Application Form

Last Name:	First Name:	Middle Name:

Address:

City:	State:	Zip Code:	Telephone:

Date of Birth:	Place of Birth:	Citizenship:

Highest Degree Attained:
   High School Diploma
   Bachelor's Degree
   Master's Degree
   Ph.D.
	List Schools Attended (include years attended):

List Specific Computer Skills:

List Relevant Computer Experience:

References (list name, title, and current mailing address):

1.

2.

3.

FIGURE 4.17   Document for Practice Exercise 5

6. Graphics: A table may contain anything—text, graphics, or numbers as shown by the document in Figure 4.18, which displays a hypothetical computer advertisement. It's not complicated; in fact, it was really very easy; just follow the steps below:

   a. Create a 7 × 4 table.

   b. Merge all of the cells in row one and enter the heading. Merge all of the cells in row two and type the text describing the sale.

   c. Use the Clip Gallery to insert a picture into the table. (Various computer graphics are available in the Business and Technology categories.)

   d. Enter the sales data in rows three through seven of the table; all entries are centered within the respective cells.

   e. Change the font, colors, and formatting, then print the completed document. Use any format you think is appropriate.

Of course, it isn't quite as simple as it sounds, but we think you get the idea. Good luck and feel free to improve on our design. Color is a nice touch, but it is definitely not required. You might also make your table more realistic by going to the Web and searching for current prices and configurations. Go to the Exploring Windows home page (www.prenhall.com/grauer), click on Additional Resources, then click the link to PC Buying Guide as one source of information.

Computers To Go

Our tremendous sales volume enables us to offer the fastest, most powerful series of Pentium and Pentium Pro computers at prices almost too good to be true. Each microprocessor is offered in a variety of configurations so that you get exactly what you need. All configurations include a local bus video, a 17-inch monitor, a mouse, and Windows 95.

Capacity	Configuration 1 16 Mb RAM 1.6 Gb Hard Drive	Configuration 2 32 Mb RAM 2.5 Gb Hard Drive	Configuration 3 64 Mb RAM 4 Gb Hard Drive
Pentium w/MMX – 166 MHz	$1,599	$2,199	$3,099
Pentium w/MMX – 200 MHz	$1,799	$2,399	$3,299
Pentium Pro – 180 MHz	$1,999	$2,599	$3,499
Pentium Pro – 200 MHz	$2,199	$2,799	$3,699

FIGURE 4.18   Document for Practice Exercise 6

Milestones in Communications

We take for granted immediate news of everything that is going on in the world, but it was not always that way. Did you know, for example, that it took five months for Queen Isabella to hear of Columbus' discovery, or that it took two weeks for Europe to learn of Lincoln's assassination? We've done some research on milestones in communications and left the file for you (Milestones in Communications). It runs for two, three, or four pages, depending on the formatting, which we leave to you. We would like you to include a header, and we think you should box the quotations that appear at the end of the document (it's your call as to whether to separate the quotations or group them together). Please be sure to number the completed document and don't forget a title page.

The Term Paper

Go to your most demanding professor and obtain the formatting requirements for the submission of a term paper. Be as precise as possible; for example, ask about margins, type size, and so on. What are the requirements for a title page? Is there a table of contents? Are there footnotes or endnotes, headers or footers? What is the format for the bibliography? Summarize the requirements, then indicate the precise means of implementation within Microsoft Word.

Tips for Windows 95

Open the *Tips for Windows 95* document that can be found in the Exploring Windows folder. The tips are not formatted so we would like you to use the Auto-Format command to create an attractive document. There are lots of tips so a table of contents is also appropriate. Add a cover page with your name and date, then submit the completed document to your instructor.

Word Outlines and PowerPoint Presentations

A Word document can be the basis of a PowerPoint presentation, provided the document has been formatted to include styles. Each paragraph formatted according to the Heading 1 style becomes the title of a slide, each paragraph formatted with the Heading 2 style becomes the first level of text, and so on.

Use the *Milestones in Communications* document in the Exploring Word folder as the basis of a PowerPoint presentation (see the first case study). Use the AutoFormat command to apply the necessary styles, pull down the File menu, select the Send To command, then choose Microsoft PowerPoint. Your system will start PowerPoint, then convert the styles in the Word document to a PowerPoint outline. Complete the presentation based on facts in the Word document, then submit the completed presentation to your instructor.

DESKTOP PUBLISHING: CREATING A NEWSLETTER

After reading this chapter you will be able to:

1. Design and implement a multicolumn newsletter; explain how sections are used to vary the number of columns in a document.
2. Describe one advantage and one disadvantage of using the Newsletter Wizard as opposed to creating a newsletter from scratch.
3. Define a pull quote and a reverse; explain how to implement these features using Microsoft Word.
4. Use the Borders and Shading command to emphasize a selected article.
5. Define typography; explain how styles can be used to implement changes in typography throughout a document.
6. Use the Insert Picture command to insert clip art into a document; explain how the Format Picture command is used to move and size a graphic.
7. Discuss the importance of a grid in the design of a document; describe the use of white space as a design element.

OVERVIEW

Desktop publishing evolved through a combination of technologies including faster computers, laser printers, and sophisticated page composition software to manipulate text and graphics. Desktop publishing was initially considered a separate application, but today's generation of word processors has matured to such a degree, that it is difficult to tell where word processing ends and desktop publishing begins. Microsoft Word is, for all practical purposes, a desktop publishing program that can be used to create all types of documents.

205

The essence of *desktop publishing* is the merger of text with graphics to produce a professional-looking document without reliance on external services. Desktop publishing will save you time and money because you are doing the work yourself rather than sending it out as you did in traditional publishing. That is the good news. The bad news is that desktop publishing is not as easy as it sounds, precisely because you are doing work that was done previously by skilled professionals. Nevertheless, with a little practice, and a basic knowledge of graphic design, which we include in this chapter, you will be able to create effective and attractive documents.

Our discussion focuses on desktop publishing as it is implemented in Microsoft Word. We show you how to design a multicolumn document, how to import clip art and other objects, and how to position those objects within a document. The chapter also reviews material from earlier chapters on bullets and lists, borders and shading, and section formatting, all of which will be used to create a newsletter.

THE NEWSLETTER

The chapter is built around the newsletter in Figure 5.1. The newsletter itself describes the basics of desktop publishing and provides an overview of the chapter. The material is presented conceptually, after which you implement the design in two hands-on exercises. We provide the text and you do the formatting. The first exercise creates a simple newsletter from copy that we provide. The second exercise uses more sophisticated formatting as described by the various techniques mentioned within the newsletter. Many of the terms are new, and we define them briefly in the next few paragraphs.

A *reverse* (light text on a dark background) is a favorite technique of desktop publishers to emphasize a specific element. It is used in the *masthead* (the identifying information) at the top of the newsletter and provides a distinctive look to the publication. The number of the newsletter and the date of publication also appear in the masthead in smaller letters.

A *pull quote* is a phrase or sentence taken from an article to emphasize a key point. It is typically set in larger type, often in a different typeface and/or italics, and may be offset with parallel lines at the top and bottom.

A *dropped-capital letter* is a large capital letter at the beginning of a paragraph. It, too, catches the reader's eye and calls attention to the associated text.

Clip art, used in moderation, will catch the reader's eye and enhance almost any newsletter. It is available from a variety of sources including the *Microsoft Clip Gallery,* which is included in Office 97. Clip art can also be downloaded from the Web, but be sure you are allowed to reprint the image.

Borders and shading are effective individually, or in combination with one another, to emphasize important stories within the newsletter. Simple vertical and/or horizontal lines are also effective. The techniques are especially useful in the absence of clip art or other graphics and are a favorite of desktop publishers.

Lists, whether bulleted or numbered, help to organize information by emphasizing important topics. A *bulleted list* emphasizes (and separates) the items. A *numbered list* sequences (and prioritizes) the items and is automatically updated to accommodate additions or deletions.

All of these techniques can be implemented with commands you already know, as you will see in the hands-on exercise, which follows shortly.

Creating a Newsletter

Volume I, Number 1   Spring 1997

Desktop publishing is easy, but there are several points to remember. This chapter will take you through the steps in creating a newsletter. The first hands-on exercise creates a simple newsletter with a masthead and three-column design. The second exercise creates a more attractive document by exploring different ways to emphasize the text.

Clip Art and Other Objects

Clip art is available from a variety of sources. You can also use other types of objects such as maps, charts, or organization charts, which are created by other applications, then brought into a document through the Insert Object command. A single dominant graphic is usually more appealing than multiple smaller graphics.

Techniques to Consider

Our finished newsletter contains one or more examples of each of the following desktop publishing techniques. Can you find where each technique is used, and further, explain, how to implement that technique in Microsoft Word?
1. Pull Quotes
2. Reverse
3. Drop Caps
4. Tables
5. Styles
6. Bullets and Numbering
7. Borders and Shading

Newspaper-Style Columns

The essence of a newsletter is the implementation of columns in which text flows continuously from the bottom of one column to the top of the next. You specify the number of columns, and optionally, the space between columns. Microsoft Word does the rest. It will compute the width of each column based on the number of columns and the margins.

Beginners often specify margins that are too large and implement too much space between the columns. Another way to achieve a more sophisticated look is to avoid the standard two-column design. You can implement columns of varying width and/or insert vertical lines between the columns.

The number of columns will vary in different parts of a document. The masthead is typically a single column, but the body of the newsletter will have two or three. Remember, too, that columns are implemented at the section level and hence, section breaks are required throughout a document.

Typography

Typography is the process of selecting typefaces, type styles, and type sizes, and is a critical element in the success of any document. Type should reinforce the message and should be consistent with the information you want to convey. More is not better, especially in the case of too many typefaces and styles, which produce cluttered documents that impress no one. Try to limit yourself to a maximum of two typefaces per document, but choose multiple sizes and/or styles within those typefaces. Use boldface or italics for emphasis, but do so in moderation, because if you use too many different elements, the effect is lost.

A pull quote adds interest to a document while simultaneously emphasizing a key point. It is implemented by increasing the point size, changing to italics, centering the text, and displaying a top and bottom border on the paragraph.

Use Styles as Appropriate

Styles were covered in the previous chapter, but that does not mean you cannot use them in conjunction with a newsletter. A style stores character and/or paragraph formatting and can be applied to multiple occurrences of the same element within a document. Change the style and you automatically change all text defined by that style. You can also use styles from one edition of your newsletter to the next to ensure consistency.

Borders and Shading

Borders and shading are effective individually or in combination with one another. Use a thin rule (one point or less) and light shading (five or ten percent) for best results. The techniques are especially useful in the absence of clip art or other graphics and are a favorite of desktop publishers.

FIGURE 5.1   The Newsletter

Typography

Typography is the process of selecting typefaces, type styles, and type sizes, and it is a critical, often subtle, element in the success of a document. Good typography goes almost unnoticed, whereas poor typography calls attention to itself and detracts from a document. Our discussion uses basic terminology, which we review below.

A *typeface* (or *font*) is a complete set of characters (upper- and lowercase letters, numbers, punctuation marks, and special symbols). Typefaces are divided into two general categories, serif and sans serif. A *serif typeface* has tiny cross lines at the ends of the characters to help the eye connect one letter with the next. A *sans serif typeface* (sans from the French for *without*) does not have these lines. A commonly accepted practice is to use serif typefaces with large amounts of text and sans serif typefaces for smaller amounts. The newsletter in Figure 5.1, for example, uses *Times New Roman* (a serif typeface) for the text and *Arial* (a sans serif typeface) for the headings.

Type size is a vertical measurement and is specified in points. One *point* is equal to $\frac{1}{72}$ of an inch. The text in most documents is set in 10- or 12-point type. (The book you are reading is set in 10-point.) Different elements in the same document are often set in different type sizes to provide suitable emphasis. A variation of at least two points, however, is necessary for the difference to be noticeable. The headings in the newsletter, for example, were set in 12-point type, whereas the text of the articles is in 10-point type.

The introduction of columns into a document poses another concern in that the type size should be consistent with the width of a column. Nine-point type, for example, is appropriate in columns that are two inches wide, but much too small in a single-column term paper. In other words, longer lines or wider columns require larger type sizes. Conversely, the shorter the line or narrower the column, the smaller the point size. A related rule is to avoid very narrow columns (less than two inches) because narrow columns are choppy and difficult to read. Overly wide columns or very long lines are just as bad because the reader can easily get lost.

We reiterate that there are no hard and fast rules for the selection of type, only guidelines and common sense. You will find that the design that worked so well in one document may not work at all in a different document. Indeed, good typography is often the result of trial and error, and we encourage you to experiment freely.

TYPOGRAPHY TIP: USE RESTRAINT

More is not better, especially in the case of too many typefaces and styles, which produce cluttered documents that impress no one. Try to limit yourself to a maximum of two typefaces per document, but choose multiple sizes and/or styles within those typefaces. Use boldface or italics for emphasis, but do so in moderation, because if you emphasize too many elements the effect is lost.

The Columns Command

The columnar formatting in a newsletter is implemented through the *Columns command* as shown in Figure 5.2. Start by selecting one of the preset designs and Microsoft Word takes care of everything else. It calculates the width of each col-

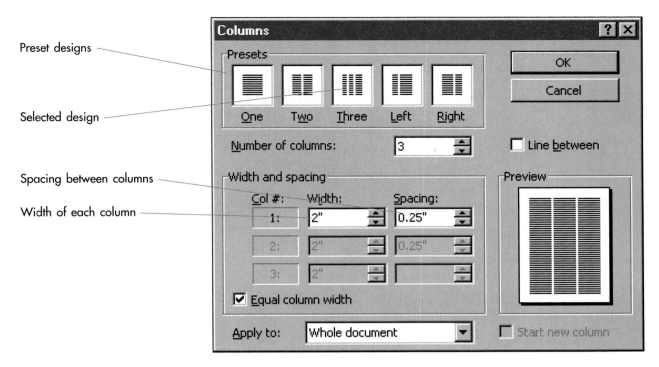

Preset designs

Selected design

Spacing between columns

Width of each column

FIGURE 5.2   The Columns Command

umn based on the number of columns, the left and right margins on the page, and the specified (default) space between columns.

Consider, for example, the dialog box in Figure 5.2 in which the preset design of three equal columns is selected with a spacing of ¼ inch between each column. The 2-inch width of each column is computed automatically based on left and right margins of 1 inch each and the ¼-inch spacing between columns. The width of each column is computed by subtracting the sum of the margins and the space between the columns (a total of 2½ inches in this example) from the page width of 8½ inches. The result of the subtraction is 6 inches, which is divided by 3, resulting in a column width of 2 inches.

You can change any of the settings in the Columns dialog box and Word will automatically make the necessary adjustments. The newsletter in Figure 5.1, for example, uses a two-column layout with wide and narrow columns. We prefer this design to columns of uniform width, as we think it adds interest to our document. Note, too, that once columns have been defined, text will flow continuously from the bottom of one column to the top of the next

Return for a minute to the newsletter in Figure 5.1, and notice that the number of columns varies from one part of the newsletter to another. The masthead is displayed over a single column at the top of the page, whereas the remainder of the newsletter is formatted in two columns of different widths. The number of columns is specified at the section level, and thus a **section break** is required whenever the column specification changes. (Section formatting was described in the previous chapter in conjunction with changing margins, headers and footers, page numbering, size, and orientation.)

THE NEWSLETTER WIZARD

At first glance the **Newsletter Wizard** appears to answer the prayers of the would-be desktop publisher. The Newsletter Wizard asks you a series of questions as shown in Figure 5.3, then creates a template for you on which to base a document.

(a) The Newsletter Wizard

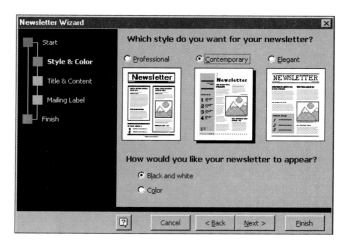

(b) Choose the Style and Color

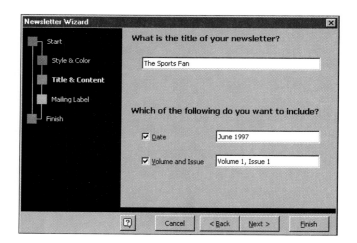

(c) Choose the Title

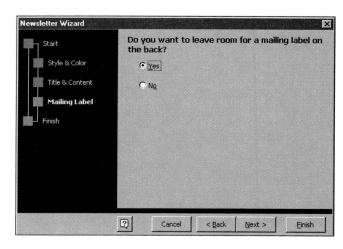

(d) Specify a Mailing Label

(e) The Completed Template

FIGURE 5.3   The Newsletter Wizard

The Newsletter Wizard provides a considerable amount of flexibility, as can be inferred from the screens in Figure 5.3a, b, c, and d, which let you specify the style, number of columns, title, and elements to include. The resulting template in Figure 5.3e is based on your answers, and further, incorporates good typography and other elements of graphic design.

What, then, is the drawback, and why would you not use the Newsletter Wizard for every newsletter you create? The problem is one of adaptability in that the wizard may not be suitable for the newsletter you wish to create. What if you wanted to include two graphics rather than one, or you wanted the graphics in a different position? What if you needed a newsletter with columns of varying width or you wanted to include a pull quote or a reverse?

You could, of course, use the template created by the wizard as the starting point for the newsletter, then execute the necessary commands in Word to modify the document according to your specifications. You will find, however, that it is just as easy to create the newsletter from the beginning and bypass the wizard entirely. You will wind up with a superior document that is exactly what you need, not what the wizard thinks you need. Creating a newsletter is a lot easier than you might imagine, as you will see in the following hands-on exercise.

HANDS-ON EXERCISE 1

Newspaper Columns

Objective: To create a basic newsletter through the Format columns command; to use section breaks to change the number of columns within a document. Use Figure 5.4 as a guide in the exercise.

STEP 1: The Page Setup Command

➤ Start Word. Open the **Text for Newsletter document** in the Exploring Word folder. Save the document as **Modified Newsletter** so that you can return to the original document if necessary.

➤ Pull down the **File menu.** Click **Page Setup** to display the Page Setup dialog box in Figure 5.4a. Change the top, bottom, left, and right margins to .75 as shown in the figure. (Press the **Tab key** to move from one text box to another.)

➤ Click **OK** to accept these settings and close the Page Setup dialog box. If necessary, click the **Page Layout View button** above the status bar. Set the magnification (zoom) to **Page Width.**

CHANGE THE MARGINS

The default margins of 1 inch at the top and bottom of a page, and 1¼ inches on the sides, are fine for a typical document. A multicolumn newsletter, however, looks better with smaller margins, which in turn enables you to create wider columns. Margins are defined at the section level, and hence it's easiest to change the margins at the very beginning, when a document consists of only a single section.

Change margins to .75"

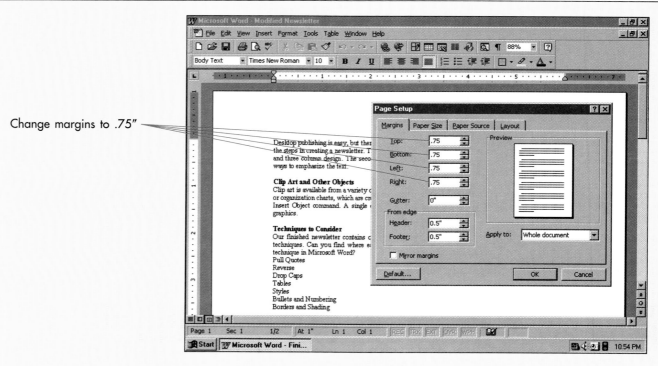

(a) The Page Setup Command (step 1)

FIGURE 5.4   Hands-on Exercise 1

STEP 2: Check the Document

➤ Pull down the **Tools menu,** click **Options,** click the **Spelling and Grammar tab,** and select the option for **Standard writing style.** Click **OK** to close the Options dialog box.

➤ Click the **Spelling and Grammar button** on the Standard toolbar to check the document for errors.

➤ The first error detected by the spelling and grammar check is the omitted hyphen between the words *three* and *column* as shown in Figure 5.4b. (This is a subtle mistake and emphasizes the need to check a document using the tools provided by Word.) Click **Change** to accept the indicated suggestion.

➤ Continue checking the document, accepting (or rejecting) the suggested corrections as you see fit.

➤ Save the document.

USE THE SPELLING AND GRAMMAR CHECK

Our eyes are less discriminating than we would like to believe, allowing misspellings and simple typos to go unnoticed. To prove the point, count the number of times the letter f appears in this sentence, *"Finished files are the result of years of scientific study combined with the experience of years."* The correct answer is six, but most people find only four or five. Checking your document takes only a few minutes. Do it!

Spelling and
Grammar button

Detected errors

Suggested correction

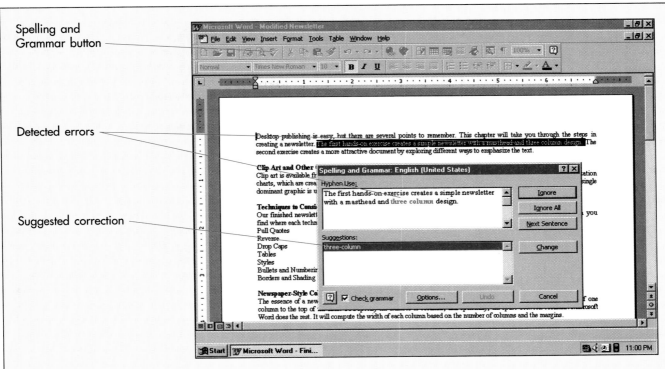

(b) Check the Document (step 2)

FIGURE 5.4   Hands-on Exercise 1 (continued)

STEP 3: Implement Newspaper Columns

➤ Pull down the **Format menu.** Click **Columns** to display the dialog box in Figure 5.4c. Click the **Presets icon** for **Two.** The column width for each column and the spacing between columns will be determined automatically from the existing margins.

➤ If necessary, clear the **Line Between box.** Click **OK** to accept the settings and close the Columns dialog box.

➤ The text of the newsletter should be displayed in two columns. If you do not see the columns, it is probably because you are in the wrong view. Click the **Page Layout View button** above the status bar to change to this view.

THE COLUMNS BUTTON

The Columns button on the Standard toolbar is the fastest way to create columns in a document. Click the button, drag the mouse to choose the number of columns, then release the mouse to create the columns. The toolbar lets you change the number of columns, but not the spacing between columns. The toolbar is also limited in that you cannot create columns of different widths or select a line between columns.

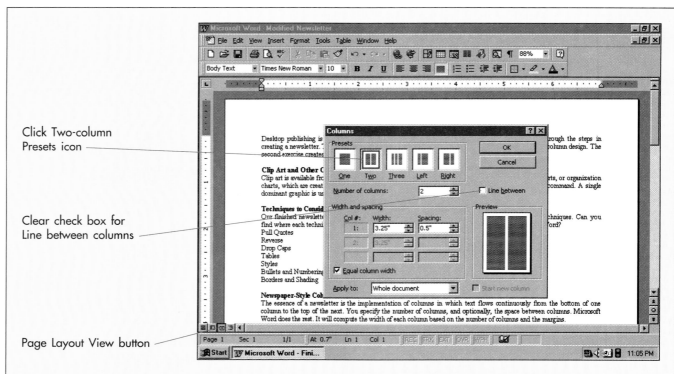

Click Two-column
Presets icon

Clear check box for
Line between columns

Page Layout View button

(c) Implement Newspaper Columns (step 3)

FIGURE 5.4   Hands-on Exercise 1 (continued)

STEP 4: Balance the Columns

➤ Use the **Zoom box** on the Standard toolbar to zoom to **Whole Page** to see the entire newsletter as shown in Figure 5.4d. Do not be concerned if the columns are of different lengths.

➤ Press **Ctrl+End** to move the insertion point to the end of the document. Pull down the **Insert menu.** Click **Break** to display the Break dialog box in Figure 5.4d. Select the **Continuous option button** under Section breaks.

➤ Click **OK** to accept the settings and close the dialog box. The columns should be balanced, although one column may be one line longer than the other.

USE THE RULER TO CHANGE COLUMN WIDTH

Click anywhere within the column whose width you want to change, then point to the ruler and click and drag the right margin (the mouse pointer changes to a double arrow) to change the column width. Changing the width of one column in a document with equal-sized columns changes the width of all other columns so that they remain equal. Changing the width in a document with unequal columns changes only that column. You can also double click the top of the ruler to display the Page Setup dialog box, then click the Margins tab to change the left and right margins, which in turn will change the column width.

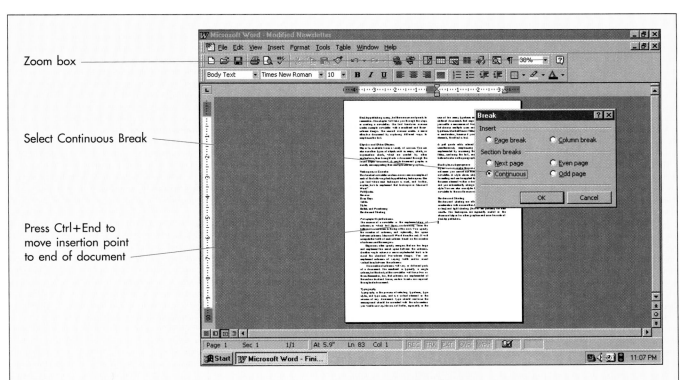

Zoom box

Select Continuous Break

Press Ctrl+End to move insertion point to end of document

(d) Balance the Columns (step 4)

FIGURE 5.4   Hands-on Exercise 1 (continued)

STEP 5: Create the Masthead

➤ Use the Zoom box on the Standard toolbar to change to **Page Width.** Click the **Show/Hide ¶ button** to display the paragraph and section marks.

➤ Press **Ctrl+Home** to move the insertion point to the beginning of the document. Pull down the **Insert menu,** click **Break,** select the **Continuous option button,** and click **OK.** You should see a double dotted line indicating a section break as shown in Figure 5.4e.

➤ Click immediately to the left of the dotted line, which will place the insertion point to the left of the line. Check the status bar to be sure you are in section one.

➤ Change the format for this section to a single column by clicking the **Columns button** on the Standard toolbar and selecting one column. (Alternatively, you can pull down the **Format menu,** click **Columns,** and choose **One** from the Presets column formats.)

➤ Type **Creating a Newsletter** and press the **enter key** twice. Select the newly entered text, click the **Center button** on the Formatting toolbar. Change the font to **48 point Arial Bold.**

➤ Save the newsletter.

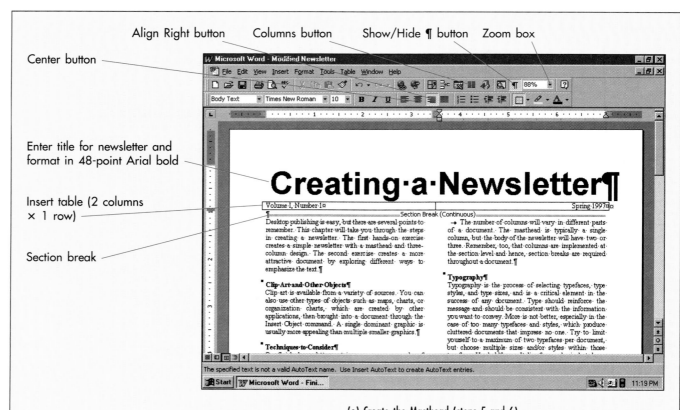

Center button — Align Right button — Columns button — Show/Hide ¶ button — Zoom box

Enter title for newsletter and format in 48-point Arial bold

Insert table (2 columns × 1 row)

Section break

(e) Create the Masthead (steps 5 and 6)

FIGURE 5.4   Hands-on Exercise 1 (continued)

COLUMNS AND SECTIONS

Columns are implemented at the section level and thus a new section is required whenever the number of columns changes within a document. Select the text that is to be formatted in columns, click the Columns button on the Standard toolbar, then drag the mouse to set the desired number of columns. Microsoft Word will automatically insert the section breaks before and after the selected text.

STEP 6: Create the Masthead (Continued)

➤ Click underneath the masthead (to the left of the section break). Pull down the **Table menu,** click **Insert Table,** and insert a table with one row and two columns as shown in Figure 5.4e.

➤ Click in the left cell of the table. Type **Volume I, Number 1.** Click in the right cell (or press the **Tab key** to move to this cell and type the current semester (for example, **Spring 1997**). Click the **Align Right button** on the Standard toolbar to realign the text.

➤ Save the newsletter.

LEFT ALIGNED	CENTERED	RIGHT ALIGNED

Many documents call for left, centered, and/or right aligned text on the same line, an effect that is achieved through setting tabs, or more easily through a table. To achieve the effect shown at the top of this box, create a 1 × 3 table (one row and three columns), type the text in the three cells as needed, then use the buttons on the Formatting toolbar to left-align, center, and right-align the respective cells. Select the table, pull down the Format menu, click Borders and Shading, then specify None as the Border setting.

STEP 7: Create a Reverse

➤ Press **Ctrl+Home** to move the insertion point to the beginning of the newsletter. Click anywhere within the title of the newsletter.

➤ Pull down the **Format menu,** click **Borders and Shading** to display the Borders and Shading dialog box, then click the **Shading tab** as shown in Figure 5.4f.

➤ Click the **drop-down arrow** in the Style list box (in the Patterns area) and select **Solid (100%)** shading. Click **OK** to accept the setting and close the dialog box. Click elsewhere in the document to see the results.

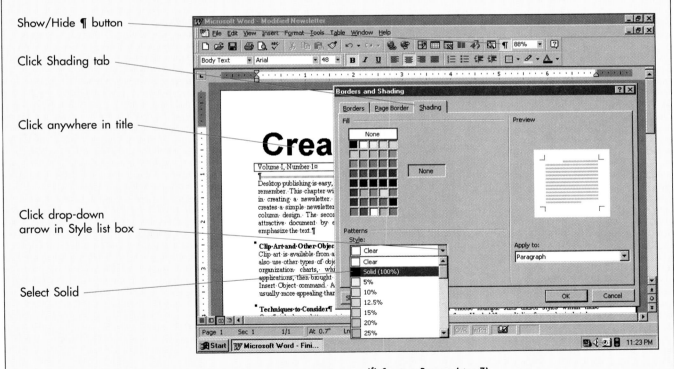

Show/Hide ¶ button

Click Shading tab

Click anywhere in title

Click drop-down arrow in Style list box

Select Solid

(f) Create a Reverse (step 7)

FIGURE 5.4   Hands-on Exercise 1 (continued)

- ➤ The final step is to remove the default border that appears around the table. Click in the selection area to the left of the table to select the entire table.
- ➤ Pull down the **Format menu,** click **Borders and Shading,** and if necessary click the **Borders tab.** Click the **None icon** in the Presets area. Click **OK.** Click elsewhere in the document to see the result.

USE COLOR REVERSES FOR EMPHASIS

White letters on a solid background (technically called a reverse) is a favorite technique of desktop publishers. It looks even better in color—if you have a color printer. Select the text, pull down the Format menu, click the Borders and Shading command, and click the Shading tab. Click the drop-down arrow in the Style list box and choose solid (100%) shading to create the reverse. Click the drop-down arrow in the Color list box and choose the background color (e.g., blue), then click OK to close the dialog box. Click and drag to select the text, click the down arrow on the Font color button on the Formatting toolbar, and select white. Click the Bold button on the Formatting toolbar, then click elsewhere in the document to see the results.

STEP 8: Modify the Heading Style

- ➤ Two styles have been implemented for you in the newsletter. Click in any text paragraph and you see the Body Text style name displayed in the Style box on the Formatting toolbar. Click in any heading and you see the Heading 1 style.
- ➤ Click and drag to select the heading **Clip Art and Other Objects.** Click the **drop-down arrow** on the Font list box and change the font to **Arial.** Change the **Font Size** to **12** point.
- ➤ Click the **Heading 1** style name within the Style list box on the Formatting toolbar. Press enter to select this style and display the Modify Style dialog box as shown in Figure 5.4g.
- ➤ The option button to update the style according to the current formatting is selected. Click **OK** to change the style, which automatically reformats every element defined by this style.
- ➤ Save the newsletter.

USE STYLES AS APPROPRIATE

Styles were covered in the previous chapter, but that does not mean you cannot use them in conjunction with a newsletter. A style stores character and/or paragraph formatting and can be applied to multiple occurrences of the same element within a document. Change the style and you automatically change all text defined by that style. You can also use the same styles from one edition of your newsletter to the next to ensure consistency.

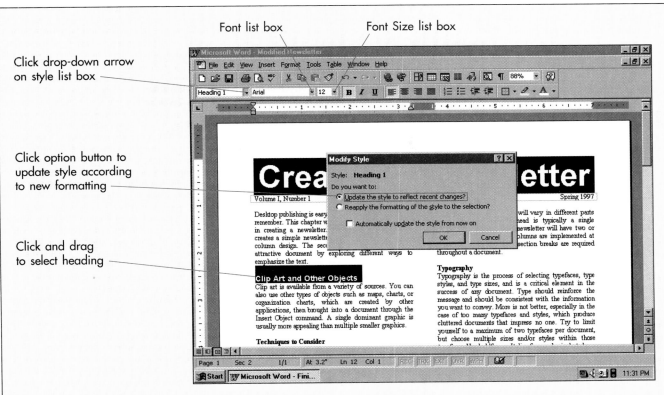

Click drop-down arrow on style list box

Font list box

Font Size list box

Click option button to update style according to new formatting

Click and drag to select heading

(g) Modify the Heading Style (step 8)

FIGURE 5.4 Hands-on Exercise 1 (continued)

STEP 9: The Print Preview Command

➤ Pull down the **File menu** and click **Print Preview** (or click the **Print Preview button** on the Standard toolbar) to view the newsletter as in Figure 5.4h. This is a basic two-column newsletter with the masthead appearing as a reverse and stretching over a single column.

➤ Click the **Print button** to print the newsletter at this stage so that you can compare this version with the finished newsletter at the end of the next exercise. Click the **Close button** on the Print Preview toolbar to close the Preview view and return to the Page Layout view.

➤ Exit Word if you do not want to continue with the next exercise at this time.

THE PRINT PREVIEW TOOLBAR

Click the Context Sensitive Help button on the extreme right of the Print Preview toolbar (the mouse pointer changes to an arrow and a question mark), then click any other button for an explanation of its function. The Shrink to Fit button is especially useful if a small portion of the newsletter spills over to a second page—click the button and it uniformly reduces the fonts throughout the document to eliminate the second page.

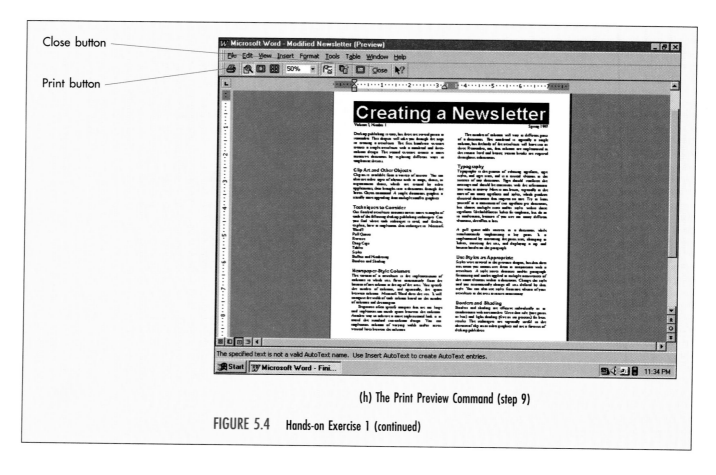

Close button

Print button

(h) The Print Preview Command (step 9)

FIGURE 5.4   Hands-on Exercise 1 (continued)

ELEMENTS OF GRAPHIC DESIGN

We trust you have completed the first hands-on exercise without difficulty and that you were able to duplicate the initial version of the newsletter. That, however, is the easy part of desktop publishing. The more difficult aspect is to develop the design in the first place because the mere availability of a desktop publishing program does not guarantee an effective document, any more than a word processor will turn its author into another Shakespeare. Other skills are necessary, and so we continue with a brief introduction to graphic design.

Much of what we say is subjective, and what works in one situation will not necessarily work in another. Your eye is the best judge of all, and you should follow your own instincts. Experiment freely and realize that successful design is the result of trial and error. Seek inspiration from others by collecting samples of real documents that you find attractive, then use those documents as the basis for your own designs.

The Grid

The design of a document is developed on a *grid,* an underlying, but *invisible,* set of horizontal and vertical lines that determine the placement of the major elements. A grid establishes the overall structure of a document by indicating the number of columns, the space between columns, the size of the margins, the placement of headlines, art, and so on. The grid does *not* appear in the printed document or on the screen.

A grid may be simple or complex, but is always distinguished by the number of columns it contains. The three-column grid of Figures 5.5a and 5.5b is one

(a) Empty Three-column Grid

No Can Do

He felt more and more pressure to play the game of not playing. Maybe that's why he stepped in front of that truck.

People wonder why people do things like this, but all you have to do is look around and see all the stress and insanity each person in responsibility is required to put up with. There is no help or end in sight. It seems that managers are managing less and shoveling the workloads on to their underlings. This seems to be the overall response to the absence of raises or benefit packages they feel are their entitlement. Something must be done now!

People wonder why people do things like this, but all you have to do is look around and see all the stress and insanity each person in responsibility is required to put up with. There is no help or end in sight. It seems that managers are managing less and shoveling the workloads on to their underlings. This seems to be the overall response to the absence of raises or benefit packages they feel are their entitlement. Something must be done now!

People wonder why people do things like this, but all you have

to do is look around and see all the stress and insanity each person in responsibility is required to put up with. There is no help or end in sight. It seems that managers are managing less and shoveling the workloads on to their underlings. This seems to be the overall response to the absence of raises or benefit packages they feel are their entitlement.

People wonder why people do things like this, but all y o u have to do is look

around and see all the stress and insanity each person in responsibility is required to put up with. There is no help or end in sight. It seems that managers are managing less and shoveling the workloads on to their underlings. This seems to be the overall response to the absence of raises or benefit packages they feel are their entitlement. Something must be done now!

People wonder why people do things like this, but all you have to do is look around and see all the stress and insanity each person in responsibility is required to put up with. There is no help or end in sight. It seems that managers are managing less. Something must be done now!

People wonder why people do things like this, but all you have to do is look around and see all the stress and insanity each person in ▼

(b) Three-column Grid

No Can Do

He felt more and more pressure to play the game of not playing. Maybe that's why he stepped in front of that truck.

People wonder why people do things like this, but all you have to do is look around and see all the stress and insanity each person in responsibility is required to put up with. There is no help or end in sight. It seems that managers are managing less and shoveling the workloads on to their underlings. This seems to be the overall response to the absence of raises or benefit packages they feel are their entitlement. Something must be done now!

People wonder why people do things like this, but all you have to do is look around and see all the stress and insanity each person in re-

sponsibility is required to put up with. There is no help or end in sight. It seems that managers are managing less and shoveling the workloads on to their underlings. This seems to be the overall response to the absence of raises or benefit packages they feel are their entitlement. Something must be done now!

People wonder why people do things like this, but all you have to do is look around and see all the stress and insanity each person in responsibility is required to put up with. There is no help or end in sight. It seems that

managers are managing less and shoveling the workloads on to their underlings. This seems to be the overall response to the absence of raises or benefit packages they feel are their entitlement. Something must be done now!

People wonder why people do things like this, but all you have to do is look around and see all the stress and insanity each person in responsibility is required to put up with. There is no help or end in sight. It seems that managers are managing less. Something must be done now!

People wonder why people do things like this, but all you have to do is look around and see all the stress and insanity each person in responsibility is required to put up with. There is no help or end in sight. It seems that manag-ing less and shoveling the workloads on to their underlings. This seems to be the overall response to the ▼

(c) Four-column Grid

People wonder why people do things like this, but all you have to do is look around and see all the stress and insanity each person in responsibility is required to put up with. There is no help or end in sight. It seems that managers are managing less and shoveling the workloads on to their underlings. This seems to be the overall response to the absence of raises or benefit packages they feel are their entitlement. Something must be done!

People wonder why people do things like this, but all you have to do is look around and see all the stress and insanity each person in responsibility is required to put up with. There is no help or end in sight. It seems that managers are managing less and shoveling the workloads on to their underlings. This seems to be the overall response to the absence of raises

People wonder why people do things like this, but all you have to do is look around and see all the stress and insanity each person in responsibility is required to put up with. There is no help or end in sight. It seems that managers are managing less and shoveling the workloads on to their underlings. This seems to be the overall response to the absence of raises or benefit packag-es they feel are their entitlement. Something must be done now!

People wonder why people do

things like this, but all you have to do is look around and see all the stress and insanity each person in responsibility is required to put up with. There is no help or end in sight. It seems that manag-ers are managing less and shoveling the workloads on to their underlings. This seems to be the overall response to the absence of raises or

He felt more and more pressure to play the game of not playing. Maybe that's why he stepped in front of that truck.

ers are managing less and shoveling the workloads on to their underlings. This seems to be the overall response to the absence of raises or

benefit packages they feel are their entitlement. Something must be done now!

People wonder why people do things like this, but all you have to do is look around and see all the stress and insanity each person in responsibility is required to put up with. There is no help or end in sight. It seems that managers are managing less and shoveling the workloads on to their underlings. This seems to be the overall response to the absence of raises or benefit packages they feel are their

entitlement. Something must be done now!

People wonder why people do things like this, but all you have to do is look around and see all the stress and insanity each person in responsibility is required to put up with. There is no help or end in sight. It seems that managers are managing less and shoveling the workloads on to their underlings. This seems to be the overall response to the absence of raises or benefit packag-es they feel are their entitlement. Something must be done!

People wonder why people do things like this, but all you have to do is look around and see all the stress and insanity each person in responsibility is required to put up with. There is no help or end in sight. It seems that managers are managing less and shoveling the workloads on to their underlings. Something must be done now!

People wonder why people do things like this, but all you have to do ▼

(d) Five-column Grid

FIGURE 5.5 The Grid System of Design

of the most common and utilitarian designs. Figure 5.5c shows a four-column design for the same document, with unequal column widths to provide interest. Figure 5.5d illustrates a five-column grid that is often used with large amounts of text. Many other designs are possible as well. A one-column grid is used for term papers and letters. A two-column, wide and narrow format is appropriate for textbooks and manuals. Two- and three-column formats are used for newsletters and magazines.

The simple concept of a grid should make the underlying design of any document obvious, which in turn gives you an immediate understanding of page composition. Moreover, the conscious use of a grid will help you organize your material and result in a more polished and professional-looking publication. It will also help you to achieve consistency from page to page within a document (or from issue to issue of a newsletter). Indeed, much of what goes wrong in desktop publishing stems from failing to follow or use the underlying grid.

Clip Art

Clip art is available from a variety of sources including the Microsoft Clip Gallery. The complete gallery, contained on the Office 97 CD, is a wonderful resource with more than 3,000 clip art images and almost 150 photographs. The Clip Gallery can be accessed in a variety of ways, most easily through the ***Insert Picture command.*** Once clip art has been inserted into a document, it can be moved and sized just like any other Windows object, as will be illustrated in our next hands-on exercise.

The ***Format Picture command*** provides additional flexibility in the placement of clip art. The Wrapping tab, in the Format Picture dialog box, determines the way text is positioned around a picture. The Top and Bottom option (no wrapping) is selected in Figure 5.6a and the resulting document is shown in Figure 5.6b. The sizing handles around the clip art indicate that it is currently selected, enabling you to move and/or resize the clip art using the mouse. (You can also use the Size and Position tabs in the Format Picture dialog box for more precision with either setting.) Changing the size or position of the object, however, does not affect the way in which text wraps around the clip art.

The document in Figure 5.6c illustrates a different wrapping selection in which text is wrapped on both sides. Figure 5.6c also uses an option on the Colors and Lines tab to draw a blue border around the clip art. The document in Figure 5.6d eliminates the border and chooses the tight wrapping style so that the text is positioned as closely as possible to the figure in a free-form design. Choosing among the various documents in Figure 5.6 is one of personal preference. Our point is simply that Word provides multiple options, and it is up to you, the desktop publisher, to choose the design that best suits your requirements.

Emphasis

Good design makes it easy for the reader to determine what is important. As indicated earlier, emphasis can be achieved in several ways, the easiest being variations in type size and/or type style. Headings should be set in type sizes (at least two points) larger than body copy. The use of **boldface** is effective as are *italics,* but both should be done in moderation. (UPPERCASE LETTERS and underlining are alternative techniques that we believe are less effective.)

Boxes and/or shading call attention to selected articles. Horizontal lines are effective to separate one topic from another or to call attention to a pull quote. A reverse can be striking for a small amount of text. Clip art, used in moderation, will catch the reader's eye and enhance almost any newsletter.

Top and Bottom Wrapping Style is selected

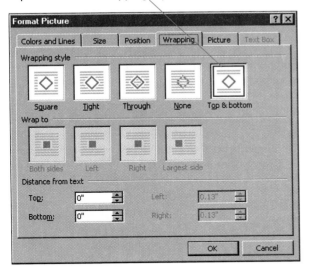

(a) Wrapping Tab

(b) Top and Bottom Wrapping

(c) Square Wrapping (both sides)

(d) Tight Wrapping (both sides)

FIGURE 5.6   The Format Picture Command

Complete the Newsletter

Objective: To insert clip art into a newsletter; to format a newsletter using styles, borders and shading, pull quotes, and lists. Use Figure 5.7.

STEP 1: Change the Column Layout

➤ Open the **Modified Newsletter** from the previous exercise. Click in the masthead and change the number of this edition from 1 to **2.**

➤ Click anywhere in the body of the newsletter. The status bar should indicate that you are in the second section. Pull down the **Format menu.** Click **Columns** to display the dialog box in Figure 5.7a. Click the **Left Preset icon.**

➤ Change the width of the first column to **2.25** and the space between columns to **.25.** Check (click) the **Line Between box.** Click **OK.** Save the newsletter.

Click Left Presets icon

Click check box to create a Line Between the columns

Change column width to 2.25"

Change space between columns to .25"

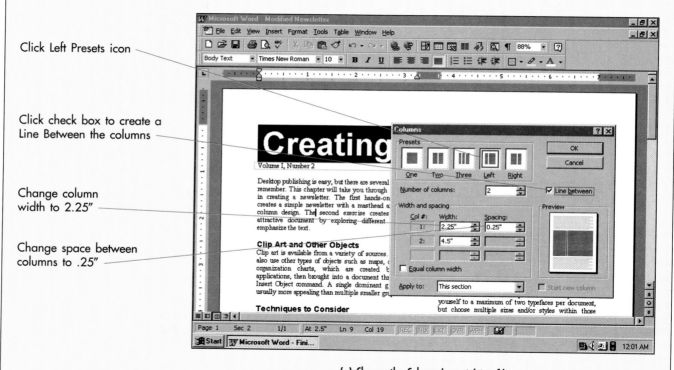

(a) Change the Column Layout (step 1)

FIGURE 5.7 Hands-on Exercise 2

EXPERIMENT WITH THE DESIGN

The number and width of the columns in a newsletter is the single most important element in its design. Experiment freely. Good design is often the result of trial and error.

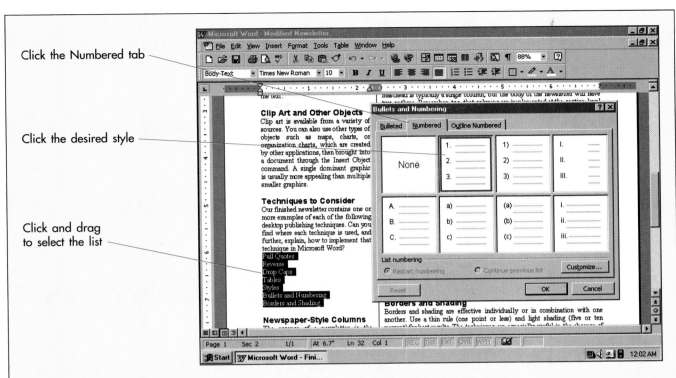

Click the Numbered tab

Click the desired style

Click and drag
to select the list

(b) Bullets and Numbering (step 2)

FIGURE 5.7   Hands-on Exercise 2 (continued)

STEP 2: Bullets and Numbering

➤ Scroll in the document until you come to the list within the **Techniques to Consider** paragraph. Select the entire list as shown in Figure 5.7b.

➤ Pull down the **Format menu** and click **Bullets and Numbering** to display the Bullets and Numbering dialog box. If necessary, click the **Numbered tab** and choose the numbering style with Arabic numbers followed by periods. Click **OK** to accept these settings and close the Bullets and Numbering dialog box.

➤ Click anywhere in the newsletter to deselect the text. Save the newsletter.

LISTS AND THE FORMATTING TOOLBAR

The Formatting toolbar contains four buttons for use with bulleted and numbered lists. The Increase Indent and Decrease Indent buttons move the selected items one tab stop to the right and left, respectively. The Bullets button creates a bulleted list from unnumbered items or converts a numbered list to a bulleted list. The Numbering button creates a numbered list or converts a bulleted list to numbers. The Bullets and Numbering buttons also function as toggle switches; for example, clicking the Bullets button when a bulleted list is already in effect will remove the bullets.

STEP 3: Insert the Clip Art

➤ Click immediately to the left of the article beginning **Clip Art and Other Objects.** Pull down the **Insert menu,** click **Picture,** then click **Clip Art** to display the Microsoft Clip Gallery. (Click **OK** if you see a dialog box reminding you that additional clip art is available on a CD-ROM.)

➤ If necessary, click the **Clip Art tab** and select (click) the **Cartoons category** as shown in Figure 5.7c. Select the **man with many hats** (or a different image if you prefer), then click the **Insert button** to place the clip art into the newsletter.

➤ The Microsoft Clip Gallery dialog box will close and the picture will appear in the newsletter. Do not be concerned about the size or position of the clip art.

Click the Clip Art tab

Click to position the insertion point

Click the Cartoons category

Click the desired clip art image

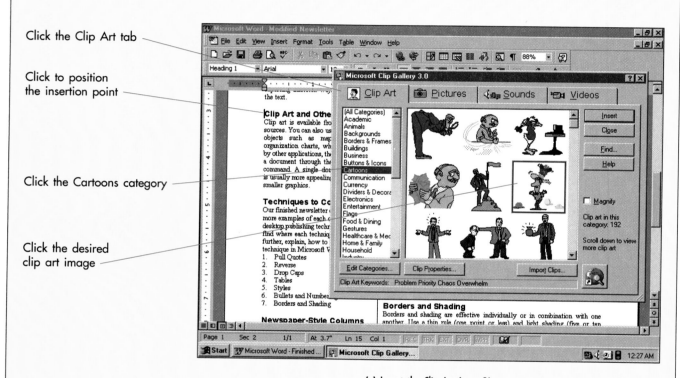

(c) Insert the Clip Art (step 3)

FIGURE 5.7   Hands-on Exercise 2 (continued)

ADDITIONAL CLIP IMAGES

The Microsoft Clip Gallery contains over 100MB of data consisting of more than 3,000 clip art images, 144 photographs, 28 sounds, and 20 video clips. Only a fraction of these are installed with Microsoft Office, but you can access the additional objects from the Office CD at any time. You can also install some or all of the objects on your hard disk, provided you have sufficient space. Start the Windows Explorer, then open the ClipArt folder on the Office CD. Double click the Setup icon to start the Setup Wizard, then follow the on-screen instructions to install the additional components you want.

STEP 4: Move and Size the Clip Art

➤ The clip art is initially too large and forces the newsletter to spill over to a second page. Click the **drop-down arrow** on the Zoom list box and select **Two Pages.** You can move and size the clip art just as you can any Windows object.

➤ To size the clip art, click anywhere within the clip art to select it and display the sizing handles. Drag a corner handle (the mouse pointer changes to a double arrow) to change the length and width of the picture simultaneously and keep the object in proportion.

➤ To move the clip art, click the object to select it and display the sizing handles. Point to any part of the object except a sizing handle (the mouse pointer changes to a four-sided arrow), then click and drag to move the clip art elsewhere in the document.

➤ It's faster, however, to use the Format Picture command. Select (click) the clip art, then pull down the **Format menu** and select the **Picture command** to display the Format Picture dialog box in Figure 5.7d.

➤ Click the **Size tab,** click in the **Width list box,** enter **1.5",** then click **OK** to accept the settings and close the Format Picture dialog box. The newsletter should fit on one page, and all of the items in the numbered list should fit in the first column. (Change the width if the figure does not fit.)

➤ Save the document.

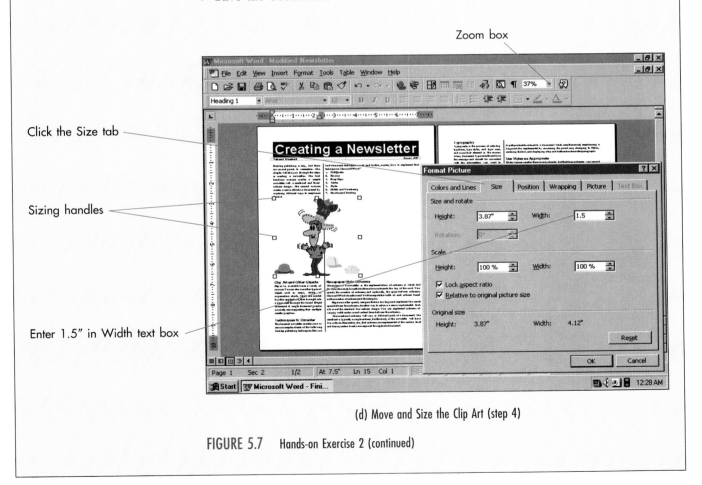

(d) Move and Size the Clip Art (step 4)

FIGURE 5.7   Hands-on Exercise 2 (continued)

THE PICTURE TOOLBAR

The Picture toolbar offers the easiest way to execute the various commands associated with a picture or clip art image. As with any toolbar, you can point to a button to display a ScreenTip containing the name of the button, which is indicative of its function. You will find buttons for wrapping and formatting a picture, a Line Styles button to place a border around a picture, and a cropping button to crop (erase) part of a picture. (If you do not see the Picture toolbar when clip art is selected, right click any visible toolbar, then toggle the Picture toolbar on.)

STEP 5: Borders and Shading

➤ Change to **Page Width** and click the **Show/Hide ¶ button** to display the paragraph marks. Press **Ctrl+End** to move to the end of the document, then select the heading and associated paragraph for Borders and Shading. (Do not select the ending paragraph mark or else the shading will continue below the section break.)

➤ Pull down the **Format menu.** Click **Borders and Shading.** If necessary click the **Borders tab** to display the dialog box in Figure 5.4e. Click the **Box icon** in the Setting area. Click the **drop-down arrow** in the Width list box and select the **1 point** line style.

Click Borders tab

Click Box icon

Click drop-down arrow to display available line widths

Click and drag to select heading and text

Do not select paragraph mark

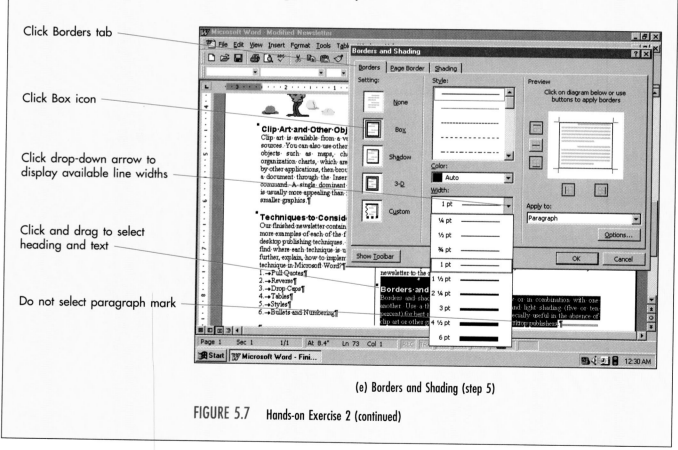

(e) Borders and Shading (step 5)

FIGURE 5.7   Hands-on Exercise 2 (continued)

➤ Click the **Shading tab.** Click the **drop-down arrow** in the Style list box (in the Patterns area) and select 5% shading. Click **OK** to accept the setting and close the dialog box.

➤ Click elsewhere in the document to see the results. The heading and paragraph should be enclosed in a border with light shading.

➤ Save the newsletter.

BORDERS AND SHADING

The Borders and Shading command takes practice, but once you get used to it you will love it. To place a border around multiple paragraphs (the paragraphs should have the same indents or else a different border will be placed around each paragraph), select the paragraphs prior to execution of the Borders and Shading command. Select (click) the line style you like, then click the Box or Shadow Preset button to place the border around the selected paragraphs. To change the border on one side, click the desired style and then click the side within the Preview area. Click OK to accept the settings and close the dialog box.

STEP 6: Create a Pull Quote

➤ Scroll to the bottom of the document until you find the paragraph describing a pull quote. Select the entire paragraph and change the text to 14-point Arial italic.

➤ Click in the paragraph to deselect the text, then click the **Center button** to center the paragraph.

➤ Click the **drop-down arrow** on the **Border button** to display the different border styles as shown in Figure 5.7f.

➤ Click the **Top Border button** to add a top border to the paragraph.

➤ Click the **Bottom border button** to create a bottom border and complete the pull quote.

EMPHASIZE WHAT'S IMPORTANT

Good design makes it easy for the reader to determine what is important. A pull quote (a phrase or sentence taken from an article) adds interest to a document while simultaneously emphasizing a key point. Boxes and shading are also effective in catching the reader's attention. A simple change in typography, such as increasing the point size, changing the typeface, and/or the use of boldface or italics, calls attention to a heading and visually separates it from the associated text.

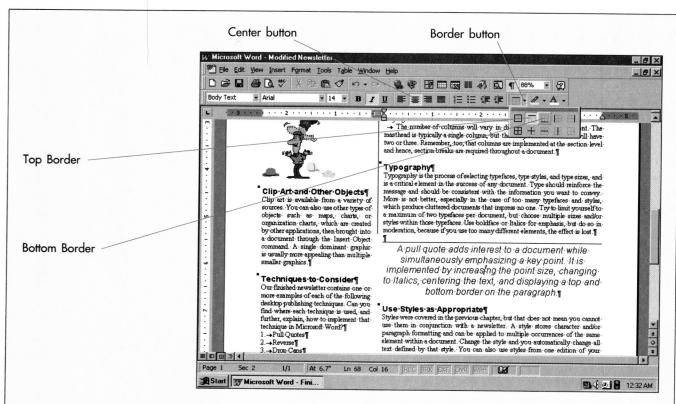

Center button   Border button

Top Border

Bottom Border

(f) Create a Pull Quote (step 6)

FIGURE 5.7   Hands-on Exercise 2 (continued)

STEP 7: Create a Drop Cap

➤ Scroll to the beginning of the newsletter. Click immediately before the D in *Desktop publishing*.

➤ Pull down the **Format menu.** Click **Drop Cap** to display the dialog box in Figure 5.7g. Click the **Position icon** for **Dropped** as shown in the figure. We used the default settings, but you can change the font, size (lines to drop), or distance from the text by clicking the arrow on the appropriate list box.

➤ Click **OK** to create the Drop Cap dialog box. Click outside the frame around the drop cap. Save the newsletter.

MODIFYING A DROP CAP

Select (click) a dropped capital letter to display a thatched border known as a frame, then click the border or frame to display its sizing handles. You can move and size a frame just as you can any Windows object; for example, click and drag a corner sizing handle to change the size of the frame (and the drop cap it contains). To delete the frame (and remove the drop cap) press the delete key.

Click the Dropped icon

Click to position insertion point to left of the "D"

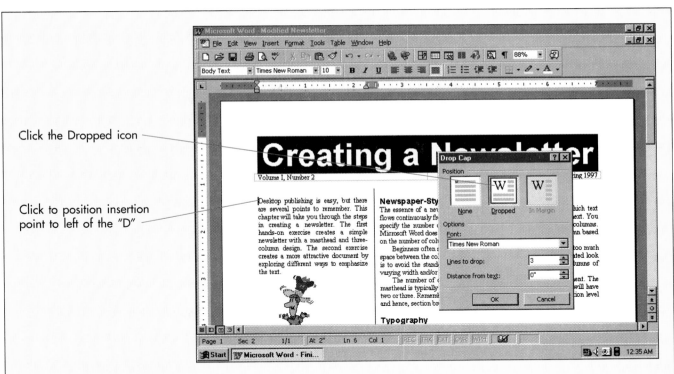

(g) Create a Drop Cap (step 7)

FIGURE 5.7   Hands-on Exercise 2 (continued)

STEP 8: The Completed Newsletter

➤ Zoom to **Whole Page** to view the completed newsletter as shown in Figure 5.7h. The newsletter should fit on a single page, but if not, there are several techniques that you can use:

- Pull down the **File menu,** click the **Page Setup command,** click the **Margins tab,** then reduce the top and/or bottom margins to .5 inch. Be sure to apply this change to the **Whole document** within the Page Setup dialog box.
- Change the **Heading 1 style** to reduce the point size to **10 points** and/or the space before the heading to **6 points.**
- Click the **Print Preview button** on the Standard toolbar, then click the **Shrink to Fit button** on the Print Preview toolbar.
- Save the document a final time. Print the completed newsletter and submit it to your instructor as proof you did this exercise. Congratulations on a job well done.

A FINAL WORD OF ADVICE

Desktop publishing is not a carefree operation. It is time-consuming to implement and you will be amazed at the effort required for even a simple document. Computers are supposed to save time, not waste it, and while desktop publishing is clearly justified for some documents, the extensive formatting it requires is not necessary for most documents. And finally, remember that the content of a document is its most important element.

Print Preview button

Zoom box

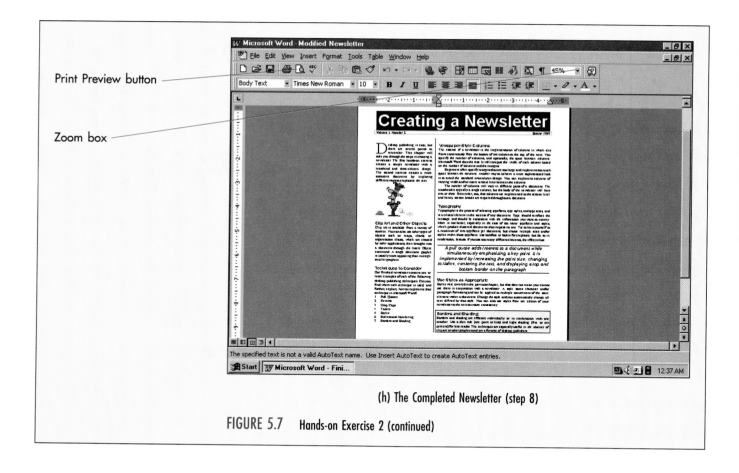

(h) The Completed Newsletter (step 8)

FIGURE 5.7   Hands-on Exercise 2 (continued)

SUMMARY

The essence of desktop publishing is the merger of text with graphics to produce a professional-looking document. Proficiency in desktop publishing requires knowledge of the associated commands in Microsoft Word, as well as familiarity with the basics of graphic design.

Typography is the process of selecting typefaces, type styles, and type sizes. A typeface (or font) is a complete set of characters (upper- and lowercase letters, numbers, punctuation marks, and special symbols). Type size is a vertical measurement and is specified in points. One point is equal to $\frac{1}{72}$ of an inch.

The design of a document is developed on a grid, an underlying but invisible set of horizontal and vertical lines that determine the placement of the major elements. A newsletter can be divided into any number of newspaper-style columns in which text flows from the bottom of one column to the top of the next. Columns are implemented by clicking the Columns button on the Standard toolbar or by selecting the Columns command from the Format menu. Sections are required if different column arrangements are present in the same document. The Page Layout view is required to see the columns displayed side by side.

Emphasis can be achieved in several ways, the easiest being variations in type size and/or type style. Boxes and/or shading call attention to selected articles in a document. Horizontal lines are effective in separating one topic from another or calling attention to a pull quote (a phrase or sentence taken from an article to emphasize a key point). A reverse (light text on a solid background) is striking for a small amount of text. Clip art, used in moderation, will catch the reader's eye and enhance almost any newsletter.

Clip art is available from a variety of sources including the Microsoft Clip Gallery, which is accessed most easily through the Insert Picture command. Once clip art has been inserted into a document, it can be moved and sized just like any other Windows object. The Format Picture command provides additional flexibility and precision in the placement of an object.

Graphic design does not have hard and fast rules, only guidelines and common sense. Creating an effective document is an iterative process and reflects the result of trial and error. We encourage you to experiment freely with different designs.

KEY WORDS AND CONCEPTS

Arial
Borders and Shading command
Bulleted list
Clip art
Columns command
Desktop publishing
Drop cap
Emphasis
Font
Format Picture command

Grid
Insert Picture command
Masthead
Microsoft Clip Gallery
Newsletter Wizard
Newspaper-style columns
Numbered list
Point size
Pull quote
Reverse

Sans serif typeface
Section break
Serif typeface
Times New Roman
Type size
Typeface
Typography

MULTIPLE CHOICE

1. Which of the following is a commonly accepted guideline in typography?
   (a) Use a serif typeface for headings and a sans serif typeface for text
   (b) Use a sans serif typeface for headings and a serif typeface for text
   (c) Use a sans serif typeface for both headings and text
   (d) Use a serif typeface for both headings and text

2. Which of the following best enables you to see a multicolumn document as it will appear on the printed page?
   (a) Normal view at 100% magnification
   (b) Normal view at whole page magnification
   (c) Page Layout view at 100% magnification
   (d) Page Layout view at whole page magnification

3. What is the width of each column in a document with two uniform columns, given 1¼-inch margins and ½-inch spacing between the columns?
   (a) 2½ inches
   (b) 2¾ inches
   (c) 3 inches
   (d) Impossible to determine

4. What is the minimum number of sections in a three-column newsletter whose masthead extends across all three columns?
   (a) One
   (b) Two
   (c) Three
   (d) Four

5. Which of the following describes the Arial and Times New Roman fonts?
   (a) Arial is a sans serif font, Times New Roman is a serif font
   (b) Arial is a serif font, Times New Roman is a sans serif font
   (c) Both are serif fonts
   (d) Both are sans serif fonts

6. How do you balance the columns in a newsletter so that each column contains the same amount of text?
   (a) Check the Balance Columns box in the Format Columns command
   (b) Visually determine where the break should go, then insert a column break at the appropriate place
   (c) Insert a continuous section break at the end of the last column
   (d) All of the above

7. What is the effect of dragging one of the four corner handles on a selected object?
   (a) The length of the object is changed but the width remains constant
   (b) The width of the object is changed but the length remains constant
   (c) The length and width of the object are changed in proportion to one another
   (d) Neither the length nor width of the object is changed

8. Which type size is the most reasonable for columns of text, such as those appearing in the newsletter created in the chapter?
   (a) 6 point
   (b) 10 point
   (c) 14 point
   (d) 18 point

9. A grid is applicable to the design of:
   (a) Documents with one, two, or three columns and moderate clip art
   (b) Documents with four or more columns and no clip art
   (c) Both (a) and (b)
   (d) Neither (a) nor (b)

10. Which of the following can be used to add emphasis to a document?
    (a) Borders and shading
    (b) Pull quotes and reverses
    (c) Both (a) and (b)
    (d) Neither (a) nor (b)

11. Which of the following is a recommended guideline in the design of a document?
    (a) Use at least three different clip art images in every newsletter
    (b) Use at least three different typefaces in a document to maintain interest
    (c) Use the same type size for the heading and text of an article
    (d) None of the above

12. Which of the following is implemented at the section level?
   (a) Columns
   (b) Margins
   (c) Both (a) and (b)
   (d) Neither (a) nor (b)

13. What is the easiest way to change the type size of various headings scattered throughout a document, each of which has been formatted with the same style?
   (a) Select the headings individually, then choose the new type size
   (b) Select the headings at the same time, then choose the new type size
   (c) Change the point size in the style, which automatically changes the headings
   (d) Retype the headings according to the new specifications

14. A reverse is implemented:
   (a) By selecting 100% shading in the Borders and Shading command
   (b) By changing the Font color to black
   (c) Both (a) and (b)
   (d) Neither (a) nor (b)

15. The Format Picture command enables you to:
   (a) Change the way in which text is wrapped around a figure
   (b) Change the size of a figure
   (c) Place a border around a figure
   (d) All of the above

ANSWERS

1. b	**6.** c	**11.** d
2. d	**6.** c	**12.** c
3. b	**8.** b	**13.** c
4. b	**9.** c	**14.** a
5. a	**10.** c	**15.** d

PRACTICE WITH MICROSOFT WORD

1. The flyers in Figure 5.8 were created using clip art from the Microsoft Clip Gallery. (We used the complete selection, which is found on the Office 97 CD, but you can use different images if ours are not available to you.) Once the clip art was brought into the document, it was moved and sized as necessary to create the documents in the figure.

   Recreate either or both of our flyers, or better yet, design your own with our text but your own layout. Alternatively, you can create a flyer for a hypothetical intramural sporting event or a fraternity or sorority rushing function. (Use the Insert Symbol command to select Greek letters from the Symbols font.) The flyers are simpler to create than a newsletter. Submit your flyers and a cover sheet to your instructor as proof you did this exercise.

UM Jazz Band
Plays Dixieland

Where: Gusman Hall

When: Friday
      November 10

Time: 8:00 PM

(a)

CIS 120 Study Sessions

For those who don't know a bit from a byte
Come to Stanford College this Tuesday night
We'll study the concepts that aren't always clear
And memorize terms that hackers hold dear

We'll hit the books from 7 to 10
And then Thursday night, we'll do it again
It can't hurt to try us - so come on by
And give the CIS tutors that old college try!

(b)

FIGURE 5.8   Screens for Practice Exercise 1

2. Figure 5.9 displays three additional mastheads suitable for the newsletter that was developed in the chapter. Each masthead was created as follows:

   a. A two-by-two table was used in Figure 5.9a in order to right justify the date of the newsletter.

   b. Microsoft WordArt was used to create the masthead in Figure 5.9c. (Use the pull-down Help menu to learn more about this application if you have not used it before.)

   c. A different font was used for the masthead in Figure 5.9b.

Choose the masthead you like best, then modify the newsletter as it existed at the end of the second hands-on exercise to include the new masthead. Submit the modified newsletter to your instructor as proof that you did the hands-on exercises in this chapter as well as this problem.

Creating a Newsletter
Volume 1, Number 1   Spring 1997

Creating a Newsletter

Creating a Newsletter

FIGURE 5.9   Mastheads for Practice Exercise 2

3. Create a newsletter containing at least one graphic image from the Microsoft Clip Gallery. The intent of this problem is simply to provide practice in graphic design. There is no requirement to write meaningful text, but the headings in the newsletter should follow the theme of the graphic.

   a. Select a graphic, then write one or two sentences in support of that graphic. If, for example, you choose a clip art image of a dog or cat, write a sentence about your pet.

   b. As indicated, there is no requirement to write meaningful text for the newsletter; just copy the sentences from part (a) once or twice to create a paragraph, then copy the paragraph several times to create the newsletter. You should, however, create meaningful headings to add interest to the document.

   c. Develop an overall design away from the computer—that is, with pencil and paper. Use a grid to indicate the placement of the articles, headings, clip art, and masthead. You may be surprised to find that it is easier to master commands in Word than it is to design the newsletter; do not, however, underestimate the importance of graphic design in the ultimate success of your document.

4. **A Guide to Smart Shopping:** This problem is more challenging than the previous exercises in that you are asked to consider content as well as design. The objective is to develop a one- (or two-) page document with helpful tips to the novice on buying a computer. We have, however, written the copy for you and put the file on the data disk.

   a. Open and print the *Chapter 5 Practice 4* document on the data disk, which takes approximately a page and a half as presently formatted. Read our text and determine the tips you want to retain and those you want to delete. Add other tips as you see fit.

   b. Examine the available clip art through the Insert Picture command or through the Microsoft Clip Gallery. There is no requirement, however, to include a graphic; that is, use clip art only if you think it will enhance the document.

   c. Consult a current computer magazine (or another source) to determine actual prices for one or more configurations, then include this information prominently in your document.

   d. Create the masthead for the document, then develop with pencil and paper a rough sketch of the completed document showing the masthead, the placement of the text, clip art, and the special of the month (the configuration in part c).

   e. Return to the computer and implement the design of part d. Try to create a balanced publication that completely fills the space allotted; that is, your document should take exactly one or two pages (rather than the page and a half in the original document on the data disk).

5. **What You Can Do with Clip Art:** We are not artistic by nature, and there is no way that we could have created an original clip art image of the man with his many hats. We did, however, create the variation shown in Figure 5.10 using various tools on the Drawing toolbar. All it took was a little imagination and a sense of what can be done.

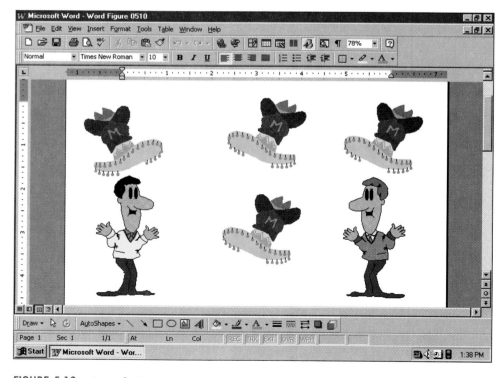

FIGURE 5.10 Screen for Practice Exercise 5

Start by inserting the clip art image into a new document and displaying the Drawing toolbar. Select the clip art image, click the drop-down arrow on the Draw button on the Drawing toolbar, and click the Ungroup command one or more times as necessary until the man and his hats are separate objects, each of which can be selected and manipulated separately. The rest is up to you. Use the ScreenTips and online help to learn about the different tools on the Drawing toolbar.

Prove to your instructor that you have done this exercise by developing a one-page document containing the original clip art and its final form. Include a brief description of what you did to create the modified image.

6. The Equation Editor: Create a simple newsletter such as the two-column design in Figure 5.11. There is no requirement to write meaningful text, as the intent of this exercise is to illustrate the Equation Editor. Thus all you need to do is write a sentence or two, then copy that sentence so that it fills the newsletter.

MATH NEWS

Basics of Algebra I

Freshman students contend with the quadratic equation in Algebra I. Freshman students contend with the quadratic equation in Algebra I. Freshman students contend with the quadratic equation in Algebra I. Freshman students contend with the quadratic equation in Algebra I. Freshman students contend with the quadratic equation in Algebra I. Freshman students contend with the quadratic equation in Algebra I. Freshman students contend with the quadratic equation in Algebra I. Freshman students contend with the quadratic equation in Algebra I. Freshman students contend with the quadratic equation in Algebra I. Freshman students contend with the quadratic equation in Algebra I. Freshman students contend with the quadratic equation in Algebra I. Freshman students contend with the quadratic equation in Algebra I. Freshman students contend with the quadratic equation in Algebra I. Freshman students contend with the quadratic equation in Algebra I.

$$x = \frac{-b \pm \sqrt{b^2 - 4ac}}{2a}$$

Freshman students contend with the quadratic equation in Algebra I. Freshman students contend with the quadratic equation in Algebra I. Freshman students contend with the quadratic equation in Algebra I. Freshman students contend with the quadratic equation in Algebra I. Freshman students contend with the quadratic equation in Algebra I. Freshman students contend with the quadratic equation in Algebra I. Freshman students contend with the quadratic equation in Algebra I. Freshman students contend with the quadratic equation in Algebra I.

Intermediate Algebra I

Freshman students contend with the quadratic equation in Algebra I. Freshman students contend with the quadratic equation in Algebra I. Freshman students contend with the quadratic equation in Algebra I. Freshman students contend with the quadratic equation in Algebra I. Freshman students contend with the quadratic equation in Algebra I.

Freshman students contend with the quadratic equation in Algebra I. Freshman students contend with the quadratic equation in Algebra I. Freshman students contend with the quadratic equation in Algebra I. Freshman students contend with the quadratic equation in Algebra I.

Basics of Algebra II

Freshman students contend with the quadratic equation in Algebra I. Freshman students contend with the quadratic equation in Algebra I. Freshman students contend with the quadratic equation in Algebra I. Freshman students contend with the quadratic equation in Algebra I. Freshman students contend with the quadratic equation in Algebra I. Freshman students contend with the quadratic equation in Algebra I. Freshman students contend with the quadratic equation in Algebra I. Freshman students contend with the quadratic equation in Algebra I. Freshman students contend with the quadratic equation in Algebra I. Freshman students contend with the quadratic equation in Algebra I. Freshman students contend with the quadratic equation in Algebra I. Freshman students contend with the quadratic equation in Algebra I. Freshman students contend with the quadratic equation in Algebra I. Freshman students contend with the quadratic equation in Algebra I.

Intermediate Algebra II

Freshman students contend with the quadratic equation in Algebra I. Freshman students contend with the quadratic equation in Algebra I. Freshman students contend with the quadratic equation in Algebra I. Freshman students contend with the quadratic equation in Algebra I. Freshman students contend with the quadratic

FIGURE 5.11   Screen for Practice Exercise 6

To create the equation, pull down the Insert menu, click the Object command, click the Create New tab, then select Microsoft Equation to start the Equation Editor. This is a new application and we do not provide instruction in its use. It does, however, follow the conventions of other Office applications, and through trial and error, and reference to the Help menu, you should be able to duplicate our equation.

Once the equation (object) has been created, you can move and size it within the document. Clicking an object selects the object and displays the sizing handles to move, size, or delete the object. Double clicking an object loads the application that created it, and enables you to modify the object using the tools of the original application.

CASE STUDIES

Before and After

The best way to learn about the do's and don'ts of desktop publishing is to study the work of others. Choose a particular type of document—for example, a newsletter, résumé, or advertising flyer, then collect samples of that document. Choose one sample that is particularly bad and redesign the document. You need not enter the actual text, but you should keep all of the major headings so that the document retains its identity. Add or delete clip art as appropriate. Bring the before and after samples to class for your professor.

Clip Art

Clip art—you see it all the time, but where do you get it, and how much does it cost? Scan the computer magazines and find at least two sources for additional clip art. Better yet, use your favorite search engine to locate additional sources of clip art on the Web. Return to class with specific information on prices and types of the clip art.

Color Separations

It's difficult to tell where word processing stops and desktop publishing begins. One distinguishing characteristic of a desktop publishing program, however, is the ability to create color separations, which in turn enable you to print a document in full color. Use your favorite search engine to learn more about the process of color separations. Summarize the results of your research in a short paper to your instructor.

Subscribe to a Newsletter

There are literally thousands of regularly published newsletters that are distributed in printed and/or electronic form. Some charge a subscription fee, but many are available just for the asking. Use your favorite search engine to locate a free newsletter in an area of interest to you. Download an issue, then summarize the results of your research in a brief note to your instructor.

CREATING A HOME PAGE: INTRODUCTION TO HTML

OBJECTIVES

After reading this chapter you will be able to:

1. Define HTML and its role on the World Wide Web; describe HTML codes and explain how they control the appearance of a Web document.
2. Use Microsoft Word to create a home page; explain the role of the Save As command in creating an HTML document.
3. Use the Insert Hyperlink command to include hyperlinks in a Web page.
4. Explain how to view the HTML source code of a document from within Microsoft Word; modify the document by changing its source code.
5. Download one or more graphics from the Web, then include those graphics in a Web document.
6. Describe the additional steps needed to place your home page on the Web so that it can be viewed by others.
7. Describe the potential benefits of an Intranet to an organization.

OVERVIEW

Sooner or later anyone who cruises the World Wide Web wants to create a *home page* of their own. That, in turn, requires a basic knowledge of *Hypertext Markup Language* (*HTML*), the language in which all Web pages are written. An HTML document consists of text and graphics, together with a set of codes (or tags), that describe how the document is to appear when viewed in a Web browser such as Internet Explorer.

In the early days of the Web, anyone creating a home page had to learn each of these codes and enter it explicitly. Today, however, it's much easier as you can use an HTML editor to generate the codes for you. Office 97 goes one step further as it enables you to create an HTML document directly in Microsoft Word. In essence, you enter the text of a document, apply basic formatting such as boldface or italics, then simply save the file as an HTML document. There are, of course, additional commands that you will need to learn, but all commands are executed from within Word, through pull-down menus, toolbars, or keyboard shortcuts.

This chapter shows you how to create a home page in Word 97, how to include graphics and other formatting effects, and how to include links to other pages. As always, the hands-on exercises are essential to our learn-by-doing philosophy, as they enable you to apply the conceptual material at the computer. The exercises are structured in such a way that you can view the Web pages you create, even if you don't have access to the Internet.

LEARN MORE ABOUT THE INTERNET

Use your favorite Web search engine to look for additional information about the Internet. One excellent place to begin is the resource page maintained by the Library of Congress at http://lcweb.loc.gov/global. This site contains links to several HTML tutorials and also provides you with information about the latest HTML standard.

INTRODUCTION TO HTML

Figure 6.1 displays a home page similar to the one you will create in the hands-on exercises, which follow shortly. Our page has the look and feel of Web pages you see when you access the World Wide Web. It includes different types of formatting, a bulleted list, underlined links, horizontal lines (rules) that separate elements on the page, and a heading displayed in a larger font. All of these elements are created by inserting codes, called **HTML tags,** into a document to identify the formatting that should be applied at that location. Figure 6.1a displays the document as it would appear when viewed using Internet Explorer. Figure 6.1b shows the underlying HTML codes (tags) that are necessary to format the page.

HTML source codes become less intimidating when you realize that the tags are enclosed in angle brackets and are used consistently from document to document. Most tags occur in pairs, at the beginning and end of the text to be formatted, with the ending code preceded by a slash. In Figure 6.1b, for example, the text *John Doe's Home Page* is enclosed within the <TITLE> and </TITLE> tags. (The function of the Title tag is to indicate the text that will be displayed in the title bar of the browser's application window when that page is accessed. Look at the title and other tags in Figure 6.1b, then observe the effect of these tags as they are read and displayed by the browser in Figure 6.1a.)

Tags can also be nested within one another. The welcome message that John has chosen to place at the top of his page is nested within codes to center (<CENTER>) and boldface (<B>) the text, as well as display it in a larger font size (<FONT SIZE=5>). Links to other pages (which are known as *hyperlinks*) are enclosed within a pair of anchor tags <A> and </A> in which you specify the URL address of the document through the HREF parameter. Note, too, that some tags, such as <P> or <HR>, appear individually to indicate a new paragraph or horizontal rule, respectively.

Text for title bar

Text is boldfaced, centered, and set in a larger font size

Links to other pages

Horizontal rule

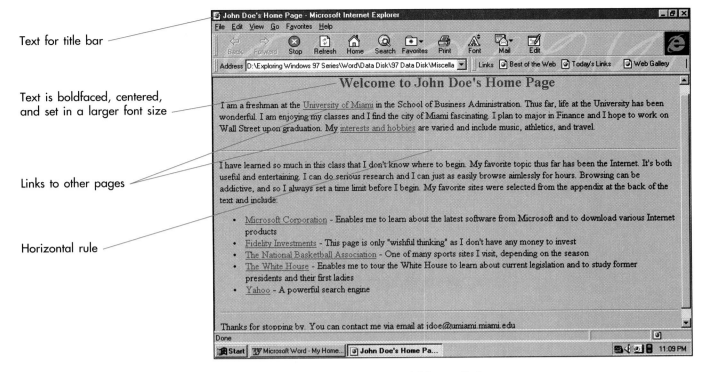

(a) Internet Explorer

Text that will appear in the title bar is enclosed in <TITLE> tags

HTML tags to boldface, establish the font size, and center the text

Ending tags

<A HREF> tag is used to specify a URL address for a hyperlink

<HR> tag specifies a horizontal rule

Ending tags

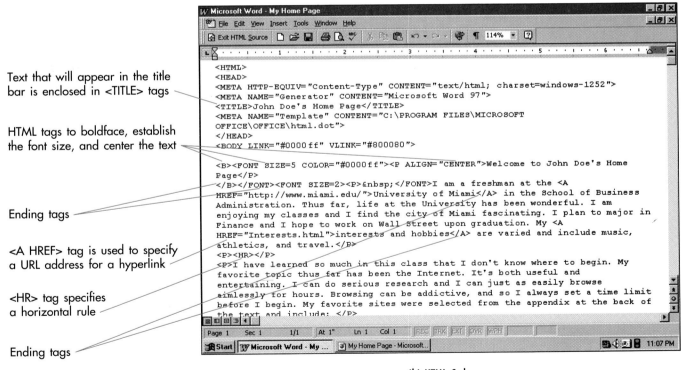

(b) HTML Codes

FIGURE 6.1   A Home Page

Fortunately, however, it is not necessary to memorize HTML tags since you can usually determine their meaning from the codes themselves. Nor is it even necessary for you to enter the tags, as Word will create an HTML document for you based on commands executed from its pull-down menus or toolbars.

THE HEAD AND THE BODY

An HTML document is composed of two parts—a head and a body. The heading contains the text that will be displayed on the browser's title bar and is found between the <HEAD> and </HEAD> tags. The main portion (body) of the document is entered between the <BODY> AND </BODY> tags, which contain the necessary codes to format the document for display on a Web browser.

Microsoft Word 97

As indicated, there are two ways to create an HTML document. The original (and more difficult) method was to enter the codes explicitly in a text editor such as Notepad. The easier technique (and the only one you need to consider) is to use Microsoft Word 97 to create the document for you without having to enter or reference the HTML tags at all.

Figure 6.2 displays the Word 97 screen used to create John Doe's home page. Look carefully and you will see that the toolbars are subtly different from those you are used to seeing. The Standard toolbar, for example, contains an additional tool, the Web Page Preview button, that enables you to see your document as it will appear in the default browser (Internet Explorer). The Formatting toolbar contains tools to increase and decrease font size, in lieu of the drop-down list box to specify a specific point size. (This is because Web documents specify a relative type size rather than an absolute type size.) The Formatting toolbar in Figure 6.2 also has tools to create a horizontal line and change the background, two techniques that are used frequently in creating Web documents.

To create a Web document, start Word in the usual fashion and enter the text of the document with basic formatting. However, instead of saving the document in the default format (as a Word 97 document), you use the *Save As command* to specify an HTML document. Microsoft Word does the rest, generating the HTML tags needed to create the document. You can continue to enter text and/or change the formatting for existing text just as you can with an ordinary Word document. You can also enter any additional HTML tags as appropriate— for example, click the Insert Hyperlink button to insert a hyperlink into a document.

Going on the Web

Once you've completed your home page, you'll want to place your page on the Web so that other people will be able to access it. This requires that you obtain an account on a Web server (typically a UNIX-based machine) with adequate disk space to hold the various pages you create. To do so, you need to check with your system administrator at school or work, or with your local Internet provider, to determine how to submit your page when it is complete.

Realize, however, that even if you do not place your page on the Web, you can still view it locally on your PC. This is the approach we follow in the next hands-on exercise, which enables you to create an HTML document and see the

Web Page Preview button

Insert Hyperlink button

Increase Font Size button

Decrease Font Size button

Horizontal Line button

Background button

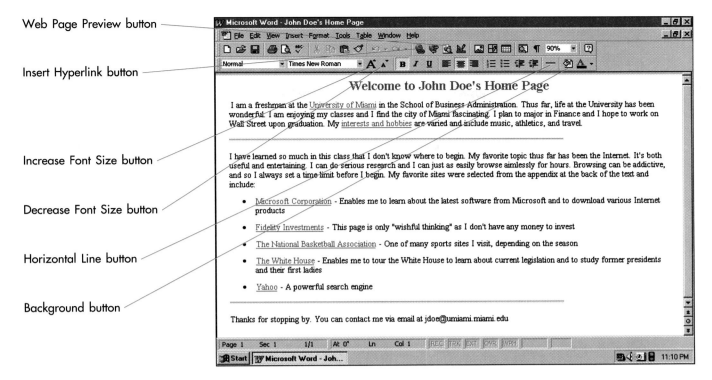

FIGURE 6.2 Microsoft Word 97

results of your effort. Your document is stored on a local drive (e.g., on drive A or drive C) rather than on an Internet server, but it can still be viewed through Internet Explorer (or any other browser). After you have completed the exercise, you (and/or your instructor) can decide whether it is worthwhile to place your page on your school or university's server, where it can be accessed by anyone.

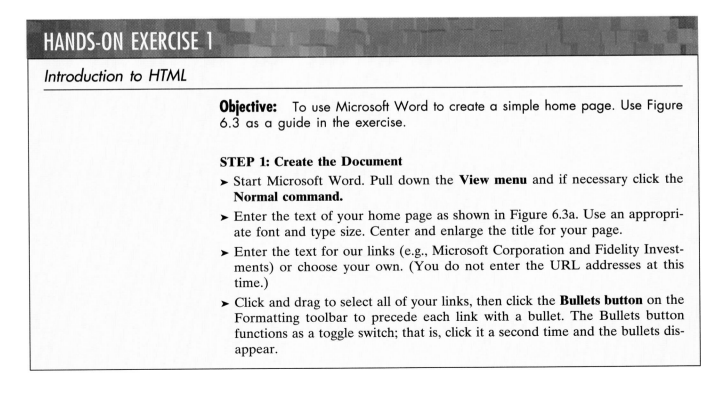

HANDS-ON EXERCISE 1

Introduction to HTML

Objective: To use Microsoft Word to create a simple home page. Use Figure 6.3 as a guide in the exercise.

STEP 1: Create the Document

➤ Start Microsoft Word. Pull down the **View menu** and if necessary click the **Normal command.**

➤ Enter the text of your home page as shown in Figure 6.3a. Use an appropriate font and type size. Center and enlarge the title for your page.

➤ Enter the text for our links (e.g., Microsoft Corporation and Fidelity Investments) or choose your own. (You do not enter the URL addresses at this time.)

➤ Click and drag to select all of your links, then click the **Bullets button** on the Formatting toolbar to precede each link with a bullet. The Bullets button functions as a toggle switch; that is, click it a second time and the bullets disappear.

Bullets button

Center and increase font size for title

Click and drag to select all the text for the links

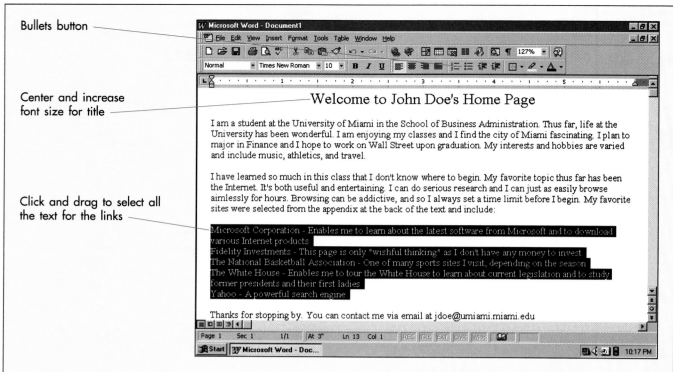

(a) Create the Document (step 1)

FIGURE 6.3 Hands-on Exercise 1

SELECT THEN DO

All formatting operations in Word take place within the context of select-then-do; that is, you select a block of text, then you execute the command to operate on that text. You may select the text in many different ways, the most basic of which is to click and drag over the desired characters. You may also take one of many shortcuts, which include double clicking on a word, pressing Ctrl as you click a sentence, and triple clicking on a paragraph.

STEP 2: Save the Document

➤ Pull down the **File menu.** Click the **Save as HTML command** to display the Save As HTML dialog box in Figure 6.3b.

- Select the appropriate drive (and optionally the folder) where you want to save your document—for example, the **Exploring Word folder** on drive A or C.

- Enter **My Home Page** as the name of the document.

- Click the **Save button** in the Save As HTML dialog box to save the document. Click **Yes** in response to the warning that indicates some formatting may be lost in converting to an HTML document.

➤ The display changes ever so slightly (the Standard and Formatting toolbars include additional buttons for use with an HTML document), but otherwise you continue to work in Word as usual.

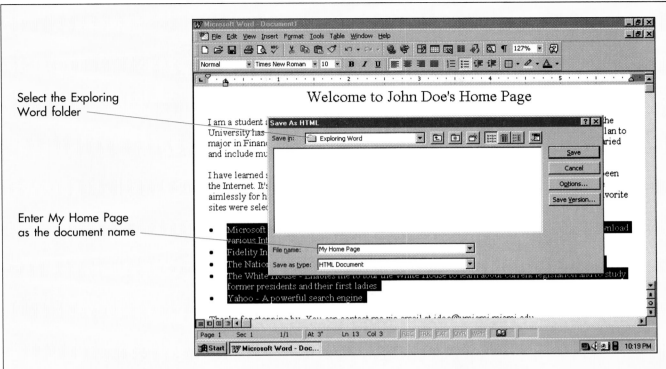

Select the Exploring
Word folder

Enter My Home Page
as the document name

(b) Save the Document (step 2)

FIGURE 6.3   Hands-on Exercise 1 (continued)

MISSING TOOLBARS

The Standard and Formatting toolbars are displayed by default, but either or both can be hidden from view. To display (or hide) a toolbar, point to any toolbar, click the right mouse button to display the Toolbar shortcut menu, then click the individual toolbars on or off as appropriate. If you do not see any toolbars at all, pull down the View menu, click Toolbars to display a dialog box listing the available toolbars, check the toolbars you want displayed, and click OK.

STEP 3: Complete the Formatting

➤ Click and drag to select the title of your document. Pull down the **Format menu,** then click **Font** to display the Font dialog box shown in Figure 6.3c.

➤ Click the **drop-down arrow** on the Font Color list box, then click **Blue** to change the color of the selected text. Click **OK** to close the dialog box.

➤ Click at the end of the first paragraph, then click the **Horizontal Line button** to insert a horizontal rule at the end of the paragraph. Click to the left of the paragraph that begins *Thanks for stopping by,* then click the **Horizontal Line button** a second time.

➤ Enter additional formatting as you see fit. Delete (or enter) blank lines before (after) the rules as necessary.

➤ Click the **Spelling and Grammar button** to check your document for spelling. Save the document.

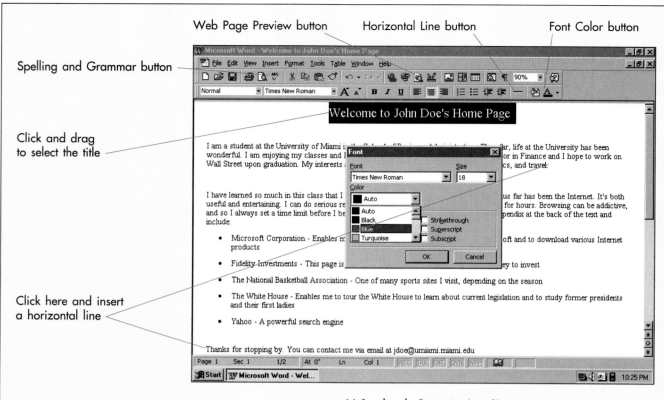

Spelling and Grammar button

Web Page Preview button — Horizontal Line button — Font Color button

Click and drag to select the title

Click here and insert a horizontal line

(c) Complete the Formatting (step 3)

FIGURE 6.3   Hands-on Exercise 1 (continued)

STEP 4: View the Completed Page

➤ Click the **Web Page Preview button** on the Standard toolbar to open the default browser (e.g., Internet Explorer) to see how the finished document will appear when viewed on the Web or a corporate Intranet. Click **OK** if asked to save the document.

➤ You should see your home page as shown in Figure 6.3d. The URL address (C:\Exploring Word\My Home Page.html) indicates that you are viewing the home page on a local drive (drive C) as opposed to an actual Web server.

➤ View your home page and write down any changes you want to make. Click the **Microsoft Word button** on the Windows 95 taskbar to return to Word in order to modify your page.

MULTITASKING

Multitasking, the ability to run multiple programs at the same time, is one of the primary advantages of the Windows environment. Each open application is represented as a button on the Windows 95 taskbar. The easiest way to switch from one open application to another is to click the appropriate button on the taskbar. You can also use the Alt+Tab shortcut that worked in Windows 3.1.

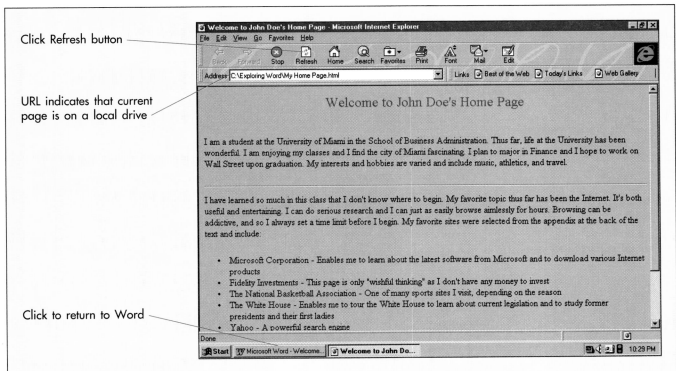

Click Refresh button

URL indicates that current page is on a local drive

Click to return to Word

(d) View the Completed Page (step 4)

FIGURE 6.3   Hands-on Exercise 1 (continued)

STEP 5: View the HTML Tags

➤ Pull down the **View menu** and click **HTML Source** to display the HTML source code as shown in Figure 6.3e. Word has created all of the necessary HTML tags for you.

➤ Delete the words **Welcome to** that appear after the <TITLE> tag. Change the word **student** to **freshman** within the body of the document. Make any other changes you want to the text of your page.

➤ Click the **Exit HTML source button** on the Standard toolbar (or pull down the **View menu** and click **Exit HTML source**), then click **Yes** when asked whether to save the changes. The HTML tags are no longer visible.

➤ Click the **Web Page Preview button** on the Standard toolbar to return to Internet Explorer. Click the **Refresh button.**

➤ The entry in the title bar has changed, as has the text in the document, corresponding to the changes you just made.

➤ Close Internet Explorer. Exit Word if you do not want to continue with the next exercise at this time.

MODIFY THE SOURCE DOCUMENT

Don't be intimidated by the HTML tags, which are quite understandable after you study them for a few minutes. You can modify an HTML document in the Source view by inserting and deleting text and/or codes. Any changes that you make are reflected automatically in the Word document.

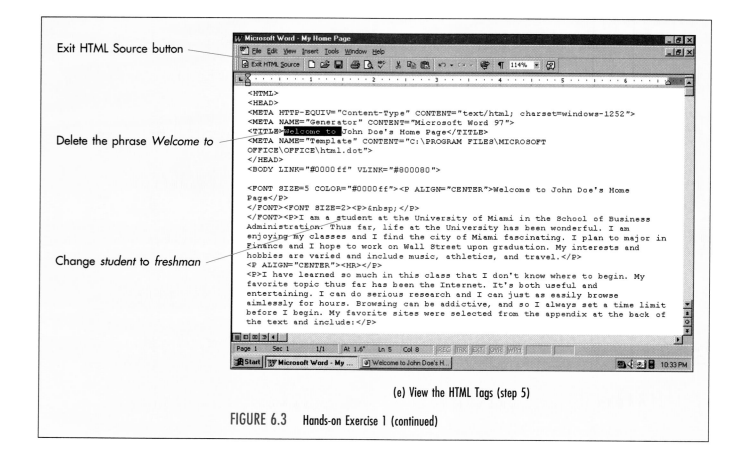

Exit HTML Source button

Delete the phrase *Welcome to*

Change *student* to *freshman*

(e) View the HTML Tags (step 5)

FIGURE 6.3 Hands-on Exercise 1 (continued)

HYPERLINKS

The hands-on exercise just completed had you create a Web page without links of any kind. What makes the Web so fascinating, however, is the ability to jump from one page to the next. Think, for a minute, of the time you have spent in exploring the Web as you clicked on one hyperlink after another. It didn't matter if the linked documents were on the same server (computer) or if they were on an entirely different computer. Either way you were able to go from one document to another simply by clicking on the links of interest to you. It's apparent, therefore, that if you are to develop a meaningful home page, you must learn how to include hyperlinks of your own.

Figure 6.4a displays your home page as it will appear at the end of the next hands-on exercise. It looks very similar to the page you just created except that it contains links to other Web documents. The links appear as underlined text, such as University of Miami or National Basketball Association. Click on a desired link and the browser (e.g., Internet Explorer) displays the associated document. Note, too, that the links (underlined text) appear in two colors, blue and magenta. A blue link indicates that the associated page has not been previously displayed. Magenta, on the other hand, indicates that the page has been viewed.

The ***Insert Hyperlink*** command enables you to create a link within your document. You need to know the URL address of the associated page, such as www.nba.com to display the home page for the National Basketball Association. You need not, however, concern yourself with the syntax of the HTML tags, as Word will prompt you for the necessary information, via the Hyperlink dialog box in Figure 6.4b.

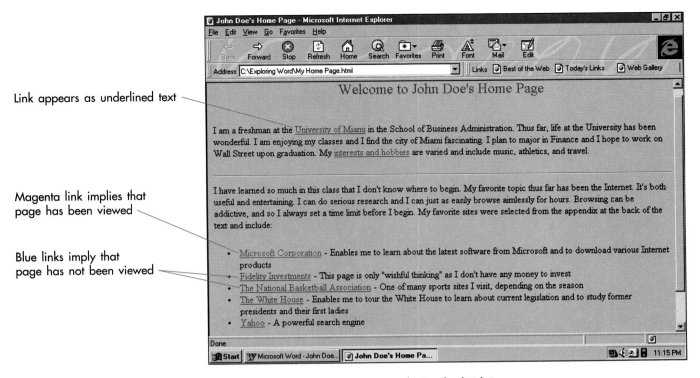

Link appears as underlined text

Magenta link implies that page has been viewed

Blue links imply that page has not been viewed

(a) The Completed Web Page

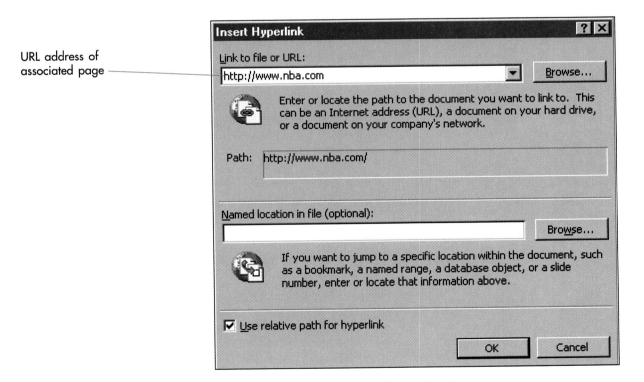

URL address of associated page

(b) External Link

FIGURE 6.4   Hyperlinks

Filename rather than URL
address indicates that link
is to a local document

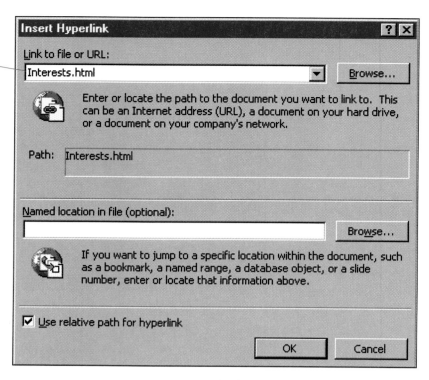

(c) Local Link

FIGURE 6.4   Hyperlinks (continued)

Figure 6.4c displays a second hyperlink dialog box but this time the link is
to a local document (a document on your PC or on the LAN to which your PC
is connected) rather than to an external Web page. The dialog box in Figure 6.4c
contains a file name (interests.html) rather than a URL address. This enables you
to link one document, such as your home page, to a second document that
describes your hobbies and interests in detail, which in turn can be linked to
another document and so on.

The following exercise has you modify the home page you created earlier to
include links to other documents. We will show you how to create two types of
links—one to a local document on your PC and another to an external document
anywhere on the Web.

THE INTRANET

The ability to create links to local documents and to view those pages
through a Web browser has created an entirely new way to disseminate information. Indeed, many organizations are taking advantage of this capability
to develop a corporate Intranet, in which Web pages are placed on a local
area network for use within the organization. The documents on an Intranet
are available only to individuals with access to the LAN on which the documents are stored. This is in contrast to loading the pages onto a Web server
where they can be viewed by anyone with access to the Web.

Objective: To create a Web page with both local and external hyperlinks. Use Figure 6.5 as a guide in the exercise.

STEP 1: Create a Second Web Document

➤ Start Word. Create a document describing your interests such as the document in Figure 6.5a. Your document does not have to be long, as its purpose is to demonstrate how you can link one Web document to another.

➤ Pull down the **File menu.** Click the **Save As HTML command** to display the Save As HTML dialog box. Save the document in the same drive and folder (e.g., the Exploring Word folder on drive C) you used in the previous exercise.

  • Enter **Interests** as the name of the document.

  • Click the **Save button** to save the document. Click **Yes** in response to the warning that indicates some formatting may be lost in conversion to an HTML document.

➤ Close the document.

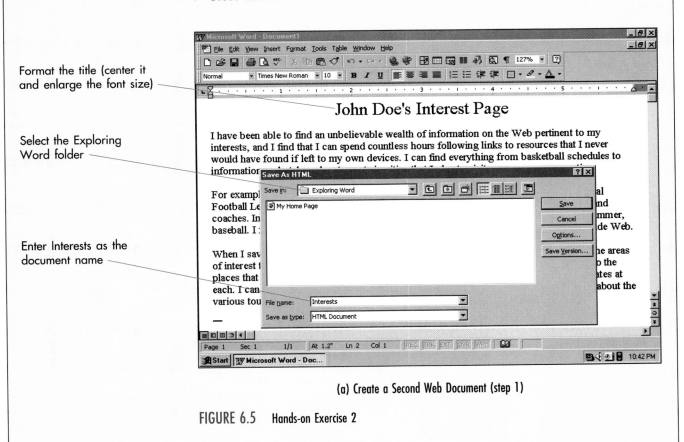

Format the title (center it and enlarge the font size)

Select the Exploring Word folder

Enter Interests as the document name

(a) Create a Second Web Document (step 1)

FIGURE 6.5   Hands-on Exercise 2

SOME FORMATTING IS LOST

The Save As command converts an existing Word document to its HTML equivalent. Some formatting (e.g., spacing before and after paragraphs) is lost in the process, but most is retained. To learn the limitations of the conversion process, pull down the Help menu, click the Contents and Index command, click the Index tab, type *formatting,* select the Web page entry under formatting, then select the topic *Word features that are different or unavailable during Web authoring.* To obtain a hard copy of the information, point anywhere in the Help window, click the right mouse button to display a shortcut menu, then click the Print Topic command.

STEP 2: Open Your Home Page

➤ Pull down the **File menu,** click **Open** (or click the **Open button** on the Standard toolbar). If necessary, change to the appropriate drive and folder (e.g., the Exploring Word folder on drive C).

➤ Click the **drop-down arrow** on the Files of type list box, then select **All Files** as shown in Figure 6.5b.

➤ Scroll until you can select **My Home Page** (the HTML document created in the first exercise), then click **Open** to open the document.

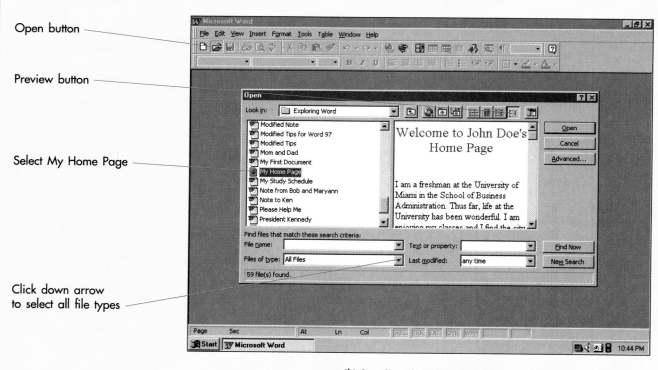

(b) Open Your Home Page (step 2)

FIGURE 6.5   Hands-on Exercise 2 (continued)

STEP 3: Create the Link

➤ Read through your home page until you come to the phrase describing your interests and hobbies at the end of the first paragraph. Click and drag to select the text **interests and hobbies.**

➤ Pull down the **Insert menu** and click **Hyperlink** (or click the **Insert Hyperlink button** on the Standard toolbar) to display the Hyperlink dialog box in Figure 6.5c.

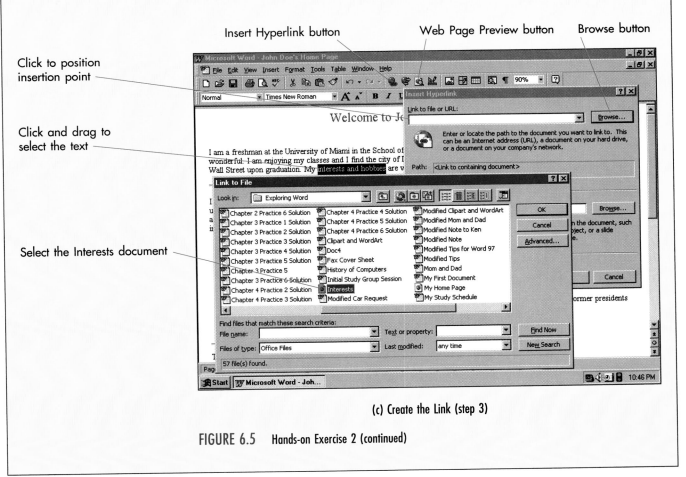

(c) Create the Link (step 3)

FIGURE 6.5   Hands-on Exercise 2 (continued)

➤ Check that the insertion point is positioned in the **Link to File** or **URL text box,** then click the **Browse button** to display the **Link to File dialog box** shown in the figure. Select (click) the **Interests** document you created earlier, then click **OK** to select the file and close the Link to File dialog box.

➤ Click **OK** to close the Hyperlink dialog box. If necessary, add a space between the link and the next word. Save the document.

HYPERLINKS BEFORE AND AFTER

Hyperlinks are displayed in different colors, depending on whether (or not) the associated page has been displayed. Pull down the Format menu and click Text Colors to display the associated dialog box. Click the drop-down arrow next to the appropriate list box to change the color associated with hyperlinks before and after they are viewed. Click OK to accept your changes and close the dialog box.

STEP 4: Test the Link

➤ Click the **Web Page Preview button** on the Standard toolbar to view your home page in Internet Explorer as shown in Figure 6.5d.

➤ The URL address (C:\Exploring Word\My Home Page.html) in the Address bar indicates that you are viewing the home page from a local drive (drive C) as opposed to an actual Web server.

URL address indicates current page is on a local drive

Click the Font button to change the font size in Internet Explorer

Point to link (mouse pointer changes to a hand) and click to view associated page

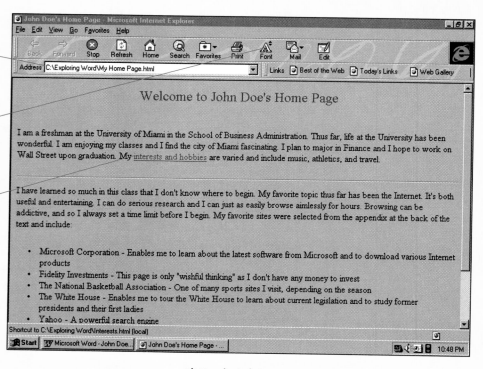

(d) Test the Link (step 4)

FIGURE 6.5   Hands-on Exercise 2 (continued)

➤ Point to the link (the mouse pointer changes to a hand to indicate a hyperlink, and the status bar displays the associated address), then click the **hobbies and interests** hyperlink you just created to view this page.

CHANGE THE FONT SIZE

Internet Explorer enables you to view and/or print a page in one of five font settings (smallest, small, medium, large, and largest). Click the Font button on the toolbar to cycle through the various settings, or alternatively, pull down the View menu, click Fonts, then click the desired font size. The setting pertains to both the displayed page as well as the printed page.

STEP 5: View Your Interests Page

➤ You should see your hobbies and interests as shown in Figure 6.5e. The URL address in Figure 6.5e (C:\Exploring Word\Interests.html) indicates that you are viewing this page from a local drive (drive C) as opposed to an actual server.

➤ Click the **Back button** on the Internet Explorer toolbar to return to your home page. Click the **Close button** to close the browser and return to Word, where you can make additional changes.

Back button

URL address indicates that current page is on a local drive

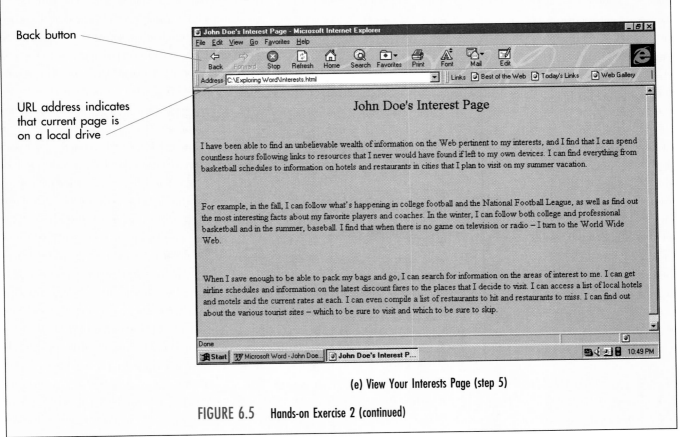

(e) View Your Interests Page (step 5)

FIGURE 6.5   Hands-on Exercise 2 (continued)

MICROSOFT ON THE WEB

Microsoft's home page (www.microsoft.com) is well worth including in any list of Web links. Not only are you able to download free clip art and other Web resources, but you also have access to the latest developments from the software giant. You can also search the Microsoft Knowledge Base for specific information on Windows or any Microsoft application.

STEP 6: Create an External Link

➤ You should see your home page displayed within Word as shown in Figure 6.5f. Click and drag to select the phrase **Microsoft Corporation.**

➤ Pull down the **Insert menu** and click **Hyperlink** (or click the **Insert Hyperlink button** on the Standard toolbar) to display the Insert Hyperlink dialog box in Figure 6.5f.

➤ Check that the insertion point is positioned in the **Link to file** or **URL text box,** then enter the URL of a specific site such as **www.microsoft.com** (the http:// is assumed).

➤ Click **OK** to close the Hyperlink dialog box. Add spaces as necessary to separate the link from the adjacent text.

➤ Add the additional links for your other interests, then save the document. The addresses in our document are: www.cbs.com, www.fidelity.com, www.nba.com, www.whitehouse.gov, and www.yahoo.com.

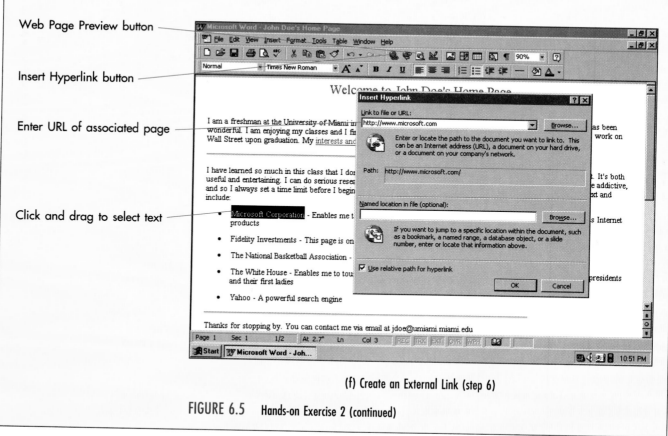

(f) Create an External Link (step 6)

FIGURE 6.5   Hands-on Exercise 2 (continued)

STEP 7: Test the External Link

➤ Click the **Web Page Preview button** on the Standard toolbar to view the document in your default browser. You should see your home page with the newly added links.

➤ Click the link to **Microsoft.** Realize, however, that unlike the link to a local document in step 5, you need access to the Internet in order for this step to work.

➤ You should see the Microsoft home page as shown in Figure 6.5g. The URL address displayed by Internet Explorer corresponds to the address you entered in the Insert Hyperlink dialog box in step 6.

➤ If you are unable to connect, it is most likely because you entered the URL incorrectly or because you are not connected to the Internet. To correct the

Back button

URL of associated page (corresponds to address entered in Insert Hyperlink dialog box)

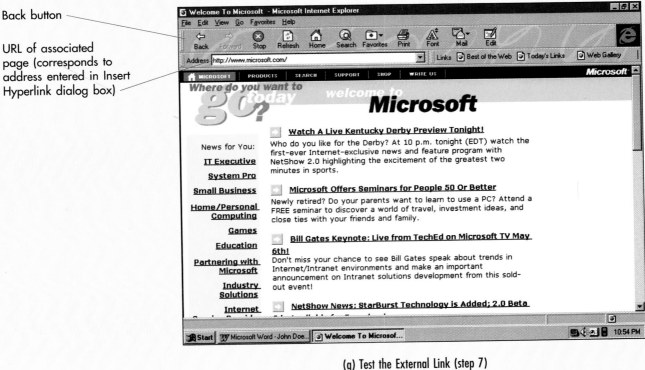

(g) Test the External Link (step 7)

FIGURE 6.5   Hands-on Exercise 2 (continued)

problem, you need to close the browser and return to Word, where you should delete the invalid link, repeat step 6, then be sure you are connected to the Internet.

➤ If you link successfully, click the **Back button** in your browser to return to your home page, then test the various other links to be sure that they are working.

➤ Exit Word and Internet Explorer if you do not want to continue with the next exercise at this time.

ADD YOUR HOME PAGE TO THE LYCOS CATALOG

After you have completed your home page and your LAN administrator has placed it on a server, you want others to be able to find it. You can add your page to various catalogs such as the Lycos Search Engine, which claims to index more than 90% of the Web. Go to www.lycos.com/ addasite.html and fill out the form. Wait a week or two, then try a search on your name. You should be cataloged on the Web!

TOWARD MORE SOPHISTICATED PAGES

You have completed two exercises and have gained valuable experience in HTML. The first exercise had you create a simple home page using commands in Microsoft Word. The second exercise showed you how to link Web pages to one another. We continue with another exercise, which reviews the earlier material and, in addition, shows you how to incorporate graphic elements into a Web page.

The document in Figure 6.6 represents the home page of a hypothetical travel agency, *World Wide Travel*. It contains hyperlinks to four additional pages, each of which describes a specific vacation. The document also contains a link (Return to Top of Page) that references a hidden ***bookmark*** at the top of the page. Bookmarks are a valuable addition to long documents that extend beyond a single screen, as they enable you to jump from one place to another within a document without having to manually scroll through the document.

The document in Figure 6.6 also contains three graphic images to enhance the page and make it more interesting. Graphics may come from a variety of sources such as commercial clip art and/or photographs, either of which may be scanned or downloaded from the Internet. (The graphics in our figure were downloaded from Microsoft's Multimedia Gallery, as will be described in the following hands-on exercise.) Remember, too, that graphics increase the time necessary to display a page, especially over a modem. Be careful, therefore, about including too many graphics or graphics with large file sizes—you don't want your user to lose interest as he or she waits for the page to load.

The ease with which you create the document in Figure 6.6 depends (in part) on your proficiency in Microsoft Word. We use the Tables feature, for example, to position the graphics within the document. We also use the Bullets and Numbering command to accentuate the different vacations. Even if you have only limited experience with Microsoft Word, however, our instructions are sufficiently detailed that you should be able to complete the exercise with little difficulty.

Hidden bookmark

World Wide Travel

(800) 123- 4567

We are a full service travel agency with trips all over the world. We cater to individuals and groups, especially campus organizations. We offer the lowest air fares and hotel accommodations and always provide the ultimate in service. We run specials all the time and urge you to consider the following:

- Honeymoon to the Bahamas
- Spring Break

- Summer Special to Europe
- See the West

Graphic images

You need identification when you travel outside the United States. Passports are not required in North America, but are for most other destinations. They take time to get, so be sure you apply for the passport well in advance of your trip.

Film and other equipment are always cheaper in the United States, so be sure to purchase all of your equipment before you leave. It's always a good idea to bring spare batteries for your camera. You can also bring postage paid envelopes to mail your film home so it will be developed and waiting for you when you return.

Hyperlink to a bookmark

Return to Top of Page

FIGURE 6.6   World Wide Web Travel Page

RESPECT THE COPYRIGHT

A copyright provides legal protection to written and artistic work, and gives the author exclusive rights to its use and reproduction. There are exceptions, however, such as the fair use exclusion, which permits you to use a portion of a work for educational, nonprofit purposes, or for the purpose of critical review or commentary. It is a complicated issue to say the least, and our advice is when in doubt, assume that you do not have permission. Go to the Copyright Web Site at http://www.benedict.com to learn more about copyright law.

Toward More Sophisticated Pages

Objective: To create a more sophisticated HTML document containing graphics, links, and bookmarks. This step requires access to the Internet in order to download material from the Web for inclusion in your document. Use Figure 6.7 as a guide in the exercise.

STEP 1: Download Web Resources

➤ Start Word, then click the **New button** on the Standard toolbar to begin a new document. Use the **Save As HTML** command to save the document as **World Wide Travel** in the same drive and folder you have used throughout the chapter.

➤ Pull down the **Insert menu,** click **Picture,** then click the **Browse Web Art Page command.** (If you do not see the Browse Web Art Page command it is because you did not save the document as an HTML file.) Click **Yes** if asked whether you want to browse the Microsoft Web site. (You must have an Internet connection to do this step.)

➤ Click the link to **IE MMGallery Themes** to display the page in Figure 6.7a. (If do not see this page try entering its address **(www.microsoft.com/workshop/design/mmgallry)** directly in the address box.

➤ Scroll down in the page until you can click the link to **Travel** to display the images for this category.

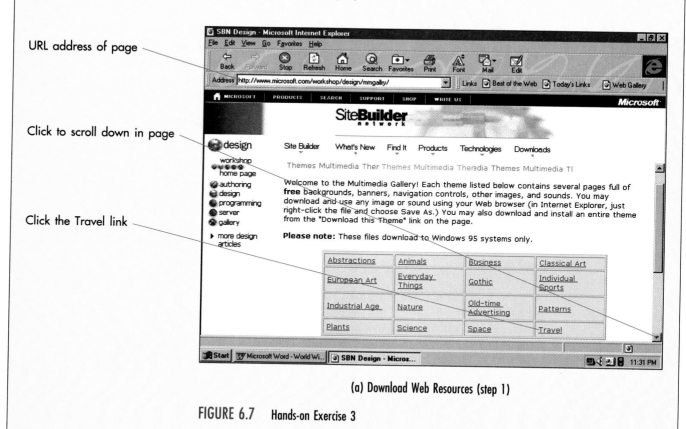

(a) Download Web Resources (step 1)

FIGURE 6.7   Hands-on Exercise 3

THE MICROSOFT SEARCH ENGINE

Microsoft is continually changing its home page and you may not find the exact links we describe. You can, however, find the equivalent information by using Microsoft's internal search engine. Go to Microsoft's home page and click the Search icon to display a search form. Enter the scope of the search (a full site search) and the key words (*Multimedia gallery*), then click the Search button. You should see one or more articles that will take you to the multimedia gallery.

STEP 2: Download the Travel Images

➤ Scroll down in the Travel page until you come to the **General Images section.** Be patient, especially if you are on a modem connection, as it takes time for the images to be displayed.

➤ Point to the image of the **Two Globes,** then click the **right mouse button** to display a shortcut menu. Click the **Save Image as** command to display the Save As dialog box in Figure 6.7b.

- Click the **drop-down arrow** in the Save in list box to select the same folder you have been using throughout the chapter.

- Change the default name *images01* to **Two Globes** (a more meaningful name). This will facilitate selecting the appropriate image later in the exercise.

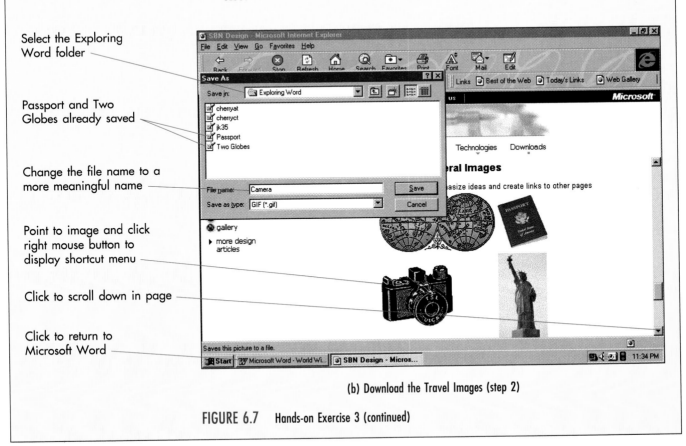

Select the Exploring Word folder

Passport and Two Globes already saved

Change the file name to a more meaningful name

Point to image and click right mouse button to display shortcut menu

Click to scroll down in page

Click to return to Microsoft Word

(b) Download the Travel Images (step 2)

FIGURE 6.7   Hands-on Exercise 3 (continued)

- Click the **Save button** to download the figure and save it on your local drive.

➤ Repeat the process to save the other two images (**Passport** and **Camera**) as shown in the figure. Now that you have the necessary resources, you are ready to create the HTML document.

DOWNLOADING A THEME

You can download an entire theme with a single command as opposed to downloading each of the objects individually. Go to the Multimedia Gallery page, click the link to the desired theme (e.g., travel), then click the link to Download this Theme, which appears at the top of the Web page. You should see the Save As dialog box. Choose the folder in which to save the file, then click the Save button to begin downloading. After downloading is complete (the process takes a few minutes), start the Windows Explorer, open the folder in which you saved the file, then double click the file to install the theme on your PC. The installation program places the objects in the Mmgallry (Multimedia Gallery) folder in the Program Files folder on drive C. See problem 4 at the end of the chapter.

STEP 3: Create the Travel Document

➤ Click the **Word button** on the Windows 95 taskbar. Pull down the **Table menu** and click the **Insert Table command** to display a table grid. Click and drag to select a one-by-two grid, then release the mouse to create a table consisting of one row and two columns.

➤ Pull down the **Tables menu** and toggle the **Show Gridlines command** on if you do not see the table.

➤ Click in the leftmost cell of the table. Type **World Wide Travel** and press the **enter key.** Enter the phone number **(800) 123-4567.**

➤ Click and drag to select **World Wide Travel,** then pull down the **Format menu.** Click **Font** and choose a larger font size (e.g., 24 points). Click **OK.** Select both lines of text and click the **Center button** on the Formatting toolbar.

➤ Pull down the **File menu** and click **Save** (or click the **Save button** on the Standard toolbar).

➤ Click below the table and click the **Horizontal Line button** on the Formatting toolbar. Enter the additional text shown in Figure 6.7c.

➤ Click the **Horizontal Line button** a second time. Your document should approximate the one in our figure.

STEP 4: Insert the Picture

➤ Click in the rightmost cell of the table. Pull down the **Insert menu** and click (or point to) **Picture,** then click **From file** to display the Insert Picture dialog box in Figure 6.7d.

➤ Click the **drop-down arrow** in the Look in list box, then select the folder containing the clip art images. (This is the folder where you saved the images in step 2.)

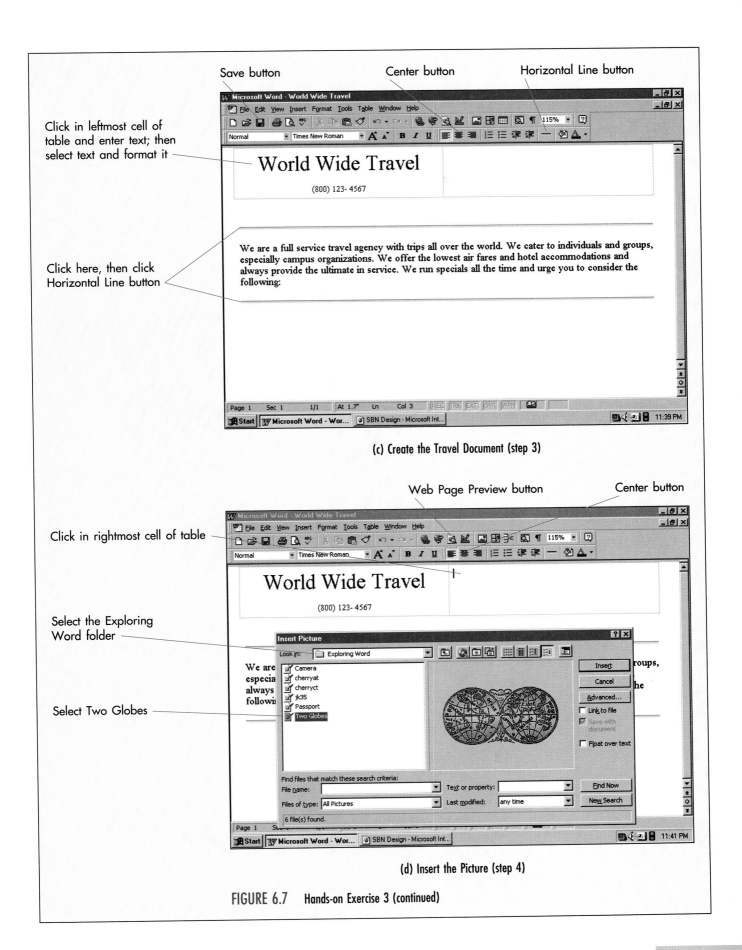

Save button   Center button   Horizontal Line button

Click in leftmost cell of table and enter text; then select text and format it

Click here, then click Horizontal Line button

(c) Create the Travel Document (step 3)

Web Page Preview button   Center button

Click in rightmost cell of table

Select the Exploring Word folder

Select Two Globes

(d) Insert the Picture (step 4)

FIGURE 6.7   Hands-on Exercise 3 (continued)

➤ Select the **Two Globes** graphic as shown in Figure 6.7d. Click **Insert** to insert the image and close the Insert Picture dialog box.

➤ Click the **Center button** on the Formatting toolbar to center the image in the cell. Save the document.

STEP 5: Change the Background

➤ Click the **Web Page Preview button** on the Standard toolbar to see how your page will appear in the default browser that is installed on your system. Click **Yes** if asked to save the document.

➤ You should see the document in Internet Explorer. The document has a gray background by default. Click the **Word button** on the Windows 95 taskbar to return to Word to change the background.

➤ Pull down the **Format menu.** Click **Background** to display the Background color palette in Figure 6.7e. Click **Fill Effects.** Click **Parchment.** Click **OK.**

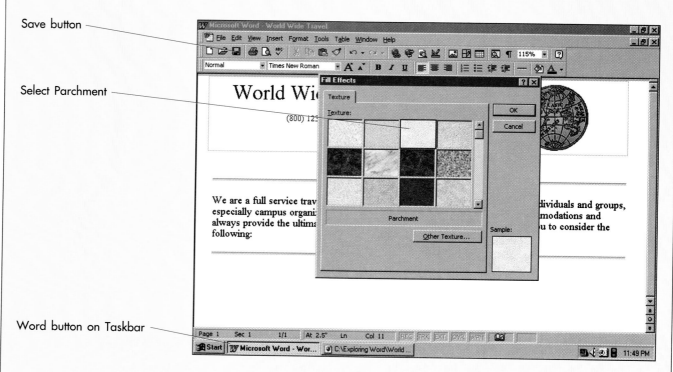

Save button

Select Parchment

Word button on Taskbar

(e) Change the Background Color (step 5)

FIGURE 6.7   Hands-on Exercise 3 (continued)

KEEP IT SIMPLE

Too many would-be designers clutter a page unnecessarily by importing a complex background, which tends to obscure the text. The best design is a simple design—either no background or a very simple pattern. We also prefer light backgrounds with dark text (e.g., black or dark blue text on a white background) as opposed to the other way around. Design, however, is subjective and there is no consensus as to what makes an attractive page. Variety is indeed the spice of life.

➤ Save the document. Click the **Web Page Preview button** on the Standard toolbar to reactivate the browser, then click the **Refresh button** to obtain the most recent copy of the document. You should see the same document as before, except that the background has changed.

STEP 6: Create the Second Document

➤ Click the **Word button** on the Windows taskbar to return to Word. Click the **New button** on the Standard toolbar to start a new document, then double click the **Blank document icon** in the New dialog box.

➤ Enter the text of the document as shown in Figure 6.7f. (This is the document that will be associated with the various travel links in the main document.)

➤ Save the document as an **HTML document** called **Dream Vacation** as shown in Figure 6.7f. Be sure to save the document in the same drive and folder you have been using throughout the chapter.

➤ Click the **Background button** on the Formatting toolbar and select the same background as in the previous step.

➤ Pull down the **File menu** and click **Close** to close this document but remain in Word. Answer **Yes** if prompted to save your changes.

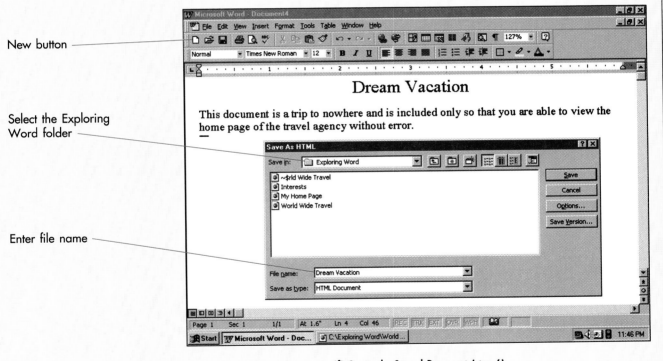

(f) Create the Second Document (step 6)

FIGURE 6.7   Hands-on Exercise 3 (continued)

STEP 7: Add the Links

➤ You should see the World Wide Travel document as before. Scroll through the document until you come to the point where you want to insert a hyperlink (above the last horizontal rule).

➤ If necessary, add a blank line, then type **Honeymoon to the Bahamas.** Click and drag to select this text as shown in Figure 6.7g.

➤ Pull down the **Insert menu** and click **Hyperlink** (or click the **Insert Hyperlink button** on the Standard toolbar) to display the Insert Hyperlink dialog box.

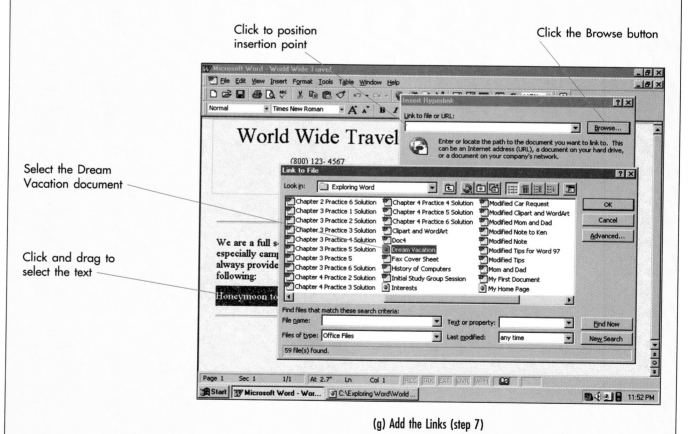

Click to position insertion point

Click the Browse button

Select the Dream Vacation document

Click and drag to select the text

(g) Add the Links (step 7)

FIGURE 6.7   Hands-on Exercise 3 (continued)

➤ Check that the insertion point is positioned in the **Link to File** or **URL text box,** then click the **Browse button** to display the **Link to File dialog box** shown in the figure.

➤ Select (click) the **Dream Vacation document** you created earlier, then click **OK** to select the file and close the Link to File dialog box.

➤ Click **OK** to close the Insert Hyperlink dialog box. You should see the under-lined link <u>Honeymoon to the Bahamas</u> in the document.

➤ Click the **Bullets button** on the Formatting toolbar to place a bullet in front of the link. Press the **enter key** to move to the next line, then add additional links for **Spring Break, Summer Special to Europe,** and **See the West.**

➤ All of your links should reference the same Dream Vacation document. (Eventually, however, you will have to create separate documents, one for each vacation. See practice exercise 1 at the end of the chapter.)

➤ Save the document after the links have been added.

PROTOTYPING

Prototyping is a widely used technique that enables an end user to experience the look and feel of a system before the system has been completed. The user is shown the highest level screen (e.g., the travel agency's home page) and provided with a set of links to partially completed documents. The user gets the sense of the eventual system even though the latter is far from finished. Prototyping also provides valuable feedback to the developer, who is able to make the necessary adjustments before any extensive work has been done.

STEP 8: Test the Links

➤ Click the **Web Page Preview button** on the Standard toolbar to view the document in your browser. Click **Yes** if prompted to save the document.

➤ You should see the travel document in your Web browser as shown in Figure 6.7h. The URL address (C:\Exploring Word\World Wide Travel.html) that is displayed in the Location text box indicates that you are viewing the page from a local drive (drive C) as opposed to an actual Web server.

➤ Point to the first link (the mouse pointer changes to a hand to indicate a link), then click the **Honeymoon to the Bahamas** hyperlink you just created to change to view the Dream Vacation page.

➤ Click the **Back button** on the Internet Explorer toolbar to return to the home page for the travel agency. Select (click) a different link to once again display the Dream Vacation page. Click the **Back button** to return to the home page.

➤ Continue testing in this fashion until you are satisfied your links are working. Click the **Word button** on the Windows 95 taskbar to return to Word in order to complete the home page for the travel agency.

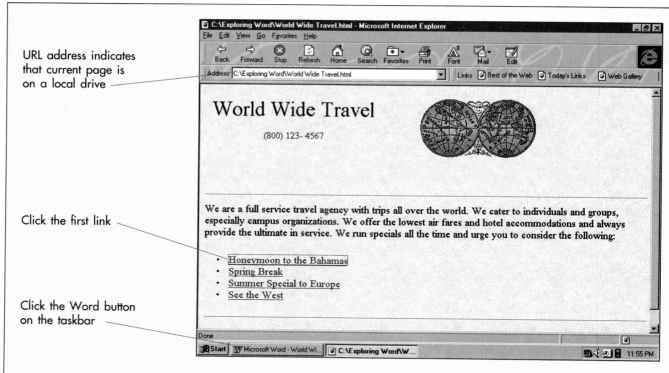

URL address indicates
that current page is
on a local drive

Click the first link

Click the Word button
on the taskbar

(h) Test the Links (step 8)

FIGURE 6.7 Hands-on Exercise 3 (continued)

OBTAINING A PASSPORT

You can't obtain a passport online, but you can get all of the information you need. Go to travel.state.gov, the home page of the Bureau of Consular Affairs in the U. S. Department of State, then click the link to Passport Information to learn how to apply for a passport. You will be able to download an actual passport application with detailed instructions including a list of the documents you need to supply. You can also access a nationwide list of places where you can apply.

STEP 9: Complete the Document

➤ You should be back in Word as shown in Figure 6.7i. Click below the second horizontal rule.

➤ Pull down the **Table menu** and click the **Insert Table command** to display a grid. Click and drag to select a two-by-two grid, then release the mouse to create the table.

➤ Click in the left cell of the first row and insert the Passport graphic you downloaded earlier.

➤ Press the **Tab** or **right arrow key** to move to the next cell in that row and enter the text shown in Figure 6.7i.

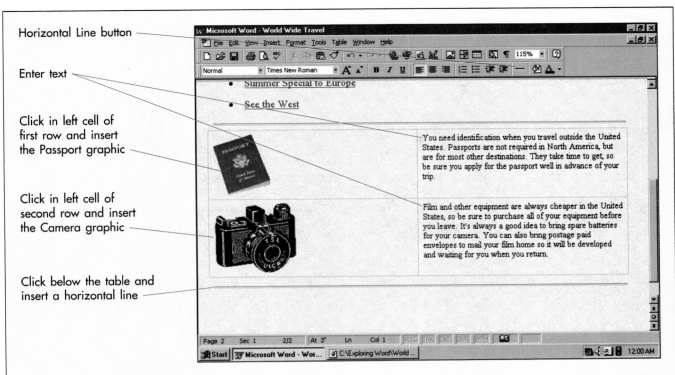

Horizontal Line button

Enter text

Click in left cell of
first row and insert
the Passport graphic

Click in left cell of
second row and insert
the Camera graphic

Click below the table and
insert a horizontal line

(i) Complete the Document (step 9)

FIGURE 6.7   Hands-on Exercise 3 (continued)

➤ Complete the second row of the table by entering the camera graphic and associated text.

➤ Click below the table, then click the **Horizontal Line button** to insert the horizontal line at the bottom of the document. Save the document.

THE UNDO COMMAND

The Undo command enables you to undo the last 100 changes to a document. Click the drop-down arrow next to the Undo button to produce a list of your previous actions, then click the action you want to undo, which also undoes all of the preceding commands. Undoing the fifth command in the list, for example, will also undo the preceding four commands.

STEP 10: Add a Bookmark

➤ Creating a bookmark and a link that points to it is a two-step process (the second step is shown in Figure 6.7j). You start by creating the bookmark itself (which in our example is hidden at the top of the page), then you create the link(s) to the bookmark elsewhere in the document.

➤ To create the bookmark:

• Press **Ctrl+Home** to move to the top of the page. Pull down the **Insert menu** and click **Bookmark** to display the Bookmark dialog box.

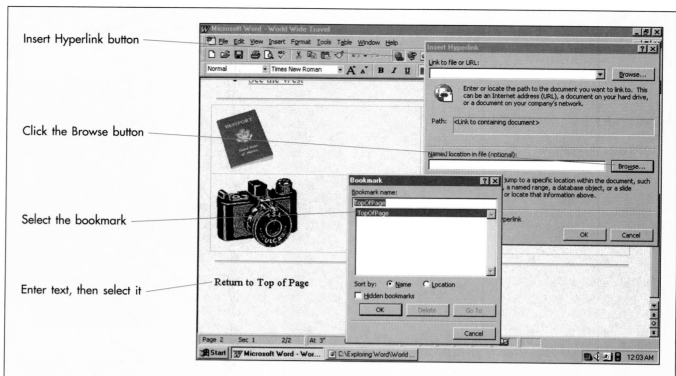

Insert Hyperlink button

Click the Browse button

Select the bookmark

Enter text, then select it

(j) Add a Bookmark (step 10)

FIGURE 6.7   Hands-on Exercise 3 (continued)

- Enter **TopOfPage** (spaces are not allowed) as the name of the bookmark, then click the **Add button** to add the bookmark and close the dialog box. (The bookmark is visible in the HTML source but not in the document.)

➤ To create the link to the bookmark:

- Press **Ctrl+End** to move to the end of the document (the place where you want the reference to the bookmark). Type **Return to Top of Page,** then select the text.

LEARN FROM OTHERS

You can incorporate elements from existing Web pages into your own documents. Once you find a Web page of interest to you, pull down the View menu in your browser, then select the Source command to view the underlying HTML codes. Click and drag to select the codes you need, press Ctrl+C to copy the code to the Windows clipboard, then return to Word and the document on which you are working. Pull down the View menu from within Word, select HTML Source to view the source code for your page, then press Ctrl+V to paste the codes into your document. *Do not, however, incorporate copyrighted material into your document.*

- Click the **Insert Hyperlink button** to display the Insert Hyperlink dialog box, then click the **Browse button** next to the Named Location in File text box. Select the bookmark you just created (TopOfPage). Click **OK.**
- Click **OK** to close the Insert Hyperlink dialog box.

➤ You now have a link to jump from the bottom of your page to the top. Save the completed document.

STEP 11: Preview in the Browser

➤ Click the **Web Page Preview button** to preview the document. Check each of the links to be sure they work.

➤ Proofread the document, making note of any changes, then close the browser and return to Word to make corrections as necessary. Return to the browser to verify that the corrections have taken effect.

➤ Return to Word. Pull down the **File menu** and click the **Print Preview command** to see the entire document as shown in Figure 6.7k.

➤ Click the **Magnifier button** to turn the magnifier on, then click the page to increase (decrease) the magnification of the document.

➤ Click the **Print button** to print the document and submit it to your instructor. Congratulations on a job well done. Bon Voyage!

Zoom box

Magnifier button

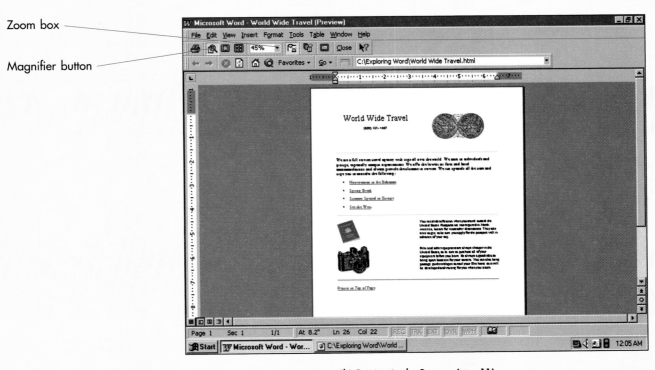

(k) Preview in the Browser (step 11)

FIGURE 6.7   Hands-on Exercise 3 (continued)

Hypertext Markup Language (HTML) is the language used to create a Web page. In essence, HTML consists of a set of codes that format a document for display on the World Wide Web. There are two ways to create a document containing HTML tags. The original (and more difficult) method was to explicitly enter the text and codes in a text editor such as Notepad. The easier technique (and the only one you need to consider) is to use Microsoft Word and have it create the HTML tags for you.

To create a Web document, start Word in the usual fashion and enter the text of the document with basic formatting. Pull down the File menu and click the Save As command, then specify HTML document as the file type. Microsoft Word does the rest, generating the HTML tags needed to create the document. You can continue to enter text and/or change the formatting for existing text just as you can with an ordinary Word document.

Tables facilitate the creation of more complex documents. The Insert Hyperlink command is used to link a document to other pages. Clip art and other graphics are inserted into a document through the Insert Picture command.

After a home page is created, it has to be placed on a Web server or local area network so that other people will be able to access it. This, in turn, requires you to check with your system administrator if, in fact, your page is to become part of the World Wide Web or a corporate Intranet. Even if your page is not placed on the Web, you can still view it locally on your PC through a Web browser.

KEY WORDS AND CONCEPTS

Bookmark
Browser
Graphics
Home page
HTML tags
Hyperlink
Hypertext Markup
  Language (HTML)

Insert Hyperlink
  Command
Insert Picture
  Command
Internet Explorer
Intranet
Microsoft Multimedia
  Gallery

Save As command
Tables command
Tag

MULTIPLE CHOICE

1. Which of the following requires you to enter HTML tags explicitly in order to create a Web document?
   (a) A text editor such as the Notepad accessory
   (b) Word 97
   (c) Both (a) and (b) above
   (d) Neither (a) nor (b) above

2. Which of the following is true about the Formatting toolbar in Word 97?
   (a) It is displayed with Word documents but not with HTML documents
   (b) It is displayed with HTML documents but not with Word documents
   (c) It is displayed with both types of documents, and further it displays the identical buttons regardless of the type of document
   (d) It is displayed with both types of documents, but displays different buttons depending on the type of document

3. Which of the following is true about the Standard toolbar in Word 97?
   (a) It is displayed with Word documents but not with HTML documents
   (b) It is displayed with HTML documents but not with Word documents
   (c) It is displayed with both types of documents, and further it displays the identical buttons regardless of the type of document
   (d) It is displayed with both types of documents, but displays different buttons depending on the type of document

4. What is the easiest way to switch back and forth between Word and Internet Explorer, given that both are open?
   (a) Click the appropriate button on the Windows 95 taskbar
   (b) Click the Start button, click Programs, then choose the appropriate program
   (c) Minimize all applications to display the Windows 95 desktop, then double click the icon for the appropriate application
   (d) All of the above are equally convenient

5. The Format Background command:
   (a) Enables you to change the background color of a Web document
   (b) Enables you to change the texture of a Web document
   (c) Both (a) and (b)
   (d) Neither (a) nor (b)

6. All of the following tags require a matching code except:
   (a) <HR>
   (b) <TITLE>
   (c) <CENTER>
   (d) <A>

7. When should you click the Refresh button on the Internet Explorer toolbar?
   (a) Whenever you visit a new Web site
   (b) Whenever you return to a Web site within a session
   (c) Whenever you view a document on a corporate Intranet
   (d) Whenever you return to a document within a session and the document has changed during the session

8. Which of the following codes creates a horizontal rule across a page in an HTML document?
   (a) <HR>
   (b) <HL>
   (c) <P>
   (d) <UL>

9. How do you view the HTML tags for a Web document from within Word?
   (a) Pull down the View menu and select the HTML Source command
   (b) Pull down the File menu, click the Save As command, and specify HTML as the file type
   (c) Click the Web Page Preview button on the Standard toolbar
   (d) All of the above

10. Which of the following was the source of the clip art used to create the travel document in the chapter?
    (a) The Microsoft Clip Gallery that is included with Office 97
    (b) The Multimedia Gallery on the Microsoft Web site
    (c) The clip art home page at www.clipart.com
    (d) The clip art collection of the Smithsonian Institution

11. Which of the following is required to jump to another section of the same HTML document?
    (a) A bookmark
    (b) An ordered list of the document's contents
    (c) An anchored graphic image
    (d) All of the above

12. Where will the text enclosed in the <TITLE> </TITLE> tags appear when an HTML document is displayed using a Web browser?
    (a) In the title bar
    (b) At the top of the document
    (c) Both (a) and (b) above
    (d) Neither (a) nor (b) above

13. Which of the following statements regarding HTML tags is true?
    (a) They cannot be created in Word 97
    (b) They cannot be viewed in Word 97
    (c) They cannot be viewed in Internet Explorer
    (d) None of the above

14. Internet Explorer can display an HTML page that is stored on:
    (a) A local area network as part of a company's Intranet
    (b) A web server as part of the World Wide Web
    (c) Drive A or drive C of a standalone PC
    (d) All of the above

15. How do you convert an existing Word document to its HTML equivalent?
    (a) Click the Save button on the Standard toolbar
    (b) Pull down the File menu, click the Save As command, then specify an HTML file type
    (c) Both (a) and (b)
    (d) Neither (a) nor (b)

ANSWERS

1. a	**6.** a	**11.** a
2. d	**7.** d	**12.** a
3. d	**8.** a	**13.** d
4. a	**9.** a	**14.** d
5. c	**10.** b	**15.** b

PRACTICE WITH MICROSOFT WORD

1. The Travel Agent: Create a page for at least two additional excursions for use with the travel page(s) created in the chapter. Figure 6.8, for example, creates the page for the *Honeymoon to the Bahamas* link and incorporates a graphic from the Microsoft Clip Gallery. You might also consult the Virtual Tourist Web site (www.vtourist.com/vt) for information about other destinations.

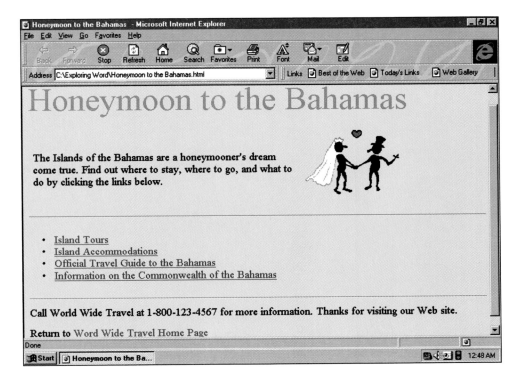

FIGURE 6.8   Screen for Practice Exercise 1

2. The Multimedia Gallery: Figure 6.9 displays a banner from three different themes within the Microsoft Multimedia Gallery. Use one of these banners (or select another banner of your own choosing) as the basis for a Web page. Design is important, so make the page as attractive as you can. Submit a copy of the completed page to your instructor for inclusion in a class contest to determine the most attractive banner.

3. Milestones in Communications: The availability of HTML facilitates the creation of interactive documents such as the document in Figure 6.10. The author used Microsoft Word to create *Milestones in Communications*, then used the Save As command to convert the Word document to its HTML equivalent. Next he bookmarked each of the nine events and created a table of bookmarks at the beginning of the document. And finally, he created a common *Return to Milestones* bookmark (not shown in the figure), which appears at the end of each event. The result is an interactive document that lets the user browse through it.

(a) Travel Banner

(b) European Art Banner

(c) Science Banner

FIGURE 6.9   Banners for Practice Exercise 2

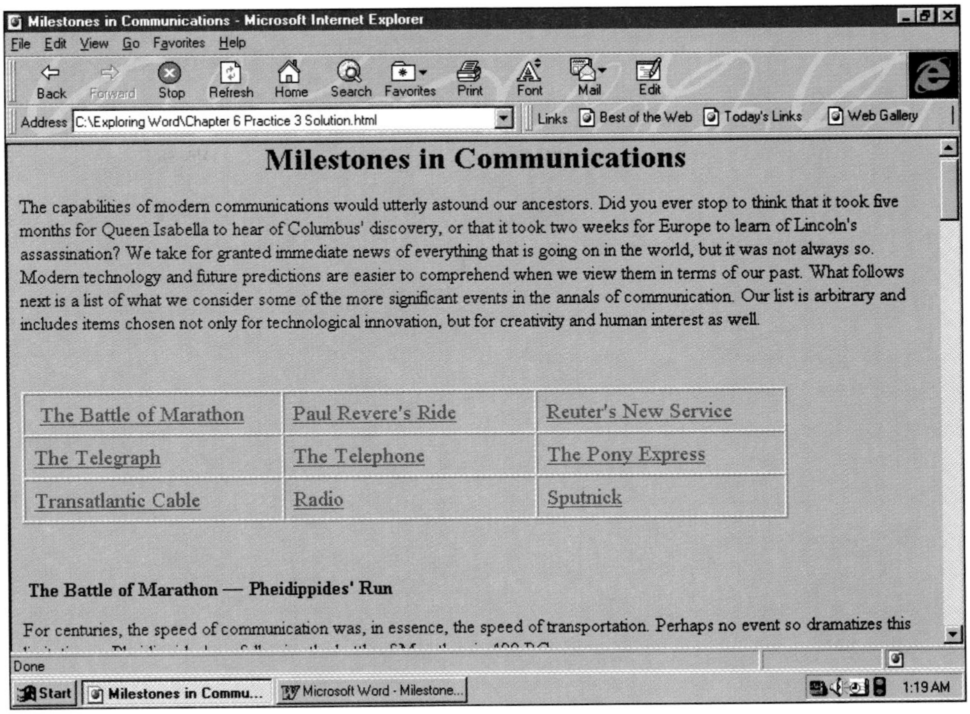

FIGURE 6.10   Screen for Practice Exercise 3

Create your own interactive document containing at least four bookmarks, or alternatively, duplicate the document in Figure 6.10. You can find the text for the document in the file *Milestones in Communications,* which is found in the *Exploring Word* folder.

4. Downloading a theme: The chapter described how to download individual images from the Microsoft Multimedia Gallery for inclusion in a Web document. It's often easier, however, to download an entire theme as shown in Figure 6.11. Go to the Multimedia Gallery as described in the third hands-on exercise, select a theme that interests you, then create a Web document based on that theme.

5. The Web Page Wizard: Figure 6.12 displays one of several templates that can be selected using the Web Page Wizard in Word 97. Pull down the File menu, click New to display the New dialog box, click the Web Pages tab, then double click the icon for the Web Page Wizard. Create a Web page based on one of the existing templates and submit it to your instructor as proof you did the exercise. Include a reference on your page to the specific Wizard, together with a sentence or two describing your impression of the Wizard.

6. Update the Wizard: Microsoft is continually updating its Web site with new templates, styles, and so on. Pull down the Help menu, click Microsoft on the Web, then click Free Stuff to connect to the Microsoft Web site. Scroll down the page until you can click the link to Word Web Page Wizard Accessories to display a page similar to Figure 6.13. Download the latest offering, then incorporate that material into the document created in the previous exercise.

FIGURE 6.11   Screen for Practice Exercise 4

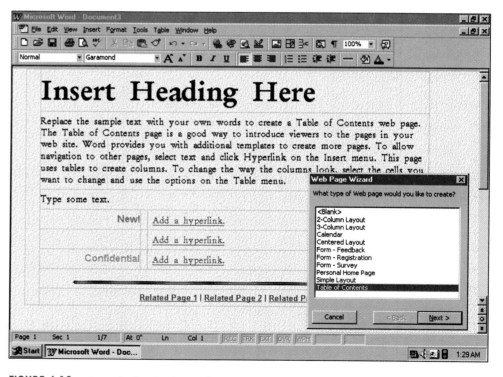

FIGURE 6.12   Screen for Practice Exercise 5

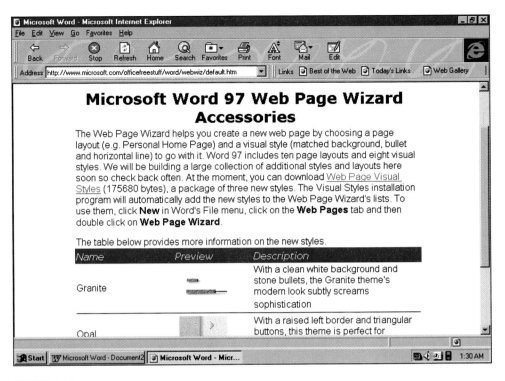

FIGURE 6.13   Screen for Practice Exercise 6

CASE STUDIES

Designer Home Pages

Everyone has a personal list of favorite Web sites, but have you ever thought seriously about what makes an attractive Web page? Is an attractive page the same as a useful page? Try to develop a set of guidelines for a designer to follow as he or she creates a Web site, then incorporate these guidelines into a brief report for your instructor. Support your suggestions by referring to specific Web pages that you think qualify for your personal "Best (Worst) of the Web" award.

Employment Opportunities

The Internet abounds with employment opportunities, help-wanted listings, and places to post your résumé. Your home page reflects your skills and experience to the entire world, and represents an incredible opportunity never before available to college students. You can encourage prospective employers to visit your home page, and make contact with hundreds more companies than would otherwise be possible. Update your home page to include a link to your résumé, and then surf the Net to find places to register it.

Forms in HTML Documents

Many Web pages require you to enter information into a text box, then submit that information to a Web server. Every time you use a search engine, for example, you enter key words into a form, which transmits your request to the search engine. Other common forms include a guest book where you register as having visited the site. Including a form on a page is not difficult but it does require additional knowledge of HTML. Use an appropriate search engine to see what you can find about forms, then summarize your results in a note to your instructor.

The Contest

Almost everyone enjoys some form of competition. Ask your instructor to choose a theme for a Web site such as a school club, and to declare a contest in the class to produce the "best" document. Submit your entry, but write your name on the back of the document so that it can be judged anonymously. Your instructor may want to select a set of semi-finalists, then distribute copies of those documents so that the class can vote on the winner.

Front Page 97

Microsoft Word 97 is an excellent way to begin creating Web documents. It is only a beginning, however, and there are many specialty programs that offer significantly more capability. One such product is Front Page 97, a product aimed at creating a Web site as opposed to isolated documents. Search the Web for information on Front Page 97, then summarize your findings in a short note to your instructor. Be sure to include information on capabilities that are included in Front Page that are not found in Word.

APPENDIX A: OBJECT LINKING AND EMBEDDING

OVERVIEW

OLE

The ability to create a document containing data (objects) from multiple applications is one of the primary advantages of the Windows environment. The memo in Figure A.1, for example, was created in Microsoft Word, and it contains a worksheet from Microsoft Excel. **Object Linking and Embedding** (abbreviated OLE and pronounced "OH-lay") is the means by which you insert an object from a source file (e.g., an Excel workbook) into a destination file (e.g., a Word document).

The essential difference between linking and embedding is whether the object in the destination file maintains a connection to the source file. A **linked** object maintains the connection. An **embedded object** does not. A linked object can be associated with many different destination files that do not contain the object per se, but only a representation of the object as well as a pointer (link) to the source file containing the object. Any change to the object in the source file is reflected automatically in every destination file that is linked to that object. An embedded object, however, is contained entirely within the destination file. Changes to the object in the destination file are *not* reflected in the source file.

The choice between linking and embedding depends on how the object will be used. Linking is preferable if the object is likely to change and the destination file requires the latest version. Linking should also be used when the same object is placed in many documents, so that any change to the object has to be made in only one place. Embedding is preferable if you intend to edit the destination file on a computer other than the one on which it was created.

The exercise that follows shows you how to create the compound document in Figure A.1. The exercise uses the **Insert Object command** to embed a copy of the Excel worksheet into a Word document. Once an object has been embedded into a document, it can be modified

Lionel Douglas

402 Mahoney Hall • Coral Gables, Florida 33124

June 25, 1997

Dear Folks,

I heard from Mr. Black, the manager at University Commons, and the apartment is a definite for the Fall. Ken and I are very excited, and can't wait to get out of the dorm. The food is poison, not that either of us are cooks, but anything will be better than this! I have been checking into car prices (we are definitely too far away from campus to walk!), and have done some estimating on what it will cost. The figures below are for a Jeep Wrangler, the car of my dreams:

Price of car	$11,995			
Manufacturer's rebate	$1,000			
Down payment	$3,000		**My assumptions**	
Amount to be financed	$7,995		Interest rate	7.90%
Monthly payment	$195		Term (years)	4
Gas	$40			
Maintenance	$50			
Insurance	$100			
Total per month	$385			

My initial estimate was $471 based on a $2,000 down payment and a three year loan at 7.9%. I know this is too much so I plan on earning an additional $1,000 and extending the loan to four years. That will bring the total cost down to a more manageable level (see the above calculations). If that won't do it, I'll look at other cars.

Lionel

FIGURE A.1 A Compound Document

through *in-place editing.* In-place editing enables you to double click an embedded object (the worksheet) and change it, using the tools of the source application (Excel). In other words, you remain in Microsoft Word, but you have access to the Excel toolbar and pull-down menus. In-place editing modifies the copy of the embedded object in the destination file. It does *not* change the original object because there is no connection (or link) between the source file (if indeed there is a source file) and the destination file.

HANDS-ON EXERCISE 1

Embedding

Objective: To embed an Excel worksheet into a Word document; to use in-place editing to modify the worksheet within Word. Use Figure A.2 as a guide in the exercise.

STEP 1: Open the Word Document

➤ Start Word. Open the **Car Request document** in the **Exploring Word folder.** Zoom to **Page Width** so that the display on your monitor matches ours.

➤ Save the document as **Modified Car Request** so that you can return to the original document if you edit the duplicated file beyond redemption.

➤ Point to the date field, click the **right mouse button** to display the shortcut menu in Figure A.2a, then click the **Update Field command.**

THE DATE FIELD

The Insert Date and Time command enables you to insert the date as a specific value (the date on which a document is created) or as a field. The latter will be updated automatically whenever the document is printed or when the document is opened in Page Layout view. Opening the document in the Normal view requires the date field to be updated manually.

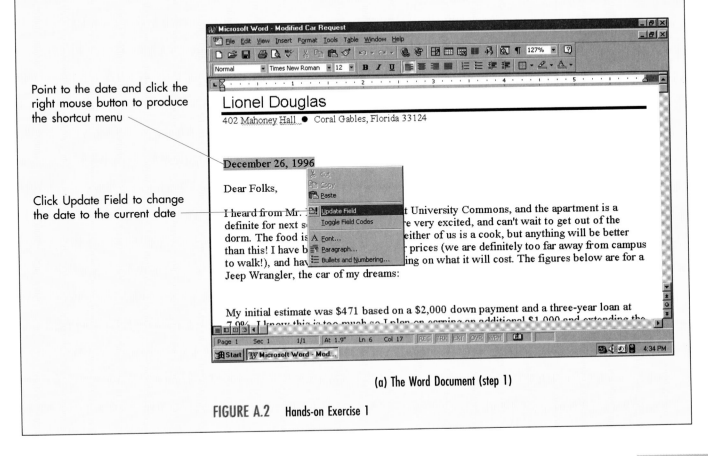

Point to the date and click the right mouse button to produce the shortcut menu

Click Update Field to change the date to the current date

(a) The Word Document (step 1)

FIGURE A.2   Hands-on Exercise 1

APPENDIX A: OBJECT LINKING AND EMBEDDING   **285**

STEP 2: Insert an Object

➤ Click the blank line above paragraph two as shown in Figure A.2b. This is the place in the document where the worksheet is to go.

➤ Pull down the **Insert menu**, and click the **Object command** to display the Object dialog box in Figure A.2b.

➤ Click the **Create from File tab,** then click the **Browse command button** in order to open the Browse dialog box and select the object.

➤ Click (select) the **Car Budget workbook** (note the Excel icon), which is in the Exploring Word folder.

➤ Click **OK** to select the workbook and close the Browse dialog box.

Click the Create from File tab

Click the Browse button

Click to select Car Budget

Click on the blank line above paragraph two

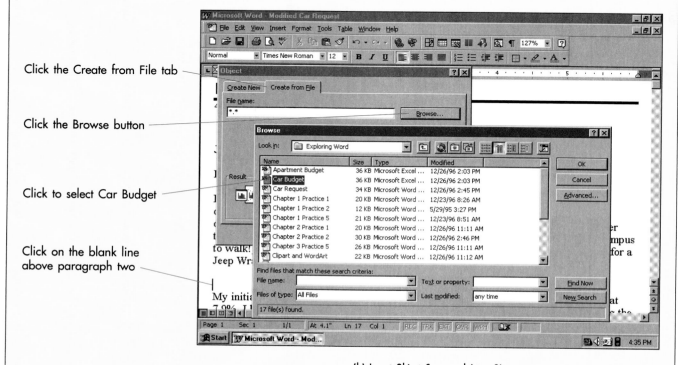

(b) Insert Object Command (step 2)

FIGURE A.2   Hands-on Exercise 1 (continued)

STEP 3: Insert an Object (continued)

➤ The file name of the object (Car Budget.xls) has been placed into the File Name text box, as shown in Figure A.2c.

➤ Verify that the Link to File and Display as Icon check boxes are clear and that the Float over text box is checked.

➤ Note the description at the bottom of the Object dialog box, which indicates that you will be able to edit the object using the application that created the source file.

➤ Click **OK** to insert the Excel worksheet into the Word document. Save the document.

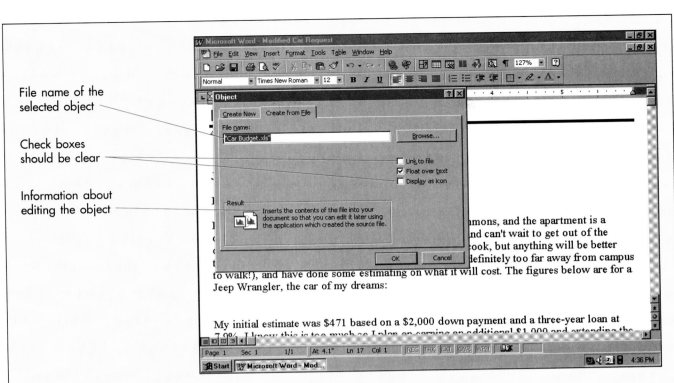

File name of the
selected object

Check boxes
should be clear

Information about
editing the object

(c) Insert Object Command, continued (step 3)

FIGURE A.2   Hands-on Exercise 1 (continued)

STEP 4: Position the Worksheet

➤ The worksheet should appear within the Word document. If necessary, click (select) the worksheet to display the sizing handles as shown in Figure A.2d.

➤ To move the worksheet:

- Point to any part of the worksheet except a sizing handle (the mouse pointer changes to a four-sided arrow), then click and drag to move the worksheet.

➤ To size the worksheet:

- Drag a corner handle (the mouse pointer changes to a double arrow) to change the length and width simultaneously and keep the worksheet in proportion.
- Drag a handle on the horizontal or vertical border to change one dimension only (which distorts the worksheet).

➤ Click anywhere in the document, except for the worksheet. The sizing handles disappear and the worksheet is no longer selected.

➤ If necessary, click above and/or below the worksheet, then press the **enter key** to insert a blank line(s) for better spacing.

➤ Save the document.

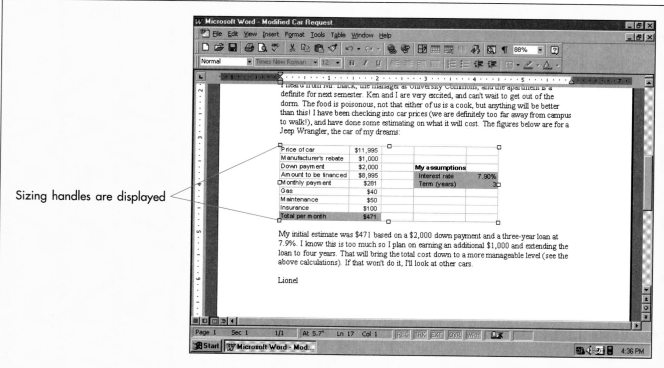

Sizing handles are displayed

(d) Position the Worksheet (step 4)

FIGURE A.2   Hands-on Exercise 1 (continued)

TO CLICK OR DOUBLE CLICK

Clicking an object selects the object and displays the sizing handles, which let you move and/or size the object. Double clicking an object starts the application that created the object and enables you to modify the object using that application. Double click a worksheet, for example, and you start Microsoft Excel from where you can modify the worksheet without exiting from Microsoft Word.

STEP 5: In-place Editing

➤ We will change the worksheet to reflect Lionel's additional $1,000 for the down payment. Double click the worksheet object to edit the worksheet in place.

➤ Be patient as this step takes a while, even on a fast machine. The Excel grid, consisting of the row and column labels, will appear around the worksheet, as shown in Figure A.2e.

➤ You are still in Word, as indicated by the title bar (Microsoft Word - Modified Car Request), but the Excel toolbars are displayed.

➤ Click in cell **B3,** type the new down payment of **$3,000,** and press **enter.**

➤ Click in cell **E5,** type **4,** and press **enter.** The Monthly payment (cell B5) and Total per month (cell B9) drop to $195 and $385, respectively.

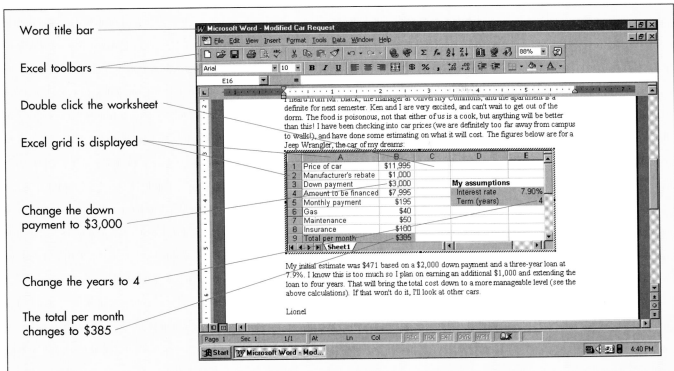

Word title bar

Excel toolbars

Double click the worksheet

Excel grid is displayed

Change the down payment to $3,000

Change the years to 4

The total per month changes to $385

(e) In-place Editing (step 5)

FIGURE A.2   Hands-on Exercise 1 (continued)

IN-PLACE EDITING

In-place editing enables you to edit an embedded object using the toolbar and pull-down menus of the original application. Thus, when editing an Excel worksheet embedded into a Word document, the title bar is that of Microsoft Word, but the toolbars and pull-down menus are from Excel. There are, however, two exceptions; the File and Window menus are from Microsoft Word, so that you can save the compound document and/or arrange multiple documents.

STEP 6: The Completed Document

➤ Click anywhere outside the worksheet to deselect it. Press **Ctrl+Home** to move to the beginning of the document, then scroll as necessary to view the completed Word document as shown in Figure A.2f.

➤ Pull down the **File menu** and click **Save** (or click the **Save button** on the Standard toolbar).

➤ Pull down the **File menu** a second time. Click **Exit** if you do not want to continue with the next hands-on exercise once this exercise is completed. Otherwise click **Close** to remove the document from memory but leave Word open.

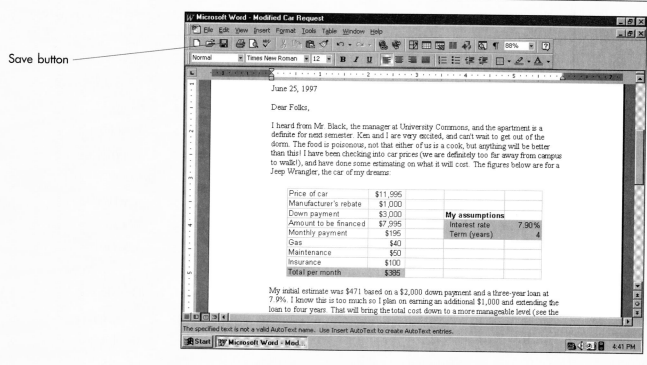

Save button

(f) The Completed Word Document (step 6)

FIGURE A.2 Hands-on Exercise 1 (continued)

STEP 7: View the Original Object

➤ Click the **Start Button,** click (or point to) the **Programs menu,** then click **Microsoft Excel** to open the program.

➤ If necessary, click the **Maximize button** in the application window so that Excel takes the entire desktop, as shown in Figure A.2g.

➤ Pull down the **File menu** and click **Open** (or click the **Open button** on the Standard toolbar) to display the Open dialog box.

- Click the **drop-down arrow** on the Look In list box. Click the appropriate drive, drive C or drive A, depending on the location of your data.
- Double click the **Exploring Word folder** to make it the active folder.
- Click (select) **Car Budget** to select the workbook that we have used throughout the exercise.
- Click the **Open command button** to open the workbook, as shown in Figure A.2g.
- Click the **Maximize button** in the document window (if necessary) so that the document window is as large as possible.

➤ You should see the original (unmodified) worksheet, with a down payment of $2,000, a three-year loan, a monthly car payment of $281, and total expenses per month of $471. The changes that were made in step 6 were made to the compound document and are *not* reflected in the source file.

➤ Pull down the **File menu.** Click **Exit** to exit Microsoft Excel.

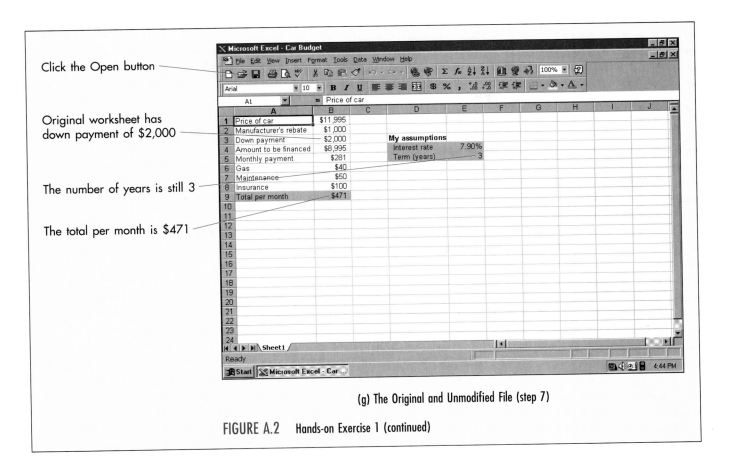

Click the Open button

Original worksheet has
down payment of $2,000

The number of years is still 3

The total per month is $471

(g) The Original and Unmodified File (step 7)

FIGURE A.2   Hands-on Exercise 1 (continued)

LINKING

The exercise just completed used embedding rather than linking to place a copy of the Excel worksheet into the Word document. The last step in the exercise demonstrated that the original worksheet was unaffected by changes made to the embedded copy within the compound document (destination file).

Linking is very different from embedding as you shall see in the next exercise. Linking maintains a dynamic connection between the source and destination files. Embedding does not. With linking, the object created by the source application (e.g., an Excel worksheet) is tied to the destination file (e.g., a Word document) in such a way that any changes in the Excel worksheet are automatically reflected in the Word document. The Word document does not contain the worksheet per se, but only a representation of the worksheet, as well as a pointer (or link) to the Excel workbook.

Linking requires that an object be saved in its own file because the object does not actually exist within the destination file. Embedding, on the other hand, lets you place the object directly in a destination file without having to save it as a separate file. (The embedded object simply becomes part of the destination file.)

Consider now Figure A.3, in which the same worksheet is linked to two different documents. Both documents contain a pointer to the worksheet, which may be edited by double clicking the object in either document. Alternatively, you may open the source application and edit the object directly. In either case, changes to the Excel workbook are reflected in every destination file that is linked to the workbook.

Lionel Douglas

402 Mahoney Hall • Coral Gables, Florida 33124

Dear Mom and Dad,

Enclosed please find the budget for my apartment at University Commons. As I told you before, it's a great apartment and I can't wait to move.

	Total	Individual
Rent	$895	$298
Utilities	$125	$42
Cable	$45	$15
Phone	$60	$20
Food	$600	$200
Total		$575
Persons	3	

I really appreciate everything that you and Dad are doing for me. I'll be home next week after finals.

Lionel

(a) First Document (Mom and Dad)

Lionel Douglas

402 Mahoney Hall • Coral Gables, Florida 33124

Dear Ken,

I just got the final figures for our apartment next year and am sending you an estimate of our monthly costs. I included the rent, utilities, phone, cable, and food. I figure that food is the most likely place for the budget to fall apart, so learning to cook this summer is critical. I'll be taking lessons from the Galloping Gourmet, and suggest you do the same. Enjoy your summer and Bon Appetit.

	Total	Individual
Rent	$895	$298
Utilities	$125	$42
Cable	$45	$15
Phone	$60	$20
Food	$600	$200
Total		$575
Persons	3	

Guess what - the three bedroom apartment just became available which saves us more than $100 per month over the two bedroom we had planned to take. Jason Adler has decided to transfer and he can be our third roommate.

Lionel

(b) Second Document (Note to Ken)

	Total	Individual
Rent	$895	$298
Utilities	$125	$42
Cable	$45	$15
Phone	$60	$20
Food	$600	$200
Total		$575
Persons	3	

(c) Worksheet (Apartment Budget)

FIGURE A.3   Linking

The next exercise links a single Excel worksheet to two different Word documents. During the course of the exercise both applications (Word and Excel) will be explicitly open, and it will be necessary to switch back and forth between the two. Thus, the exercise also demonstrates the multitasking capability within Windows and the use of the taskbar to switch between the open applications.

Linking

Objective: To demonstrate multitasking and the ability to switch between applications; to link an Excel worksheet to multiple Word documents. Use Figure A.4 as a guide in the exercise.

STEP 1: Open the Word Document

➤ Check the taskbar to see whether there is a button for Microsoft Word indicating that the application is already active in memory. Start Word if you do not see its button on the taskbar.

➤ Open the **Mom and Dad document** in the **Exploring Word folder** as shown in Figure A.4a. The document opens in the Normal view (the view in which it was last saved). If necessary, zoom to **Page Width** so that the display on your monitor matches ours.

➤ Save the document as **Modified Mom and Dad.**

Click here to zoom to Page Width

Lionel is a proper name and is flagged as a misspelling

Click the start button

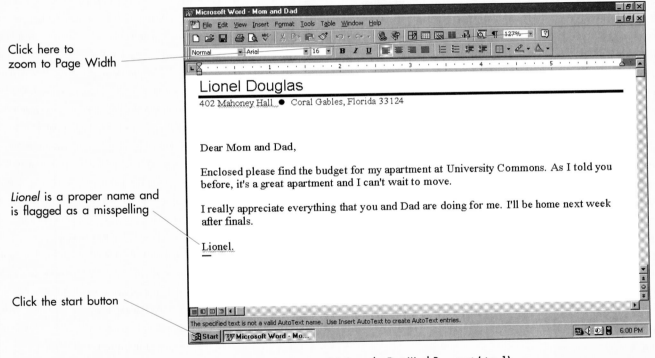

(a) Open the First Word Document (step 1)

FIGURE A.4 Hands-on Exercise 2

STEP 2: Open the Excel Worksheet

➤ Click the **Start button,** click (or point to) the **Programs menu,** then click **Microsoft Excel** to open the program.

➤ If necessary, click the **Maximize button** in the application window so that Excel takes the entire desktop. Click the **Maximize button** in the document window (if necessary) so that the document window is as large as possible.

➤ The taskbar should now contain buttons for both Microsoft Word and Microsoft Excel. Click either button to move back and forth between the open applications. End by clicking the Microsoft Excel button, since you want to work in that application.

➤ Pull down the **File menu** and click **Open** (or click the **Open button** on the Standard toolbar) to display the Open dialog box in Figure A.4b.

➤ Click the **drop-down arrow** on the Look In list box. Click the appropriate drive, drive C or drive A, depending on the location of your data. Double click the **Exploring Word folder** to make it the active folder. Double click **Apartment Budget** to open the workbook.

Click the Open button

Select the Exploring Word folder

Double click Apartment Budget to open it

Taskbar has buttons for Word and Excel

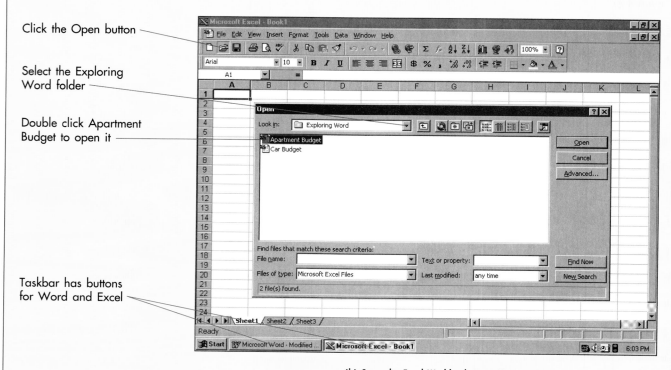

(b) Open the Excel Workbook (step 2)

FIGURE A.4   Hands-on Exercise 2 (continued)

THE COMMON USER INTERFACE

The *common user interface* provides a sense of familiarity from one Windows application to the next. Even if you have never used Excel, you will recognize many of the elements present in Word. Both applications share a common menu structure with consistent ways to execute commands from those menus. The Standard and Formatting toolbars are present in both applications. Many keyboard shortcuts are also common—for example Ctrl+Home and Ctrl+End to move to the beginning and end of a document.

STEP 3: Copy the Worksheet to the Clipboard

➤ Click in cell **A1**. Drag the mouse over cells **A1 through C9** so that the entire worksheet is selected as shown in Figure A.4c.

➤ Point to the selected cells, then click the **right mouse button** to display the shortcut menu shown in the figure. Click **Copy.** A moving border appears around the selected area in the worksheet, indicating that it has been copied to the clipboard.

➤ Click the **Microsoft Word button** on the Windows taskbar to return to the Word document.

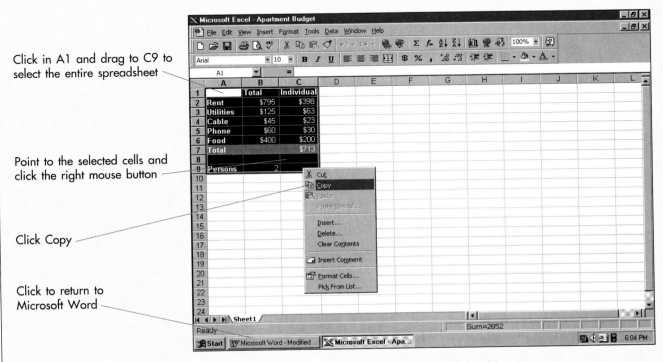

Click in A1 and drag to C9 to select the entire spreadsheet

Point to the selected cells and click the right mouse button

Click Copy

Click to return to Microsoft Word

(c) Copy the Worksheet to the Clipboard (step 3)

FIGURE A.4   Hands-on Exercise 2 (continued)

THE WINDOWS TASKBAR

Multitasking, the ability to run multiple applications at the same time, is one of the primary advantages of the Windows environment. Each button on the taskbar appears automatically when its application or folder is opened and disappears upon closing. (The buttons on are resized automatically according to the number of open windows.) You can customize the taskbar by right clicking an empty area to display a shortcut menu, then clicking the Properties command. You can resize the taskbar by pointing to its inside edge, then dragging when you see a double-headed arrow. You can also move the taskbar to the left or right edge of the desktop, or to the top of the desktop, by dragging a blank area of the taskbar to the desired position.

STEP 4: Create the Link

➤ Click in the document between the two paragraphs. Press **enter** to enter an additional blank line.

➤ Pull down the **Edit menu.** Click **Paste Special** to produce the dialog box in Figure A.4d.

➤ Click the **Paste Link option button.** Click **Microsoft Excel Worksheet Object.** Click **OK** to insert the worksheet into the document. You may want to insert a blank line before and/or after the worksheet to make it easier to read.

➤ Save the document containing the letter to Mom and Dad.

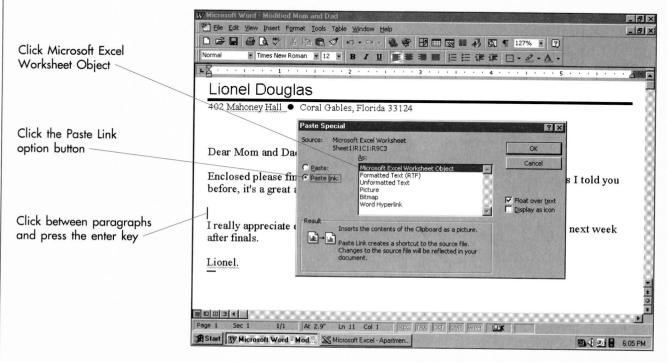

Click Microsoft Excel Worksheet Object

Click the Paste Link option button

Click between paragraphs and press the enter key

(d) Create the Link (step 4)

FIGURE A.4   Hands-on Exercise 2 (continued)

LINKING VERSUS EMBEDDING

The ***Paste Special command*** will link or embed an object, depending on whether the Paste Link or Paste Option button is checked. Linking stores a pointer to the source file containing the object together with a reference to the source application. Changes to the object are automatically reflected in all destination files that are linked to the object. Embedding stores a copy of the object with a reference to the source application. Changes to the object within the destination file, however, are not reflected in the original object. Linking and embedding both allow you to double click the object in the destination file to edit the object by using the tools of the source application.

STEP 5: Open the Second Word Document

➤ Open the **Note to Ken document** in the **Exploring Word folder.** Save the document as **Modified Note to Ken** so that you can always return to the original document.

➤ The Apartment Budget worksheet is still in the clipboard since the contents of the clipboard have not been changed. Click at the end of the first paragraph (after the words Bon Appetit). Press the **enter key** to insert a blank line after the paragraph.

➤ Pull down the **Edit menu.** Click **Paste Special.** Click the **Paste Link option button.** Click **Microsoft Excel Worksheet Object.** Click **OK** to insert the worksheet into the document, as shown in Figure A.4e.

➤ If necessary, enter a blank line before or after the object to improve the appearance of the document. Save the document.

➤ Click anywhere on the worksheet to select the worksheet, as shown in Figure A.4e. The message on the status bar indicates you can double click the worksheet to edit the object.

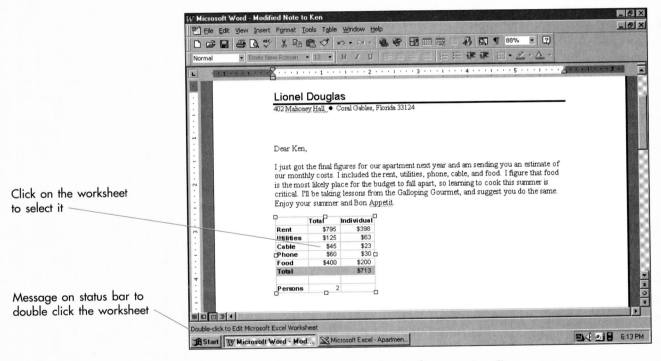

Click on the worksheet to select it

Message on status bar to double click the worksheet

(e) Open the Second Document (step 5)

FIGURE A.4   Hands-on Exercise 2 (continued)

STEP 6: Modify the Worksheet

➤ The existing spreadsheet indicates the cost of a two-bedroom apartment, but you want to show the cost of a three-bedroom apartment. Double click the worksheet in order to change it.

➤ The system pauses (the faster your computer, the better) as it switches back to Excel. Maximize the document window.

➤ Cells **A1 through C9** are still selected from step 3. Click outside the selected range to deselect the worksheet. Press **Esc** to remove the moving border.

- ➤ Click in cell **B2.** Type **$895** (the rent for a three-bedroom apartment).
- ➤ Click in cell **B6.** Type **$600** (the increased amount for food).
- ➤ Click in cell **B9.** Type **3** to change the number of people sharing the apartment. Press **enter.** The total expenses (in cell C9) change to $575, as shown in Figure A.4f.
- ➤ Save the worksheet.

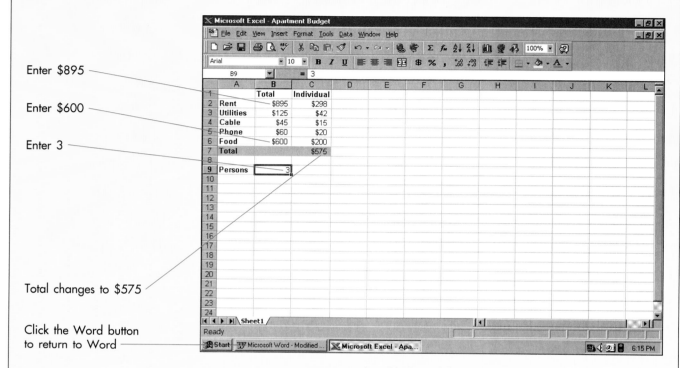

(f) Modify the Worksheet (step 6)

FIGURE A.4   Hands-on Exercise 2 (continued)

STEP 7: View the Modified Document

- ➤ Click the **Microsoft Word button** on the taskbar to return to Microsoft Word and the note to Ken, as shown in Figure A.4g.
- ➤ The note to Ken displays the modified worksheet because of the link established earlier.
- ➤ Click below the worksheet and add the additional text shown in Figure A.4g to let Ken know about the new apartment.
- ➤ Save the document.

STEP 8: View the Completed Note to Mom and Dad

- ➤ Pull down the **Window menu.** Click **Modified Mom and Dad** to switch to this document as shown in Figure A.4h.
- ➤ The note to your parents also contains the updated worksheet (with three roommates) because of the link established earlier.
- ➤ Save the completed document.

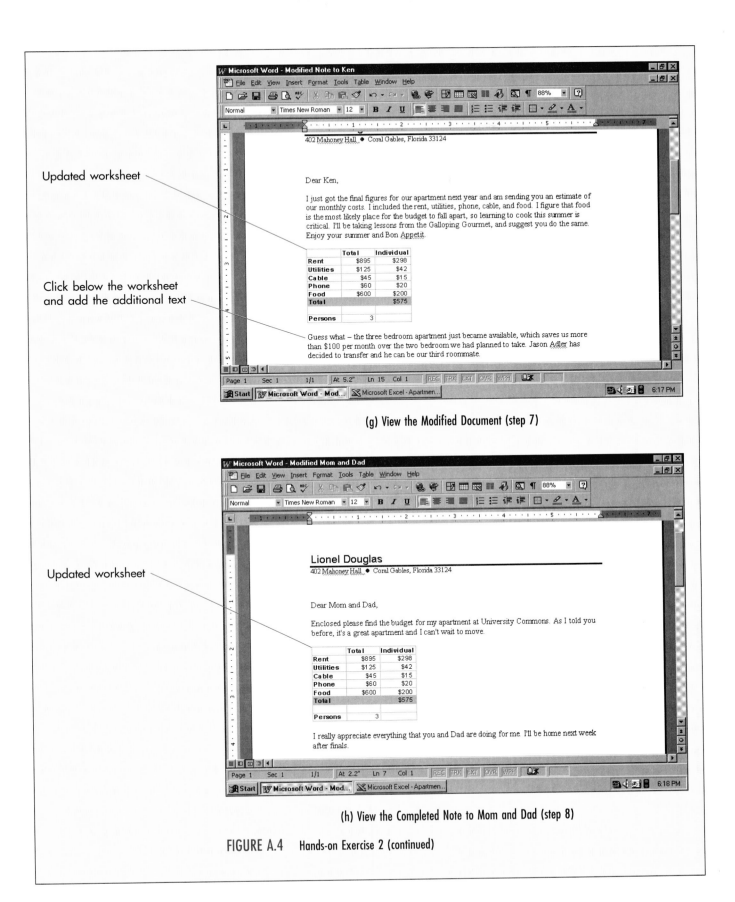

Updated worksheet

Click below the worksheet and add the additional text

(g) View the Modified Document (step 7)

Updated worksheet

(h) View the Completed Note to Mom and Dad (step 8)

FIGURE A.4   Hands-on Exercise 2 (continued)

ALT+TAB STILL WORKS

Alt+Tab was a treasured shortcut in Windows 3.1 that enabled users to switch back and forth between open applications. The shortcut also works in Windows 95. Press and hold the Alt key while you press and release the Tab key repeatedly to cycle through the open applications. Note that each time you release the Tab key, the icon of a different application is selected in the small rectangular window that is displayed in the middle of the screen. Release the Alt key when you have selected the icon for the application you want.

STEP 9: Exit Word

➤ Exit Word. Save the files if you are requested to do so. The button for Microsoft Word disappears from the taskbar.

➤ Exit Excel. Save the files if you are requested to do so. The button for Microsoft Excel disappears from the taskbar.

SUMMARY

The essential difference between linking and embedding is that linking does not place an object into the destination file (compound document), but only a pointer (link) to that object. Embedding, on the other hand, places (a copy of) the object into the destination file. Linking is dynamic whereas embedding is not.

Linking requires that an object be saved in its own (source) file, and further that the link between the source file and the destination file be maintained. Linking is especially useful when the same object is present in multiple documents, because any subsequent change to the object is made in only one place (the source file), but will be automatically reflected in the multiple destination files.

Embedding does not require an object to be saved in its own file because the object is contained entirely within the destination file. Thus, embedding lets you distribute a copy of the destination file, without including a copy of the source file, and indeed, there need not be a separate source file. You would not, however, want to embed the same object into multiple documents because any subsequent change to the object would have to be made in every document.

KEY WORDS AND CONCEPTS

Common user interface
Compound document
Embedding
In-place editing

Insert Object command
Linking
Multitasking

Object linking and
   embedding (OLE)
Paste Special command

APPENDIX B:
TOOLBAR SUMMARY

OVERVIEW

Microsoft Word has 16 predefined toolbars that provide access to commonly used commands. The toolbars are displayed in Figure B.1 and are listed here for convenience. They are the Standard, Formatting, AutoText, Control toolbox, Database, Drawing, Forms, Microsoft, Picture, Reviewing, Shadow Settings, Tables and Borders, Visual Basic, Web, WordArt, and 3-D Settings toolbars.

The Standard and Formatting toolbars are displayed by default immediately below the menu bar. The other predefined toolbars are displayed (hidden) at the discretion of the user. Six additional toolbars are displayed automatically when their corresponding features are in use. These toolbars appear (and disappear) automatically and are shown in Figure B.2. They are the Equation Editor, Header/Footer, Macro, Mail Merge, Master Document, and Outlining toolbars.

The buttons on the toolbars are intended to indicate their functions. Clicking the Printer button, for example, executes the Print command. If you are unsure of the purpose of any toolbar button, point to it, and a ScreenTip will appear that displays its name.

You can display multiple toolbars at one time, move them to new locations on the screen, or customize their appearance. To display or hide a toolbar, pull down the View menu and click the Toolbars command. Select (deselect) the toolbar(s) that you want to display (hide). The selected toolbar(s) will be displayed in the same position as when last displayed. You may also point to any toolbar and click with the right mouse button to bring up a shortcut menu.

Toolbars are either docked (along the edge of the window) or floating (in their own window). A toolbar moved to the edge of the window will dock along that edge. A toolbar moved anywhere else in the window will float in its own window. Docked toolbars are one tool wide (high), whereas floating toolbars can be resized by clicking and dragging a border or corner as you would with any window. To move a docked toolbar, click and drag the move handle (the pair of parallel lines) at the left of the toolbar. To move a floating toolbar, drag its title bar to its new location.

Standard Toolbar

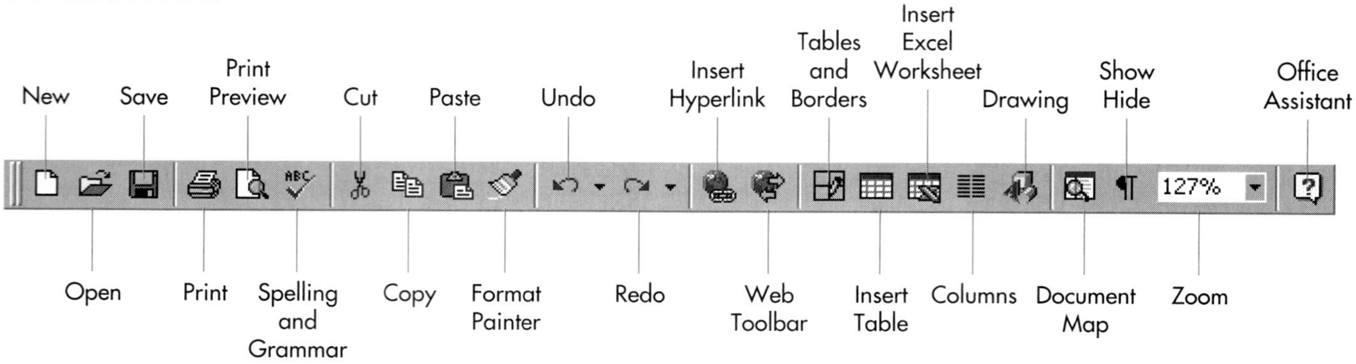
New
Save
Print Preview
Cut
Paste
Undo
Insert Hyperlink
Tables and Borders
Insert Excel Worksheet
Drawing
Show Hide
Office Assistant
127%
Open
Print
Spelling and Grammar
Copy
Format Painter
Redo
Web Toolbar
Insert Table
Columns
Document Map
Zoom

Formatting Toolbar

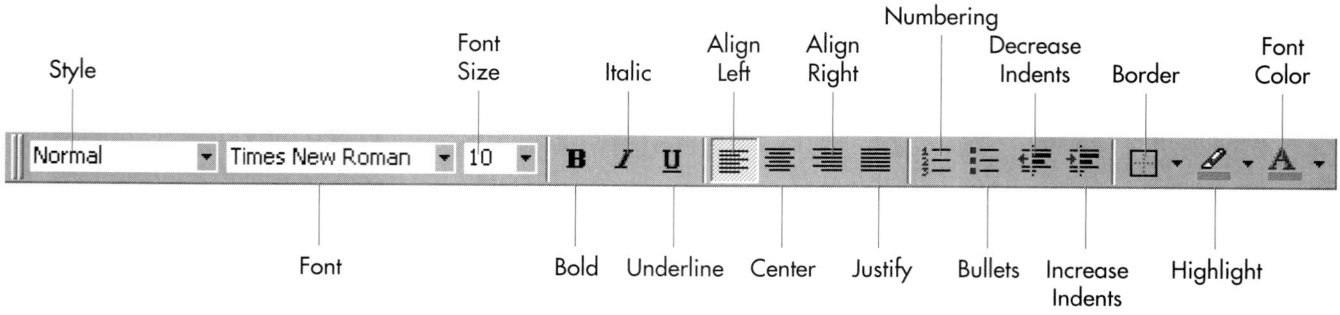
Style
Font Size
Italic
Align Left
Align Right
Numbering
Decrease Indents
Border
Font Color
Normal
Times New Roman
10
Font
Bold
Underline
Center
Justify
Bullets
Increase Indents
Highlight

AutoText Toolbar

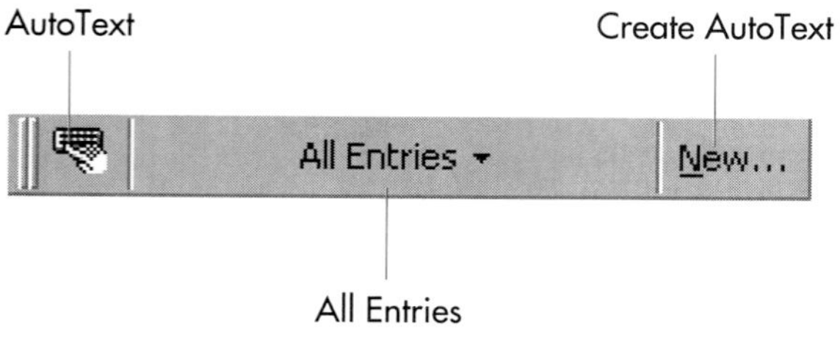
AutoText
Create AutoText
All Entries
New...
All Entries

Database Toolbar

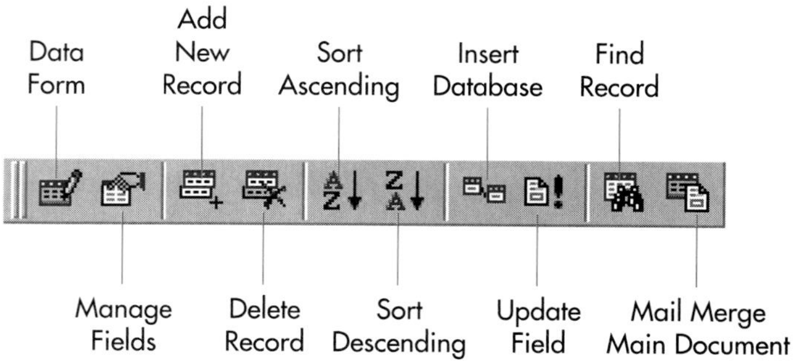
Data Form
Add New Record
Sort Ascending
Insert Database
Find Record
Manage Fields
Delete Record
Sort Descending
Update Field
Mail Merge Main Document

Control Toolbox

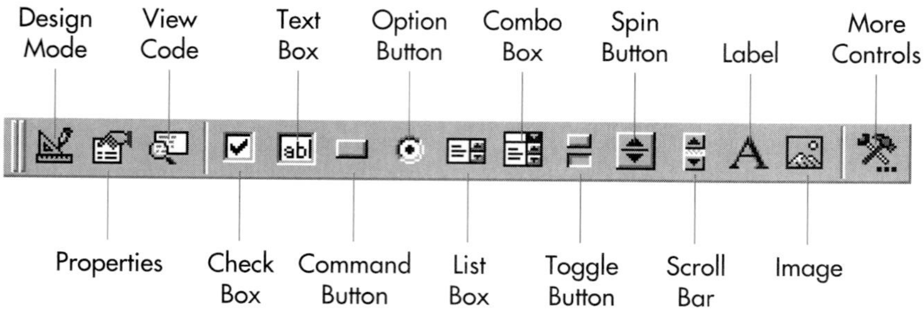
Design Mode
View Code
Text Box
Option Button
Combo Box
Spin Button
Label
More Controls
Properties
Check Box
Command Button
List Box
Toggle Button
Scroll Bar
Image

FIGURE B.1

Drawing Toolbar

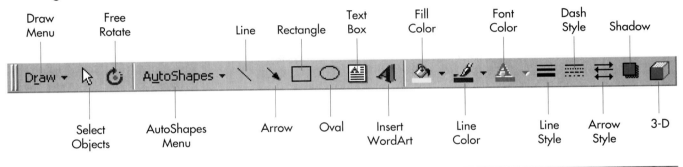

Forms Toolbar

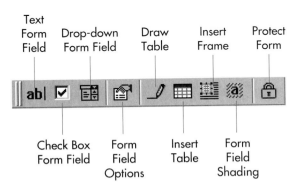

Microsoft Toolbar

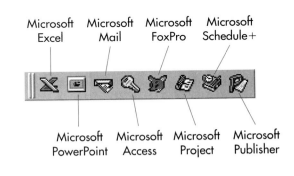

Picture Toolbar

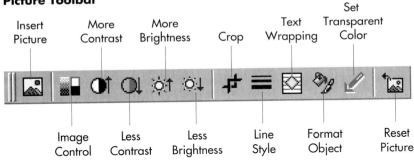

Reviewing Toolbar

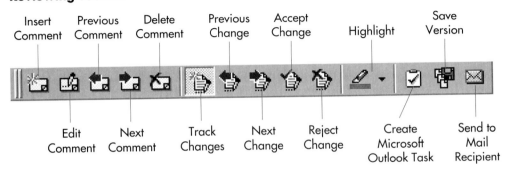

FIGURE B.1 (continued)

Shadow Settings Toolbar

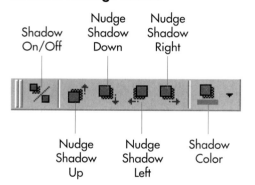

Shadow On/Off — Nudge Shadow Down — Nudge Shadow Right

Nudge Shadow Up — Nudge Shadow Left — Shadow Color

Visual Basic Toolbar

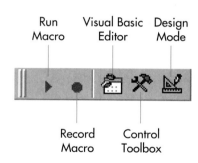

Run Macro — Visual Basic Editor — Design Mode

Record Macro — Control Toolbox

Tables and Borders Toolbar

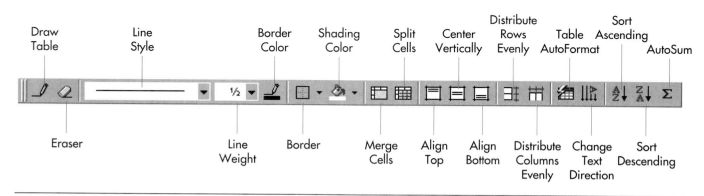

Draw Table — Line Style — Border Color — Shading Color — Split Cells — Center Vertically — Distribute Rows Evenly — Table AutoFormat — Sort Ascending — AutoSum

Eraser — Line Weight — Border — Merge Cells — Align Top — Align Bottom — Distribute Columns Evenly — Change Text Direction — Sort Descending

Web Toolbar

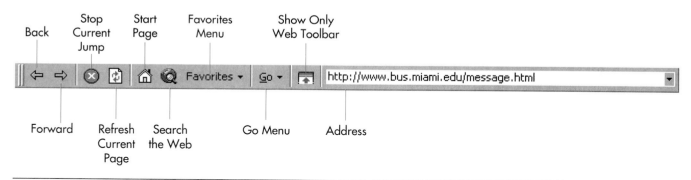

Back — Stop Current Jump — Start Page — Favorites Menu — Show Only Web Toolbar

http://www.bus.miami.edu/message.html

Forward — Refresh Current Page — Search the Web — Go Menu — Address

WordArt Toolbar

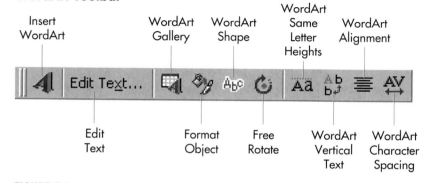

Insert WordArt — WordArt Gallery — WordArt Shape — WordArt Same Letter Heights — WordArt Alignment

Edit Text — Format Object — Free Rotate — WordArt Vertical Text — WordArt Character Spacing

FIGURE B.1   (continued)

3-D Settings Toolbar

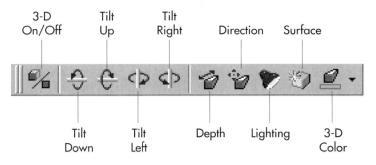

FIGURE B.1   (continued)

Equation Editor Toolbar

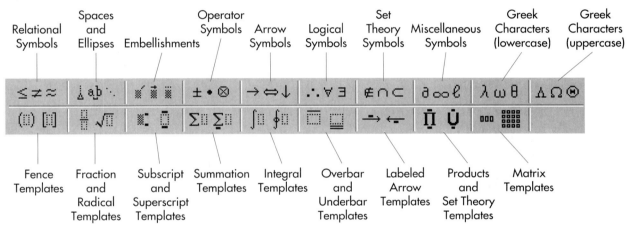

Header/Footer Toolbar

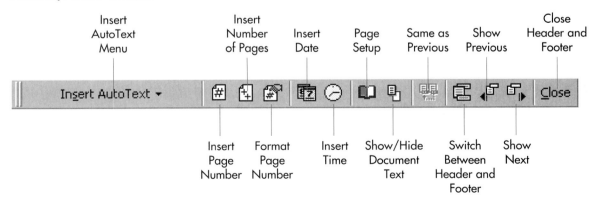

FIGURE B.2

Macro Toolbar

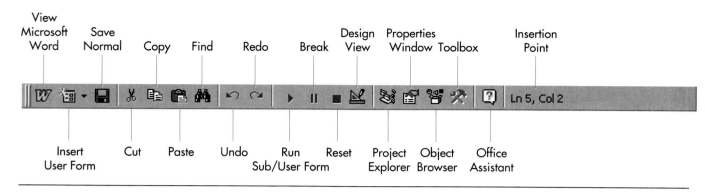

Labels (top): View Microsoft Word, Save Normal, Copy, Find, Redo, Break, Design View, Properties Window, Toolbox, Insertion Point

Labels (bottom): Insert User Form, Cut, Paste, Undo, Run Sub/User Form, Reset, Project Explorer, Object Browser, Office Assistant

Mail Merge Toolbar

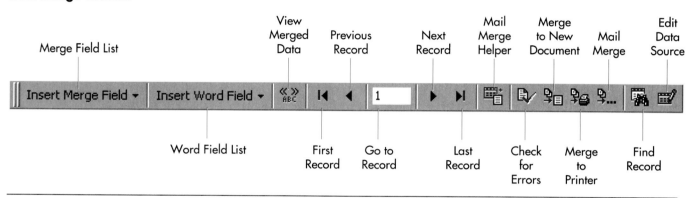

Labels (top): Merge Field List, View Merged Data, Previous Record, Next Record, Mail Merge Helper, Merge to New Document, Mail Merge, Edit Data Source

Labels (bottom): Word Field List, First Record, Go to Record, Last Record, Check for Errors, Merge to Printer, Find Record

Master Document Toolbar

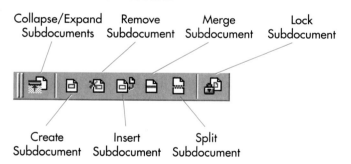

Labels (top): Collapse/Expand Subdocuments, Remove Subdocument, Merge Subdocument, Lock Subdocument

Labels (bottom): Create Subdocument, Insert Subdocument, Split Subdocument

Outlining Toolbar

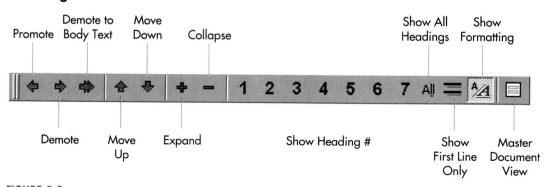

Labels (top): Promote, Demote to Body Text, Move Down, Collapse, Show All Headings, Show Formatting

Labels (bottom): Demote, Move Up, Expand, Show Heading #, Show First Line Only, Master Document View

FIGURE B.2   (continued)

APPENDIX C: MAIL MERGE

C

OVERVIEW

A *mail merge* takes the tedium out of sending *form letters,* as it creates the same letter many times, changing the name, address, and other information as appropriate from letter to letter. You might use a mail merge to look for a job upon graduation, when you send essentially the same letter to many different companies. The concept is illustrated in Figure C.1, in which John Smith drafts a letter describing his qualifications, then merges that letter with a set of names and addresses, to produce the individual letters.

The mail merge process uses two files as input, a main document and a data source. A set of form letters is created as output. The *main document* (e.g., the cover letter in Figure C.1a) contains standardized text together with one or more *merge fields* that indicate where variable information is to be inserted into the individual letters. The *data source* (the set of names and addresses in Figure C.1b) contains the information that varies from letter to letter.

The first row in the data source is called the header row and identifies the fields in the remaining rows. Each additional row contains the data to create one letter and is called a *data record.* Every data record contains the same fields in the same order—for example, Title, First-Name, LastName, and so on.

The main document and the data source work in conjunction with one another, with the merge fields in the main document referencing the corresponding fields in the data source. The first line in the address of Figure C.1a, for example, contains the entries in angled brackets, <<Title>> <<FirstName>> <<LastName>>. (These entries are not typed explicitly but are entered through special commands as described in the hands-on exercise that follows shortly.) The merge process examines each record in the data source and substitutes the appropriate field values for the corresponding merge fields as it creates the individual form letters. For example, the first three fields in the first record will

John H. Smith

426 Jenny Lake Drive • Coral Gables, FL 33146 • (305) 666-4801

May 11, 1997

«Title» «FirstName» «LastName»
«JobTitle»
«Company»
«Address1»
«City», «State» «PostalCode»

Dear «Title» «LastName»:

I am writing to inquire about a position with «Company» as an entry level computer programmer. I have just graduated from the University of Miami with a Bachelor's Degree in Computer Information Systems (May, 1997) and I am very interested in working for you. I have a background in both microcomputer applications (Windows 95, Word, Excel, PowerPoint, and Access) as well as extensive experience with programming languages (Visual Basic, C++ and COBOL). I feel that I am well qualified to join your staff as over the past two years I have had a great deal of experience designing and implementing computer programs, both as a part of my educational program and during my internship with Personalized Computer Designs, Inc.

I am eager to put my skills to work and would like to talk with you at your earliest convenience. I have enclosed a copy of my résumé and will be happy to furnish the names and addresses of my references, if you so desire. You may reach me at the above address and phone number. I look forward to hearing from you.

Sincerely,

John Smith

(a) The Main Document

FIGURE C.1   The Mail Merge

produce *Mr. Jason Frasher.* The same fields in the second record will produce *Ms. Elizabeth Schery,* and so on.

In similar fashion, the second line in the address of the main document contains the *<<JobTitle>>* field. The third line contains the *<<Company>>* field. The fourth line references the *<<Address1>>* field, and the last line contains the *<<City>>, <<State>,* and *<<PostalCode>>* fields. The salutation repeats the *<<Title>>* and *<<LastName>>* fields. The first sentence uses the *<<Company>>* field a second time. The mail merge prepares the letters one at a time, with one letter created for every record in the data source until the file of names and addresses is exhausted. The individual form letters are shown in Figure C.1c. Each letter begins automatically on a new page.

Title	FirstName	LastName	JobTitle	Company	Address1	City	State	PostalCode
Mr.	Jason	Frasher	President	Frasher Systems	100 S. Miami Avenue	Miami	FL	33103
Ms.	Elizabeth	Schery	Director of Personnel	Custom Computing	8180 Kendall Drive	Miami	FL	33156
Ms.	Lauren	Howard	President	Unique Systems	475 LeJeune Road	Coral Gables	FL	33146

(b) The Data Source

John H. Smith

426 Jenny Lake Drive • Coral Gables, FL 33146 • (305) 666-4801

May 11, 1997

Mr. Jason Frasher
President
Frasher Systems
100 S. Miami Avenue
Miami, FL 33103

Dear Mr. Frasher:

I am writing to inquire about a position
programmer. I have just graduated from
Computer Information Systems (May,
have a background in both microcompu
PowerPoint, and Access) as well as ex
(Visual Basic, C++ and COBOL). I fe
past two years I have had a great deal
programs, both as a part of my educatio
Personalized Computer Designs, Inc.

I am eager to put my skills to work and
convenience. I have enclosed a copy o
and addresses of my references, if you
and phone number. I look forward to h

Sincerely,

John Smith

John H. Smith

426 Jenny Lake Drive • Coral Gables, FL 33146 • (305) 666-4801

May 11, 1997

Ms. Elizabeth Schery
Director of Personnel
Custom Computing
8180 Kendall Drive
Miami, FL 33156

Dear Ms. Schery:

I am writing to inquire about a position with Custom Computing as an entry level computer
programmer. I have just graduated from
Computer Information Systems (May, 19
have a background in both microcompute
PowerPoint, and Access) as well as exte
(Visual Basic, C++ and COBOL). I feel
past two years I have had a great deal of
programs, both as a part of my education
Personalized Computer Designs, Inc.

I am eager to put my skills to work and
convenience. I have enclosed a copy of
and addresses of my references, if you s
and phone number. I look forward to hea

Sincerely,

John Smith

John H. Smith

426 Jenny Lake Drive • Coral Gables, FL 33146 • (305) 666-4801

May 11, 1997

Ms. Lauren Howard
President
Unique Systems
475 LeJeune Road
Coral Gables, FL 33146

Dear Ms. Howard:

I am writing to inquire about a position with Unique Systems as an entry level computer
programmer. I have just graduated from the University of Miami with a Bachelor's Degree in
Computer Information Systems (May, 1997) and I am very interested in working for you. I
have a background in both microcomputer applications (Windows 95, Word, Excel,
PowerPoint, and Access) as well as extensive experience with programming languages
(Visual Basic, C++ and COBOL). I feel that I am well qualified to join your staff as over the
past two years I have had a great deal of experience designing and implementing computer
programs, both as a part of my educational program and during my internship with
Personalized Computer Designs, Inc.

I am eager to put my skills to work and would like to talk with you at your earliest
convenience. I have enclosed a copy of my résumé and will be happy to furnish the names
and addresses of my references, if you so desire. You may reach me at the above address
and phone number. I look forward to hearing from you.

Sincerely,

John Smith

(c) The Printed Letters

FIGURE C.1   The Mail Merge (continued)

FILE DESIGN

The zip code should be defined as a separate field in the data source in order to sort on zip code and take advantage of bulk mail. A person's first and last name should also be defined separately, so that you have access to either field, perhaps to create a friendly salutation such as Dear Joe or to sort on last name.

MAIL MERGE HELPER

The implementation of a mail merge in Microsoft Word is easy, provided you understand the basic concept. In essence, there are three things you must do:

1. Create and save the main document
2. Create and save the data source
3. Merge the main document and data source to create the individual letters

The Mail Merge command is located in the Tools menu. Execution of the command displays the **Mail Merge Helper,** which lists the steps in the mail merge process and guides you every step of the way.

The screen in Figure C.2 shows the Mail Merge Helper as it appears after steps 1 and 2 have been completed. The main document is the file *Modified Form Letter.doc.* The data source is the file *Names and Addresses.doc.* All that remains is to merge the files and create the individual form letters. The options in effect

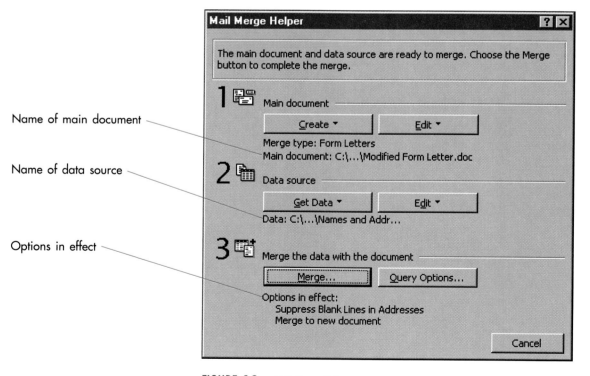

FIGURE C.2   Mail Merge Helper

indicate that the letters will be created in a new document and that blank lines, if any, in addresses (e.g., a missing company or title) will be suppressed. The Query Options command button lets you select and/or *sort* the records in the data source prior to the merge. These options are discussed after the hands-on exercise.

PAPER MAKES A DIFFERENCE

Most of us take paper for granted, but the right paper can make a significant difference in the effectiveness of a document. Reports and formal correspondence are usually printed on white paper, but you would be surprised how many different shades of white there are. Other types of documents lend themselves to colored paper for additional impact. In short, the choice of paper you use is far from an automatic decision. Our favorite source for paper is a company called PAPER DIRECT (1-800-APAPERS). Ask for a catalog, then consider the use of a specialty paper the next time you have an important project, such as the cover letter for your résumé.

HANDS-ON EXERCISE 1

Mail Merge

Objective: To create a main document and associated data source; to implement a mail merge and produce a set of form letters. Use Figure C.3 as a guide in the exercise.

STEP 1: Open the Cover Letter
➤ Open the **Form Letter document** in the **Exploring Word Folder** as shown in Figure C.3a. (The dialog box will not yet be displayed.)
  • If necessary, pull down the **View menu** and click **Page Layout** (or click the **Page Layout button** above the status bar).
  • If necessary, click the **Zoom Control arrow** to change to **Page Width.**
➤ Save the document as **Modified Form Letter** so that you can return to the original document if necessary.

THE LETTER WIZARD

It is the rare individual who has never been confronted by writer's block and the frustration of a blank screen and a flashing cursor. The Letter Wizard is Microsoft's attempt to get you started. Pull down the File menu, click New, click the Letters & Faxes tab in the New dialog box, then double click the Letter Wizard. The Wizard asks you a series of questions about the type of letter you want to write, then supplies a template for you to complete. It will even let you choose one of several prewritten letters, including a résumé cover letter. It's not perfect, but it is a starting point, and that may be all you need.

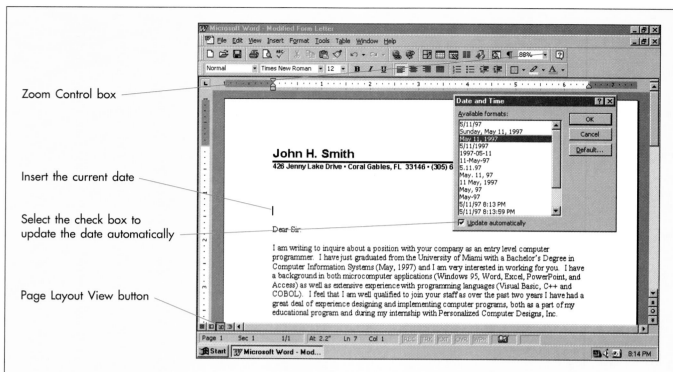

Zoom Control box

Insert the current date

Select the check box to
update the date automatically

Page Layout View button

(a) Insert Today's Date (step 2)

FIGURE C.3   Hands-on Exercise 1

STEP 2: Insert Today's Date

➤ Click to the left of the "D" in Dear Sir, then press **enter** twice to insert two lines. Press the **up arrow** two times to return to the first line you inserted.

➤ Pull down the **Insert menu** and click the **Date and Time command** to display the dialog box in Figure C.3a.

➤ Select (click) the date format you prefer and, if necessary, check the box to update the date automatically. Click **OK** to close the dialog box.

FIELD CODES VERSUS FIELD RESULTS

All fields are displayed in a document in one of two formats, as a *field code* or as a *field result.* A field code appears in braces and indicates instructions to insert variable data when the document is printed; a field result displays the information as it will appear in the printed document. You can toggle the display between the field code and field result by selecting the field and pressing Shift+F9 during editing.

STEP 3: Create the Main Document

➤ Pull down the **Tools menu.** Click **Mail Merge.** Click the **Create command button** under step 1 to create the main document as shown in Figure C.3b.

➤ Click **Form Letters,** then click **Active Window** to indicate that you will use the Modified Form Letter document (in the active window) as the main document.

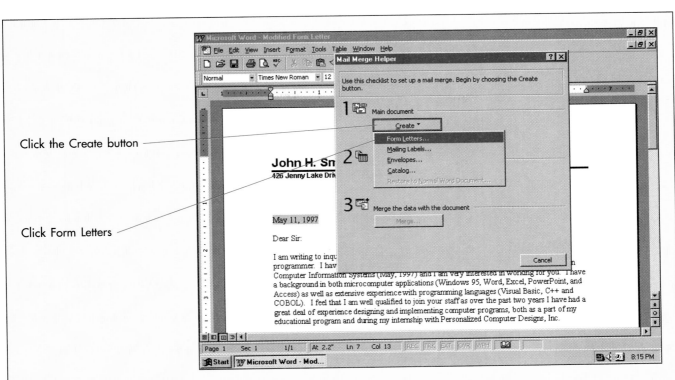

Click the Create button

Click Form Letters

(b) Create the Main Document (step 3)

FIGURE C.3   Hands-on Exercise 1 (continued)

STEP 4: Create the Data Source

➤ Click **Get Data** under step 2, then click **Create Data Source** to display the dialog box in Figure C.3c.

➤ Word provides commonly used field names for the data source, but not all of the data fields are necessary. Click **Address2,** then click the **Remove Field Name command button.** Delete the Country, HomePhone, and WorkPhone fields in similar fashion.

➤ Click **OK** to complete the definition of the data source. You will then be presented with the Save As dialog box as you need to save the data source.

➤ Type **Names and Addresses** in the File Name text box as the name of the data source. Click **Save** to save the file.

➤ You will see a message indicating that the data source does not contain any data records. Click **Edit Data Source** in order to add records at this time.

STEP 5: Add the Data

➤ Enter data for the first record. Type **Mr.** in the Title field. Press **Tab** to move to the next (FirstName) field, and type **Jason.** Continue in this fashion until you have completed the first record as shown in Figure C.3d.

➤ Click **Add New** to enter the data for the next person to receive the letter:

- Ms. Elizabeth Schery
- Director of Personnel
- Custom Computing
- 8180 Kendall Drive
- Miami, FL 33156

Click Get Data

Click Remove
Field Name button

Click Address2

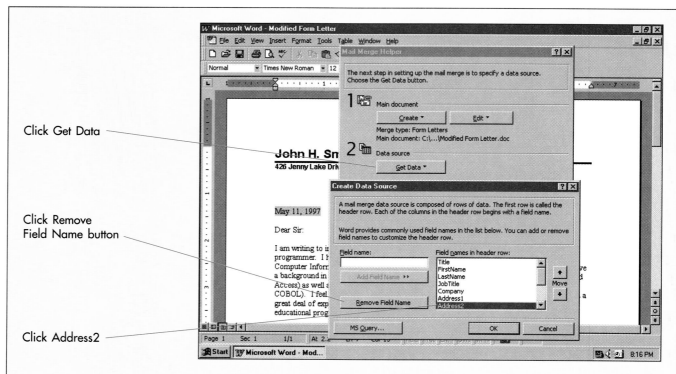

(c) Create the Data Source (step 4)

Enter the data for the first
record, pressing Tab to
move from field to field

Click Add New to
add a new record

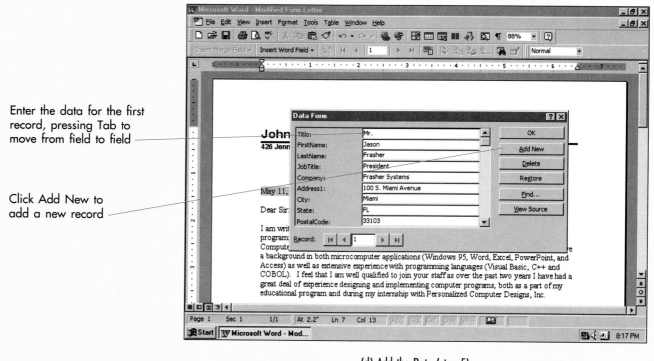

(d) Add the Data (step 5)

FIGURE C.3   Hands-on Exercise 1 (continued)

➤ Click **Add New** to enter the data for the third and last recipient:
- Ms. Lauren Howard
- President
- Unique Systems
- 475 LeJeune Road
- Coral Gables, FL 33146

➤ Click **OK** to end the data entry and return to the main document. The Mail Merge toolbar is displayed immediately below the Formatting toolbar.

STEP 6: Add the Data Fields

➤ Click in the main document immediately below the date. Press **enter** to leave a blank line between the date and the first line of the address.

➤ Click the **Insert Merge Field button** on the Merge toolbar. Click **Title** from the list of fields within the data source. The title field is inserted into the main document and enclosed in angled brackets as shown in Figure C.3e.

➤ Press the **space bar** to add a space between the words. Click the **Insert Merge Field button** a second time. Click **FirstName**. Press the **space bar.**

➤ Click the **Insert Merge Field button** again. Click **LastName.**

➤ Press **enter** to move to the next line. Enter the remaining fields in the address as shown in Figure C.3e. Be sure to add a comma after the **City field** as well as a space.

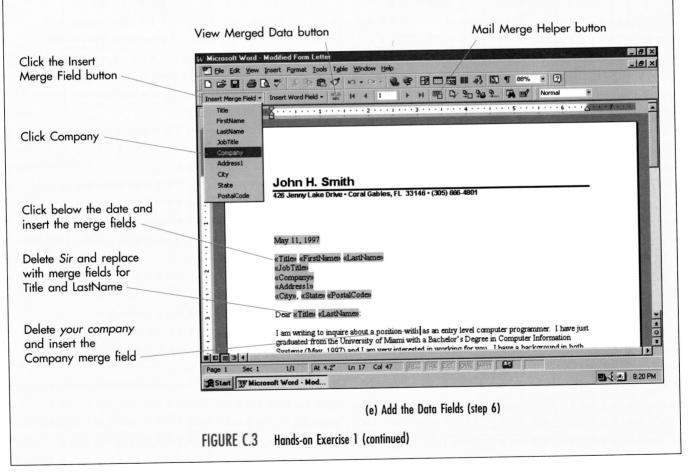

(e) Add the Data Fields (step 6)

FIGURE C.3 Hands-on Exercise 1 (continued)

➤ Delete the word "Sir" in the salutation and replace it with the **Title** and **Last-Name fields.**

➤ Delete the words "your company" in the first sentence and replace them with the **Company field.**

➤ Save the main document.

STEP 7: The Mail Merge Toolbar

➤ The Mail Merge toolbar enables you to preview the form letters before they are created.

➤ Click the **<<abc>> button** on the Merge toolbar to display field values rather than field codes; you will see Mr. Jason Frasher instead of <<Title>> <<First-Name>> <<LastName>>, etc.

➤ The **<<abc>> button** functions as a toggle switch. Click it once and you switch from field codes to field values; click it a second time and you go from field values back to field codes. End with the field values displayed.

➤ Look at the text box on the Mail Merge toolbar, which displays the number 1 to indicate that the first record is displayed. Click the ▶ **button** to display the form letter for the next record (Ms. Elizabeth Schery in our example).

➤ Click the ▶ **button** again to display the form letter for the next record (Ms. Lauren Howard). The toolbar indicates you are on the third record. Click the ◀ **button** to return to the previous (second) record.

➤ Click the |◀ **button** to move directly to the first record (Jason Frasher). Click the ▶| **button** to display the form letter for the last record (Lauren Howard).

➤ Toggle the **<<abc>> button** to display the field codes.

STEP 8: The Mail Merge Helper

➤ Click the **Mail Merge Helper button** on the Merge toolbar to display the dialog box in Figure C.3f.

➤ The Mail Merge Helper shows your progress thus far:

• The main document has been created and saved as Modified Form Letter.

• The data source has been created and saved as Names and Addresses.

➤ Click the **Merge command button** to display the dialog box in Figure C.3g.

EDIT THE DATA SOURCE

Click the Mail Merge Helper button to display a dialog box with information about the mail merge, click the Edit command button under Data Source, then click the file containing the data source. Click the View Source command button to see multiple records in the data source displayed within a table; the first row contains the field names, and each succeeding row contains a data record. Edit the data source, then pull down the Window menu and click the name of the file containing the main document to continue working on the mail merge.

STEP 9: The Merge

➤ The selected options in Figure C.3g should already be set:

• If necessary, click the **arrow** in the Merge To list box and select New document.

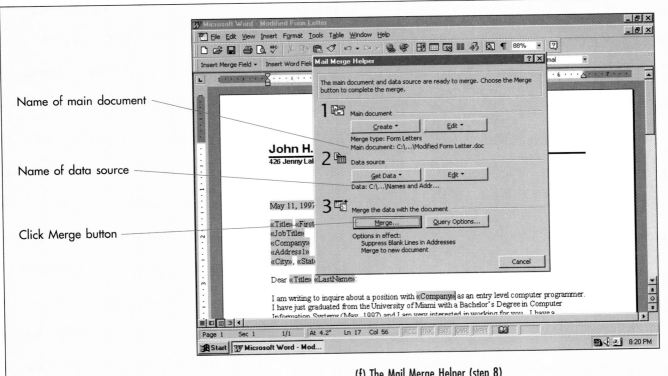

Name of main document

Name of data source

Click Merge button

(f) The Mail Merge Helper (step 8)

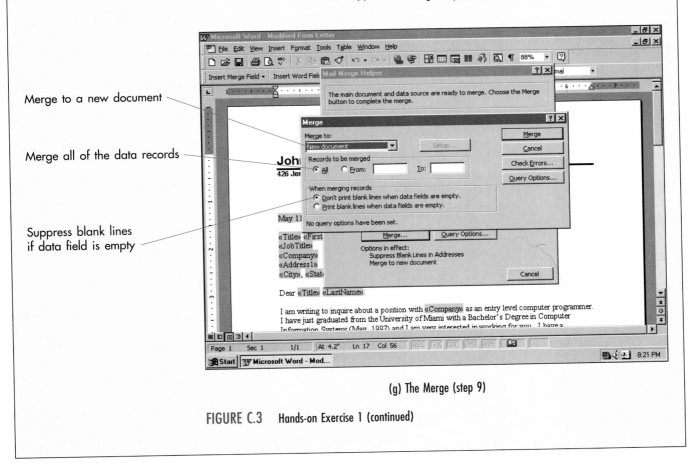

Merge to a new document

Merge all of the data records

Suppress blank lines
if data field is empty

(g) The Merge (step 9)

FIGURE C.3   Hands-on Exercise 1 (continued)

- If necessary, click the **All options button** to include all records in the data source.
- If necessary, click the **option button** to suppress blank lines if data fields are empty.

➤ Click the **Merge command button.** Word pauses momentarily, then generates the three form letters in a new document.

STEP 10: The Individual Form Letters

➤ The title bar of the active window changes to Form Letters1. Scroll through the letters to review them individually.

➤ Pull down the **View menu.** Click **Zoom.** Click **Many Pages.** Click the **monitor icon,** then click and drag within the resulting dialog box to display three pages side by side. Click **OK.** You should see the three form letters as shown in Figure C.3h.

➤ Print the letters.

➤ Pull down the **File menu** and click **Exit** to exit Word. Pay close attention to the informational messages that ask whether to save the modified file(s):
- There is no need to save the merged document (Form Letters1) because you can always re-create the merged letters, provided you have saved the main document and data source.
- Save the Modified Form Letter and Names and Addresses documents if you are asked to do so.

➤ Congratulations on a job well done. Good luck in your job hunting!

Title bar indicates
FormLetters1

Print button

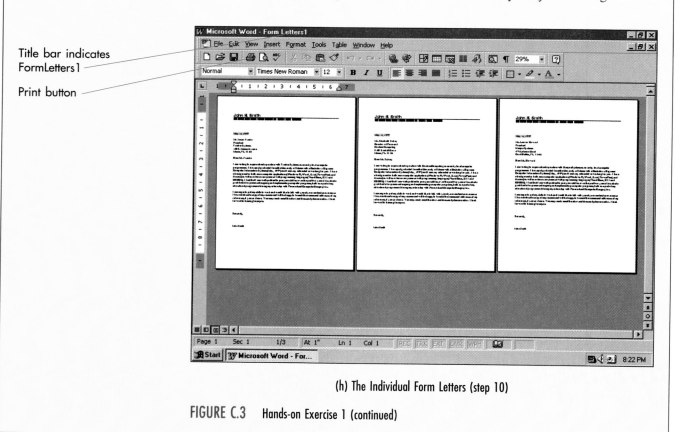

(h) The Individual Form Letters (step 10)

FIGURE C.3   Hands-on Exercise 1 (continued)

PREREQUISITES: ESSENTIALS OF WINDOWS 95

OBJECTIVES

After reading this appendix you will be able to:

1. Describe the objects on the Windows desktop; describe the programs available through the Start button.
2. Explain the function of the minimize, maximize, restore, and close buttons; move and size a window.
3. Discuss the function of a dialog box; describe the elements in a dialog box and the various ways in which information is supplied.
4. Use the Help menu to learn about features in Windows 95; format a floppy disk and implement a screen saver by following instructions from the Help menu.
5. Use the Internet Explorer to access the Internet and download the practice files for the *Exploring Windows* series.
6. Use Windows Explorer to locate a specific file or folder; describe the views available for Windows Explorer.
7. Describe how folders are used to organize a disk; create a new folder; copy and/or move a file from one folder to another.
8. Delete a file, then recover the deleted file from the Recycle Bin.

OVERVIEW

Windows 95 is a computer program (actually many programs) that controls the operation of your computer and its peripherals. **Windows 97** improves on Windows 95 to bring elements of the Internet to the desktop. Windows 97 was not available when we went to press, but we expect it to follow the same conventions as Windows 95. Thus, our introduction applies to both, as it emphasizes the common features of file management in support of Microsoft Office 97. (Microsoft Office runs equally well under Windows 95, Windows 97, or Windows NT.)

One of the most significant benefits of the Windows environment is the common user interface and consistent command structure that is imposed on every Windows application. Once you learn the basic concepts and techniques, you can apply that knowledge to every Windows application. This appendix teaches you those concepts so that you will be able to work productively in the Windows environment. It is written for you, the computer novice, and assumes no previous knowledge about a computer or about Windows. Our goal is to get you "up and running" as quickly as possible so that you can do the work you want to do.

We begin with an introduction to the Windows desktop, the graphical user interface that lets you work in intuitive fashion by pointing at icons and clicking the mouse. We identify the basic components of a window and describe how to execute commands and supply information through various elements in a dialog box. We introduce you to My Computer, an icon that is present on every Windows desktop, then show you how to use My Computer to access the various components of your system.

The appendix also shows you how to manage the hundreds (indeed, thousands) of files that are stored on the typical system. We show you how to create a new folder (the electronic equivalent of a manila folder in a filing cabinet) and how to move or copy a file from one folder to another. We show you how to rename a file, how to delete a file, and how to recover a deleted file from the Recycle Bin.

The appendix also contains four hands-on exercises, which enable you to apply the conceptual discussion in the text at the computer. The exercises are essential to the learn-by-doing philosophy we follow throughout the *Exploring Windows* series.

THE DESKTOP

Windows creates a working environment for your computer that parallels the working environment at home or in an office. You work at a desk. Windows operations take place on the ***desktop.***

There are physical objects on a desk such as folders, a dictionary, a calculator, or a phone. The computer equivalents of those objects appear as ***icons*** (pictorial symbols) on the desktop. Each object on a real desk has attributes (properties) such as size, weight, and color. In similar fashion, Windows assigns properties to every object on its desktop. And just as you can move the objects on a real desk, you can rearrange the objects on the Windows desktop.

Figure 1a displays the desktop when Windows is first installed on a new computer. This desktop has only a few objects and is similar to the desk in a new office, just after you move in. Figure 1b displays a different desktop, one with several open windows, and is similar to a desk during the middle of a working day. Do not be concerned if your Windows desktop is different from ours. Your real desk is arranged differently from those of your friends, and so your Windows desktop will also be different.

The simplicity of the desktop in Figure 1a helps you to focus on what is important. The ***Start button,*** as its name suggests, is where you begin. Click the Start button (mouse operations are described on page 9) and you see a menu that lets you start any program (e.g., Microsoft Word or Microsoft Excel) on your computer. The Start button also contains a ***Help command*** through which you can obtain information about every aspect of Windows.

Each icon on the desktop in Figure 1a provides access to an important function within Windows. ***My Computer*** enables you to browse the disk drives and optional CD-ROM drive that are attached to your computer. ***Network Neighborhood*** extends your view of the computer to include the accessible drives on the network to which your machine is attached, if indeed it is part of a network. (You

Double click to browse disk drives

Double click to access network drives

Double click to recover deleted files

Double click to start the Internet Web browser

Click the Start button to display a menu

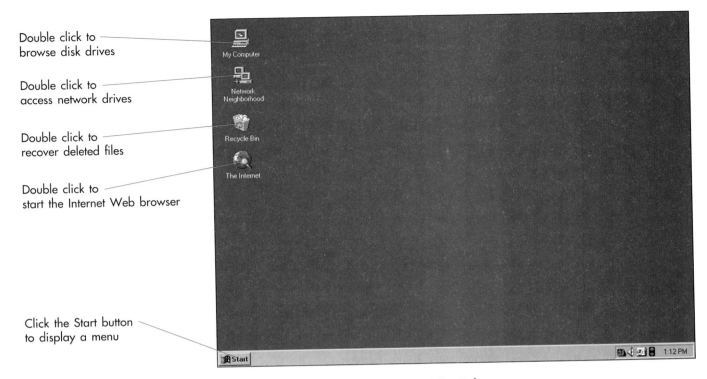

(a) New Desktop

Microsoft Word is in memory

Microsoft Excel is in memory

Internet Web browser is in memory

My Computer is in memory and shows disk drives and folders

Taskbar shows all programs currently in memory

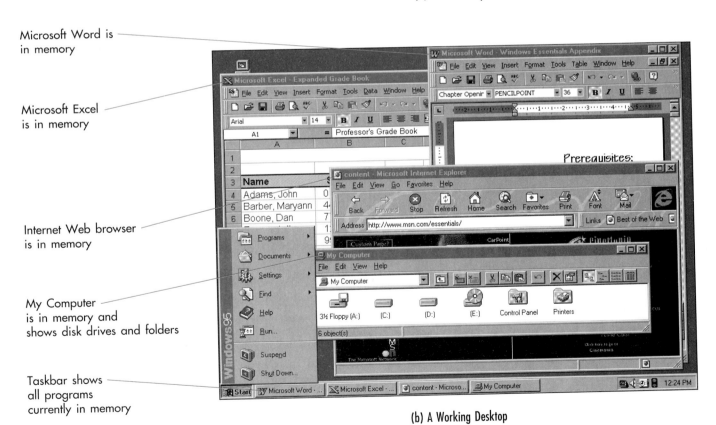

(b) A Working Desktop

FIGURE 1   The Windows Desktop

will not see this icon if you are not connected to a network.) The **Recycle Bin,** described later in the appendix, allows you to recover a file that was previously deleted. Double clicking the **Internet icon** starts the Web browser and initiates a connection to the Internet (assuming you have the necessary hardware).

Each icon on the desktop in Figure 1a opens into a window containing additional objects when you open (double click) the icon. Double click My Computer in Figure 1a, for example, and you see the objects contained in the My Computer window of Figure 2. The contents of the My Computer window depend on the hardware of the specific computer system. Our system, for example, has one floppy drive, two hard (fixed) disks, and a CD-ROM. The My Computer window also contains the Control Panel and Printer folders, which allow access to functions that control other elements in the environment on your computer. (A **folder,** called a directory under MS-DOS, may in turn contain other folders and/or individual files.)

The desktop in Figure 1b contains additional windows that display programs that are currently in use. Each window has a title bar that displays the name of the program and the associated document. You can work in any window as long as you want, then switch to a different window. **Multitasking,** the ability to run several programs at the same time, is one of the major benefits of the Windows environment. It lets you run a word processor in one window, a spreadsheet in a second window, surf the Internet in a third window, play a game in a fourth window, and so on.

The **taskbar** at the bottom of the desktop shows all of the programs that are currently active (open in memory). It contains a button for each open program and lets you switch back and forth between those programs by clicking the appropriate button. The taskbar in Figure 1a does not contain any buttons (other than the Start button) since there are no open applications. The taskbar in Figure 1b, however, contains four additional buttons, one for each open window.

ANATOMY OF A WINDOW

Figure 2 displays two views of the My Computer window and labels its essential elements. Every window has the same components as every other window, which include a title bar, a minimize button, a maximize or restore button, and a close button. Other elements that may be visible include a horizontal and/or vertical scroll bar, a menu bar, a status bar, and a toolbar. Every window also contains additional objects (icons) that pertain specifically to the programs or data associated with that window.

The **title bar** appears at the top of the window and displays the name of the window—for example, My Computer in both Figures 2a and 2b. The icon at the extreme left of the title bar provides access to a control menu that lets you select operations relevant to the window. The **minimize button** shrinks the window to a button on the taskbar. The **maximize button** enlarges the window so that it takes up the entire desktop. The **restore button** (not shown in Figure 2) appears instead of the maximize button after a window has been maximized, and restores the window to its previous size. The **close button** closes the window and removes it from the desktop.

The **menu bar** appears immediately below the title bar and provides access to pull-down menus (as discussed later in the appendix). A **toolbar** appears below the menu bar and lets you execute a command by clicking a button as opposed to pulling down a menu. The **status bar** at the bottom of the window displays information about the window as a whole or about a selected object within a window.

A **vertical** (or **horizontal**) **scroll bar** appears at the right (or bottom) border of a window when its contents are not completely visible and provides access

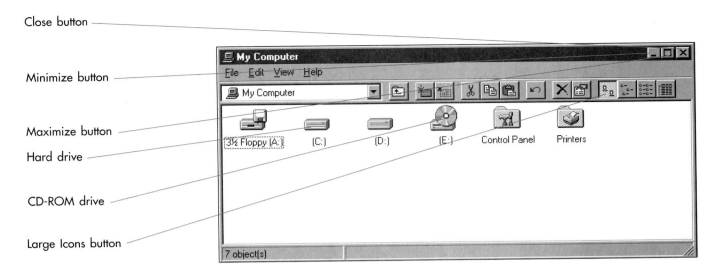

Close button

Minimize button

Maximize button

Hard drive

CD-ROM drive

Large Icons button

(a) Large Icons View

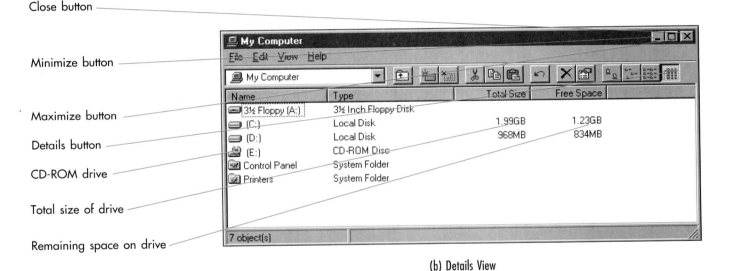

Close button

Minimize button

Maximize button

Details button

CD-ROM drive

Total size of drive

Remaining space on drive

(b) Details View

FIGURE 2   Anatomy of a Window

to the unseen areas. Scroll bars do not appear in Figure 2 since all six objects in the window are visible.

The objects in any window can be displayed in four different views according to your preference or need. The choice between the views depends on your personal preference. You might, for example, choose the **Large Icons view** in Figure 2a if there are only a few objects in the window. The **Details view** in Figure 2b displays additional information about each object including the type of object, the total size of the disk, and the remaining space on the disk. You switch from one view to the next by choosing the appropriate command from the View menu or by clicking the corresponding button on the toolbar.

Moving and Sizing a Window

A window can be sized or moved on the desktop through appropriate actions with the mouse. To **size a window,** point to any border (the mouse pointer changes to a double arrow), then drag the border in the direction you want to go—inward to shrink the window or outward to enlarge it. You can also drag a corner (instead of a border) to change both dimensions at the same time. To **move a window** while retaining its current size, click and drag the title bar to a new position on the desktop.

Pull-down Menus

The menu bar provides access to **pull-down menus** that enable you to execute commands within an application (program). A pull-down menu is accessed by clicking the menu name or by pressing the Alt key plus the underlined letter in the menu name; for example, press Alt+V to pull down the View menu. Three pull-down menus associated with My Computer are shown in Figure 3.

The commands within a menu are executed by clicking the command or by typing the underlined letter (for example, C to execute the Close command in the File menu) once the menu has been pulled down. Alternatively, you can bypass the menu entirely if you know the equivalent keystrokes shown to the right of the command in the menu (e.g., Ctrl+X, Ctrl+C, or Ctrl+V to cut, copy, or paste as shown within the Edit menu).

A **dimmed command** (e.g., the Paste command in the Edit menu) means the command is not currently executable, and that some additional action has to be taken for the command to become available.

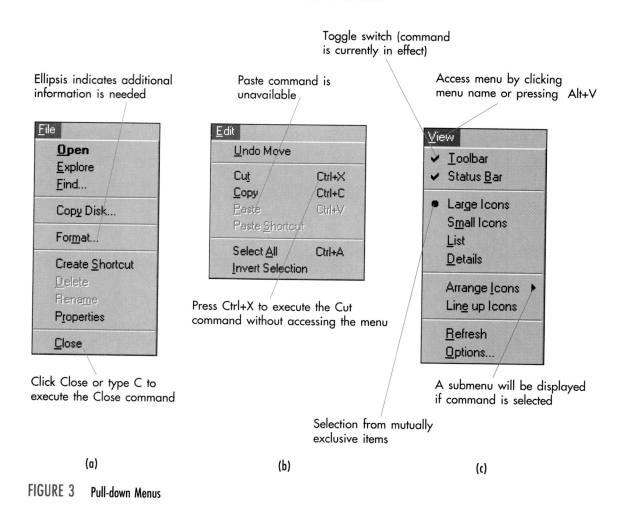

(a)   (b)   (c)

FIGURE 3   Pull-down Menus

An *ellipsis* (...) following a command indicates that additional information is required to execute the command; for example, selection of the Format command in the File menu requires the user to specify additional information about the formatting process. This information is entered into a dialog box (discussed in the next section), which appears immediately after the command has been selected.

A *check* next to a command indicates a toggle switch, whereby the command is either on or off. There is a check next to the Toolbar command in the View menu of Figure 3, which means the command is in effect (and thus the toolbar will be displayed). Click the Toolbar command and the check disappears, which suppresses the display of the toolbar. Click the command a second time and the check reappears, as does the toolbar in the associated window.

A *bullet* next to an item (e.g., Large Icons in Figure 3c) indicates a selection from a set of mutually exclusive choices. Click another option within the group (e.g., Small Icons) and the bullet will disappear from the previous selection (Large Icons) and appear next to the new selection (Small Icons).

An *arrowhead* after a command (e.g., the Arrange icons command in the View menu) indicates that a *submenu* (also known as a cascaded menu) will be displayed with additional menu options.

Dialog Boxes

A *dialog box* appears when additional information is needed to execute a command. The Format command, for example, requires information about which drive to format and the type of formatting desired.

Option (radio) buttons indicate mutually exclusive choices, one of which must be chosen—for example, one of three Format Type options in Figure 4a. Click a button to select an option, which automatically deselects the previously selected option.

Check boxes are used instead of option buttons if the choices are not mutually exclusive or if an option is not required. Multiple boxes can be checked as in Figure 4a, or no boxes may be checked as in Figure 4b. Individual options are selected (cleared) by clicking the appropriate check box.

A *text box* is used to enter descriptive information—for example, Bob's Disk in Figure 4a. A flashing vertical bar (an I-beam) appears within the text box when the text box is active, to mark the *insertion point* for the text you will enter.

A *list box* displays some or all of the available choices, any one of which is selected by clicking the desired item. A *drop-down list box,* such as the Capacity list box in Figure 4a, conserves space by showing only the current selection. Click the arrow of a drop-down list box to display the list of available options. An *open list box,* such as those in Figure 4b, displays multiple choices at one time. (A scroll bar appears within an open list box if some of the choices are not visible and provides access to the hidden choices.)

A *tabbed dialog box* provides multiple sets of options. The dialog box in Figure 4c, for example, has two tabs, each with its own set of options. Click either tab (the General tab is currently selected) to display the associated options.

The *What's This button* (a question mark at the right end of the title bar) provides help for any item in the dialog box. Click the button, then click the item in the dialog box for which you want additional information. The *Close button* (the X at the extreme right of the title bar) closes the dialog box.

All dialog boxes also contain one or more *command buttons,* the functions of which are generally apparent from the specific button's name. The Start button, in Figure 4a, for example, initiates the formatting process. The OK command button in Figure 4b accepts the settings and closes the dialog box. The Cancel button does just the opposite—it ignores (cancels) any changes made to the settings, then closes the dialog box without further action.

Click here to see other options

Drop-down list box shows current selection only

Option buttons indicate mutually exclusive choices

Text box is used to enter descriptive information

Check boxes indicate choices that are not mutually exclusive

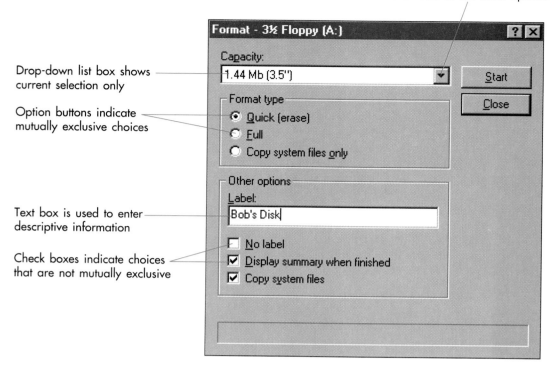

(a) Option Boxes and Check Boxes

Command buttons

Open list box displays multiple options

Scroll bar indicates that not all options are visible

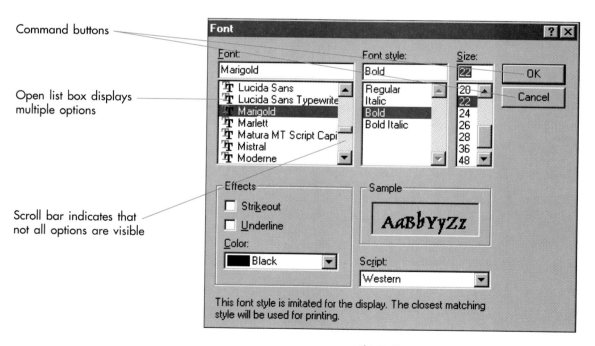

(b) List Boxes

FIGURE 4   Dialog Boxes

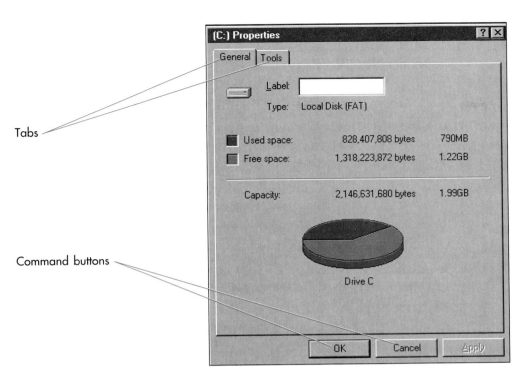

Tabs

Command buttons

(c) Tabbed Dialog Box

FIGURE 4   Dialog Boxes (continued)

THE MOUSE

The mouse is indispensable to Windows and is referenced continually in the hands-on exercises throughout the text. There are four basic operations with which you must become familiar:

- To *point* to an object, move the mouse pointer over the object.
- To *click* an object, point to it, then press and release the left mouse button; to *right click* an object, point to the object, then press and release the right mouse button.
- To *double click* an object, point to it, then quickly click the left button twice in succession.
- To *drag* an object, move the pointer to the object, then press and hold the left button while you move the mouse to a new position.

The mouse is a pointing device—move the mouse on your desk and the *mouse pointer,* typically a small arrowhead, moves on the monitor. The mouse pointer assumes different shapes according to the location of the pointer or the nature of the current action. You will see a double arrow when you change the size of a window, an I-beam as you insert text, a hand to jump from one help topic to the next, or a circle with a line through it to indicate that an attempted action is invalid.

The mouse pointer will also change to an hourglass to indicate that Windows is processing your command, and that no further commands may be issued until the action is completed. The more powerful your computer, the less frequently the hourglass will appear, and conversely, the less powerful your system, the more you see the hourglass.

Microsoft has created a new mouse for Office 97. The mouse contains a wheel between the left and right buttons, allowing you to scroll through a document by rotating the wheel forward or back. You can also increase (or decrease) the magnification by holding the Ctrl key as you rotate the wheel on the mouse. Additional information is available from the IntelliPoint Online User's Guide. (Click the Start button, point to Programs, point to Microsoft Input Devices, and then point to Mouse.)

The Mouse Versus the Keyboard

Almost every command in Windows can be executed by using either the mouse or the keyboard. Most people start with the mouse but add keyboard shortcuts as they become more proficient. There is no right or wrong technique, just different techniques, and the one you choose depends entirely on personal preference in a specific situation. If, for example, your hands are already on the keyboard, it is faster to use the keyboard equivalent. Other times, your hand will be on the mouse and that will be the fastest way.

In the beginning, you may wonder why there are so many different ways to do the same thing, but you will eventually recognize the many options as part of Windows' charm. It is not necessary to memorize anything, nor should you even try; just be flexible and willing to experiment. The more you practice, the sooner all of this will become second nature to you.

THE HELP MENU

Windows has an extensive *Help menu* that contains information about virtually every topic in Windows. We believe that the best time to learn about Help is when you begin your study of Windows. Help is available at any time, and is accessed most easily by clicking the *Help command* on the Start menu, which displays the Help Topics dialog box in Figure 5.

The *Contents tab* in Figure 5a is similar to the table of contents in an ordinary book. The major topics are represented by books, each of which can be opened to display additional topics. These topics may be viewed and/or printed to access the indicated information.

The *Index tab* in Figure 5b is analogous to the index of an ordinary book. Type the first several letters of the topic you want to look up, click the topic when it appears in the window, then click the Display button to view the information. The Help screens are task-specific and provide easy-to-follow instructions.

The *Find tab* (not shown in Figure 5) contains a more extensive listing of entries than does the Index tab. It lets you enter a specific word (or Windows term), then it returns every Help screen that contains that word.

The Microsoft Web site provides information beyond that found in the Help menu. Go to the Microsoft home page (www.microsoft.com), then click the Support tab where you choose the application. You will find articles about new features in the application, answers to frequently asked questions, as well as the knowledge base used by Microsoft support engineers.

Contents tab is selected

Books represent major topics

Open book displays more specific topics

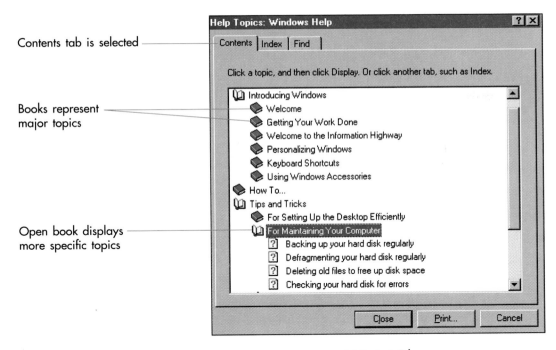

(a) Contents Tab

Index tab is selected

Type first letters of topic

Click desired topic

Click Display button

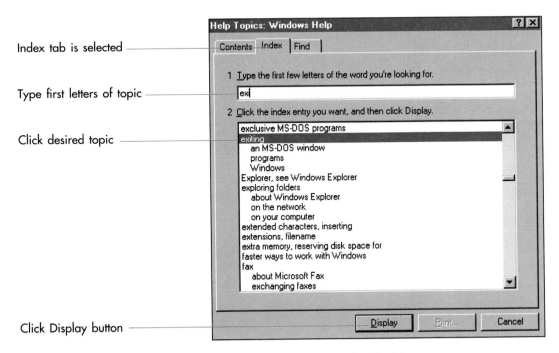

(b) Index Tab

FIGURE 5   The Help Command

FORMATTING A FLOPPY DISK

You will soon begin to work on the computer, which means that you will be using various applications to create different types of documents. Each document is saved in its own file and stored on disk, either on a hard disk (e.g., drive C) if you have your own computer, or on a floppy disk (drive A) if you are working in a computer lab at school.

Even if you have your own machine, however, you will want to copy files from the hard disk to a floppy disk for backup. Thus, you need to purchase a floppy disk(s), and further, you need to format the floppy disk so that it will be able to store the files you create. (You can purchase preformatted floppy disks, but it is very easy to format your own, and we provide instructions in the hands-on exercise that follows.) Be aware, however, that formatting erases any data that was previously on a disk, so be careful not to format a disk with important data (e.g., one containing today's homework assignment).

Formatting is accomplished through the *Format command.* The process is straightforward and has you enter all of the necessary information into a dialog box. One of the box's options is to copy system files onto the disk while formatting it. These files are necessary to start (boot) your computer, and if your hard disk were to fail, you would need a floppy disk with the system (and other) files in order to start the machine. (See Help for information on creating a *boot disk* containing the system files.) For ordinary purposes, however, you do not put the system files on a floppy disk because they take up space you could use to store data.

FORMAT AT THE PROPER CAPACITY

A floppy disk should be formatted at its rated capacity or else you may be unable to read the disk. There are two types of 3½-inch disks, double-density (720KB) and high-density (1.44MB). The easiest way to determine the type of disk you have is to look at the disk itself for the label DD or HD, for double- and high-density, respectively. You can also check the number of square holes in the disk; a double-density disk has one, whereas a high-density disk has two.

LEARNING BY DOING

Learning is best accomplished by doing, and so we come to the first of four hands-on exercises in this appendix. The exercises enable you to apply the concepts you have learned, then extend those concepts to further exploration on your own. The exercise welcomes you to Windows 95, shows you how to open, move, and size a window on the desktop, how to format a floppy disk, and how to use Help to install a screen saver.

A *screen saver* is a special program that protects your monitor by producing a constantly changing pattern after a designated period of inactivity. It is a delightful way to personalize your computer and an excellent illustration of how the Help menu can aid you in accomplishing a specific task. The answer to almost everything you need to know is found in one type of help or another. Start with the Help menu, then go to the Microsoft web site (www.microsoft.com) if you need additional information.

Welcome to Windows

Objective: To turn on the computer and start Windows; to use the Help facility; to open, move, and size a window; and to format a floppy disk. Use Figure 6 as a guide in the exercise.

STEP 1: Start the Computer

➤ The floppy drive should be empty prior to starting your machine. This ensures that the system starts by reading files from the hard disk (which contains the Windows files) as opposed to a floppy disk (which does not).

➤ The number and location of the on/off switches depend on the nature and manufacturer of the devices connected to the computer. The easiest possible setup is when all components of the system are plugged into a surge protector, in which case only a single switch has to be turned on. In any event, turn on the monitor, printer, and system unit.

➤ Your system will take a minute or so to get started after which you should see the desktop in Figure 6a. Do not be concerned if the appearance of your desktop is different from ours.

➤ You may see additional objects on the desktop in Windows 95 and/or the active desktop content in Windows 97.

Click the Start button
to see a menu

(a) Start the Computer (step 1)

FIGURE 6   Hands-on Exercise 1

STEP 2: Open My Computer

➤ Point to the **My Computer icon,** click the **right mouse button,** then click the **Open command** from the shortcut menu. (Alternatively, you can double click the icon to open it directly.)

➤ My Computer will open into a window as shown in Figure 6b. Do not be concerned if the contents of your window or its size and position on the desktop are different from ours.

➤ Pull down the **View menu** (point to the menu and click). Make or verify the following selections (you have to pull down the menu each time you choose a different command):

  • The **Toolbar command** should be checked. The Toolbar command functions as a toggle switch. Click the command and the toolbar is displayed; click the command a second time and the toolbar disappears.

  • The **Status bar command** should be checked. The status bar command also functions as a toggle switch.

  • **Large Icons** should be selected as the current view.

➤ Click the **Details button** on the toolbar to change to this view. Click the **Large Icons button** to return to this view.

➤ Pull down the **View menu** a final time. Click the **Arrange Icons command** and (if necessary) click the **AutoArrange command** so that a check appears.

➤ Click outside the menu (or press the **Esc key**) if the command is already checked.

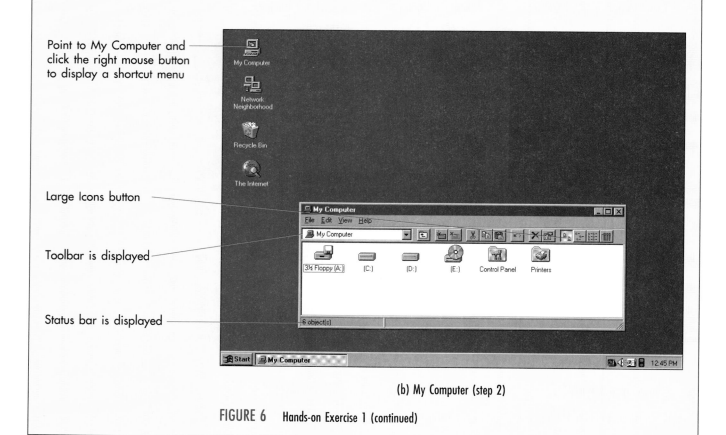

Point to My Computer and click the right mouse button to display a shortcut menu

Large Icons button

Toolbar is displayed

Status bar is displayed

(b) My Computer (step 2)

FIGURE 6   Hands-on Exercise 1 (continued)

DESIGNATING THE DEVICES ON A SYSTEM

The first (usually only) floppy drive is always designated as drive A. (A second floppy drive, if it were present, would be drive B.) The first (often only) hard disk on a system is always drive C, whether or not there are one or two floppy drives. A system with one floppy drive and one hard disk (today's most common configuration) will contain icons for drive A and drive C. Additional hard drives (if any) and/or the CD-ROM are labeled from D on.

STEP 3: Move and Size a Window

➤ Click the **maximize button** so that the My Computer window expands to fill the entire screen.

➤ Click the **restore button** (which replaces the maximize button and is not shown in Figure 6c) to return the window to its previous size.

➤ Click the **minimize button** to shrink the My Computer window to a button on the taskbar. Click the My Computer button to reopen the window.

➤ Move and size the My Computer window on your desk to match the display in Figure 6c:

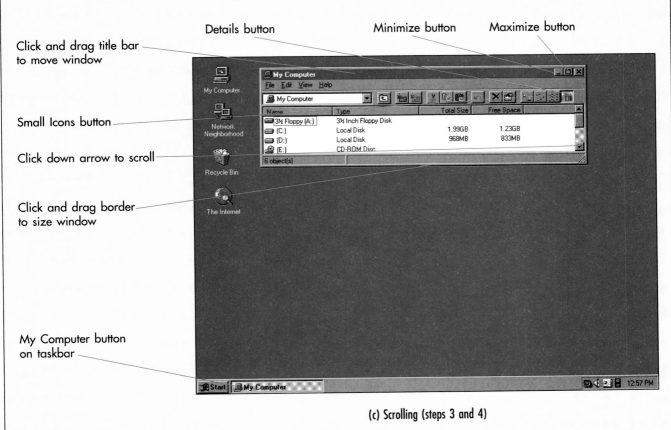

(c) Scrolling (steps 3 and 4)

FIGURE 6   Hands-on Exercise 1 (continued)

- To change the width or height of the window, click and drag a border (the mouse pointer changes to a double arrow) in the direction you want to go; drag the border inward to shrink the window or outward to enlarge it.
- To change the width and height at the same time, click and drag a corner rather than a border.
- To change the position of the window, click and drag the title bar.

➤ Click the **minimize button** to shrink the My Computer window to a button on the taskbar. My Computer is still open and remains active in memory.

➤ Click the **My Computer button** on the taskbar to reopen the window.

THE CONTROL PANEL

The Control Panel contains the utility programs (tools) used to change the hardware and/or software settings for the devices on your system (e.g., modem, monitor, mouse, and so on). Double click the Control Panel icon within My Computer to open the Control Panel window, then double click the icon of the device whose settings you want to modify. Additional information can be obtained through the Help facility.

STEP 4: Scrolling

➤ Pull down the **View menu** and click **Details** (or click the Details button on the toolbar). You are now in the Details view as shown in Figure 6c.

➤ If necessary, click and drag the bottom border of the window inward so that you see the vertical scroll bar in Figure 6c. The scroll bar indicates that the contents of the window are not completely visible.

➤ Click the **down arrow** on the scroll bar. The top line (for drive A) disappears from view and a new line containing the Control Panel comes into view.

➤ Click the **down arrow** a second time, which brings the Printers folder into view at the bottom of the window as the icon for drive C scrolls off the screen.

➤ Click the **Small icons** button on the toolbar. The scroll bar disappears because the contents of the window become completely visible.

➤ Click the **Details button** on the toolbar. The scroll bar returns because you can no longer see the complete contents. Move and/or size the window to your personal preference.

SCREENTIPS

Point to any button on the toolbar and Windows displays a ScreenTip containing the name of the button, which is indicative of its function. You can also point to other objects on the desktop to see similar ScreenTips. Point to the clock at the right end of the taskbar, for example, and you will see a ScreenTip with today's date. Point to the Start button and you will see a ScreenTip telling you to click here to begin.

STEP 5: Online Help

➤ Click the **Start button** on the taskbar, then click the **Help command** to display the Help Topics dialog box in Figure 6d.

➤ Click the **Index tab** as shown in Figure 6d. Type **For** (the first letters in formatting, the topic you are searching for). The Help system automatically displays the topics beginning with the letters you enter.

➤ Click **Disks** (under formatting) from the list of displayed topics, then click the **Display command button** (or double click the topic to avoid having to click the command button).

➤ The Help Topics dialog box is replaced by a Windows Help window with instructions on how to format a floppy disk.

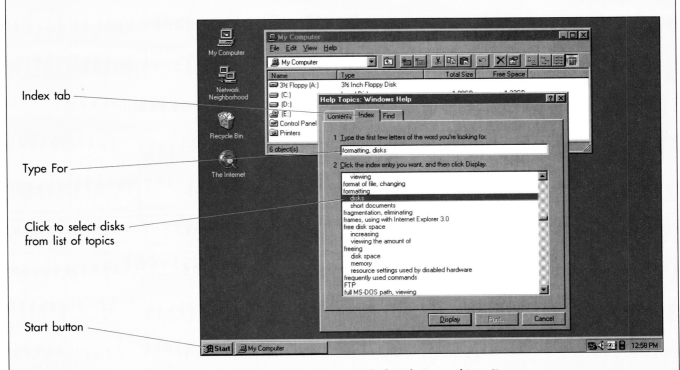

Index tab

Type For

Click to select disks from list of topics

Start button

(d) The Help Command (step 5)

FIGURE 6   Hands-on Exercise 1 (continued)

PRINT THE HELP TOPIC

You can print the contents of any Help window by pointing anywhere within the window and clicking the right mouse button to display a shortcut menu. Click Print Topic, then click the OK command button in the resulting dialog box to print the topic.

STEP 6: Format a Floppy Disk

➤ Place a floppy disk in drive A. Remember, formatting erases everything on the disk, so be sure that you do not need anything on the disk you are about to format. Read the instructions in the Help window in Figure 6.3e, then follow our instructions, which provide more detail.

➤ Click the icon for **drive A.** Pull down the **File menu** and click **Format.** You will see the dialog box in Figure 6e.

   • Set the **Capacity** to match the floppy disk you purchased (1.44MB for a high-density disk and 720KB for a double-density disk).

   • Click the **Full option button** to choose a full format. This option is well worth the extra time as it ensures the integrity of your disk.

   • Click the **Label text box** if it's empty or click and drag over the existing label if there is an entry. Enter a new label (containing up to 11 characters) such as **Bob's Disk** as shown in Figure 6e.

   • Click the **Start command button** to begin the formatting operation. This will take about a minute and you can see the progress of the formatting process at the bottom of the dialog box.

➤ After the formatting process is complete, you will see an informational dialog box with the results of the formatting operation. Read the information, then click the **Close command button** to close the informational dialog box.

➤ Close the Format dialog box. Close the Help window.

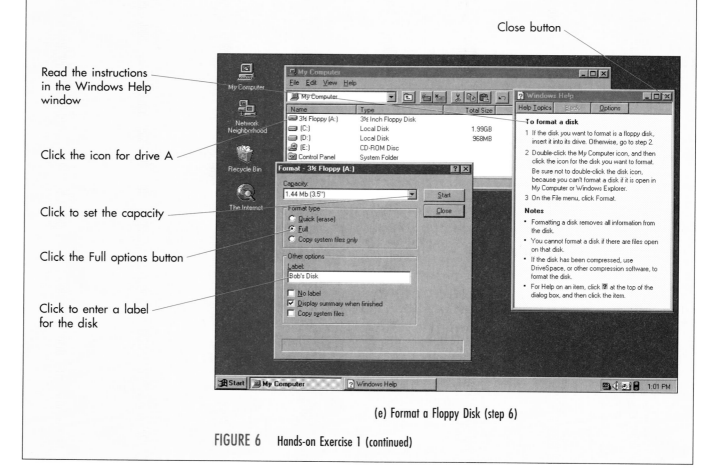

Read the instructions in the Windows Help window

Click the icon for drive A

Click to set the capacity

Click the Full options button

Click to enter a label for the disk

Close button

(e) Format a Floppy Disk (step 6)

FIGURE 6   Hands-on Exercise 1 (continued)

WHAT'S THIS?

The What's This button (a question mark) appears in the title bar of almost every dialog box. Click the question mark, then click the item you want information about (which then appears in a pop-up window). To print the contents of the pop-up window, click the right mouse button inside the window, and click Print Topic. Click outside the pop-up window to close the window and continue working.

STEP 7: Implement a Screen Saver

➤ If you are working in a lab environment, it is possible that your network administrator has disabled the ability to implement a screen saver, and that you will be unable to complete this step. If this is true at your site, skip the instructions below and go to step 8.

➤ Click the **Start button,** click the **Help command** to display the Help Topics dialog box, then click the **Index tab.** Type **Scr** (the first letters in *screen,* the topic you are searching for).

➤ Click **Screen Savers** from the list of displayed topics, then click the **Display button.** (You can also double click the topic to avoid having to click the command button.)

➤ You will see a second dialog box listing the available topics under Screen Savers. **Double click** the topic that begins **Protecting your screen.** You should see the Help window in Figure 6f. Click the **shortcut jump button** to display the Display Properties dialog box.

➤ Click the **drop-down arrow** in the Screen Saver box to display the available screen savers. Click one or more of the available screen savers until you come to one you like.

➤ Click the **OK command button** to accept the screen saver and exit the dialog box. Click the **Close button** to close the Windows Help window.

PROPERTIES EVERYWHERE

The fastest way to implement a screen saver (or to change the color or other properties of the desktop) is to display the Properties dialog box for the desktop. Point to the desktop, click the right mouse button to display a context-sensitive menu, then click Properties to open the Display Properties dialog box. Click the Screen Saver tab, make the appropriate selections, then click OK to accept the settings and close the dialog box.

STEP 8: Exit Windows

➤ Click the **Start button,** then click the **Shut Down command.** You will see a dialog box asking whether you're sure that you want to shut down the computer. (The option button to shut down the computer is already selected.)

➤ Click the **Yes command button,** then wait as Windows gets ready to shut down your system. Wait until you see another screen indicating that it is OK to turn off the computer.

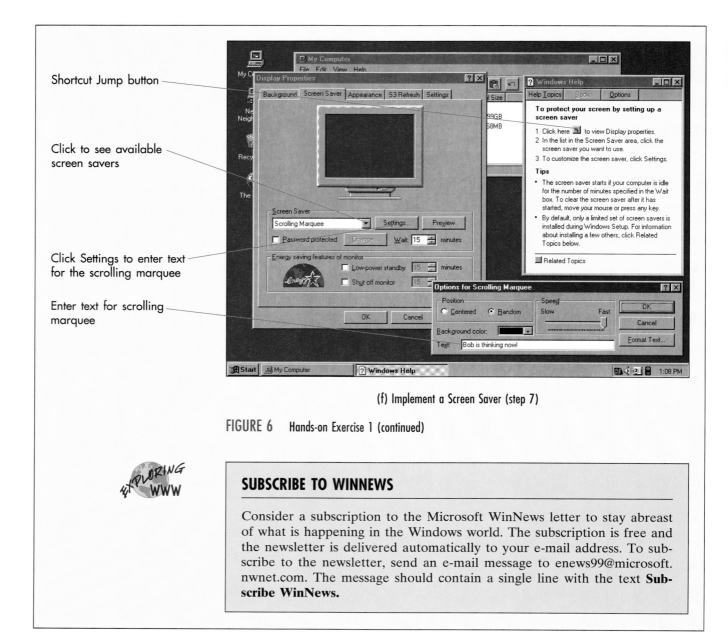

Shortcut Jump button

Click to see available screen savers

Click Settings to enter text for the scrolling marquee

Enter text for scrolling marquee

(f) Implement a Screen Saver (step 7)

FIGURE 6   Hands-on Exercise 1 (continued)

EXPLORING WWW

SUBSCRIBE TO WINNEWS

Consider a subscription to the Microsoft WinNews letter to stay abreast of what is happening in the Windows world. The subscription is free and the newsletter is delivered automatically to your e-mail address. To subscribe to the newsletter, send an e-mail message to enews99@microsoft. nwnet.com. The message should contain a single line with the text **Subscribe WinNews.**

FILES AND FOLDERS

The ultimate purpose of any computer system is to do useful work. This, in turn, requires the acquisition of various application software, such as Microsoft Office. Each document, spreadsheet, presentation, or database that you create is stored in a file on a disk, be it a hard disk or a floppy disk. It is important, therefore, that you understand the basics of file management so that you will be able to retrieve these files at a later time.

A *file* is data that has been given a name and stored on disk. There are, in general, two types of files, *program files* and *data files.* Microsoft Word and Microsoft Excel are program files. The documents and spreadsheets created by these programs are data files. A *program file* is executable because it contains instructions that tell the computer what to do. A *data file* is not executable and can be used only in conjunction with a specific program.

A file must have a name so that it can be identified. The file name can contain up to 255 characters and may include spaces and other punctuation. (This is very different from the rules that existed under MS-DOS, which limited file names to eight characters followed by an optional three-character extension.) Long file names permit descriptive entries such as *Term Paper for Western Civilization* (as opposed to a more cryptic *TPWCIV* that would be required under MS-DOS).

Files are stored in **folders** to better organize the hundreds (often thousands) of files on a hard disk. A Windows folder is similar in concept to a manila folder in a filing cabinet and contains one or more documents (files) that are somehow related to each other. An office worker stores his or her documents in manila folders. In Windows, you store your data files (documents) in electronic folders on disk.

Folders are the key to the Windows storage system. You can create any number of folders to hold your work just as you can place any number of manila folders into a filing cabinet. You can create one folder for your word processing documents and a different folder for your spreadsheets. Alternatively, you can create a folder to hold all of your work for a specific class, which may contain a combination of word processing documents and spreadsheets. The choice is entirely up to you and you can use any system that makes sense to you. Anything at all can go into a folder—program files, data files, even other folders.

Figure 7 displays two views of a folder containing six documents. The name of the folder (Homework) appears in the title bar next to the icon of an open folder. The minimize, maximize, and close buttons appear at the right of the title bar. A toolbar appears below the menu bar in each view.

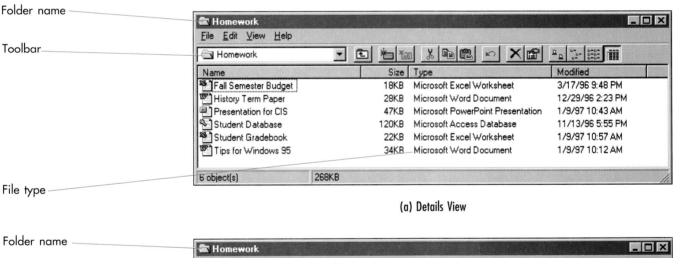

(a) Details View

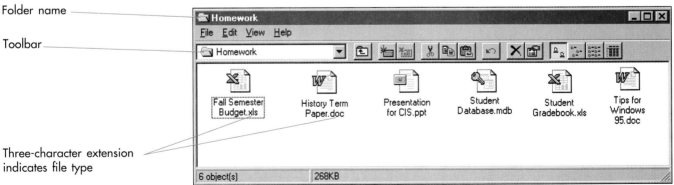

(b) Large Icons View

FIGURE 7   The Homework Folder

The Details view in Figure 7a displays a small icon representing the application that created the file. It also shows the name of each file in the folder (note the descriptive file name), the file size, the type of file, and the date and time the file was last modified. Figure 7b illustrates the Large Icons view, which displays only the file name and an icon representing the application that created the file. The choice between views depends on your personal preference. (A Small Icons view and List view are also available.)

File Type

Every data file has a specific *file type* that is determined by the application used to create the file. One way to recognize the file type is to examine the Type column in the Details view as shown in Figure 7a. The History Term Paper, for example, is a Microsoft Word document. The Student Gradebook is a Microsoft Excel worksheet.

You can also determine the file type (or associated application) from any view by examining the application icon displayed next to the file name. Look carefully at the icon next to the History Term Paper in Figure 7a, for example, and you will recognize the icon for Microsoft Word. The application icon is recognized more easily in the Large Icons view in Figure 7b.

Still another way to determine the file type is through a three-character extension, which is appended to the file name. (A period separates the filename from the extension.) Each application has a unique extension that is automatically assigned to the file name when the file is created. DOC and XLS, for example, are the extensions for Microsoft Word and Excel, respectively. The extension may be suppressed or displayed according to an option in the View menu of My Computer (or the Windows Explorer), but is best left suppressed in Windows 95/97.

My Computer

It is important to be able to locate a folder and/or its documents so that you can retrieve a document and go to work. Assume, for example, that you are looking for a term paper in American History that you began yesterday and saved in a folder called Homework. You know the folder is somewhere on drive C, but you are not quite sure where. You need to locate the folder in order to open the term paper and continue working. One way to accomplish this is through My Computer as shown in Figure 8.

You begin by double clicking the My Computer icon on the desktop to open the My Computer window and display the devices on your system. Next, you double click the icon for drive C since it contains the folder you are looking for. This opens a second window, which displays all of the folders on drive C. And finally, you double click the icon for the Homework folder to open a third window containing the documents in the Homework folder. Once in the Homework folder, you can double click the icon of an existing document, which starts the associated application and opens the document, enabling you to begin work.

The Exploring Windows Practice Files

There is only one way to master Windows 95 and that is to practice at the computer. One of the most important skills you need to acquire is that of file management; that is, you must be proficient in moving and copying files from one drive (or folder) to another. To do so requires that you have a series of files with which to work. Accordingly, we have created a set of practice files that we reference in the next several hands-on exercises. Your instructor will make these files available to you in a variety of ways:

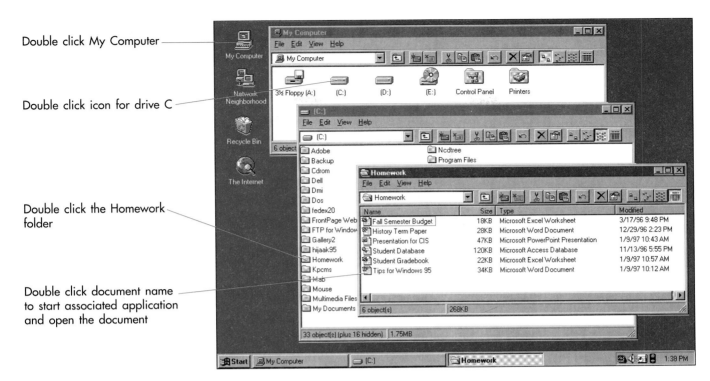

Double click My Computer

Double click icon for drive C

Double click the Homework folder

Double click document name to start associated application and open the document

FIGURE 8   Browsing My Computer

- The files can be downloaded from our Web site, as described in the next hands-on exercise. This assumes you have access to the Internet, and further, that you have a basic proficiency with a browser such as the *Internet Explorer.*
- The files might be on a network drive, in which case you can use My Computer (or the Windows Explorer, which is discussed later in the chapter) to copy the files from the network drive to a floppy disk. The procedure to do this is described in hands-on exercise 3 later in the chapter.
- There may be an actual data disk in the computer lab. Go to the lab with a floppy disk, then use the Copy Disk command to duplicate the data disk to create a copy for yourself.

It doesn't matter how you obtain the practice files, only that you are able to do so. Indeed, you may try different techniques in order to gain additional practice with the Windows environment. All three methods will place the practice files on a floppy disk; hence you need the formatted floppy disk that was created in the first hands-on exercise. Note, too, the techniques described in the hands-on exercises apply to the practice files for any book in the *Exploring Windows* series.

THE EXPLORING WINDOWS SERIES

The text you are reading is one of several books in the *Exploring Windows* series, many of which reference a series of practice files for use with the hands-on exercises. One way to access these files is from the Prentice Hall Web site at www.prenhall.com/grauer. You can also go to Bob Grauer's home page (www.bus.miami.edu/~rgrauer) and click the *Exploring Windows* link. Bob's home page also provides links to the classes he is teaching at the University of Miami.

The Practice Files (via the World Wide Web)

Objective: To download the practice files from the *Exploring Windows* Web site. The exercise requires a formatted floppy disk and access to the Internet. Use Figure 9 as a guide in the exercise.

STEP 1: The *Exploring Windows* Series

➤ Start Internet Explorer. If you are working in class, your instructor will provide additional instructions. At home, however, it is incumbent on you to be able to know how to access the Internet.

➤ If necessary, click the **maximize button** so that the Internet Explorer takes the entire desktop. Enter the address of the site you want to visit as shown in Figure 9a.

• Pull down the **File menu,** click the **Open command** to display the Open dialog box, and enter **www.prenhall.com/grauer** (the http:// is assumed). Click **OK.**

• *Or,* click in the **Address box** below the toolbar, which automatically selects the current address (so that whatever you type replaces the current address). Enter the address of the site you want to visit, **www.prenhall.com/grauer** (the http:// is assumed). Press the **enter key.**

➤ You should see the *Exploring Windows* home page as shown in Figure 9a. Click the book **Exploring Office 97** to display the page for this series. Click the link to **Office 97.**

Enter the address of the site you want to visit

Click the link to Office 97

(a) The *Exploring Windows* series (step 1)

FIGURE 9   Hands-on Exercise 2

UNABLE TO LOCATE SERVER OR SERVER NOT RESPONDING

Two things must occur in order for Internet Explorer to display the requested document—it must locate the server on which the document is stored, and it must be able to connect to that computer. The error message "Unable to Locate Server" will appear if you enter the Web address incorrectly. Click the Address bar and re-enter the Web address, being sure to enter it correctly. You may also see the message "Server Down or Not Responding," which implies that Internet Explorer located the server but was unable to connect because the site is busy. This means that too many visitors are already there and you need to try again later in the day.

STEP 2: Download the Practice Files

➤ You should see a screen listing the various books for Office 97. Click the link to **Windows Prerequisites** to display the screen in Figure 9b. (The Save As dialog box is not yet visible.)

➤ Click **prerequisites.exe** (the file you will download to your PC). The File Download window opens, and after a few seconds, an Internet Explorer dialog box opens as well. The option button to **Save it to disk** is selected. Click **OK** to display the Save As dialog box in Figure 9b:

• The **desktop** is selected as the destination in the Save in box. If this is not the case, click the **drop-down arrow** on the Save in box and select the desktop. Click **Save** to download the file.

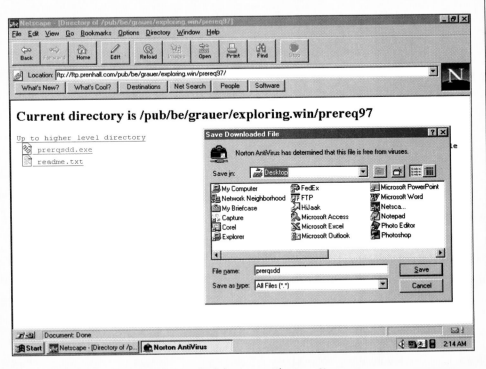

(b) Download the Practice Files (step 2)

FIGURE 9   Hands-on Exercise 2 (continued)

- If you are unable to save to the desktop because your network administrator has disabled this capability at your site, select drive A in the Save in box instead of the desktop (place a formatted floppy disk in drive A).

➤ The File Download window will reappear on your screen and show you the process of the downloading operation. Be patient, as this may take a few minutes. (The Exploring Prerequisites file is 52KB in size.) The File Download window will close automatically when downloading is complete.

➤ Minimize (do not close) Internet Explorer. The Internet Explorer window shrinks to a button on the taskbar, but the application remains open in memory. (We return to Internet Explorer in step 5.)

ABOUT INTERNET EXPLORER

Pull down the Help menu and click About Internet Explorer to see which version of the Internet Explorer you are using. Our exercises were done with Version 3.00, but you may have a later version if you installed the software after publication of our text. The command structure may vary slightly from one version to the next, but you should be able to complete the exercise without a problem, as long as you are running Version 3.00 or higher.

STEP 3: Install the Practice Files

➤ Double click the **Prerequisites icon** from the desktop or drive A, depending on where you downloaded the file.

- If you downloaded the file to the desktop, the Prerequisites icon should be visible on the desktop and you can simply double click the icon.
- If you downloaded the file to a floppy disk, double click the **My Computer icon** on the desktop to open the My Computer window, double click the icon for **drive A,** then double click the **Prerequisites icon.**

➤ You will see a dialog box thanking you for selecting the *Exploring Windows* series. Click **OK** when you have finished reading the dialog box to begin (or cancel) the installation.

FILE COMPRESSION

Software and other files are typically compressed to reduce the amount of storage space a file requires on disk and/or the time it takes to download the file. In essence, you download a compressed file from a Web site, then you uncompress the file on a local drive. Ideally a compressed file is created as a self-extracting (executable) file as opposed to a zip file, which requires a utility program outside Windows 95. Our files are executable. Thus, all you have to do is double click the executable file after it has been downloaded, and it will automatically install (uncompress) the practice files for you.

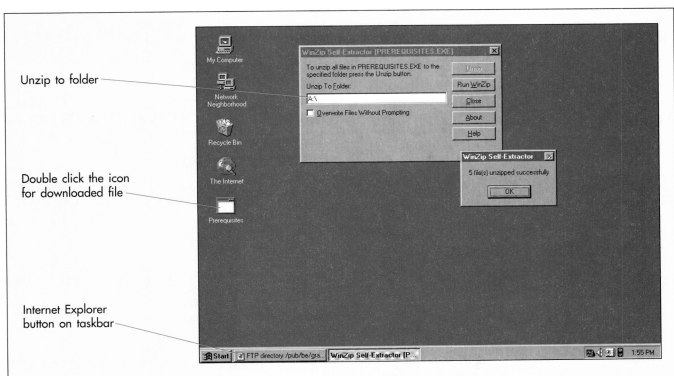

Unzip to folder

Double click the icon
for downloaded file

Internet Explorer
button on taskbar

(c) Install the Practice Files (step 3)

FIGURE 9   Hands-on Exercise 2 (continued)

➤ If necessary, place a floppy disk in drive A, then verify that the Unzip to Folder text box is specified as **A:** (the floppy disk). If it is not, enter **A:** in the text box as shown in Figure 9c.

➤ Click the **Unzip button** to extract the practice files and copy them into the designated folder.

➤ Click **OK** after you see the message indicating that the files have been unzipped successfully. Close the WinZip dialog box.

➤ The practice files have been extracted and copied to drive A.

STEP 4: Open My Computer

➤ Double click **My Computer** to open the My Computer window in Figure 9d. If necessary, pull down the **View menu** to display the toolbar. Click the **Large Icons view.**

➤ Double click the icon for **drive A** to open a second window, which displays the contents of drive A. Use the **View menu** to display the toolbar, then change to the **Details view.**

➤ You should see five files, which are the practice files on the data disk. (There are three Word files, one Excel file, and one PowerPoint file.) These are the files that will be used in a hands-on exercise later in the chapter.

➤ Select (click) the **Prerequisites icon** on the desktop. Press the **Del key** to erase this file as it is no longer needed. Click **Yes** when asked whether to remove this file.

➤ Close the windows for drive A and My Computer as they are no longer needed in this exercise.

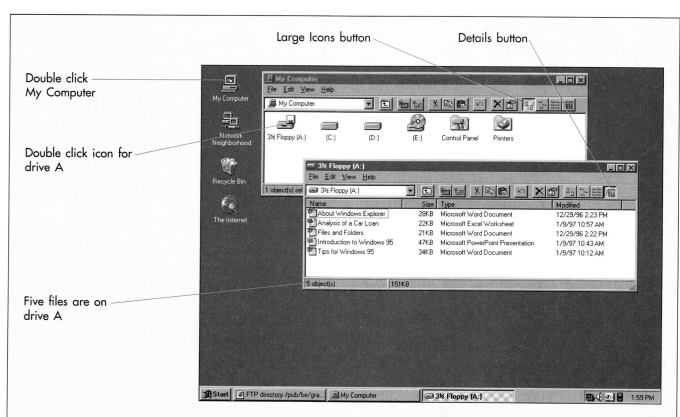

Double click
My Computer

Large Icons button

Details button

Double click icon for
drive A

Five files are on
drive A

(d) Open My Computer (step 4)

FIGURE 9   Hands-on Exercise 2 (continued)

ONE WINDOW OR MANY

By default, My Computer opens a new window every time you open a new drive or folder. The multiple windows can clutter a desktop rather quickly, and hence you may prefer to change the display in the current window to the new drive or folder rather than open a new window. Pull down the View menu, click Options, click the Folder tab, then click the option button to browse folders using a single window.

STEP 5: Microsoft on the Web

➤ Click the **Internet Explorer button** on the taskbar to return to Internet Explorer. Click in the **Address box** below the toolbar. Enter **www.microsoft. com** Press the **enter key.**

➤ You should see Microsoft's home page. Click the link to **Products,** then scroll until you can click the link to **Windows 95** to display the page in Figure 9e.

➤ Your screen will be different from ours, as Microsoft is continually updating its information. Click any links that appeal to you to view additional information that is available from Microsoft via the Web.

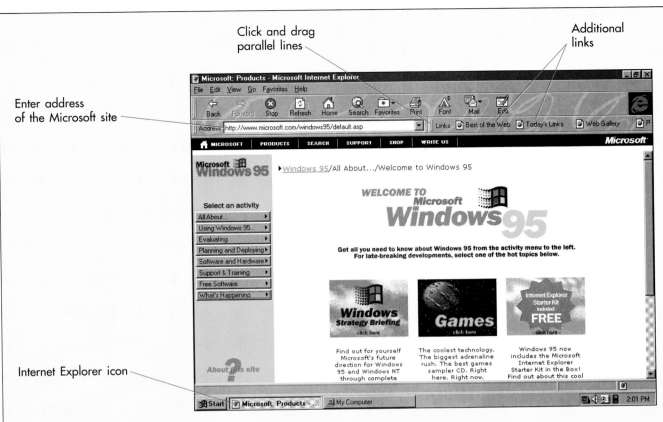

Enter address of the Microsoft site

Click and drag parallel lines

Additional links

Internet Explorer icon

(e) Windows 95 Home Page (step 5)

FIGURE 9   Hands-on Exercise 2 (continued)

➤ You may also want to view additional sites suggested by Internet Explorer. If necessary, click and drag the parallel lines that appear to the right of the address box (the mouse pointer changes to a two-headed arrow) to display additional links.

➤ Click the **Best of the Web** or the **Today's Links button** to explore the current cool sites suggested by Internet Explorer.

➤ We don't know what you will find, but you can expect something interesting every day.

➤ Click the hyperlinks that interest you and off you go. Happy surfing!

SET A TIME LIMIT

We warn you that the Web is addictive, and that once you start surfing, it is difficult to stop. We suggest, therefore, that you set a time limit before you begin, and that you stick to it. Tomorrow is another day, with new places to explore.

One of the most important skills you need to acquire is the ability to locate a specific folder or file so that you can go to work. In essence you need to be able to copy, move, rename, and even delete the various files and folders on your system. There are two basic ways to accomplish these tasks. You can use My Computer to open successive windows until you come to the file or folder you are looking for. Alternatively, you can use the *Windows Explorer* to locate the object by navigating the hierarchical structure of your system. The difference between the two is shown in Figure 10.

Assume, for example, that you are taking five classes this semester, and that you are using the computer in each course. You've created a separate folder to hold the work for each class and have stored the contents of all five folders on a single floppy disk. Assume further that you need to retrieve your third English assignment so that you can modify it and submit the revised version.

You can use My Computer to browse the system as shown in Figure 10a. You would start by opening My Computer, double clicking the icon for drive A to open a second window, then double clicking the icon for the English folder to display its documents. The process is intuitive, but it can quickly lead to a desktop cluttered with open windows. And what if you next needed to work on a paper for Art History? That would require you to open the Art History folder, which produces yet another open window on the desktop.

The Windows Explorer in Figure 10b offers a more sophisticated way to browse the system, as it shows both the hierarchy of folders and the contents of the selected folder. The Explorer window is divided into two panes. The left pane contains a *tree diagram* of the entire system showing all drives and, optionally, the folders in each drive. One (and only one) object is always selected in the left pane, and its contents are displayed automatically in the right pane.

Look carefully at the tree diagram in Figure 10b and note that the English folder is currently selected. The icon for the selected folder is an open folder to differentiate it from the other folders, which are closed and are not currently selected. The right pane displays the contents of the selected folder (English in Figure 10b) and is seen to contain three documents, Assignments 1, 2, and 3. The right pane is displayed in the Details view, but could just as easily have been displayed in another view (e.g., Large or Small Icons) by clicking the appropriate button on the toolbar.

As indicated, only one folder can be selected (open) at a time in the left pane, and its contents are displayed in the right pane. To see the contents of a different folder (e.g., Accounting), you would click the Accounting folder, which automatically closes the English folder and opens the Accounting folder.

The tree diagram in the left pane displays the drives and their folders in hierarchical fashion. The desktop is always at the top of the hierarchy and contains My Computer, which in turn contains various drives, each of which contains folders, which in turn contain documents and/or additional folders. Each object may be expanded or collapsed by clicking the plus or minus sign, respectively.

Look again at the icon next to My Computer in Figure 10b and you see a minus sign, indicating that My Computer has been expanded to show the various drives on the system. There is also a minus sign next to the icon for drive A to indicate that it too has been expanded to show the folders on the disk. Note, however, the plus sign next to drives C and D, indicating that these parts of the tree are currently collapsed and thus their subordinates are not visible.

A folder may contain additional folders and thus individual folders may also be expanded or collapsed. The minus sign next to the Finance folder in Figure 10b, for example, shows that the folder has been expanded and contains two

Double click My Computer

Double click icon for drive A

Double click icon for English folder

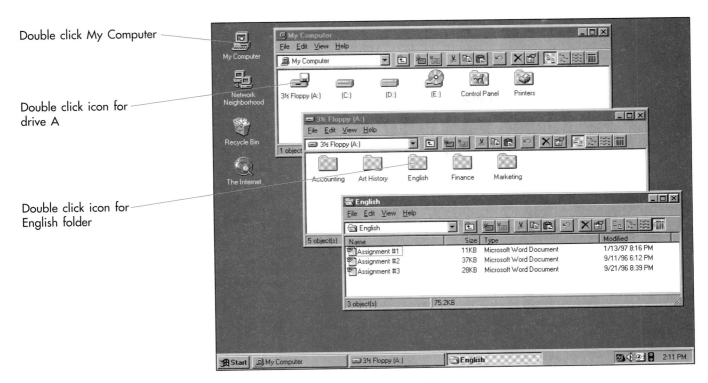

(a) My Computer

Tree diagram

Contents pane displays contents of selected folder

Minus sign indicates drive/folder is expanded (subordinates are visible)

Currently selected folder

No subordinates exist

Plus signs indicate drive/folder is collapsed (subordinates are not visible)

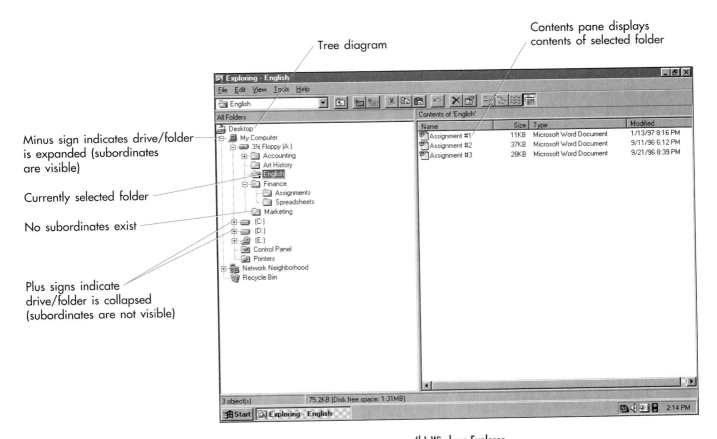

(b) Windows Explorer

FIGURE 10   Working with Files and Folders

additional folders, for Assignments and Spreadsheets, respectively. The plus sign next to the Accounting folder, however, indicates the opposite; that is, the folder is collapsed and its subordinate folders are not currently visible. A folder with neither a plus or minus sign, such as Art History or Marketing, does not contain additional folders and cannot be expanded or collapsed.

The advantage of the Windows Explorer over My Computer is the uncluttered screen and ease with which you switch from one folder to the next. If, for example, you wanted to see the contents of the Art History folder, all you would do would be to click its icon in the left pane, which automatically changes the display in the right pane to show the documents in Art History. The Explorer also makes it easy to move or copy a file from one folder or drive to another, as you will see in the hands-on exercise, which follows shortly.

ORGANIZE YOUR WORK

Organize your folders in ways that make sense to you, such as a separate folder for every class you are taking. You can also create folders within folders; for example, a correspondence folder may contain two folders of its own, one for business correspondence and one for personal letters. Use descriptive names for your folders so that you will remember their contents. (A name may contain up to 255 characters, including spaces.)

The Practice Files

As indicated, there are several ways to obtain the practice files associated with the various books in the *Exploring Windows* series. You can download the files from our Web site as described in the previous hands-on exercise. Alternatively, you can use the Windows Explorer to copy the files from a network drive (at school) to a floppy disk, as will be demonstrated in the following hands-on exercise.

The Windows Explorer is especially useful for moving or copying files from one folder or drive to another. You simply select (open) the folder that contains the file, use the scroll bar in the left pane (if necessary) so that the destination folder is visible, then click and drag the file(s) from the right pane to the destination folder. The Explorer is a powerful tool, but it takes practice to master.

EXPLORE THE PRACTICE FILES

The practice files are intended to teach you the basics of file management, but they are also interesting in and of themselves. The *Tips for Windows 95* document, for example, contains several tips that appeared throughout this appendix. The *Introduction to Windows 95* presentation summarizes much of the material in this appendix. *Analysis of a Car Loan* is an Excel workbook that computes a monthly car payment based on the cost of a car and the parameters of a loan. Double click any of these files from within the Windows Explorer to start the application and load the document.

The Practice Files (via a local area network)

Objective: To use the Windows Explorer to copy the practice files from a network drive to a floppy disk. The exercise requires a formatted floppy disk and access to a local area network. Use Figure 11 as a guide in the exercise.

STEP 1: Start the Windows Explorer

➤ Click the **Start Button,** click (or point to) the **Programs command,** then click **Windows Explorer** to start this program. Click the **maximize button** so that the Explorer takes the entire desktop as shown in Figure 11a. Do not be concerned if your screen is different from ours.

➤ Make or verify the following selections using the **View menu.** (You have to pull down the View menu each time you choose a different command.)

- The **Toolbar command** should be checked.
- The **Status bar command** should be checked.
- The **Large Icons view** should be selected.

➤ Click (select) the **Desktop icon** in the left pane to display the contents of the desktop in the right pane.

➤ Our desktop contains only the icons for My Computer, Network Neighborhood, the Recycle Bin, and the Internet icon. Your desktop may have different icons, but your screen should otherwise match Figure 11a.

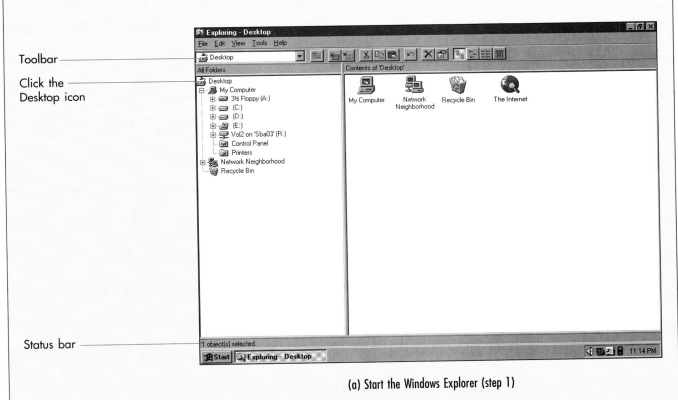

(a) Start the Windows Explorer (step 1)

FIGURE 11   Hands-on Exercise 3

FILE EXTENSIONS

Long-time DOS users remember a three-character extension at the end of a file name to indicate the file type—for example, DOC or XLS to indicate a Word document or Excel workbook, respectively. The extensions are displayed or hidden according to the option you establish through the View menu of the Windows Explorer. Pull down the View menu, click the Options command to display the Options dialog box, click the View tab, then check (or clear) the box to hide (or show) MS-DOS file extensions. Click OK to accept the setting and exit the dialog box. We prefer to hide the extensions.

STEP 2: Additional Practice

➤ The objective of this exercise is to obtain the practice files by copying files from a local area network (such as a computer lab at school) using the Windows Explorer. If you already downloaded the practice files from our Web site in the previous hands-on exercise, you can:

  • Use the practice files you already have and go to step 6 to continue with this exercise, *or*

  • Erase all of the files on your floppy disk (just reformat the disk), then proceed with steps 3 through 5 in this exercise.

➤ We suggest you continue with step 3 in order to practice with the Windows Explorer.

THE QUICK FORMAT COMMAND

The fastest way to erase the entire contents of a floppy disk is to use the Quick Format command. Start the Windows Explorer and select any drive except the floppy drive. (You cannot format a floppy disk in drive A when drive A is selected). Point to the icon for drive A in the left pane, click the right mouse button to display a shortcut menu, then click the Format command to display the Format dialog box. Click the option button for the Quick (erase) Format, then click the Start button to format the disk and erase its contents.

STEP 3: Collapse the Individual Drives

➤ Click the **minus** (or the plus) **sign** next to My Computer to collapse (or expand) My Computer and hide (display) the objects it contains.

➤ Toggle the signs back and forth a few times for practice. End with a minus sign next to the My Computer icon as shown in Figure 11b.

➤ Place a formatted floppy disk in drive A, then click the **plus sign** next to drive A. The plus sign disappears, as drive A does not have any folders.

Click icon to select drive A

Click the plus sign to expand drive

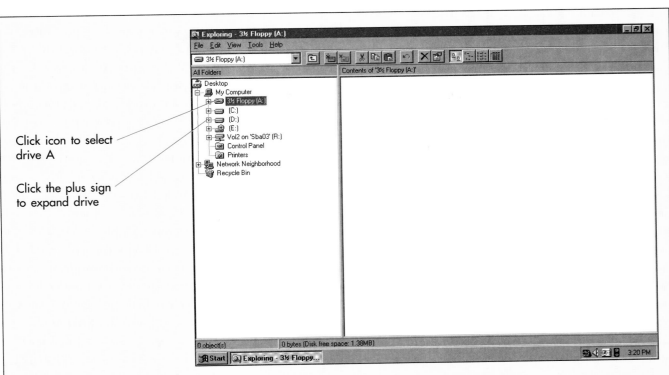

(b) Collapse the Individual Drives (step 3)

FIGURE 11   Hands-on Exercise 3 (continued)

> Click the **plus** (minus) **sign** next to the other drives to toggle back and forth between expanding (collapsing) the individual drives on your system.

> End this step with every drive collapsed; that is, there should be a **plus sign** next to every drive, as shown in Figure 11b.

> Click the drive icon next to drive A to select the drive and display its contents in the right pane. The disk does not contain any files, and hence the right pane is empty.

THE PLUS AND MINUS SIGN

Any drive, be it local or on the network, may be expanded or collapsed to display or hide its contents. A minus sign indicates that the drive has been expanded and that its folders are visible. A plus sign indicates the reverse; that is, the device is collapsed and its folders are not visible. Click either sign to toggle to the other. Clicking a plus sign, for example, expands the drive, then displays a minus sign next to the drive to indicate that the folders are visible. Clicking a minus sign has the reverse effect— it collapses the drive, hiding its folders.

STEP 4: Select the Network Drive

> Click the **plus sign** for the network drive, which contains the files you are to copy (e.g., drive R in Figure 11c). Select (click) the **Exploring Prerequisites**

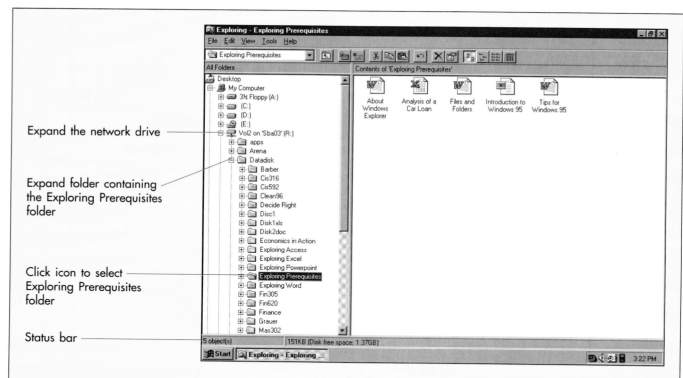

Expand the network drive

Expand folder containing
the Exploring Prerequisites
folder

Click icon to select
Exploring Prerequisites
folder

Status bar

(c) Select the Exploring Prerequisites Folder (step 4)

FIGURE 11   Hands-on Exercise 3 (continued)

folder to select this folder. (You may need to expand other folders on the network drive as per instructions from your professor.) Note the following:

- The Exploring Prerequisites folder is highlighted in the left pane, its icon has changed to an open folder, and its contents are displayed in the right pane.

- The status bar indicates that the folder contains five objects and the total file size is 151KB.

➤ Click the icon next to any other folder to select the folder, which in turn deselects the Exploring Prerequisites folder. (Only one folder in the left pane can be selected at a time.) Reselect (click) the **Exploring Prerequisites folder** and its contents are again visible in the right pane.

➤ Pull down the **View menu** and select **Details** (or click the **Details button** on the toolbar) to change to the Details view. This enables you to see the file sizes of the individual files.

THE VIEW MENU

The objects in any window can be displayed in four different views—Large Icons, Small Icons, Details, and List—according to your preference or need. The choice of views depends on your personal preference. You can change from one view to another from the View menu, or by clicking the appropriate button on the toolbar. (Windows 97 provides access to a fifth view, the Web view, which displays the addresses of recently visited Web sites.)

STEP 5: Copy the Individual Files

➤ Select (click) the file **About Windows Explorer,** which highlights the file as shown in Figure 11d. The Exploring Prerequisites folder is no longer highlighted because a different object has been selected. The folder is still open, however, and its contents are displayed in the right pane.

➤ Click and drag the selected file in the right pane to the **drive A icon** in the left pane:

  • You will see the ⊘ symbol as you drag the file until you reach a suitable destination (e.g., until you point to the icon for drive A). The ⊘ symbol will change to a plus sign when the icon for drive A is highlighted, indicating that the file can be copied successfully.

  • Release the mouse to complete the copy operation. You will see a pop-up window, which indicates the progress of the copy operation. This may take several seconds, depending on the size of the file.

➤ Select (click) the file **Tips for Windows 95,** which automatically deselects the previously selected file (About Windows Explorer). Copy the selected file to drive A by dragging its icon from the right pane to the drive A icon in the left pane.

➤ Copy the three remaining files to drive A as well. (You can select multiple files at the same time by pressing and holding the **Ctrl key** as you click each file in turn. Point to any of the selected files, then click and drag the files as a group.)

➤ Select (click) drive **A** in the left pane, which in turn displays the contents of the floppy disk in the right pane. You should see the five files you have copied to drive A.

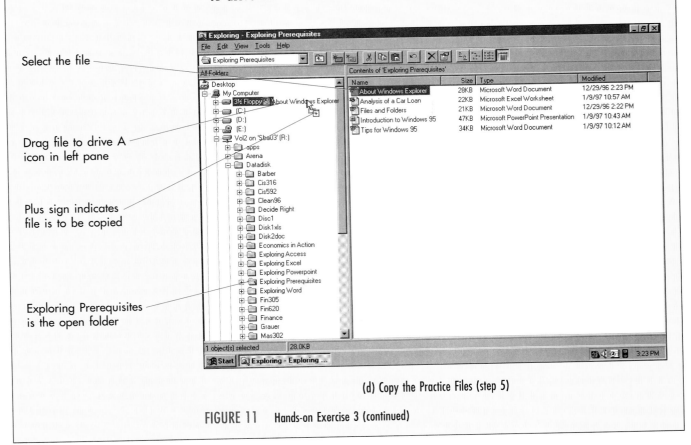

(d) Copy the Practice Files (step 5)

FIGURE 11   Hands-on Exercise 3 (continued)

SELECT MULTIPLE FILES

Selecting (clicking) one file automatically deselects the previously selected file. You can, however, select multiple files by pressing and holding the Ctrl key as you click each file in succession. You can also select multiple files that are adjacent to one another by using the Shift key; that is, click the icon of the first file, then press and hold the Shift key as you click the icon of the last file. You can also select every file in a folder through the Select All command in the Edit menu (or by clicking in the right pane and pressing Ctrl+A).

STEP 6: Check Your Work

➤ Prove to your instructor that you have done the exercise correctly by capturing the Exploring Windows screen, which appears on your monitor. The easiest way to do this is to use the Paint accessory as shown in Figure 11e. Accordingly:

- Press the **Print Screen key** to copy the current screen display to the clipboard (an area of memory that is available to every Windows application). Nothing appears to have happened, but the screen has in fact been copied to the clipboard.

- Click the **Start button,** click **Programs,** click **Accessories,** then click **Paint** to open the Paint accessory. If necessary, click the **maximize button** so that the Paint window takes the entire desktop.

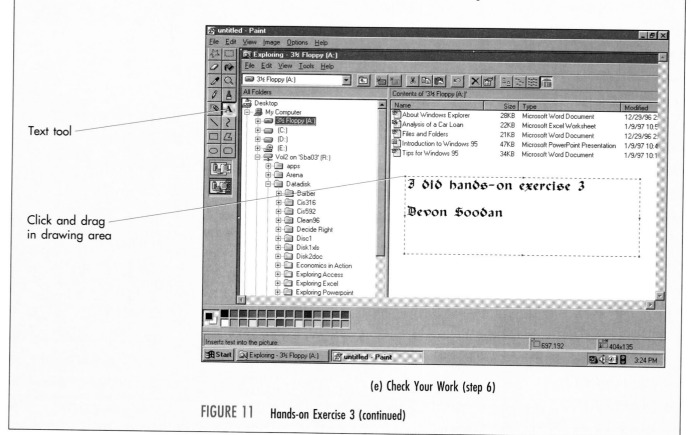

(e) Check Your Work (step 6)

FIGURE 11   Hands-on Exercise 3 (continued)

- Pull down the **Edit menu.** Click **Paste** to copy the screen from the clipboard to the drawing.
- Click the **text tool** (the capital A), then click and drag in the drawing area to create a dotted rectangle that will contain the message to your instructor. Type the text indicating that you did your homework. Click outside the rectangle to deselect it.
- Pull down the **File menu** and click the **Page Setup** command to display the Page Setup dialog box. Click the Landscape option button. Change the margins to one inch all around. Click **OK.**
- Pull down the **File menu** a second time. Click **Print.** Click **OK.** Click the **Close button** to exit Paint. Click **No** if asked to save the file.

➤ Close the Windows Explorer. Exit Windows if you do not want to continue with the next exercise at this time.

THE PAINT ACCESSORY

The Paint Accessory is included in Windows 95 and is an ideal way to create simple (or, depending on your ability, complex) drawings. There is also a sense of familiarity because the Paint accessory shares the common user interface of every Windows application, which includes a title bar, menu bar, minimize, restore, and close buttons, and vertical and horizontal scroll bars. You may also recognize a familiar command structure. The Print and Paste commands, for example, are found in the File and Edit menus, respectively, in Paint, as they are in every Windows application.

THE BASICS OF FILE MANAGEMENT

The exercise just completed had you copy the practice files from a drive on a local area network to your own floppy disk. As you grow to depend on the computer, you will create files of your own in various applications (e.g., Word or Excel). Learning how to manage those files is one of the most important skills you can acquire. This section describes the basic operations you will use.

Moving and Copying a File

Moving and copying a file from one location to another is the essence of file management. It is accomplished most easily by clicking and dragging the file icon from the source drive or folder, to the destination drive or folder, within the Windows Explorer. There is a subtlety, however, in that the result of dragging a file (whether the file is moved or copied) depends on whether the source and destination are on the same or different drives. Dragging a file from one folder to another folder on the same drive moves the file. Dragging a file to a folder on a different drive copies the file. (You can also click and drag a folder, in which case every file in that folder is moved or copied as per the rule for an individual file.)

This process is not as arbitrary as it may seem. Windows assumes that if you drag an object (a file or folder) to a different drive (e.g., from drive C to drive A), you want the object to appear in both places. Hence, the default action when you click and drag an object to a different drive is to copy the object. You can, however, override the default and move the object by pressing and holding the Shift key as you drag.

Windows also assumes that you do not want two copies of an object on the same drive as that would result in wasted disk space. Thus, the default action when you click and drag an object to a different folder on the same drive is to move the object. You can override the default and copy the object by pressing and holding the Ctrl key as you drag. It's not as complicated as it sounds, and you get a chance to practice in the hands-on exercise, which follows shortly.

Deleting Files

The *Delete command* deletes (removes) a file from a disk. The command can be executed in different ways, most easily by selecting a file, then pressing the Del key. Even after a file is deleted, however, you can usually get it back because it is not physically deleted from the hard disk, but moved instead to the Recycle Bin from where it can be recovered.

The *Recycle Bin* is a special folder that contains all files that were previously deleted from any hard disk on your system. Think of the Recycle Bin as similar to the wastebasket in your room. You throw out (delete) a report by tossing it into a wastebasket. The report is gone (deleted) from your desk, but you can still get it back by taking it out of the wastebasket as long as the basket wasn't emptied. The Recycle Bin works the same way. Files are not deleted from the hard disk per se, but are moved instead to the Recycle Bin from where they can be restored to their original location.

The Recycle Bin will eventually run out of space, in which case the files that have been in the Recycle Bin the longest are deleted to make room for additional files. Once a file is deleted from the Recycle Bin, however, it can no longer be recovered, as it has been physically deleted from the hard disk. Note, too, that the protection afforded by the Recycle Bin does not extend to files deleted from a floppy disk. Such files can be recovered, but only through utility programs outside of Windows 95.

Backup

It's not a question of whether it will happen, but when—hard disks die, files are lost, or viruses may infect a system. It has happened to us and it will happen to you, but you can prepare for the inevitable by creating adequate backup *before* the problem occurs. The essence of a backup strategy is to decide which files to back up, how often to do the backup, and where to keep the backup. Once you decide on a strategy, follow it, and follow it faithfully!

Our strategy is very simple—back up what you can't afford to lose, do so on a daily basis, and store the backup away from your computer. You need not copy every file, every day. Instead copy just the files that changed during the current session. Realize, too, that it is much more important to back up your data files than your program files. You can always reinstall the application from the original disks, or if necessary, go to the vendor for another copy of an application. You, however, are the only one who has a copy of the term paper that is due tomorrow. Forewarned is forearmed.

Write Protection

A floppy disk is normally *write-enabled* (the square hole is covered) so that you can change the contents of the disk. Thus, you can create (save) new files to a write-enabled disk and/or edit or delete existing files. Occasionally, however, you

Click and drag the About Windows Explorer file

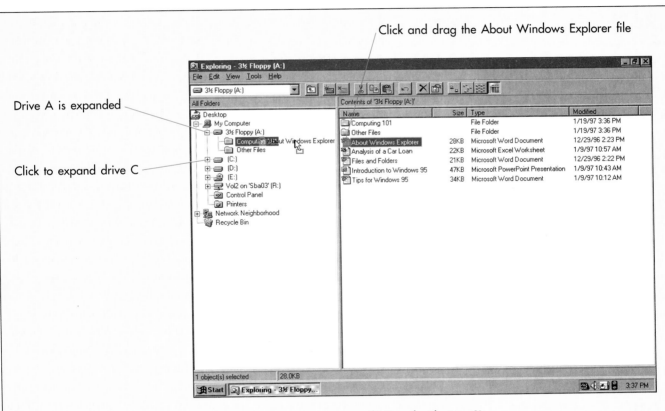

Drive A is expanded

Click to expand drive C

(b) Move the Files (step 2)

FIGURE 12   Hands-on Exercise 4 (continued)

> Click and drag the **Tips for Windows 95 icon** and the **Files and Folders icon** to the **Computing 101 folder** to move these files into the folder.
> Click the **Computing 101 icon** in the left pane to select the folder and display its contents in the right pane. You should see the three files that were just moved.
> Click the icon for **drive A** in the left pane, then click and drag the remaining files, **Analysis of a Car Loan** and **Introduction to Windows 95** to the **Other Files folder.**

USE THE RIGHT MOUSE BUTTON

The result of dragging a file with the left mouse button depends on whether the source and destination folders are on the same or different drives. Dragging a file to a folder on a different drive copies the file. Dragging the file to a folder on the same drive moves the file. If you find this hard to remember, and most people do, click and drag with the right mouse button to display a shortcut menu asking whether you want to copy or move the file. This simple tip can save you from making a careless (and potentially serious) error. Use it!

STEP 3: Copy a Folder

➤ If necessary, click the **plus sign** next to the icon for drive C to expand the drive and display its folders as shown in Figure 12c.

➤ Do *not* click the folder icon for drive C, as drive A is to remain selected. (You can expand or collapse an object without selecting it.)

➤ Point to the **Computing 101 folder** in either pane, click the **right mouse button** and drag the folder to the icon for **drive C** in the left pane, then release the mouse to display a shortcut menu. Click the **Copy Here** command.

➤ You should see the Copy files dialog box as the individual files within the folder are copied from drive A to drive C.

Point to Computing 101 folder, then click right mouse button and drag to icon for drive C

Click Copy Here

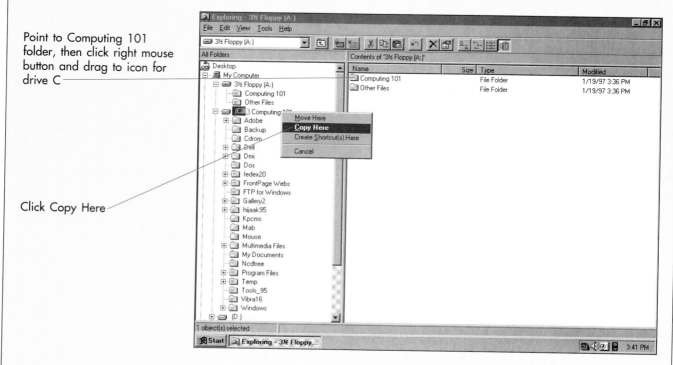

(c) Copy a Folder (step 3)

FIGURE 12   Hands-on Exercise 4 (continued)

CUSTOMIZE THE EXPLORER WINDOW

Increase (or decrease) the size of the left pane within the Explorer Window by dragging the vertical line separating the left and right panes in the appropriate direction. You can also drag the right border of the various column headings (Name, Size, Tip, and Modified) in the right pane to increase (or decrease) the width of the column in order to see more (or less) information in that column. Double click the right border of a column heading to automatically adjust the column width to accommodate the widest entry in that column.

> If you see the Confirm Folder Replace dialog box, it means that the previous student forgot to delete the Computing 101 folder when he or she did this exercise. Click the **Yes to All button** so that the files on your floppy disk will replace the previous versions on drive C.

> Please remember to **delete** the Computing 101 folder on drive C, as described in step 8 at the end of the exercise.

STEP 4: Modify a Document

> Click (select) the **Computing 101 folder** on drive C to open the folder as shown in Figure 12d. The contents of this folder are shown in the right pane.

> Double click the **About Windows Explorer** file to open the file and edit the document. Press **Ctrl+End** to move to the end of the document. Add the sentence shown in Figure 12d followed by your name. (See boxed tip on page 46 if you are unable to read the document.)

> Pull down the **File menu** and click **Save** to save the modified file (or click the **Save button** on the Standard toolbar). Pull down the **File menu** and click **Exit** to exit from Microsoft Word.

> The entire Windows Explorer window is again visible. Pull down the **View menu** and click **Refresh** (or press the **F5 key**) to update the contents of the right pane. The date and time associated with the About Windows Explorer file has been changed to indicate that the file has just been modified.

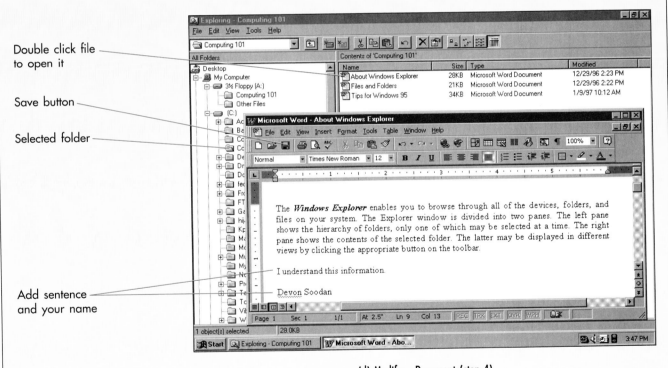

Double click file to open it

Save button

Selected folder

Add sentence and your name

(d) Modify a Document (step 4)

FIGURE 12   Hands-on Exercise 4 (continued)

FILE FORMATS ARE INCOMPATIBLE

If you are unable to open the Word document in our exercise, it is because you are using Microsoft Word 7.0 (also known as Microsoft Word for Windows 95) rather than Word 97. The new release can read documents created in the earlier version, but the converse is not true—that is, Word 7.0 cannot read documents created by Word 97. (Our file was created in Word 97.) The incompatibility between Office 97 and its predecessor Office 95 is a potential problem for millions of users.

STEP 5: Copy (Back Up) a File

➤ Verify that the **Computing 101 folder** on drive C is the active folder as denoted by the open folder icon. Click and drag the icon for the **About Windows Explorer** file from the right pane to the **Computing 101 folder** on **drive A** in the left pane.

➤ You will see the message in Figure 12e, indicating that the folder (drive A) already contains a file called About Windows Explorer and asking whether you want to replace the existing file.

➤ Click **Yes** because you want to replace the previous version of the file on drive A with the updated version on drive C.

➤ You have just backed up the file; in other words, you have created a duplicate copy of a file on drive C on drive A. Thus, you can use the floppy disk to restore the file should anything happen to drive C.

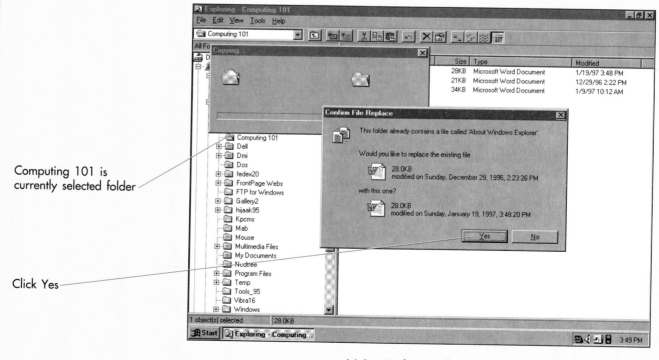

Computing 101 is currently selected folder

Click Yes

(e) Copy (Back Up) a File (step 5)

FIGURE 12   Hands-on Exercise 4 (continued)

COPYING FROM ONE FLOPPY DISK TO ANOTHER

You've learned how to copy a file from drive C to drive A, or from drive A to drive C, but how do you copy a file from one floppy disk to another? It's easy when you know how. Place the first floppy disk in drive A, select drive A in the left pane of the Explorer windows, then copy the file(s) from the right pane to a temporary folder on drive C in the left pane. Remove the first floppy disk, and replace it with the second. Press the F5 key to refresh the display in the right pane. Select the temporary folder on drive C in the left pane, then click and drag the file(s) from the left pane to the floppy disk in the right pane.

STEP 6: Delete a Folder

➤ Select (click) the **Computing 101 folder** on drive C in the left pane. Pull down the **File menu** and click **Delete** (or press the **Del key**).

➤ You will see the dialog box in Figure 12f asking whether you are sure you want to delete the folder (that is, send the folder and its contents to the Recycle Bin). Note the green recycle logo within the box, which implies that you will be able to restore the file.

➤ Click **Yes** to delete the folder. The folder disappears from drive C. Pull down the **Edit menu.** Click **Undo Delete.** The deletion is cancelled and the folder reappears in the left pane.

Select the Computing 101 folder

Click Yes

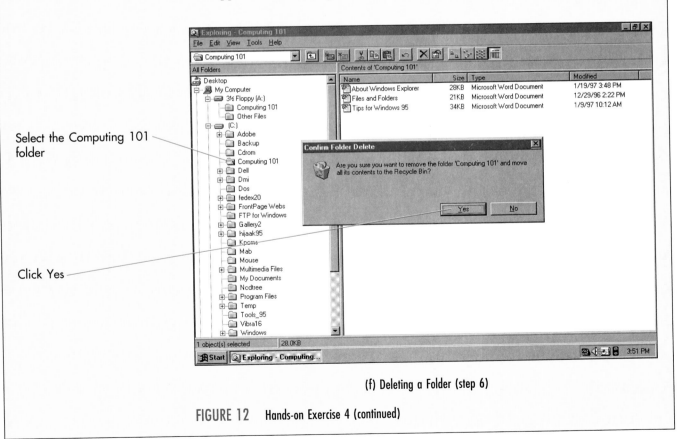

(f) Deleting a Folder (step 6)

FIGURE 12   Hands-on Exercise 4 (continued)

STEP 7: The Recycle Bin

➤ If necessary, select the **Computing 101 folder** on drive C in the left pane. Select (click) the **About Windows Explorer** file in the right pane. Press the **Del key,** then click **Yes** when asked whether to delete the file.

➤ Double click the **Recycle Bin icon** on the desktop if you can see its icon, *or* Double click the **Recycled icon** within the window for drive C. (You may have to scroll in order to see the icon.)

➤ The Recycle Bin contains all files that have been previously deleted from drive C, and hence you may see a different number of files than those displayed in Figure 12g.

➤ Point to the **About Windows Explorer** file, click the **right mouse button** to display the shortcut menu in Figure 12g, then click **Restore.** The file disappears from the Recycle Bin because it has been returned to the Computing 101 folder. Select the folder and verify the file is back.

Point to file and click right mouse button to display shortcut menu

Click Restore

Click Recycle Bin icon

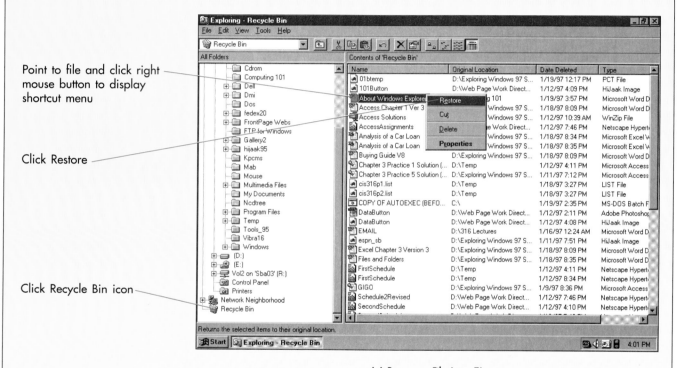

(g) Recover a File (step 7)

FIGURE 12   Hands-on Exercise 4 (continued)

STEP 8: Complete the Exercise

➤ Delete the **Computing 101 folder** on **drive C** as a courtesy to the next student.

➤ Click the **Computing 101 folder** on drive A in the left pane. Repeat the steps described on page 38 to capture the screen and prove to your instructor that you did the exercise.

➤ Exit Windows. Congratulations on a job well done. You have mastered the basics and are ready to begin working in Microsoft Office.

INDEX